Artwork by Susan H. Cooley-Gilliom

Updated Third Edition

AMERICAN RIVER INSIDER'S GUIDE TO

Recreation, Ecology and Cultural History of the North, Middle & South Forks

This 2013 edition is published by Protect American River Canyons.

3 4 5 6 7 8 9 10

ISBN: 978-0-9912364-0-4

Published by Protect American River Canyons (PARC)
www.parc-auburn.org
P. O. Box 9312, Auburn, CA 95604

With generous assistance from the Sierra Nevada Conservancy
Sierra Nevada Conservancy's Mission: To initiate, encourage, and support efforts that improve the environmental, economic and social well-being of the Sierra Nevada region, its communities, and the citizens of California.

With generous assistance from the Emigrant Trails Greenway Trust
Working with land trusts and other conservation organizations to protect open space and promote trails in the American, Bear, and Truckee River watersheds of the Sierra Nevada.

With generous assistance from the New World Library
Books that change lives.
www.newworldlibrary.com

Printed by APi-Marketing • www.api-marketing.com
Established in 1946, we're a full service commercial printer that's proud of our staff, position in the community and our ability to make our customers look good.

Guidebook and cover design by Mystic Design, Inc. • www.mysticdesign.net
With 25+ years experience in graphic design and illustration, it's been our rare privilege to work with Eric Peach on this guidebook. It's taken 3½ years to complete this edition and through it all, we've been humbled, yet proud, to work alongside such dedicated volunteers and truly lovely people.

Grateful acknowledgment is made to the following for permission to reprint copyrighted material or material controlled by them:

© ASRA Canyon Keepers; *American River Canyon Hikes.*

© John Muir Laws illustrations & Heyday Books; *The Laws Field Guide to the Sierra Nevada.*

© John Cassidy, editor; South Fork American River descriptions and history from *A Guide to Three Rivers.*

© Richard Simpson and *Sierra Heritage Magazine*; use of the abridged *Ooti: A Maidu Legacy.*

© Malcolm Margolin & Heyday Books; *Native American Stories* and *The Way We Lived: California Indian Reminiscences, Stories and Songs.*

© University of California Press; *The Tribes of California* by Stephen Powers and four songs from *The Songs of the Gold Rush* by Dwyer and Lingenfelter.

© Placer County Historical Society; re-issued *History of Placer County.*

© 1990 by The Mountaineers, Seattle, WA and Chris Stall for animal track illustrations on pages 22, 34, 57, 60, 63, 102, 115 & 117, reprinted with permission of the publisher: *Animal Tracks of Southern California* (and *Animal Tracks of the Mid-Atlantic States*).

Printed on recycled paper.

Deep Appreciation to Our Generous Contributors

Deep appreciation and concern for the future of the American River watershed brought authors and artists together to create this book. It is in the same spirit of cooperation and stewardship that PARC dedicates profits from the sale of this book to conservation and education programs in the pursuit of the permanent protection of the American River canyons. We hope the canyons and rivers that have so inspired us can be preserved and enhanced for all generations to come.

Artwork by Juan Peña

Writers & Editors

Bill Carnazzo
Bill Center
Mo Daley
Marc Davis
Bill Deitchman
Tony DeRiggi
John Donovan
Bill Drake
Gary Estes
Jim Ferris
Eric Gerstung
Ron Gould
Roger & Sue Groghan
Vince Haughey
Mimi Jenrick
Mike Kempf
John Kipping
Mark Leder-Adams
Rodi Lee
Mike Lynch
Stephanie Mandel
Malcolm Margolin
Eugene Markley
Laurel Mathe
Joe Medeiros
Jane Mulder
Eric Peach
Jasper Peach
Paula Peach
Tom Petersen
Harry C. Peterson
Leo Polansky
Diane Poslosky
Stephen Powers
Sandra Reeves
Richard Simpson
Ron Stork
Bill Templin
Alice Tenscher-Dunbar
Laird Thompson
Russell Towle
Shelia Toner
Otis Wollan
Tim Woodall
Terry Wright

Photos & Graphics

Auburn Journal
LeeAnn Bigley
Kim Brown
Guy Colwell
Susan Cooley-Gilliom
Chet Dunbar
Gary Hughes
Michael Kirby
John Kipping
Diane Krage
John Muir Laws
Mark Leder-Adams
Andy Lukkonen
Mike Lynch
Bill Mash
Laurel Mathe
Hank Meals
Heather Mehl
Stan Padilla
Eric Peach
Juan Peña
Placer County Museums
Rapid Shooters
Deren Ross
Richard Simpson
Gus Thomson
Madge Ward
Charles L. Weed
Otis Wollan
Bureau of Reclamation

Front Cover Photographs:

Gary Hughes • Eric Peach

Back Cover Photographs:

Gary Hughes • Richard Simpson • Eric Peach
Bill Mash • John Muir Laws • Placer Co. Museums

TABLE OF CONTENTS

Continued

CHAPTER 3: AMERICAN RIVER ECOLOGY

CHAPTER 4: AMERICAN RIVER HISTORY

APPENDICES

A Special Thanks …

Contributed by the PARC Board Members

Works of art spring from the inspired vision of artists who view the world around them and try to capture their vision for others to experience. Eric Peach is the artist behind the completely revised third edition of this guidebook and his deep personal connection to the canyons of the American River is reflected on virtually every page.

Eric and his wife Paula have lived on the canyon rim in Auburn for more than three decades, and have spent countless hours exploring the American River canyons. Eric's understanding and appreciation of the canyons' natural wonders is unmatched, and his selfless devotion to preserving and sharing this special place with others has been remarkable. As a ceramic artist and teacher, Eric has also found ways to creatively interpret the beauty found within the canyons, and to help others do the same. A humble and soft-spoken man, Eric will be the first to give credit to others who contributed their time and talents to producing this guidebook. Nevertheless, without Eric's devotion and creative energy this ambitious project simply would not have been possible. We, the other board members of Protect American River Canyons (PARC), want the reader to know who provided the artistic vision and passion for producing this guidebook. With deep admiration and respect, we dedicate this book to Eric Peach.

"Paula and I are humbled by this dedication bestowed upon us by the PARC Board. We would like to thank the board and all the unsung river lovers who quietly take such good care of the river without us ever knowing who you are. We all benefit from your efforts. ***You are our heroes!****"*

~ Eric & Paula Peach

Tim Woodall, Eric & Paula Peach at the 2011 PARC Confluence Festival.

Paula and Eric Peach hiking the trails.

Photographs courtesy of Gary Hughes

AUBURN STATE RECREATION AREA

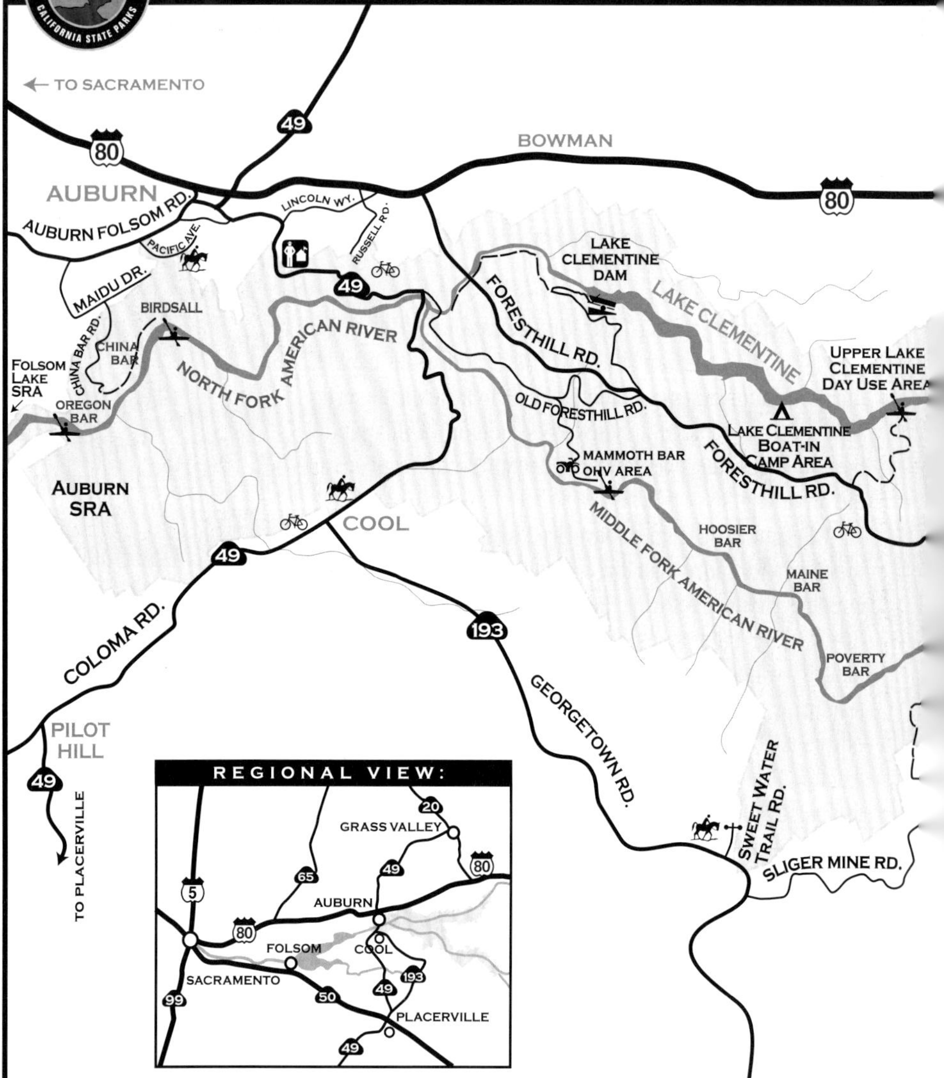

AUBURN STATE RECREATION AREA:
Address: 501 El Dorado St., Auburn, CA 95603
Website: www.parcs.ca.gov
Email: asra@parks.ca.gov
Phone: (530) 885-4527
ASRA Park Seasonal Hours: www.parcs.ca.gov

USEFUL CONTACT INFORMATION:
CalFire: (530) 823-4904
CA Dept. of Fish & Wildlife: (916) 358-2900
Placer County Visitor Center: (530)887-2111
Auburn Area Chamber of Commerce: (530) 885-5616

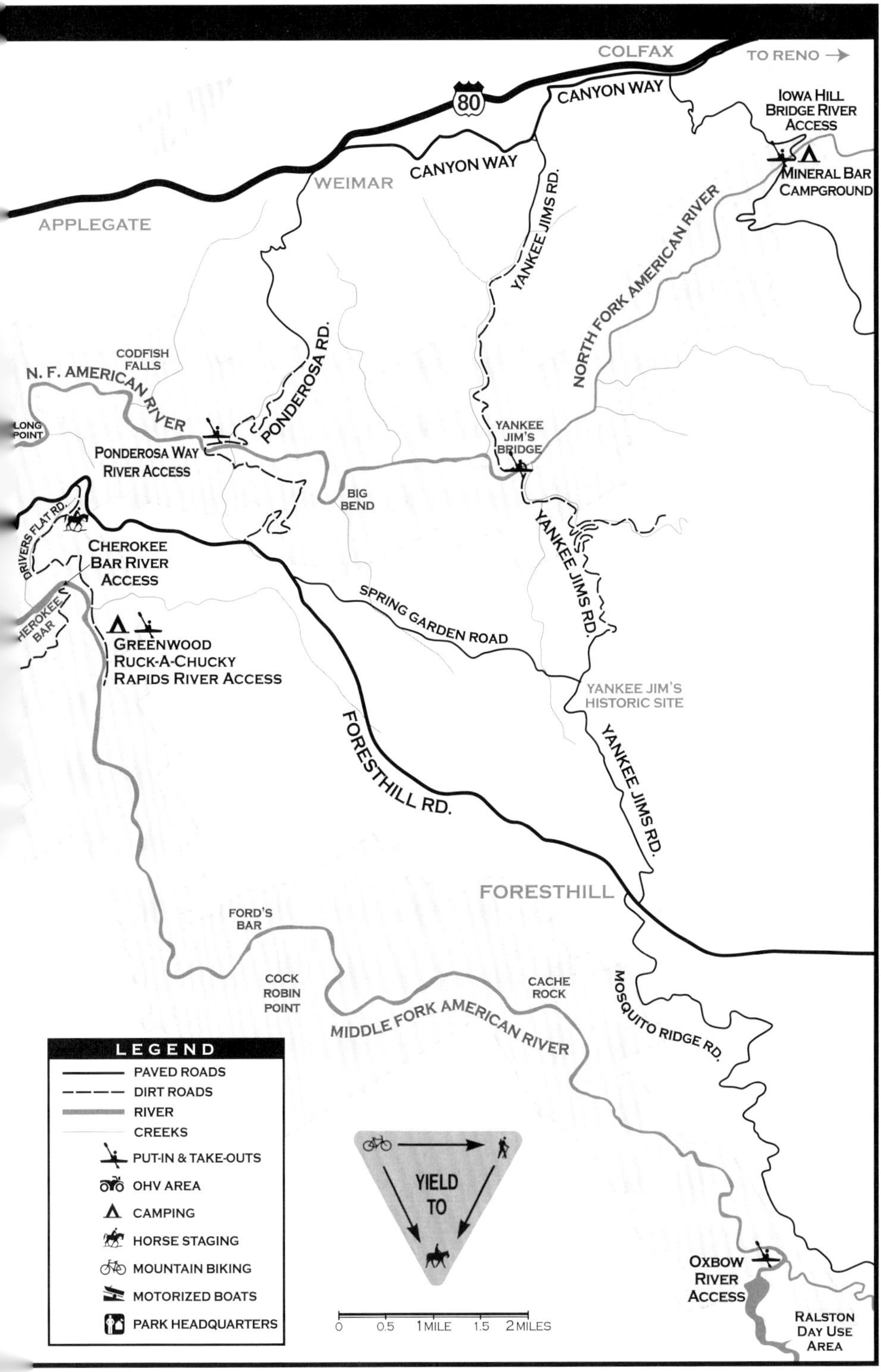

COLFAX
TO RENO →
80
CANYON WAY
IOWA HILL BRIDGE RIVER ACCESS
MINERAL BAR CAMPGROUND
CANYON WAY
WEIMAR
APPLEGATE
YANKEE JIMS RD.
NORTH FORK AMERICAN RIVER
PONDEROSA RD.
CODFISH FALLS
N. F. AMERICAN RIVER
LONG POINT
PONDEROSA WAY RIVER ACCESS
YANKEE JIM'S BRIDGE
BIG BEND
DRIVERS FLAT RD.
CHEROKEE BAR RIVER ACCESS
CHEROKEE BAR
GREENWOOD RUCK-A-CHUCKY RAPIDS RIVER ACCESS
SPRING GARDEN ROAD
YANKEE JIMS RD.
YANKEE JIM'S HISTORIC SITE
FORESTHILL RD.
YANKEE JIMS RD.
FORESTHILL
FORD'S BAR
COCK ROBIN POINT
CACHE ROCK
MOSQUITO RIDGE RD.
MIDDLE FORK AMERICAN RIVER
LEGEND
PAVED ROADS
DIRT ROADS
RIVER
CREEKS
PUT-IN & TAKE-OUTS
OHV AREA
CAMPING
HORSE STAGING
MOUNTAIN BIKING
MOTORIZED BOATS
PARK HEADQUARTERS
YIELD TO
0 0.5 1 MILE 1.5 2 MILES
OXBOW RIVER ACCESS
RALSTON DAY USE AREA

The Auburn State Recreation Area

The wild running rivers of the Mother Lode are a unique and rich natural resource. For thousands of years, the American River has been a natural paradise, a place of wild beauty and home to the original Southern Maidu Nisenan inhabitants. Only one hundred and sixty years ago the river and canyons were crowded with hard-living gold miners seeking their fortune in gold.

Safety First

As always nowadays, we're well advised to offer a disclaimer. We must tell you we take no responsibility for your safety as you use the river and trail guides in this book. Take care, go easily and lightly, and if you are inexperienced, seek someone who is knowledgeable to give you a hand. Enjoy!

When the abundant gold fields were exhausted, there were few that braved the steep canyon trails to enjoy the lush riparian river banks and crystal clear waters below.

Today, however, these rivers have been rediscovered. The Auburn State Recreation Area (ASRA) was established in 1977 along 48 miles of the North & Middle Forks of the American River that were intended to be inundated by the proposed Auburn Dam. Managed by the California Department of Parks and Recreation, under contract with the U.S. Bureau of Reclamation, the ASRA consists of approximately 30,000 acres of federally owned land in the North and Middle Forks canyons.

Each year close to a million visitors come to enjoy over 100 miles of trails for hikers, runners, mountain bikers and equestrians. They also come for whitewater boating, fishing, swimming, rock climbing, picnicking and much more in the American River canyonlands–one of Northern California's most beautiful landscapes.

The numbers of visitors to these canyons increases each year, despite a Bureau of Reclamation's management plan that

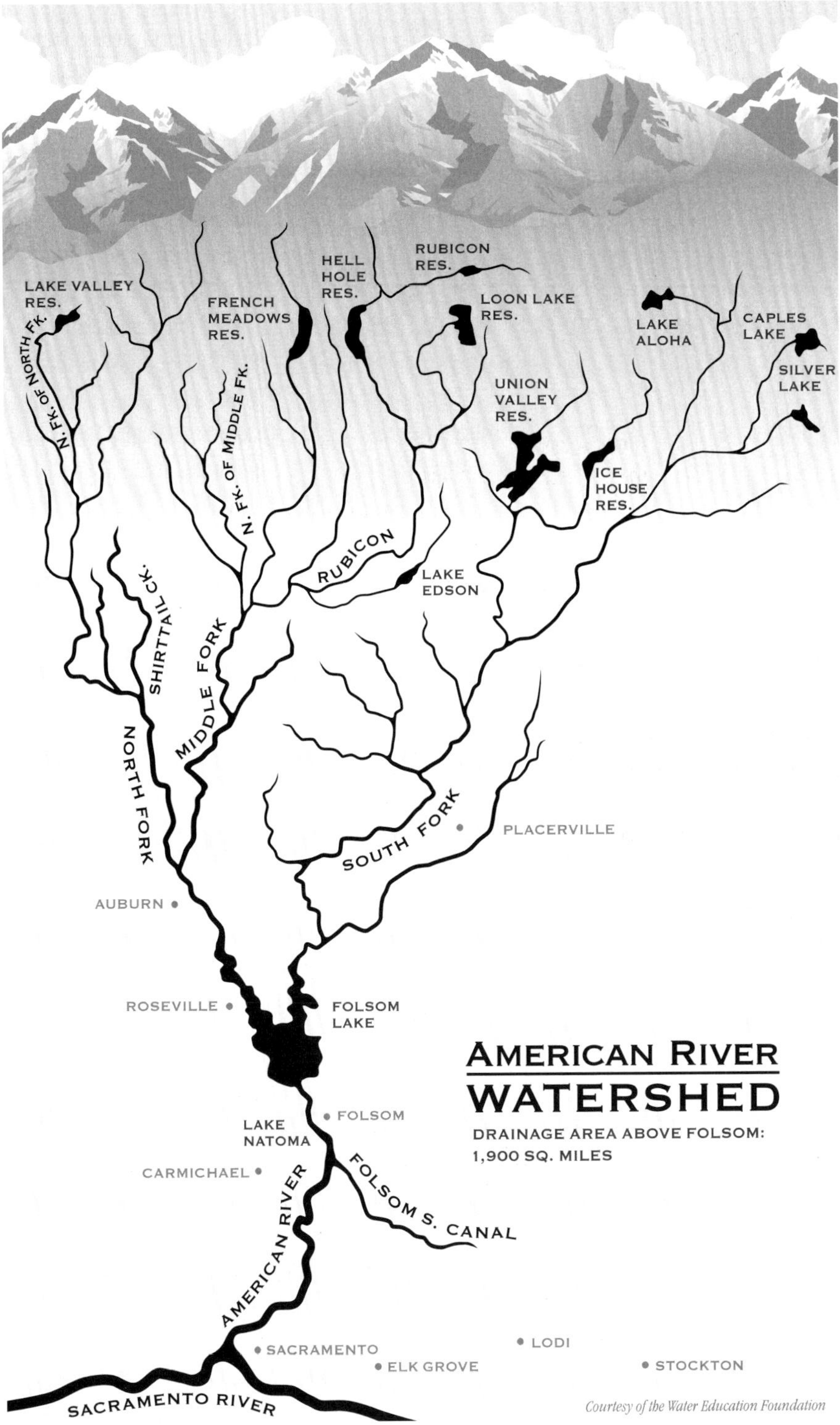

Courtesy of the Water Education Foundation

The rivers in their purity.

discourages access and keeps the canyons in a holding pattern for the proposed Auburn Dam. Historic trail systems are well developed and invite exploration. The Auburn Dam site has been restored and replaced with the China Bar Whitewater Park and a new Placer County Water Agency pumping station. This Sierra Foothill region is less than a one hour drive from Sacramento. International events like the Tevis Cup Horse Race and the Western States 100 Mile Run draw hundreds of hardy participants and thousands of spectators. Ongoing improvement to access roads, combined with facility improvements, creates an extraordinarily wide variety of recreational opportunities.

These rivers and canyons are wonderful. Some areas are easy to enjoy while others are physically demanding. Many recreationists are seeking more rigorous experiences, more intense challenges, and more time close to genuine wildlands and whitewater.

As our urban congestion grows, we feel the need to be in wilderness. The quality of our experiences in the canyons draws us back to renew our spirits ... now excitement and challenge, now gentle solitude, a moment's exchange with a deer or a heron or a flicker or an otter.

As we are becoming increasingly distracted by our high-tech devices and demands of work, these moments in wilderness reconnect us to the beauty and the complexity of our natural world. We can take a moment to breathe freely, to think and dream, and to be grateful for the beauty all around us: the blessings of the rivers of the Mother Lode.

An appreciation of the history of geologic time, up through the Native California cultures to the gold mining era, to the present day, helps us understand the changes that have happened in the canyons.

Despite the beauty and popularity of the American River Canyons, their future remains threatened. Auburn Dam remains a congressionally authorized project and if built, would inundate all stretches of the North and Middle Forks of the American that are described in this book – 48 miles of river in all. The authors of this book write in the faith that Auburn Dam will not be built. We know well that the highest and best use of the canyons is to enjoy them as they are. We are unanimous in urging permanent protection of the American River Canyons. Please see the appendix, starting on page 399, for information on the Auburn Dam and proposals to protect the canyons.

We extend to you, our reader, the warmest invitation to use this guidebook to find out for yourself. Explore the river and canyons. The reward awaits you.

This Charles Weed photograph of Maine Bar was taken in 1858, when the population of the Middle Fork River was almost 10,000 men and a few women. The river was flumed and the hills stripped for lumber and firewood.

This photo of Maine Bar was taken in 1977, from the exact vantage point of the 1858 Weed photo. The canyonlands have nearly recovered from the Gold Rush years. Trees again grow on the hillsides and the river runs clear.

The Rivers in Their Purity

Let's go back and take a look at the canyons and rivers as they were before the European culture arrived. This passage was written by Myron Angel nearly 150 years ago, quoted from *The History of Placer County, California* by Thompson and West, 1882:

"The river canons, where the old bars were located, were romantic places previous to being disturbed and torn up by the gold-digger. The water was as clear as crystal, and above each ripple or rapid place was a long, deep pool, with water blue as turquoise, swarming with fish. Salmon at that time ran up all the streams as far as they could get, until some perpendicular barrier which they could not leap prevented further progress. Before the falls at Murderer's Bar was cut down, during spawning time, the salmon would accumulate so thickly in a large pool just below, that they were taken in great numbers by merely attaching large iron hooks to a pole, running it down in the water, and suddenly jerking it up through the mass. And that place was not an exceptional one; it was so at all places where there was any obstruction to free running. During these times, the Indians supplied themselves with fish, which they dried in the sun. Trout similar to those now in Lake Tahoe [Lahaugnton cutthroat] were also plentiful, and the writer has caught them with hook and line weighing as high as ten pounds in the North Fork, above Kelley's Bar.

Upon every little bend or plat of land bordering the streams, grew the white ash, alder, maple, laurel, honeysuckle and rank ferns and mosses, with other indigenous shrubs and plants, while every projecting boulder in the river-bed was the home of the broad-leaved water plant. Tussocks of rank bunch-grass covered the bottoms, and wild grapevines clambered over every convenient tree. The water ousel, a little dark-colored bird, flitted from place to place in search of food, and the vigilant kingfisher darted from his perch on overhanging limb into the clear water and rose again with some finny victim in his beak. Deer wandered unscared amid these beauteous scenes, for there were none to do them harm. When first dug over, the old river bars were simply beds of clean-washed gravel, containing gold–natural ground-sluices–where nature had been for untold ages at work, and the innumerable fierce floods had so thoroughly washed away the finer alluvium and abraded material, that what remained, after getting below the surface soil, would scarcely roil the element in which the miner washed it.

Such was the condition of the California streams when the gold-seeker first approached them–things of rare beauty, joyous to behold, inconceivable to those who only know them as they are found today treeless, mud-laden, turgid, filthy, and fishless; with matchless beauty gone, and natural purity forever lost, prostituted to the unchaste uses of mankind in the acquirement of an artificial wealth made absolutely necessary by the civilization of the age."

The power of nature to heal wounds has proven Myron Angel wrong; the natural purity was not "forever lost." Today the canyons are restored to much of their original beauty.

SPIRIT RIVER

WE GIVE THANKS TO YOU

RIVER SPIRIT
RIVER SPIRIT
forever flowing
translucent currents
etched into stone
flowing motion
flowing motion

SINGING RIVER
SINGING RIVER
moving quickly,
called into being
unchallenged rapids
slowly collecting
into pools

Photos courtesy of Tumele Miwok Dancers

GENERATIONS
GENERATIONS
we have seen
we are seeing
we will see

SPIRIT WATER *being drawn down*
from the mountains and on down to the sea.

~ *Stan Padilla*

American River Confluence Festival:

Where the Community Comes Together to Celebrate the River

Community members gather during the dedication and celebration of the American River Overlook mosaic sign at the 2007 16th annual Confluence Festival. The sign, designed by Virginia Dains, is made of hundreds of clay fish created at community workshops.

Confluence watercolor by local artist, Juan Peña

Since 1998, local artist and designer, Laurel Mathe, has illustrated the annual Confluence Festival posters and t-shirts.

Over 20 Years of Confluence Festivals

This annual family-friendly festival sponsored by PARC since 1991, offers fun recreational, nature and art activities in a unique river village setting. This celebration also features entertainment, music, food and relevant information exhibits.

CHAPTER ONE

Hit The Trails!

Introduction to Auburn State Recreation Area's Trails of the North and Middle Forks of the American River

By Eric Peach, Sheila Toner, Jim Ferris, Ron Gould, Tom Petersen and Evan Jones

One of the most popular ways to enjoy the Auburn SRA trails is by hiking, running, mountain biking or horseback riding the miles and miles of river-canyons trails. Stunning scenic beauty and biological diversity await the curious explorer. For others the steep canyon trails represent opportunity for rigorous physical challenges and adventure. For all it is a priceless time to be close to nature. This chapter is written for those who wish to immerse themselves in the vast Auburn State Recreation Area trails system to experience diverse natural history, rich, colorful cultural history and the spectacular scenery of the river and canyons. The trails are also a path to other recreational pursuits like snorkeling, fishing, climbing, wildlife viewing, gold panning and much more. Naturalists, scientists and artists find inspiration in the nature and scenery found along the canyon trails.

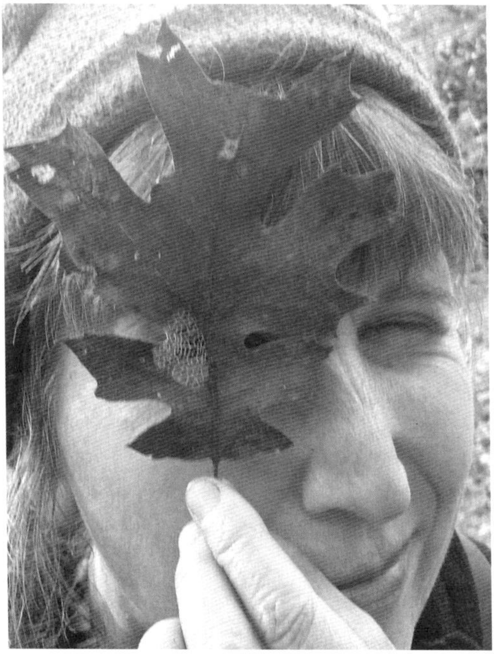

Most of the trails described in this chapter are a diverse mixture of Indian trails, miner's trails, ditches, wagon supply roads and modern firebreak roads and trails. Some of the trails can be combined into longer loop hikes or car shuttles may be set up for longer one-way hikes. Much of the maintenance is taken up by individual, enlightened trail volunteers as well as hiker, runner, equestrian, and mountain bike rider

"Come forth into the light of things. Let nature be your teacher."
– William Wordsworth

groups. Auburn SRA rangers and staff manage all trail maintenance and construction work performed by volunteer groups and individuals.

This trail chapter does not give an exhaustive description of any trail, but instead provides sufficient information to enable perceptive users to select trails for their level of ability and interest. Starting points, type of use, some historical background and natural features of interest are noted in each trail description. The time it takes to complete a trail depends on the hiker's physical condition and level of interest in features.

The trails are open year round although some access roads are subject to seasonal closure, such as Upper Clementine, Ruck-A-Chucky and China Bar day use areas. Auburn SRA lands are managed by CA State Parks for the Bureau of Reclamation and Bureau of Land Management (BLM). Some land is private property. Stay on the road or trail when crossing private property.

Native American

with weight on heels
i step down dusty trail
beneath pine and oak
sampling manzanita's sweet, globular flowers
until canyon bottoms out
at bouldered river banks
of ancient maidu
puma and forty-niner still
i leap
into cool, turquoise pool
surface as lungs give out
a warrior's bowl
crawl into granite slab
and warm
this baptismal rite
repeated along up river scramble
until day darkens into night
and i lie gazing
at pine tree tops
fingering the sky
tickling Orion at the belly
and listen
to the American River
giggling

- Rob Hanson

Using The Trails: A Few Tips

1. Plan your hike. Check out trail guides and maps. Allow plenty of time, especially in hot weather. For a more satisfying experience, don't hurry.

2. Carry your own water. There is no guarantee that the water in streams and rivers is free of animal or human contamination. For longer hikes consider carrying a water filter.

3. Carry a comfortable pack. Consider the essential items such as snacks, first aid, flashlight, knife, matches, and maps, as well as sunblock, mosquito repellent and recreational gear. Hiking poles are popular on steep rocky trails.

4. Stay on the trail. This is usually a simple matter, but some seldom-used trails are faint and can be confused with game trails. Don't cut switchbacks.

5. Keep your bearings. Trails may be confusing where there are multiple intersecting trails. Carry maps or GPS devices. On longer cross-country adventures use the Indian method of looking back frequently.

6. Stay together. Keep within site of each other especially when hiking with children. Don't hike alone!

7. Conserve your energy. While the elevations are not high, the steep trails with southern exposure can be hot in the summer. Pace yourself whether on foot, horseback or bike. Know your limitations.

8. Be careful with fire. Camp in designated areas only. Fire is generally not allowed except in designated camping areas. In other areas fires are not allowed from the onset of summer until the first good rain. Fire permits must be obtained from CALFIRE. Know the rules!

9. Protect the wildlife, scenery and historic sites. Law protects historic sites! Take pictures not artifacts. Don't litter! Protect the wildlife and scenery.

10. Enjoy and go lightly!

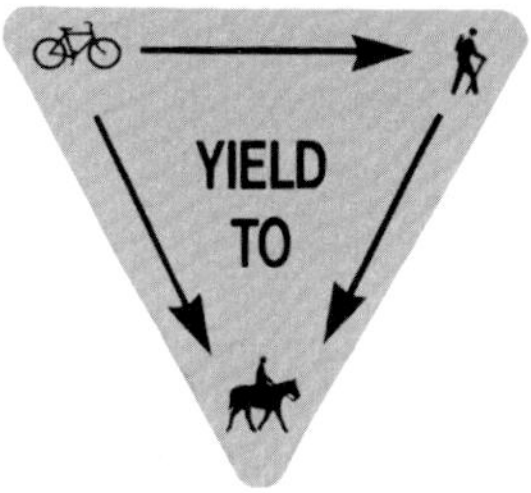

Trail Etiquette:

- Dogs should be leashed.
- Hikers yield to equestrians.
- Bikers yield to hikers and equestrians.
- Go slow. Be safe.

Auburn State Recreation Area Trail Map

An essential topographic companion to this guidebook, this map features access roads, trails, major river rapids and river mileage in the ASRA.

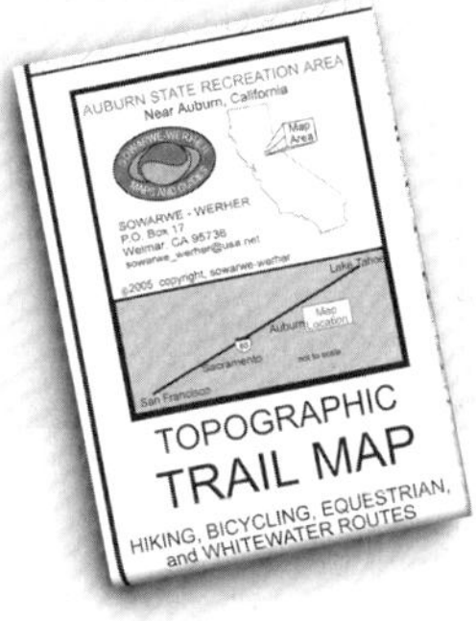

OTHER CAUTIONS

Strong River Currents

More people die from drowning in the Auburn SRA than any other cause. Use caution in or near the water at all times. The currents are strong and cold, especially in the spring. Water levels fluctuate on the Middle Fork American River from upstream hydro releases. Hypothermia is a real immediate danger in cold water. Do not mix alcohol with river related activities. Life jackets, officially known as Personal Flotation Devices (PFDs), are highly recommended for all. A limited number of PFDs are available for children to borrow in the popular Confluence and Upper Lake Clementine swimming areas.

Mountain Lions

If you come into contact with a cougar that does not run away, stay calm, stand your ground and don't back down! Back away slowly if possible and if safe to do so. Pick up children, but **DO NOT BEND DOWN, TURN YOUR BACK, OR RUN**. Running triggers an innate predatory response in cougars which could lead to an attack.

Raise your voice and speak firmly. Raise your arms to make yourself look larger, clap your hands, and throw something you might have in your hands, such as a water bottle. Again, do not bend over to pick up a stone off the ground. This action may trigger a pounce response in a cougar.

In the very unusual event that a cougar attacks you, fight back. People have successfully fought off cougars with rocks and sticks. Try to remain standing and get up if you fall to the ground.

Rattlesnakes

Look before you step or reach for a handhold in rocks. In spring, sunny rocks and paths are likely places to encounter

these canyon residents. In summer, warm rocks in the shade are favorite spots. Be alert when gathering firewood or walking at night. **STAY CALM** if bitten. Getting the victim to medical emergency is more important than any other first aid. Try not to exert the bitten area. Cutting and suction treatments are not advised by medical experts unless medical help is many hours away.

Abandoned Mines: Stay Out And Stay Alive

Our rich gold mining history has left many abandoned underground mine shafts, some with hidden openings that drop hundreds of feet down. Rotting timbers and unstable rock formations make cave-ins a real danger. Lethal concentrations of deadly gases can accumulate in underground passages, and total darkness and debris add to the hazards.

Poison Oak

Learn to recognize poison oak's three lobed leaves. It grows abundantly throughout the Sierra foothills. All parts of the plant at all times of the year contain a resinous sap that can cause severe blisters on skin and mucous membranes within one to several days of contact. The sap is most toxic during spring or summer. Many people are severely allergic to it. Wear long pants and sleeves when around it and avoid petting animals or handling clothing that has come in contact with it. Carry a tube of poison oak soap in your pack to wash off the sap from your skin.

The Mighty Tick

Ixodes pacificus, the western black-legged tick, that transmits Lyme disease or *Anaplasmos* through its bite, is found throughout the Auburn SRA. *Dermacentor* ticks may also carry Rocky Mountain spotted fever or *Tularemaia*.

Lyme Disease is a debilitating disease that in its advanced stages can affect joints, muscles, memory, mood and more. Not all ticks carry the disease, but even the bite of the pinhead sized nymph can transmit the disease. Consult a physician for diagnosis. Blood tests can help with diagnosis or, if possible, save the tick to bring in for a lab analysis. Lyme disease is treated with antibiotics.

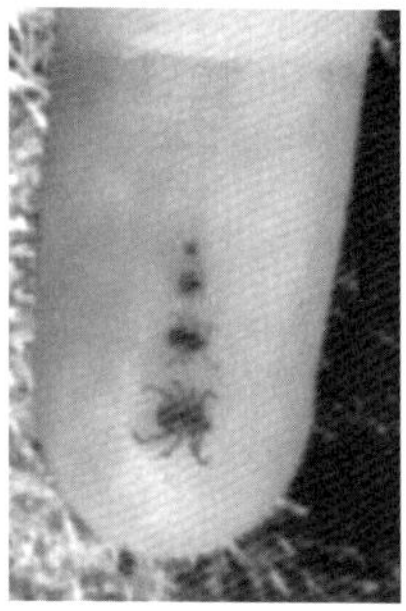

Ticks have three life stages: larva, nymph, and adult male and female.

To help avoid tick bites:

- Checking clothing and body frequently for ticks, during and after hikes.
- Wear long sleeves.

- Tuck trouser cuffs in socks especially when hiking in grassy or brushy areas.
- Repellents are available for clothing and skin.

Prompt removal of ticks can help prevent disease transmission!

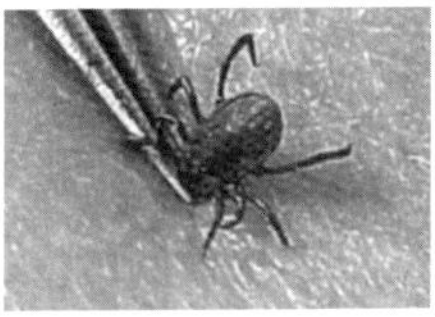

Extracting a tick with tweezers.

To remove a tick:

- Use tweezers to grab the tick as close to your skin as possible.
- Pull the tick firmly, straight out away from the skin (do not jerk, twist or burn the tick).
- Wash hands and the bite site with soap and water after the tick is removed and apply an antiseptic to the bite site.
- See your doctor if you develop a rash or flu-like symptoms within 30 days after a tick bite.

For more information contact the California Department of Public Health at www.dhs.ca.gov, phone 916-552-9730, or contact your local health department. Information on Lyme Disease is also available through the non-profit www.LymeDisease.org website.

California Black Bears

Bear tracks

Respect the Bear! The best way to avoid conflicts with bears is to prevent it. The American River canyons are home to a large California black bear population. Their color ranges from jet-black, brown, cinnamon to blonde. Bear attacks are rare.

To lessen the chances of conflict follow these guidelines when in bear habitat:

Hiking: Don't hike alone. Never approach a bear. Keep your distance. Don't let yourself come between a cub and its mother. If a bear approaches, clap and talk loudly, make yourself appear bigger. Protect children; put yourself between them and the bear. Running away could stimulate the bear's instinct to chase. If a bear attacks, research indicates it's best to fight back, throw rocks and sticks or whatever objects may be near.

Camping: Store food and toiletries away from your sleeping area suspended in a tree at least 10 feet above the ground, 4 feet from the trunk on a branch less than 4 inches in diameter. Bear resistant containers can also be effective. Pack garbage out or place in bear proof receptacles.

Mother California black bears are protective of their cubs. Absolutely do not allow yourself to come between a mother bear and her cubs.

CAMPING INFORMATION

Camping is only allowed in the following designated areas:

Mineral Bar Campground:
18 campsites on the North Fork are located at the Iowa Hill Road river crossing.

Ruck-A-Chucky Campground:
5 campsites on the Middle Fork are located on Drivers Flat Road next to the river.

Boat-in Lake Clementine Camping:
16 primitive campsites are located at the upper end of the lake. To reserve camping at Lake Clementine phone the statewide reservation number at 1-800-444-7275. All other camping is on a first come first served basis.

Primitive Camping is only allowed by a special permit issued at ASRA Park Headquarters, phone 530-885-4527.

ASRA Park Regulations:

- **Pets on a leash** are allowed in most areas of the park. Pets are not allowed in some day-use areas. Check the park signs.
- **Limited seasonal hunting** is allowed in some areas for designated species. Check with ASRA headquarters for open areas and times.
- **Alcohol is banned** from many of the popular ASRA day-use areas. Check the park signs.

Things To Do While Hiking with Children of All Ages

By Eric and Paula Peach

Several years ago a group of us were on a Protect American River Canyons' outing at Shirttail Creek near Devil's Falls on Yankee Jim's Road close to the North Fork of the American River. As we stopped to rest and cool off at the falls, the children heard a burst of chirping coming from behind the falls. Their attention focused on the chirping and they observed a water ouzel bird, also known as the "California dipper," which flew to a mossy nest behind the falls carrying aquatic insects for the baby dippers. The parents returned time-and-time-again and each time the nest came to life with chirping applause mingling with the sweet, liquid music of the falls. Balancing the kids on our shoulders, like circus acrobats, we observed three hungry baby dipper heads with open beaks waiting for the next course of bug treats. We have since returned many times to enjoy the 'Devil's Falls Dipper' sonata.

Because of their natural curiosity, hiking with children is fun. Playing nature games brings us closer together and opens our senses.

Nature Treasure Hunt

Kids love a treasure hunt. Have them carefully gather items on a list.

Shed Snakeskin	*Dried Flower*	*Acorn Cap*	*Berries*	*Seed*
Rough-Edged Leaf	*Noisemaker*	*Butterfly Wing*	*Feather*	*Shell*
Something Furry	*Piece of Moss*	*Piece of Bark*	*Rock*	
Smooth-Edged Leaf	*Something that does not belong in nature*			

Once the hunt is over and the collected items are displayed, discuss their interrelationships in the American River ecosystem.

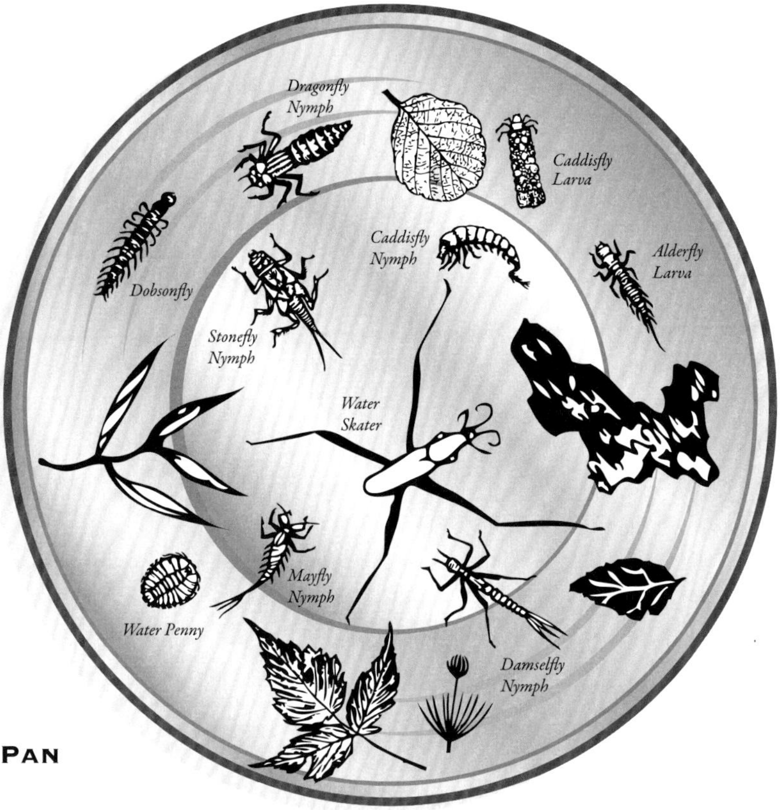

Gold Pan Soup

Purchase an inexpensive gold pan and spray-paint the bottom white. Go to a stream (Shirttail Creek is a good one), and turn over the rocks in a riffle area or at the edge of the pool, stirring up the water a bit. With a fine mesh net, catch the debris and shake it into your gold pan.

With a little luck, your stream soup will contain algae, bits of leaves, and tiny aquatic invertebrates which graze on the algae. There may be water penny larva, ancient-looking caddis fly larva (they glue together grains of sand and wood debris into fine tube houses attached to rocks), damsel fly larva, crane fly egg rafts, or stone fly larva. These ferocious-looking bugs are actually harmless and make excellent trout bait.

Look at your gold pan soup again, this time for the interrelationships. The water and sunshine feed the trees and shrubs along the stream, leaves and other organic material drop into the stream, decay into the nutrients that feed the algae which the aquatic invertebrates consume. Fish feed on the insects, both in their larval form in the water and in their adult form as flying insects.

Blindfold Walk

Another fun game with a group of children and adults is to walk wearing blindfolds. Have people pair up and blindfold a partner. One partner is to carefully lead the other along an easy trail and brings the blindfolded person interesting objects to guess, or guides them to touch, smell or listen to natural objects along the trail.

Usually when someone is blindfolded their sense of smell and touch are heightened. The nose of your blindfolded partner is sure to twitch when presented with leaves from the California bay tree or a mockorange flower.

Animal Charades

This game is fun for groups while gathered for lunch. Simply have one or more of the hikers imitate the body movements of an animal or insect. The rest try to guess the identity of the animal or insect being acted out.

Wildflower Fun

Long-beaked filaree scissors

Kids love to explore the world of plants and wildflowers. The classic is long-beaked filaree scissors. Simply push one of the long, needle-like seed pods through another to make a pair of scissors.

For a musical instrument the common henbit makes a perfect trumpet whistle. Pluck a miniature lavender flower from the cluster. Suck the nectar from the tubular base and blow gently through the tube for your new high-pitched whistle.

Did you know there is a wolf's claw hidden in the lupine flower? It might take a couple of tries to reveal the claw. Find a bush lupine with mature flowers. Gently pushing the flower back should reveal the claw protruding from inside the flower.

Once you have developed an interest in the canyon plants, it's fun to keep a wildflower journal listing the wildflowers along a particular trail and the time of year. It's exciting to return to the same trail year after year while looking forward to finding the wildflowers on our list. Each year we add new names to our list.

CIRCLE OF FRIENDS

Match the animal with the descriptive word or words found in the middle of the circle, below, that fit them best.

Use your imagination and create your own river games!

JUNIOR RANGER PROGRAM

Offered during the summer months by the Auburn SRA is the fun and educational Junior Ranger programs for children. Activities encourage quick learning. Call SRA Headquarters 530-885-4527 for times and location.

TRAIL AT-A-GLANCE:

STAGECOACH TRAIL

DISTANCE:	2 miles; 1½ hours up, ¾ hours down (hiking)
DIFFICULTY:	Moderate up, easy down
ELEVATION CHANGE:	+/- 800'

STAGECOACH TRAIL

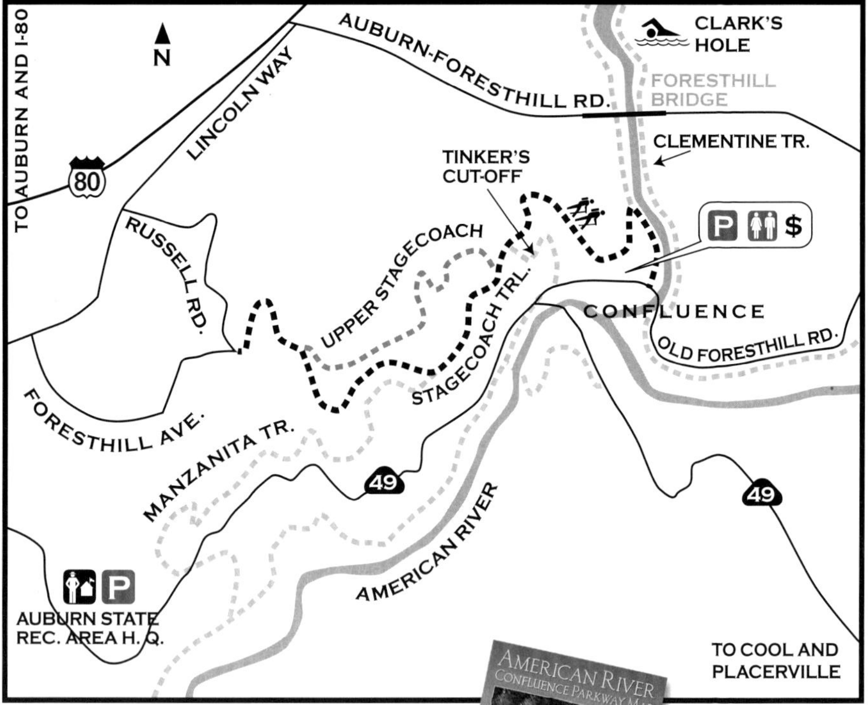

AMERICAN RIVER CONFLUENCE PARKWAY MAP

A great companion piece for your hike is PARC's partial map to the popular trails and nature guide to the flora and fauna of the Confluence Area.

The Confluence Trails

Stagecoach Trail

Trail Snapshot

This old wagon road trail offers great bird's eye views of the American River Confluence Area. Its gradual gradient provides a good aerobic workout, climbing 800 feet in 2 miles from the Confluence to the top where it intersects with Russell Road at gate (#138). Many walk from Russell Road down and back. The history of this trail dates back to the mid-1800s (see sidebar on page 31). The trail climbs through riparian corridors, as well as some typical foothill oak woodland areas. Many areas boast spectacular wildflower blooms in the spring. There is little shade, so take water and sunscreen on hot summer days.

Above: Louis Foscalina's North Fork Saloon.

Below: Upstream from the Mountain Quarries and Lyon's Bridges was an outdoor dance floor.

Courtesy of the Placer County Archives

Trailhead Parking

(N38-55.010; W121-02.207)

Trailhead is at the Confluence Area, 1¾ miles south of the ASRA Park Headquarters. Take Hwy. 49 from Auburn south to Old Foresthill Road at the bottom of the canyon. Continue straight for ¼ mile and park on the left. The trailhead is just beyond the parking area at green gate (#137) near a kiosk and toilet.

Stagecoach Trail

The trail begins at the Confluence area by the information kiosk and heads towards the high Foresthill Bridge. It is marked by a Stagecoach Trail to Russell Road sign. The first ¼ mile is

the steepest, but it provides good views of the North Fork American River at several spots on the right.

At about ¼ mile, the trail turns sharply left at the Stagecoach Trail sign where an old access road continues straight ahead. As you pause to catch your breath, you can almost hear the clatter of the horse's hooves and creak of the stagecoaches that once traveled this road.

A short distance up the trail, the graceful arches of Mt. Quarries R/R Bridge come into view on the left. A little further along, the appearance of ponderosa pine, big leaf maple, interior live oak, blue oak, willow, and Himalayan blackberry bushes signal the first of several riparian corridors on the trail. Here water runs year round, unlike other spots on the trail where it is only visible in winter and spring.

Soon a narrow, unmarked trail known as Tinker's Cut-off intersects on the left. A sign marks Flood Trail on the right. At the 1 mile point, a bench provides an opportunity to enjoy an impressive view of the Confluence area and the Mt. Quarries R/R Bridge. Often seen here are turkey vultures riding the thermals low overhead.

Above: The male Sonoran blue butterfly.

Below: Egg about the size of a pinhead on the liveforever leaf.

A few paces beyond the bench is the narrower, unsigned Manzanita Trail, *for hikers and bikers,* which intersects Stagecoach Trail on the left and meanders through manzanita and coyote brush down to the ASRA Park Headquarters.

Continuing up Stagecoach Trail, California poppies and lupine cover the open slopes in early spring. The liveforever succulent, with the bright yellow blooms, grows out of the rock outcrops and is the host plant for the Sonoran blue butterfly. The males have a bright orange spot on the wings. Shortly before arriving at the end of the trail, Upper Stagecoach Trail intersects on the right. At the top of the trail, there is a free public parking area.

Historical Snapshot:

Stagecoach Trail

Originally a toll road built in 1852 known as Yankee Jim's Turnpike and later as Old Stagecoach Road, the road led to a covered toll bridge over the North Fork American River just upriver from Clark's Hole and from there to the towns of Yankee Jim's and Iowa Hill. In the late 1800s, Yankee Jim's was a popular mining area and Foresthill was yet to be developed. In 1875, the original toll bridge was replaced with a wooden covered bridge. In the 1870s, tolls on the bridge ranged from 6¢ for a cow, 50¢ for a horseman to $1 for a wagon and two horses. There were numerous stagecoach hold-ups along this trail, most notably in 1873 and again in 1880.

Alternate Return Routes

(See trail guide on page 33.)

About ¼ mile down the trail, take Upper Stagecoach Trail to the left, (hikers and bikers only). This narrow trail is not as well graded as Stagecoach Trail, but offers rest and canyon views from a wooden bench chair at the top of the hill. A short distance beyond at another wooden bench, with a view of the Foresthill Bridge, there is a fork and sign noting Flood Trail straight ahead and Stagecoach Trail to the right. Turn right and descend through a grove of manzanita, or "little apples"–a tart but edible berry fruit. On the left, remnants of a stone foundation, along with non-native plants such as lilac, a field of periwinkle and apple and fig trees provide evidence of a former home site. Continue straight past the sign for Mossy Rock Trail on the left until you come to Stagecoach Trail. Turn left to return to the Confluence area.

Just ahead on the right, the unmarked and narrower Tinker's Cut-off Trail offers an alternate return route for hikers. While the top and bottom are a bit steep, it is a cooler hike on hot summer days as it switchbacks through a dense, tree-lined creek riparian area with a small pool and year-round waterfall.

Courtesy of Placer Co. Historical Society

The Auburn, Foresthill, Michigan Bluff and Colfax Stage carried both passengers and mail. The Colfax and Iowa Hill Stage No. 2, similar to the Auburn Foresthill Stage, is on display in the carriage barn at the Bernhard Museum Complex in Auburn. It is owned by the Native Sons of the Golden West.

TRAIL AT-A-GLANCE:

UPPER STAGECOACH TRAIL

DISTANCE: 1 mile one-way; ½ hour (hiking)
This does not include the distance walked on Stagecoach Trail to the trailhead.
Access to this trail is from Stagecoach Trail.

DIFFICULTY: Easy to Moderate

ELEVATION CHANGE: +/- 600'

UPPER STAGECOACH TRAIL

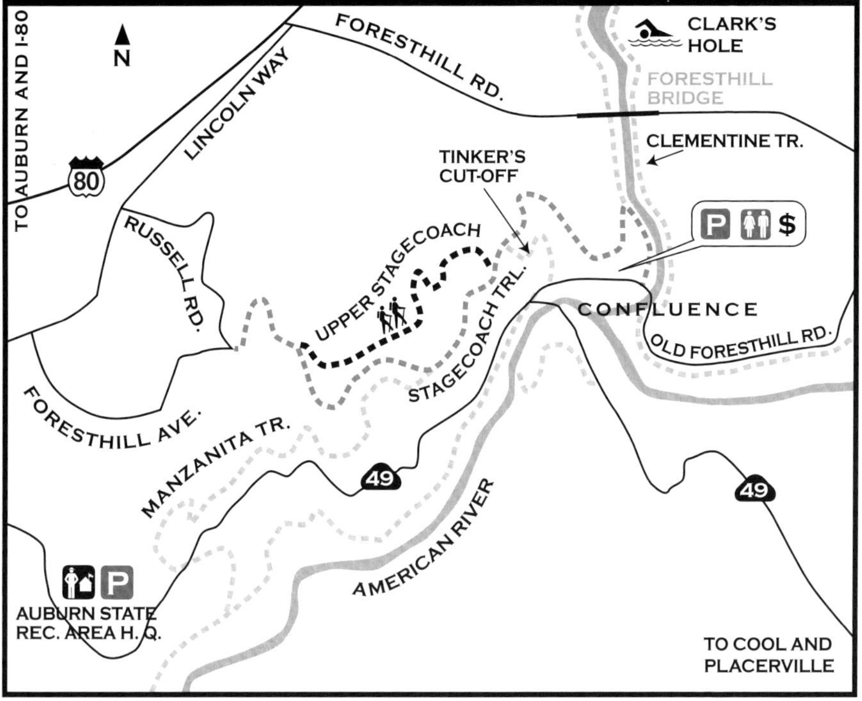

Upper Stagecoach Trail

Barn owl

TRAIL SNAPSHOT

This trail is an alternate to Stagecoach Trail. While not as wide, level or well graded as Stagecoach Trail, it provides another perspective on the canyon and has some shade. On clear days it is possible to see the snow-capped Sierra Nevada, as well as views both up and down the American River canyon. There are two locations where there are benches from which to enjoy the views along the way. The trail crosses several small oak meadows. It also provides a good view of the imposing Foresthill Bridge, (see sidebar for Lake Clementine and Clark's Hole Trail on page 49). Listen for the short soft descending whistles of the screech owl, hoots of the great horned owl or sharp screech of the barn owl at dusk.

The Canyon Keepers on a hike of Upper Stagecoach Trail.

Trailhead Parking

(N38-54.683; W121-03.257)

Parking is off Russell Road. From I-80, exit at Foresthill. Turn right *(west)* on Lincoln Way. Follow Lincoln Way for about ½ mile and turn left onto Russell Road. Drive slowly as many residents, children, and pets may be walking or biking along this narrow, rural road. After about ½ mile there is a small parking area on the left as you round a curve to the right. The trailhead is behind the parking area beyond green gate (#138).

UPPER STAGECOACH TRAIL

Upper Stagecoach Trail is usually used as an alternative route to or from Stagecoach Trail or as a shorter hike from Russell Road.

From the top of Stagecoach Trail *(off Russell Road)* proceed down Stagecoach Trail for just over a ¼ mile.

Fairy lantern

Upper Stagecoach Trail begins at the sign on your left. *(N38-54.730; W121-03.142)*. Go left up the hill at the sign for Upper Stagecoach.

Stay on the main trail. All others lead to private property or are unauthorized by State Parks.

Shortly after reaching the top of the rise, the trail comes out of the trees and shrubs into an area of small, open meadows. In less than 0.2 miles there is a nice wide wooden chair offering views of the canyon and hikers below on Stagecoach Trail. The view encompasses Hwy. 49 curving towards Cool and the Quarry Trail along the south bank of the Middle Fork American River, as well as views up the Middle Fork. The wide, steep trail that rises to the ridgeline across the canyon, at the end of the cable with the orange balls, is the Pointed Rocks Trail to Cool.

Gray Fox tracks

After passing a small meadow, but before re-entering the trees and scrubs, there is another bench with a good view of the Foresthill Bridge.

Shortly after reentering the woodlands, at ½ mile, Upper Stagecoach Trail meets Flood Trail. At the fork a sign points to Stagecoach Trail to the right and Flood Trail straight ahead. This connector down to Stagecoach is ½ mile, and is usually considered part of Upper Stagecoach Trail. Do not continue straight on Flood Trail. This narrow, overgrown, and single track trail leads up to Flood Road, a residential neighborhood with no parking. This mostly overgrown trail offers little to see.

To return to the trailhead, go right using the Stagecoach Trail loop. The beginning section of this section of trail is a rutted, single track, red clay trail through a small manzanita grove. After this, watch for a large field of periwinkle on the left. Looking behind the periwinkle, the remnants of the stone foundation of a house may be seen. A few steps further, on your left, is the start of the Mossy Rock Trail. Continue straight ahead and down. In about 0.1 mile you will reach Stagecoach Trail at a little past the halfway point. From here, turn right and return to Russell Road or turn left and follow Stagecoach Trail down to the confluence. *(See separate guide for Stagecoach Trail on page 29.)*

TRAIL AT-A-GLANCE:

Tinker's Cut-Off

DISTANCE: 0.3 of a mile one-way; ¼ hours (hiking)

DIFFICULTY: Moderate to difficult
Both top and bottom sections have been severely rutted by unauthorized bicycle use.

ELEVATION CHANGE: +/- 400'

TINKER'S CUT-OFF TRAIL

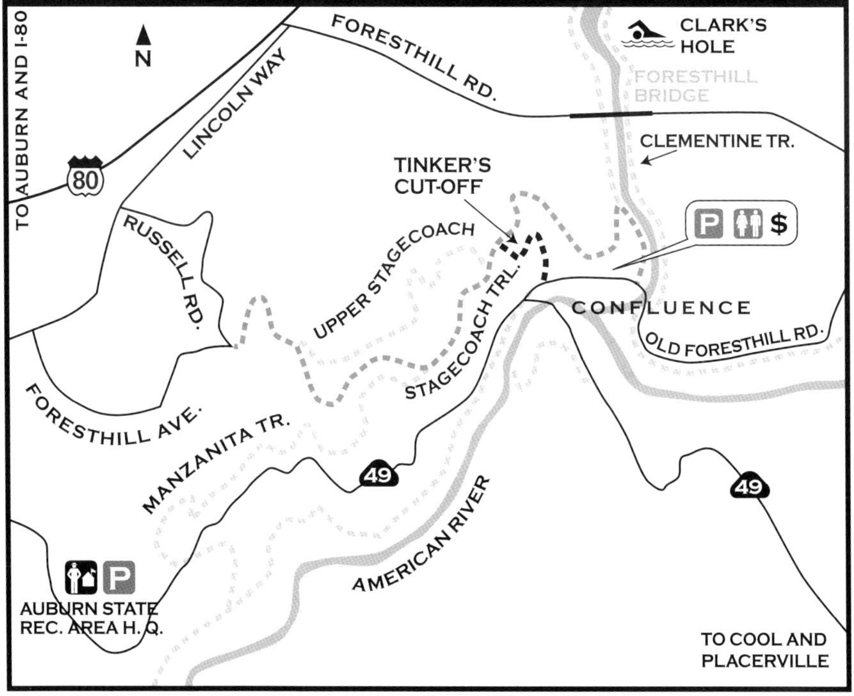

Tinker's Cut-Off

TRAIL SNAPSHOT

This single file trail offers an alternate route to and from Stagecoach Trail from the Confluence area. It follows a creek drainage through a tree-lined riparian area with a small pool and year-round waterfall. It is a popular cut-off for hikers in the summer months, providing welcome shade not always found on the Stagecoach Trail.

Trailhead Parking *(N38-54.961; W121-02.437)*

The trailhead is 1¾ miles south of the ASRA Park Headquarters in the Confluence area. Take Hwy. 49 from Auburn (south) to Old Foresthill Road at the bottom of the canyon. Park as close to the Hwy. 49 bridge to Cool as allowed. This trailhead is almost directly opposite the Hwy. 49 bridge on the Placer County or north side of the river. Looking uphill, a clear, sharp cut in the bank is visible.

The trail may also be accessed off of Stagecoach Trail. The upper trailhead for Tinker's Cut-Off is just a little less than 1 mile from the Confluence via Stagecoach Trail.

TINKER'S CUT-OFF TRAIL

Tinker's Cut-Off may be hiked up and back, but most people use it to either go up to Stagecoach Trail from the confluence or as a cut-off from Stagecoach back to the Confluence Area. The bank at the bottom has been badly eroded by unauthorized mountain biking use and there are now two paths visible on the right to loop around the steepest, narrowest portion.

Go straight up the hill to where the trail crosses a gully carrying water on a seasonal basis. As you continue up through the tall trees and dappled shade, moving water may be heard and seen bubbling over the rocks and boulders in the creek bed on the right. Just before the trail turns sharply left and away from the creek, not far below Stagecoach Trail, there is an opening on the right where there is a pleasant, mini-waterfall in the creek. This riparian oasis is a favorite spot for a break on a hot day.

As you leave the creek, the trail begins a series of switchbacks leading to Stagecoach Trail.

Upon reaching Stagecoach Trail *(see separate trail guide on page 29)*, the choices are to return back to the start or turn right and return to the Confluence area via the slightly longer, but less steep Stagecoach Trail. Or go left and continue up Stagecoach Trail to Russell Road before returning to the Confluence Area.

Below, a lunch break under the big fig tree on Manzanita Trail.

TRAIL SNAPSHOT:

All new trails in ASRA must be environmentally approved and built under state park supervision. In the past, many trails were built and maintained by individuals. One local couple, Bob and Harriet Stephens, using their own tools, cleared and created several of the popular Confluence trails in use today. Tinker's Cut-Off is named for Harriet *(Bob's nickname for his wife)*. Bob, who passed away in 2010, said, "You don't appreciate the amount of work that goes into trail-building until you've done some yourself." Today Harriet, who lives near the Stagecoach trailhead, frequently walks the trails she and Bob created together.

TRAIL AT-A-GLANCE:

PARK HQ-TO-CONFLUENCE LOOP

TRAILS INCLUDED: Park Access Trail
Western States Trail
Tinker's Cut-Off Trail
Stagecoach Trail
Manzanita Trail

DISTANCE: 3½ miles /2 hours (hiking)

DIFFICULTY: Easy to moderate
Occasionally short and steep

ELEVATION CHANGE: +/- 1000'

PARK HQ-TO-CONFLUENCE LOOP

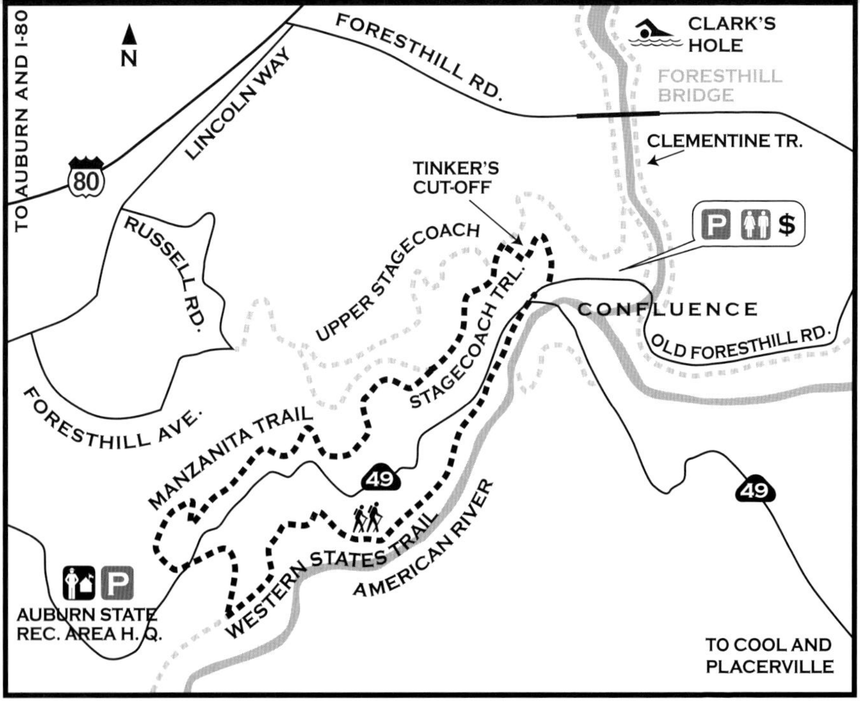

Park HQ-to-Confluence Loop

Trail Snapshot

This loop affords many beautiful views of the American River Canyon and the Confluence Area. It also includes some of the most historic trails and sites in the Confluence Area. Although the trails may be steep at times, it is mostly an easy loop through three of the common American River Canyon ecosystems: foothill woodland, riparian, and chaparral.

Trailhead Parking *(N38-54.300; W121-03.296)*

Trailhead is on Hwy. 49, opposite ASRA Park HQ, ¾ miles south of Auburn at the green gate (#136). Parking is at ASRA Park HQ. An alternate trailhead is at the Confluence area, 1½ miles south of Park HQ. Take Hwy. 49 south to Old Foresthill Road at the bottom of the canyon; go straight and park on the right just past the intersection.

Poison oak is common on most foothill trails.

Park HQ-to-Confluence Loop

The loop starts at the ASRA Park Headquarters. Carefully cross Hwy. 49 opposite the Park HQ and head down the Park Access Trail behind the metal green gate (#136). This trail is fairly steep, dropping 360 feet in less than a half mile. At the bottom of the hill, turn left onto the historic Western States Trail *(see page 97 in the WST section for more history)*. This trail follows the old Mountain Quarries R/R bed. Several old cement pilings for the railroad trestles can be seen along the trail. The cascading waterfall and wet boulder-strewn stream crossing is known as the "Black Hole of Calcutta".

The next mile is a gentle descent to the Mt. Quarries R/R Bridge *(see sidebar on page 41)*, that alternates from wide railroad bed to single track in the ravines. Side trails lead down to sandy beaches and gentle rapids on the American River, popular with sunbathers on hot summer days. Approaching the Mt. Quarries R/R Bridge, two other bridges can be seen in the distance: the Hwy. 49 Bridge and the high Foresthill Bridge.

The loop continues via an unmarked path on your left just before the Mt. Quarries R/R Bridge. This trail parallels Hwy. 49 and goes under the Hwy. 49 bridge. The metal and cement debris in the river is from the old Hwy. 49 bridge which collapsed in 1964 when the Hell Hole coffer dam failed. After reaching the road, cross to the other side and go up the steep hill just behind the green Cool/Placerville sign. This is the start of Tinker's Cut-Off *(see page 36)*. This scenic trail is steep with many switchbacks, climbing 320 feet in just 0.3 mile. It passes through thick riparian woodlands as it parallels a small creek with several tiny waterfalls (the best flows are in winter and spring).

At the top of Tinker's Cut-Off, turn left onto the historic Stagecoach Trail *(see page 29)*. This is the actual road used by stagecoaches to carry passengers between Foresthill and Auburn in the late 1800s. Its wide, gentle gradient makes it a favorite of hikers and bikers throughout the year. Continue up the hill to a bench on the left, affording an opportunity to catch your breath, enjoy the view and take more photos of the Confluence area. The high water mark of the reservoir would be just below your feet. As you sit, be thankful the Auburn Dam Reservoir did not drown the beautiful and popular Confluence Area.

The Confluence is a great place to test your panning skills.

Manzanita Trail

A few paces beyond the bench, go left on the unmarked Manzanita Trail, which intersects Stagecoach Trail at a sharp angle. Although narrower, Manzanita Trail is fairly level and meanders through manzanita groves and crosses a couple of creeks. After a mile of fairly easy hiking, the trail ends at a firebreak road just above ASRA Park HQ. Look for white cable TV boxes and then take the firebreak road on the left past some buildings to return to Park HQ.

Historical Snapshot:

Mountain Quarries Railroad Bridge

The Mountain Quarries Railroad Bridge was one of the world's longest reinforced concrete bridges when it was completed in 1912. It was used until 1940 by the Mt. Quarries Railroad to haul limestone from the nearby quarry up to the Central Pacific R/R main line in Auburn. The arched bridge has withstood several floods, including the disastrous one of 1964 resulting from the failure of Hell Hole Dam–a testament to its rugged design. In 1942, the railroad tracks were taken up for the war effort. Today, the bridge is the main artery for hikers and equestrians on the Western States Trail between Cool and Auburn. It was nicknamed "No Hands Bridge" by horsewoman Ina Robinson who rode her horse over it prior to the construction of the safety railing without holding onto the reins, shouting, "Look, no hands!" It was listed on the National Register of Historic Places in 2004.

Mountain Quarries Railroad Bridge, circa 1911

Photo by Alice Dunbar

A Confluence of recreational activities!

TRAIL AT-A-GLANCE:

Western States MQRR Bed Section

DISTANCE: 2 miles; 1 hour each way (hiking)

DIFFICULTY: Easy to moderate

ELEVATION CHANGE: +/- 500’

WESTERN STATES MQRR RAILROAD BED SECTION

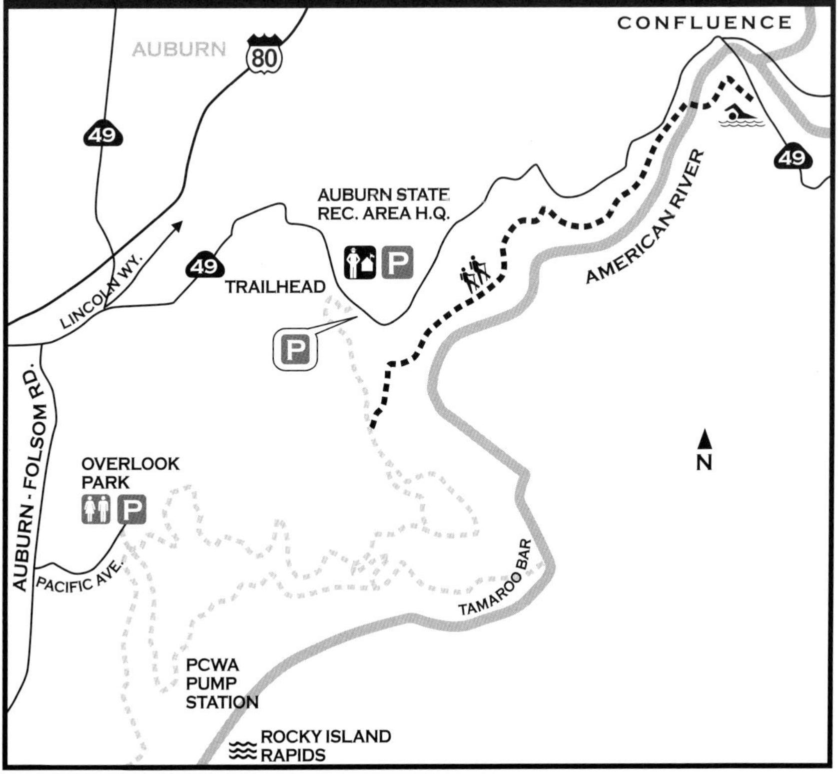

Western States Mountain Quarries Railroad Bed Section

TRAIL SNAPSHOT

This short section of the Western States Trail offers an easy outing with excellent river views of the American River. The trail follows the old Mountain Quarries Railroad roadbed for most of its route. It is fairly wide and level in most places. Users pass several reminders of the railroad along the way. The trail remains in sight of the river through its entire length. Several short spur trails lead down to the river and its many gravel bars and swimming spots.

Photo by A. C. Phelps, courtesy of Michael Lynch

Engine 103 pulls crushed limestone in four gondola cars, circa 1940

Trailhead Parking

East (Confluence Area by Hwy. 49 Bridge):

(N38-54.893; W121-02.388)

Trailhead is on Hwy. 49, 1¾ miles southeast of ASRA Park Headquarters. Take Hwy. 49 south from Auburn towards Placerville. After crossing the American River, park on right off the highway. Walk to trailhead through the green gate (#150).

West (Hwy. 49 – Robie Point trailhead):

(N38-54.001; W121-03.536)

Trailhead is accessed from parking area on Hwy. 49, southbound from Auburn ½ mi (on the right) or northbound from ASRA Park Headquarters ¼ mi (on the left). Caution: cars coming downhill are hard to see. From the parking area behind the gate (#130), walk ½ mile of Robie Point trail. The trailhead is a narrow trail on the left marked with a metal 'Trail' or WST sign. *(N38-53.707; W121-03.426)*

WESTERN STATES MQRR BED SECTION

The railroad bed section is a scenic and easily reached portion of the Western States Trail *(see page 97 in the WST section for more history)*. Leaving the Confluence Area and Hwy. 49 trailhead, one quickly arrives at the Mt. Quarries R/R Bridge.

Cliff swallows nesting on the bridge always put on a show in spring. Be sure and stop at the far end and read the plaque, outlining the history of this graceful structure. The route continues just above the American River. Along the way, the small trails on the left lead down to gravel or sand bars that serve as swimming areas in the summer. Listen for the yellow-breasted chat's whistles and brash calls coming from the willows in the late spring and early summer. The wider, main trail continues downstream. After 0.7 of a mile, the first of several concrete remains of trestle abutments will be found on the left side of the trail with the date 1921 etched on the corner. Since these remnants always mark where the railroad crossed a ravine, look for its replica on the other side. At these spots, since the trestles no longer exist, the trail leaves the original roadbed and become narrower and not as well graded as it goes up, down and around the intervening ravine. Note the various dates etched in the trestle abutments along the way.

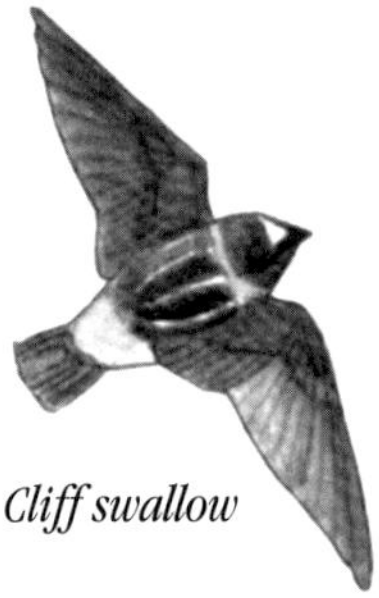
Cliff swallow

After 1 mile, the trail has a steep descent and ascent to and from a pretty area popularly known as "the Black Hole of Calcutta". As the name implies, the area is always shaded and darker than the surrounding area. Mist or spray from the graceful waterfall ensures a consistently moist and cool environment.

Leaving this oasis, the trail climbs back to the railroad bed. At 1.28 miles, the Headquarters Park Access Trail comes in on an angle on the right. Along the next stretch there is a concrete bench to enjoy river views and wildflowers in spring. At 1½ miles, the trail passes a rock outcropping on the right and the tall, somewhat pyramid shaped spire known as Eagle Rock. Don't expect eagles, but there is a good chance of finding turkey vultures.

Past the rock outcrop, in the tiny clearing on the right, shaded by a large oak, are some rotting timbers. This is all that remains of the water tower that served here as a watering stop for the MQRR steam engines. A few paces further, at 1.6 miles, is a trestle abutment from 1917. This is as far as the trail follows the old roadbed. If you are doing this as an out-and-back, this is a good turn around spot. From here the trail becomes a narrow series of zigzags through the trees up the hillside to the Robie Point Firebreak Trail. This section is muddy and slippery after heavy rains.

Reaching the Robie Point Firebreak Trail, riders go left following the WST to the staging area in Auburn. Hikers often go right for ½ mile to the parking area on Hwy. 49, a good place to leave a shuttle car.

TRAIL AT-A-GLANCE:

Robie Point Firebreak Trail

DISTANCE:	3.6 miles one way; 1½ hours each way (hiking), but a variety of shorter options are available
DIFFICULTY:	Easy to moderate
ELEVATION CHANGE:	+/- 850'

ROBIE POINT FIREBREAK TRAIL

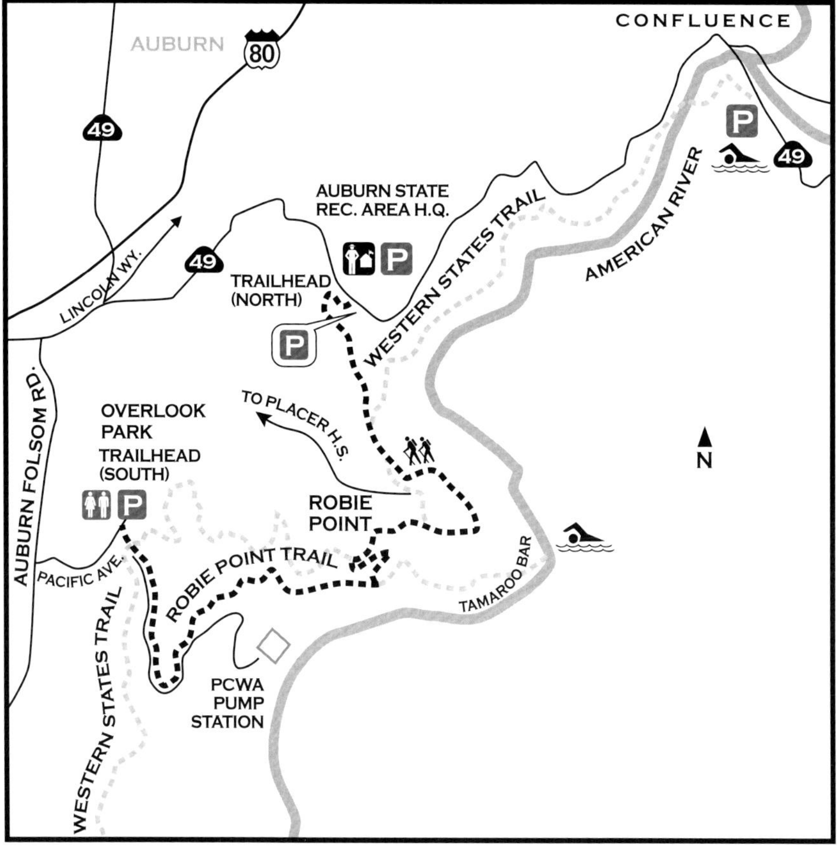

Robie Point Firebreak Trail

TRAIL SNAPSHOT

This firebreak trail is wide and well-maintained. It provides great views of the North Fork American River canyon and the Auburn Dam construction site. Although the trail is steep at the southern end, it is otherwise fairly gentle and passes through three of the most common American River canyon ecosystems: foothill woodland, riparian, and chaparral. It can be hot in the summer since there is little shade, but it is ideal in the late afternoon or early evening for a hike or ride.

Trailhead Parking

North: ***(N38-54.001; W121-03.536)***

Trailhead (north) is on Hwy. 49, southbound from Auburn, ½ of a mile (on the right) or northbound from ASRA Park Headquarters and a ¼ of a mile (on the left), behind gate (#130). Caution: cars coming downhill are hard to see on the curve.

South: ***(N38-53.245; W121-04.246)***

Trailhead (south) is at Overlook Park behind the Gold Country Fairgrounds. Take Hwy. 49 and Lincoln Way north through Auburn to Auburn-Folsom Road. Turn left onto Auburn-Folsom Road and left again at the second stoplight onto Pacific Ave. Turn right after a ½ mile into the large Overlook parking area. After parking, walk back along Pacific Avenue to the Camp Flint gate (#141) trailhead. Continue on the paved pump station road down the hill. The road splits after 100 yards; follow the left fork down the hill 0.8 mile past the electrical substation to the signed trailhead on the left.

ROBIE POINT FIREBREAK TRAIL

Starting at the Hwy. 49 north end, the Robie Point Firebreak Trail (#130), gradually descends to a small creek, passing through a densely forested oak, pine and riparian areas. The first 500 feet is paved and then turns to packed dirt. After crossing the creek, the trail soon enters the main American

River canyon with some awesome views of the North Fork American River. Looking east, you can see the snow-capped Sierra Mountains in the distance.

Hiking the Robie Point Trail.

At the 0.5 mile point, the trail merges with the historic Western States Trail (WST), which enters from the left (a narrow dirt trail). At ¾ miles, the WST splits off to the right, uphill to enter Auburn. For those wanting more of a workout, take the WST for ¼ mile up and over Robie Point. Otherwise, continue to the left on the main Robie Point Firebreak Trail around Robie Point. Birding is good around the point with ruby-crowned kinglets, spotted towhees, oak titmice and cedar waxwings in residence during various times of the year.

Just beyond the 1 mile point, evidence of the Auburn Dam construction project becomes visible. The big rock slide on the opposite side of the canyon at Salt Creek was going to be a boat ramp. The trail rejoins the WST just past the 1¼ mile point. Stay to the left at the junction of the trails.

Just beyond the 1½ mile point, the WST splits off (again) to the right and up the hill around the gate. The Robie Point Firebreak Trail continues to the left down the hill. From this vantage point you get a great view of the partially restored Auburn Dam site and PCWA pump station. The western keyway for the dam is easily visible from here, towards the right.

From this viewpoint, the Robie Point Firebreak Trail descends rapidly for the next ¼ mile. At the bottom of the hill, a side trail splits off to the left, leading down to the river to Tamaroo Bar, (¾ mile and a 400 foot descent). Robie Point Firebreak Trail continues to the right for another 1½ miles and affords even closer views of the dam construction site *(see page 399 for the history of the Auburn Dam)*. The last ¾ mile of the trail is paved and climbs over 500 feet before reaching Pacific Avenue.

TRAIL AT-A-GLANCE:

Lake Clementine and Clark's Hole Trail

DISTANCE: 1.9 miles one way; 1 hour each way (hiking)

DIFFICULTY: Easy

ELEVATION CHANGE: +/- 350'

LAKE CLEMENTINE & CLARK'S HOLE TRAIL

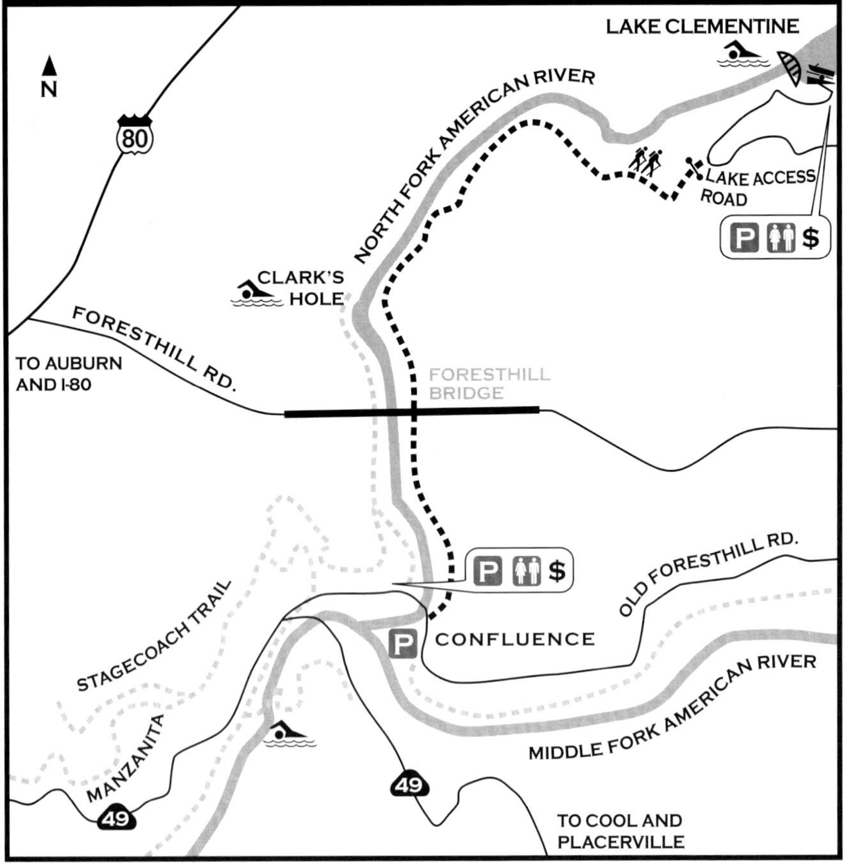

Lake Clementine and Clark's Hole Trail

TRAIL SNAPSHOT

An easy and ideal trail for a panoramic hike along the North Fork American River, mostly in the shade of conifers and oaks. Several side trails lead down to the river, the last one descending to a deep pool beneath the North Fork Dam where a spectacular year-round waterfall cascades over the dam into a summer swimming pool.

Trailhead Parking

(N38-54.941; W121-02.144)

Trailhead is at Confluence area, 1¾ miles south of ASRA Park Headquarters. Take Hwy. 49 from Auburn (south) to Old Foresthill Road at the bottom of the canyon. Continue straight for ¼ mile, cross the curved Old Foresthill Rd. Bridge, and park on the right. Trailhead is on the left across from the parking area behind the green gate (#139).

This 185 foot-long, covered North Fork bridge was a privately built toll bridge linking Auburn to the towns of Yankee Jim's, Foresthill and Michigan Bluff. Pictured in front is the Auburn-Foresthill Stage, circa 1910.

LAKE CLEMENTINE AND CLARK'S HOLE TRAIL

The Lake Clementine Trail begins at the Confluence area on the far side of the curved Old Foresthill Rd. Bridge (built in 1955). It parallels the North Fork American River upstream, river left. At ¼ mile, concrete abutments for what was known as the Steel Bridge (1911-1955), may be seen on the opposite riverbank. At ½ mile, the trail goes under the Foresthill Bridge *(see sidebar on following page)*.

At ¾ mile, Clark's Hole can be seen on the left. It is a deep and clear rock-lined swimming hole popular with locals for over one hundred years. A short side trail, on the left, leads down to the pool and a sandy beach. The summer water temperature of the river below Lake Clementine is surprisingly warm since it is fed from sun-warmed water from the surface of Lake Clementine flowing over the North Fork Dam. By contrast, the Middle Fork American River is fed from the bottom of Oxbow

Reservoir and is considerably colder.

At 1 mile, rock abutments of a wooden covered toll bridge, built in 1875 and used until 1911, are visible on the opposite riverbank. A short distance upriver, if you look carefully, you can see evidence on the opposite riverbank of abutments where three different bridges existed between 1852 and 1875.

Continuing upriver, this part of the trail uses a largely shaded roadway once the old stagecoach route connecting Auburn with the gold rush camps of Foresthill, Yankee Jim's and Iowa Hill.

Lake Clementine trail ends at Lake Clementine Road. Follow this paved road to the left for about ¼ mile and then take the unmarked side trail on the left towards the river for an exciting view of water plunging over the dam face into a summer swimming pool *(see page 76 sidebar in the Applegate to Lake Clementine Trail section)*.

TRAIL SNAPSHOT:

Foresthill Bridge

The 2,248 foot long Foresthill Bridge was designed to span the reservoir that would have resulted had the Auburn Dam been completed. (Work on the dam was discontinued in 1976.) Water was expected to reach the top of the cement piers, but today the bridge towers 730 feet above the river, making it the tallest bridge in California. It was opened in 1973 with much fanfare and has been featured in numerous movies and commercials. It has been the site for many stunts–both legal and illegal.

The California Highway Patrol helicopter removes a cargo net bag of trash collected by dedicated volunteers at the annual Earth Day American River Cleanup.

Trash thrown off the bridge creates a safety hazard for those recreating in the river and using the trails below. As part of the 2012-2014 Foresthill Bridge Seismic Retrofit Project, the bridge railing has being raised to 5½ feet to deter dumping and suicide plunges from the bridge.

TRAIL AT-A-GLANCE:

MIDDLE FORK CONFLUENCE TRAIL

DISTANCE: 1.8 mile one way; ½ hour down; 1 hour up (hiking)

DIFFICULTY: Moderate

ELEVATION CHANGE: +/- 600'

MIDDLE FORK CONFLUENCE TRAIL

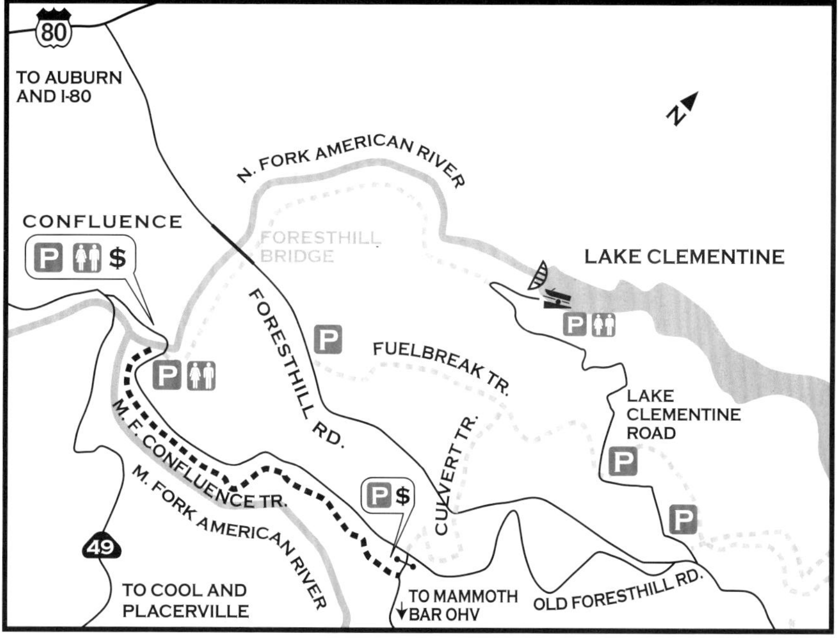

An unique view of a Foresthill Bridge base-jumper at the 2013 Adventure Auburn event.

Photo by Gary Hughes

Middle Fork Confluence Trail

TRAIL SNAPSHOT

This trail provides a short, scenic, out-and-back excursion along the north side of the Middle Fork and is dotted with wildflowers in the spring. It offers the best views of the waters of the Middle Fork American River above the Confluence Area, as well as unique views of the quarry site on the opposite bank. It is often combined with other trails to make a longer loop.

Trailhead Parking

West: ***(N38-54.940; W121-02.150)***
Trailhead (west) parking is on Old Foresthill Road at the Confluence area, 1¾ miles south of the ASRA Park Headquarters. Take Hwy. 49 from Auburn (south) to Old Foresthill Road at the bottom of the canyon. Continue straight for ¼ mile. Cross the curved Old Foresthill Bridge, and park on the right. The trailhead is between a large 'Warning Strong Current' sign and toilet. At the fork, go left on the trail above the cobble beach. This is also a very popular mountain bike trail.

East: ***(N38-55.333; W121-00.906)***
Trailhead (east), drive approximately 1½ miles up the Old Foresthill Road from the Confluence area to the entrance to the Mammoth Bar OHV Area. Park by the info panel. (This turnout also serves the trailhead for the Culvert Trail that begins across the road.) To reach the Confluence trailhead east *(N38-55.235; W121-00.739)* walk down the Mammoth Bar Road for 0.2 mile, past the self-pay kiosk for OHV's. The trailhead is on your right behind the yellow gate (#107).

MIDDLE FORK CONFLUENCE TRAIL

The Confluence Trail offers a rolling but gentle climb above the flowing waters of the Middle Fork below the Old Foresthill Road. Starting at the Confluence almost immediately below the trail, the roiling waters of the Middle Fork force their way over the bedrock at Louisiana Bar also known as J-Turn Rapid. At one time the trail was a paved road and remnants of the old asphalt may still be found. Due to its popularity with hikers and bikers going in both directions, changing road surface, dips and rises, riders often find it more challenging than hikers. Much of the trail is single track so riders need to watch speed around blind curves to avoid hitting hikers and other bikers. There are two small creek crossings along the trail.

In spring, the trail is often awash in color. California poppies and lupine paint the hillsides with color. Wild iris, lace pods, globe lilies, Indian paintbrush, twining brodea and owl clover are among the many wildflowers that may be spotted along this trail.

There are several interesting views of the limestone quarry, located above the Middle Fork on the opposite bank, near Cool *(see sidebar)*. Ahead there is a large limestone outcropping that is a continuation of the same limestone vein. There is a spur trail through the brush worth taking to explore the limestone outcrop.

The trail continues across Mammoth Bar OHV road into the OHV park where the hiker may encounter motorcycle riders. A point of interest is the rock wall that supports the trail about ¼ mile from the road crossing.

Return to the Confluence, on the same trail or go back to the Confluence by using a combination of the Culvert, Fuelbreak or Lake Clementine trails. The other option is to have a shuttle car parked at the entrance to the Mammoth Bar OHV Park.

Historical Snapshot:

The Quarry

The Quarry was first known as the Cool Cave Quarry. In the 1860s Munson Manning started a limekiln here. In 1910, the Pacific Portland Cement Company began its Mountain Quarries operation at the site. It built a railroad track and the Mountain Quarries Railroad Bridge to carry its products to the main line in Auburn. The Bureau of Reclamation bought the right of way and underground site of the Mountain Quarries when work began on the proposed Auburn Dam. Spreckles Sugar Company operated the quarry from the 1930s until 1987. Teichert is the current operator.

The quarry contains the largest exposed limestone deposit in the Sierra Nevada mountains. This limestone vein runs under the Middle Fork and is seen on the opposite bank below the Confluence Trail. This same limestone vein juts up above ground on the North Fork, notably as Lime Rock or Robbers Roost. The deposit is extremely pure with an average purity rating of 96-98%, which historically led to its use in the food and beverage industry, as well as in the production of cement.

Compare this current photo of the Quarry with the historic photo pictured in the Hawver Cave article in the Lower Middle Fork Whitewater section.

TRAIL AT-A-GLANCE:

CULVERT TRAIL

DISTANCE: 1 mile one way; ½ hour down; ¾ hour up (hiking)
Add 1 mile (½ hour) from trailhead (north)

DIFFICULTY: Moderate

ELEVATION CHANGE: +/- 650'

CULVERT TRAIL

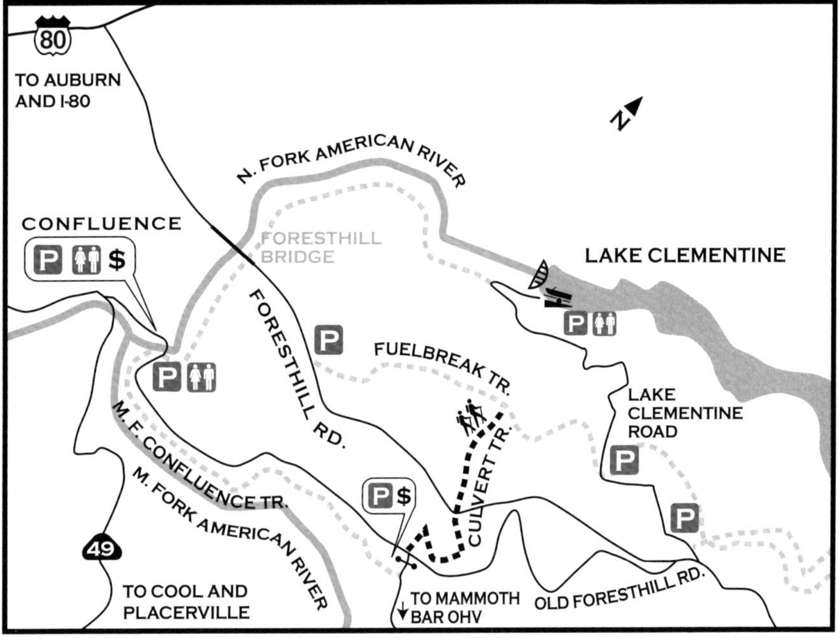

Culvert Trail

Trail Snapshot

This short trail goes under the Foresthill Road to connect the North and Middle Fork American River trails safely, without having to traverse busy Foresthill Road. It passes through rolling oak woodland and open grassland dotted with wildflowers in spring.

Trailhead Parking

North: ***(N38-55.400; W121-01.876)***
Trailhead (north) parking is on Foresthill Road 0.1 of a mile east of the Foresthill Bridge, at a large parking area on the left, just after the bridge. Access the north end of the Culvert Trail from the Fuel Break Trail behind the green gate (#114), or from the Fuel Break Trailhead on Lake Clementine Road next to the green gate (#146).

South: ***(N38-55.341; W121-00.911)***
Trailhead (south) is on Old Foresthill Road 1½ miles down Foresthill Road or 1½ miles up Old Foresthill Road from the Confluence. The trailhead is directly across from the entrance to Mammoth Bar OHV area. Currently there is free parking near the bulletin board.

Culvert Trail

A popular year-round trail, the Culvert Trail is most frequently used by hikers and bikers to extend their outing to connect with other trails, such as the Lake Clementine, Fuel Break, Lakeview Connector or Middle Fork Confluence Trails.

Bikers almost universally access it from Lake Clementine or Fuel Break Trail. Starting from the top or trailhead (north) adds a journey of one mile on the Fuel Break Trail before reaching the Culvert Trail trailhead proper *(N38-55.834; W121-01.167)*. Some bikers access it from the Lake Clementine Road terminus of the Fuel Break Trail, but parking there is limited. It is also accessed from the Confluence on the Middle Fork Confluence Trail. The trail is generally single track with occasional wider spots. In a little less than ½ mile, the long metal culvert passes under the Foresthill Road, for which the trail is named. Expect the culvert to be muddy after rain. After traversing the culvert you reach the prettiest section of the trail, opening up into large, rolling grasslands dotted with majestic blue oaks and beautiful wildflowers in the spring.

Cross the Old Foresthill Road at Mammoth Bar and continue down the paved road to connect with the Middle Fork Confluence Trail. From there it is a quick descent to the Confluence.

TRAIL AT-A-GLANCE:

FUEL BREAK TRAIL

DISTANCE: 1½ miles one way; ¾ hour (hiking)

DIFFICULTY: Easy

ELEVATION CHANGE: +/- 400'

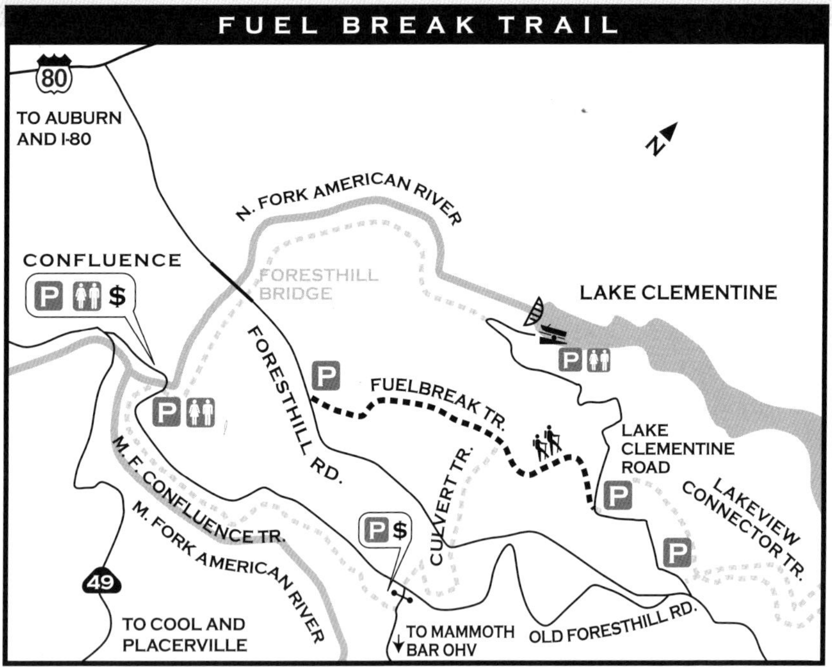

Fuel Break Trail

TRAIL SNAPSHOT

This wide easy trail passes oak meadows, foothill chaparral and woodlands and provides several nice ridge top views. It connects with Lake Clementine Road, the Culvert Trail and the Lakeview Connector Trail. It is often used in conjunction with these trails for longer excursions.

Coyote tracks

Trailhead Parking *(N 38-55-400; W121-01.876)*

Trailhead is off Foresthill Road just past the Foresthill Bridge. Take I-80 to the Foresthill Exit. Drive towards Foresthill, and in less than a mile, cross the Foresthill Bridge. Just after the bridge, the trailhead parking area is visible on the left side of the road. The trailhead is behind the green gate (#114), at the end of the parking strip farthest from the Foresthill Bridge. There is very limited parking at the terminus in a dirt turnout off the Lake Clementine Road next to a green gate (#146).

Lizard tracks

FUEL BREAK TRAIL

The Fuel Break Trail begins in the woodland meadow behind the green gate (#114), at the end of the parking strip farthest from the Foresthill Bridge. Before or after the hike, walk out onto the bridge for a bird's eye view of the confluence and North Fork.

The trail begins by climbing to the ridgeline. The steepest portion of the hike is the first ½ mile. After reaching the ridgeline, the trail levels off and begins a gradual descent. Several small oak meadows are passed along the way. These areas host nice wildflower and wild tom turkey displays in the spring.

Skunk tracks

In addition to hikers and bikers, the trail is popular with the local wildlife. They frequently use it in the early mornings and evenings, especially when the manzanita trees that line several areas of the trail are loaded with berries. They are seldom seen, but their tracks show this is a busy roadway for both large and small animals. It is an ideal place to practice reading the signs of their travels.

After a mile, the Culvert Trail branches off to the right *(see page 55)*. A few other paths will branch off along the way for short distances. Stay on the main trail that continues straight ahead. The trail ends at the paved Lake Clementine Road on the left by the large boulders marking the end of the trail. The Lakeview Connector Trail begins a few feet across and up the road *(see page 69)*.

TRAIL AT-A-GLANCE:

Pointed Rocks Trail

DISTANCE: 1.6 miles one way; 1 hour up,
¾ hours down (hiking)
A variety of loop options are available.

DIFFICULTY: Difficult to moderate

ELEVATION CHANGE: +/- 1,000’

POINTED ROCKS TRAIL

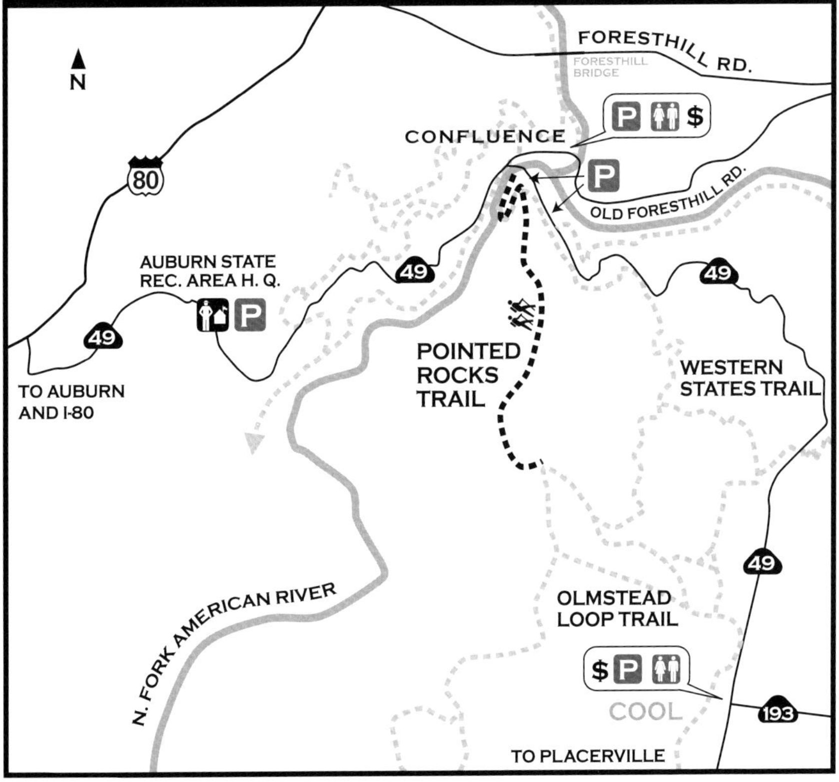

Pointed Rocks Trail

TRAIL SNAPSHOT

Bring binoculars. On clear winter days along the ridge top there are sweeping vistas including Mt. Diablo, the Sacramento Valley and the Coast Mountain Range to the west. Looking to the east, Castle Peaks and the Crystal Range of the Sierra Nevada come into view. Both the Sutter and Sierra Buttes are visible to the north. The trail is also known as Training Hill because it is so steep. It connects to the Olmstead Loop after reaching the ridge, and passing through open, rolling hills and meadows dominated by several species of oaks, and wildflowers in the spring. Stone outcroppings at the top give the trail its name.

A sunny afternoon at the Pointed Rocks.

Trailhead Parking *(N38-54.893; W121-02.388)*

Trailhead is on Hwy. 49, 1¾ miles south of ASRA Park Headquarters. Take Hwy. 49 south from Auburn towards Placerville. After crossing the American River, park on right off the highway. Walk to trailhead through the green gate (#150).

POINTED ROCKS TRAIL

This trail is sometimes referred to as 'The Training Hill' on trail markers since it offers a great workout for endurance runners and equestrians. It provides one of the steepest gradients of any trail in the area. Note: trail markers are posted at some, but not all intersections.

Walk downriver on the trail behind the green gate (#150) on Hwy. 49 on the south side of the bridge over the American River. This wide road parallels the river downstream for about 0.1 mile towards the Mountain Quarries Railroad Bridge.

Just before reaching the Mt. Quarries R/R Bridge, a narrow trail goes up the hillside on the left, look for a sign to Cool *(N38-54.801; W121-02.456)*. This is the start of the Pointed Rocks Trail and a continuation of the Western States Trail (WST). The trail immediately switchbacks and begins climbing. In less than 0.2 of a mile, the trail splits. The Pointed Rocks Trail veers up to the right while the WST continues around the ridge. Take the unsigned Pointed Rocks Trail to the right. The trail widens and starts to climb sharply.

Black-tailed jackrabbit and tracks

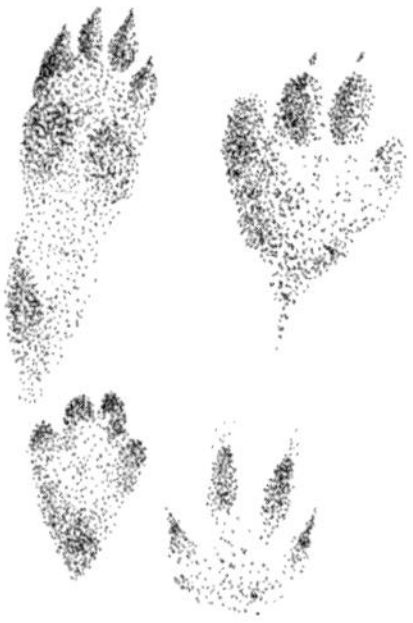

The climb is brutal. Rest and enjoy the views through openings in the trees and shrubs that border the trail. Near the top of the ridge, look back and east for views of the Sierra Mountains and the Middle Fork American River.

After reaching the ridge, the terrain flattens out and meanders through a picturesque rolling oak woodland. Watch for fine-grained stone outcroppings of pointed rocks for which the trail is named.

After reaching an oak meadow, a small footpath splits off to the left. The main, wider trail continues around this meadow, offering a panoramic view on clear days of Folsom Lake and Sacramento. Both paths soon rejoin. Occasionally black-tailed jackrabbits, wild turkeys and western bluebirds are seen in the meadow areas.

A little further along, the Pointed Rocks Trail ends at the Olmstead Loop Trail. Look to the west through the trees for views of Auburn. There are several options at this point, turn around and return to the Confluence the same way or make a loop using the WST for a gentler but longer return trip. The WST branches off the Olmstead Loop a short distance ahead on the left. It is labeled Wendell T. Robie Trail on some trail markers. The 100 mile endurance runners and riders both use this section of the WST for their annual Squaw Valley to Auburn races. Another option is to continue into Cool using the Olmstead Loop along the road-trail with the barbed wire fence where goldfinches like to warm themselves in the morning sun *(see page 62)*. Grab a bite to eat and then return the same way to the Confluence.

TRAIL AT-A-GLANCE:

OLMSTEAD LOOP TRAIL

DISTANCE:	8.6 miles; 4 hours (hiking), but a variety of shorter trail options and cutoffs are also possible
DIFFICULTY:	Easy to moderate
ELEVATION CHANGE:	+/- 370'

OLMSTEAD LOOP TRAIL

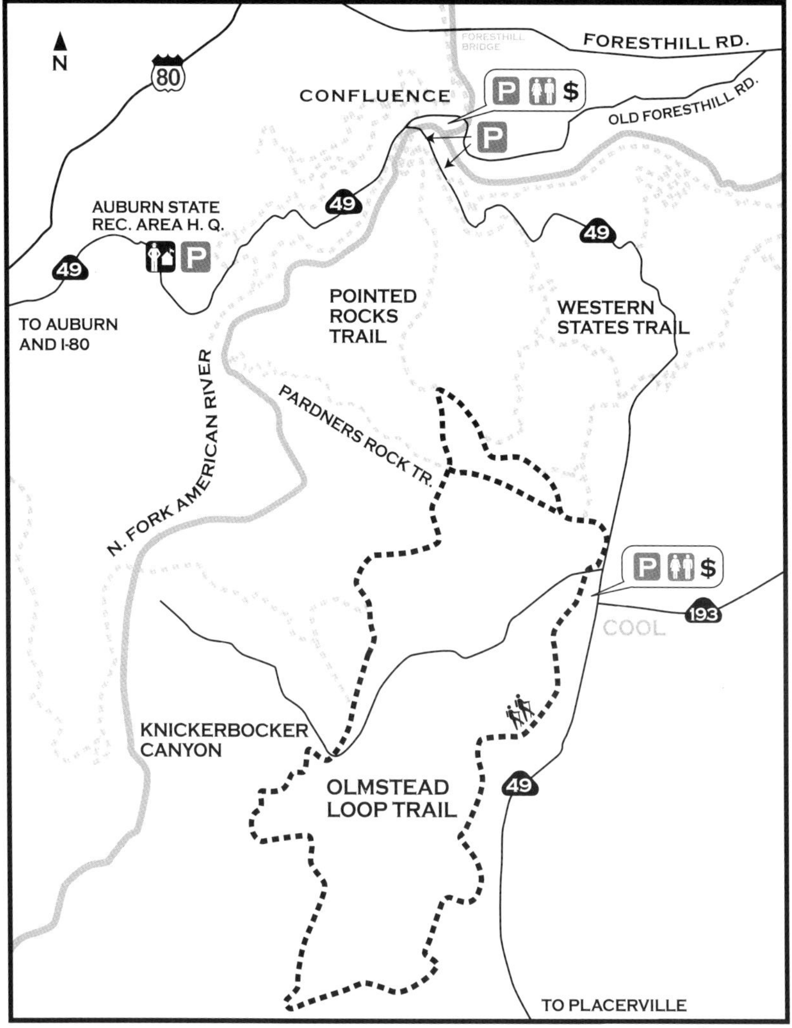

Olmstead Loop Trail

TRAIL SNAPSHOT

This beautiful loop trail, which parallels Hwy. 49 on one side and the American River Canyon on the other, passes through open, rolling hills of oaks, wildflowers and abandoned homesteads and orchards. It also includes steep canyon descents and climbs as it crosses Knickerbocker and Salt Creeks. Side trails on the canyon side offer panoramic views of the North Fork American River and of the Auburn dam construction site. Trail markers have been posted at most trail intersections.

Tandem riders race in the annual Cool Mountain Bike Race.

Trailhead Parking

(N38-53.335; W121-01.036)

Trailhead and parking are behind the fire station in Cool. Take Hwy. 49 south to Cool and turn right at St. Florien Court just before the fire station and blinking red light. This is also the Cool staging area for equestrians. Trailheads are on south and north ends of the parking area.

FATRAC: Folsom-Auburn Trail Riders Action Coalition

FATRAC is a biking organization that educates trail users about proper trail stewardship, including maintenance and trail-building techniques. www.fatrac.org

OLMSTEAD LOOP TRAIL

The Olmstead Loop Trail is especially popular for hikers, bikers and equestrians in the springtime when wildflowers are in bloom. Ponds and vernal pools are visible, and numerous species of birds can be seen. Bobcats, coyote and bear are occasionally glimpsed. The Cool Mountain Bike Race, usually held in March, uses this trail and is well known for its large amounts of flying mud.

Proceeding around the loop in a clockwise direction, most of the first section of the trail is fairly flat and meanders through a typical foothill oak woodland ecosystem. Note: bikes race in a counter-clockwise direction. It passes through sprawling hills, providing great views of the snow-capped Sierras in the distance. At about 3½ miles, the trail starts winding down through a pine forest to Knickerbocker Creek. At the creek crossing, you can enjoy the natural setting with its pools and rushing water before heading uphill again. The more adventurous may want to scramble down a faint side trail to see Knickerbocker Creek waterfalls and pools from the rim of Knickerbocker Canyon.

Continuing on the Olmstead Loop, the trail is steeper beyond Knickerbocker Creek, but after another half mile you will be at the top of a hill that affords a grand view. The trail soon crosses a wide, paved road built to provide access to the top of the foundation for the Auburn Dam. For a shortcut, take this road to the right for 1¾ miles to get back to the Cool fire station (for about a 7 mile loop). Indian grinding rocks are visible just off the paved road in the trees about ¼ mile from Cool.

The Olmstead Loop crosses the paved road and continues on for about another 4 miles. It intersects the Auburn to Cool Trail (labeled Coffer Dam Trail on the markers) twice, once before climbing up a rather steep hill and again shortly before crossing the headwaters of Salt Creek, which is at the bottom of an even steeper descent. A gradual climb leads to an intersection near an old homestead. (Note: The very obscure Pardners Rock Trail starts here, passing through the meadow before dropping steeply down to the river.) The terrain continuing on the Olmstead Loop Trail flattens out, and then another steady climb takes you to the top of a shady knoll. Here, the trail meets the Pointed Rocks Trail *(see page 59)*, which descends left to the Confluence Area.

The Olmstead Loop descends gradually after this, winding to the right in a big U-turn past outcroppings of pointed rocks. It passes two side trails that lead to the Western States Trail (labeled Wendell T. Robie Trail on the markers), which both take off to the left. Tevis Cup riders and 100 mile endurance runners use the WST for their annual Squaw Valley to Auburn races.

The trail then crosses another small knoll before returning along Hwy. 49 to the Cool fire station.

HISTORICAL SNAPSHOT:

Olmstead Loop Trail

The Olmstead Loop Trail was formerly known as the Knickerbocker Trail. It was named for the late Dan Olmstead in 1993. Olmstead was a local, avid mountain biker, hiker and bike shop owner. He dedicated himself to creating harmony between hikers, mountain bikers and equestrians, and to multi-use of trails in this area.

Equestrians and hikers enjoy the Knickerbocker Trail.

Bobcat tracks

TRAIL AT-A-GLANCE:

FORESTHILL DIVIDE LOOP TRAIL

DISTANCE:	8.2 miles; 3.7 hours (hiking) Shorter loops are also possible. Add 1 mile (0.4 hours) from Trail-head (West)
DIFFICULTY:	Easy to moderate
ELEVATION CHANGE:	+/- 320'

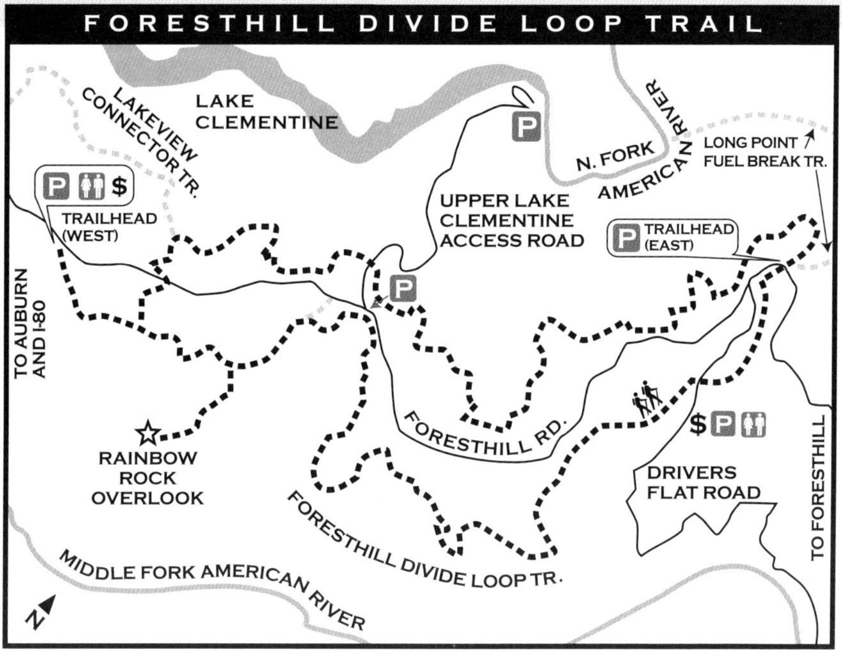

Foresthill Divide Loop Trail

TRAIL SNAPSHOT

This loop features views of both the North Fork and Middle Fork American River and Lake Clementine from the divide ridge which separates the North and Middle Forks. Straddling the Foresthill Divide at elevations ranging from 1600 to 1900 feet, it provides a diversity of flora as it meanders through five major American River Canyon ecosystems: yellow pine forest, foothill woodland, riparian and chaparral. It also passes through open meadow grasslands that overflow with wildflowers in the spring. All of the ecosystems are abundant with wild mushrooms in the wet sunny months.

Mountain bike riders usually ride in a counter-clockwise direction on the Foresthill Divide Loop Trail.

Trailhead Parking

West: (N38-56.561; W120-58.946)

Trailhead (west) is on Foresthill Road, 3½ miles east of Foresthill Bridge, at a large parking area on the right known locally as the Grizzly Bear House turnout.

East: (N38-58.433; W120-57.253)

Trailhead (east) is on Foresthill Road, 7 miles east of Foresthill Bridge (0.2 mile past Drivers Flat Road) at a large parking area on the left. Both trailheads have a port-a-potty.

FORESTHILL DIVIDE LOOP TRAIL

The Foresthill Divide Loop Trail offers a quintessential American River Canyon experience for hikers, bikers and equestrians, and it is extremely popular year round. Starting the loop at

The Upsidedown Tree

the trailhead (west) adds one mile to the 8.2 mile loop, but it is the closer trailhead coming from Auburn.

The trail begins at a green gate (#118), behind the parking area and then turns left into the shade of oak and foothill pines. About 100 yards east of the parking area, there's an old quartz rock foundation of a hotel nestled in the trees which served the gold rush era miners. The hotel was appropriately named the Grizzly Bear House because the skin of an enormous grizzly bear was once spread out on one of its walls, seeming to take the whole building in its embrace. The trail soon opens up into large, rolling grasslands dotted with majestic oaks. One is nicknamed the Upsidedown Tree as its massive, gnarly branches look like roots reaching to the sky. Gobbling wild turkeys delight canyon pilgrims with their fanciful feather displays. Matted spring grass on the fringes of tiny meadows, hidden deep within the woodlands, provide evidence of bear lairs. At ½ mile, turn right at the Drivers Flat marker, which puts you onto the 8.2 mile loop going counter-clockwise. At 1 mile, a side trail to the right leads to Rainbow Rock, an overlook with a magnificent panoramic view of the Middle Fork American River from Poverty Bar to the east and to Brown's Bar to the west. This side trail adds 0.8 of a mile round trip from Rainbow Rock and a 200 foot elevation change.

Wild turkey

Returning to the loop trail, meander on and in and out of shaded foothill woodlands and sunny chaparral dominated by manzanita, buck brush and chemise. At 1.4 miles, the trail turns right while a dirt road continues straight.

Those interested in a shorter, 3.9 mile loop should

continue straight on the dirt road; carefully cross Foresthill Road and go right for 200 yards; turn left onto Upper Lake Clementine Road and go 0.2 of a mile down the road to find the loop trail again. Turn left on the loop trail and proceed 2 miles to return to trailhead (west).

For those remaining on the 8.2 mile loop, the trail becomes narrower and more scenic. At the 2.2 mile point, there is a grand view of the Middle Fork and the Cool limestone quarry to the west. At 3 miles, a well-built wooden bridge crosses a perennial creek. Fresh mud on the trail is a puzzle of animal and human tracks. A bit further, there is a fork in the trail. Stay to the left. At 4.1 miles, either continue straight on the loop trail or turn left and proceed up Drivers Flat Road to Foresthill Road. Either way, when you get to the road, carefully cross and proceed to the parking lot at the trailhead (east). This marks the halfway point of the 8.2 miles loop trail.

From the trailhead (east), the loop trail continues left behind the parking area, passing through a few miles of dense, yellow pine forest and foothill woodlands with occasional glimpses of the North Fork. The trail crosses Upper Clementine Road through dense stands of madrone to a trail intersection. Take the left fork back to the Grizzly Bear House trailhead.

An option to access the North Fork at the east trailhead is to walk straight out the faint Long Point Fuel Break road/trail through mature black oak forest carpeted with pungent smelling mountain misery to excellent views at the North Fork canyon rim. A bulldozed firebreak trail connects to downriver bars.

Historical Snapshot:

Grizzly Bear House

In the summer of 1852 J.D. Borthwick, an English sketch artist who spent the night at the Grizzly Bear House spins this tale of a grizzly in his book *Three Years in California*, "Ursus horribilis, who after having both eyes shot out and winking a good deal, turned on his hunter pursuer, and treed him by scent. The hunter unloaded more shot balls into the grizzly until at last it fell mortally wounded."

TRAIL AT-A-GLANCE:

LAKEVIEW CONNECTOR TRAIL

DISTANCE: 3.6 miles one way; 1½ hours each way (hiking)

DIFFICULTY: Easy to Moderate

ELEVATION CHANGE: +/- 250'

LAKEVIEW CONNECTOR TRAIL

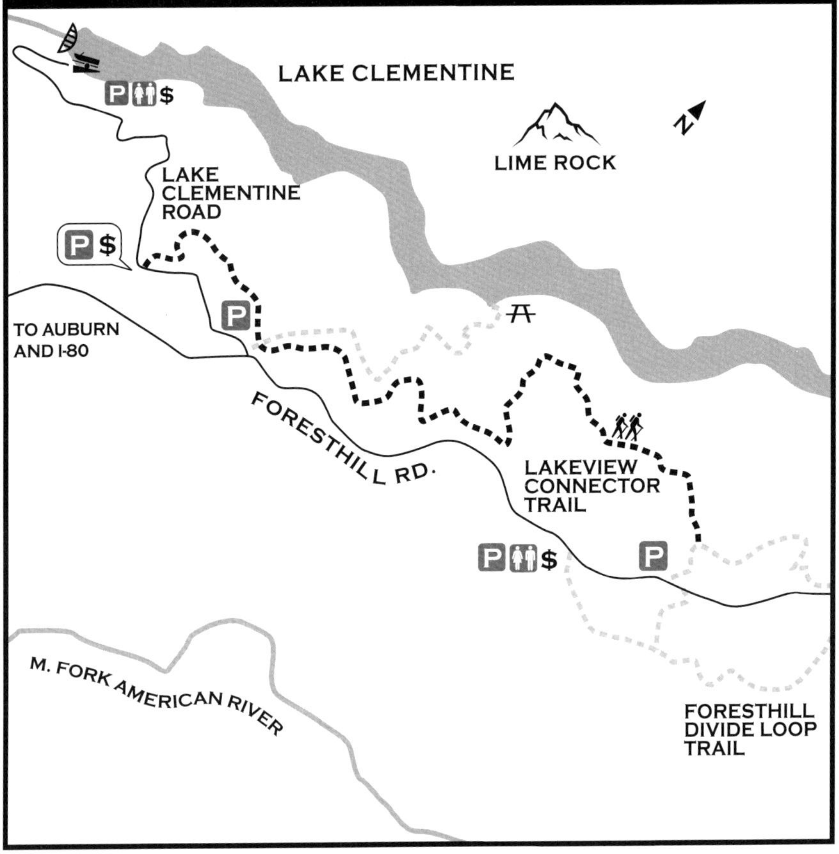

The North Fork Trails

Lakeview Connector Trail

The Colfax and Iowa Hill Stage No. 2, similar to the Auburn Foresthill Stage, is on display in the carriage barn at the Bernhard Museum Complex in Auburn. It is owned by the Native Sons of the Golden West.

Trail Snapshot

This fairly level trail connects Lake Clementine Road to the Foresthill Divide Loop Trail, meandering through chaparral areas of chemise and foothill woodlands on the south side of the North Fork canyon above Lake Clementine. The North Fork Dam completed by the Army Corps of Engineers in 1938 formed serene, picturesque Lake Clementine below. The trail also offers spectacular views of Lime Rock framed by tall stands of manzanita, madrone and black oak. Lime Rock is protected wildlife habitat and private property.

Trailhead Parking *(N38-55.972; W121-00.713)*

Trailhead is on Lake Clementine Road. From I-80, take Foresthill Exit and continue on Foresthill Road towards Foresthill for 3.2 miles; turn left on Lake Clementine Road. A tiny parking area is ½ mile ahead on left at a sharp right bend in the road. After parking, walk back up the road a few paces to the trailhead on your left. (An alternative parking area and trail entry point is ½ mile back up Lake Clementine Road–you passed it on the right just after turning off Foresthill Rd.)

LAKEVIEW CONNECTOR TRAIL

The Lakeview Connector Trail follows contours on the canyon between Lake Clementine and Foresthill Road. The vistas on this trail are outstanding. Although not visible until well along the trail, the lake and the opposite canyon can occasionally be seen through the trees.

Approximately ¾ mile in, the trail passes through chemise-covered hillsides. A little further along the trail there are large boulder outcroppings big enough to scramble onto for a better view. At the 1 mile point, the trail crosses the unmarked, but wide, Lake Clementine Access Trail *(N38-56.121; W121-00.217), (see page 72)* leading down to the lake in 1½ miles from the green gate (#115). This is also near the Lake Clementine Road and alternate trailhead and parking area.

Mushrooms are plentiful in the wet-sunny seasons on the Foresthill Divide. Gathering is not advised as correct identification between poisonous and non-poisonous species can be very, very subtle. A good beginners identification book is David Arora's All That the Rain Promises and More: A Hip Pocket Guide to Western Mushrooms.

The Lakeview Connector Trail continues straight across this trail, passing mainly through foothill woodlands that includes several stands of manzanita and madrone–both of which have distinctive reddish bark that peels off seasonally. In the spring they drop small white flowers that carpet the trail. At the 2¼ mile point, there is a bridge spanning a seasonal stream and its small riparian corridor. This is the lowest elevation on the trail. The trail then begins a steep rise for the next ½ mile, at the top of which is the best vista point on the trail, providing grand views of the lake and Lime Rock on the opposite hillside. This massive limestone outcropping is also known locally as Robbers Roost *(see sidebar)*.

The next mile is mostly in the shade, although small, open, sunny areas often have colorful displays of wildflowers in the spring or mushrooms in the wet-sunny seasons. As you approach the end of the trail, there is a small clearing and a path entering from the left. This is a cutoff to the Foresthill Divide Loop Trail going towards Driver's Flat.

A little further along, there is a larger clearing and the Lakeview Connector Trail ends at the Foresthill Divide Loop Trail "T" intersection going both left and right *(see page 65)*.

Going right on the Foresthill Divide Loop, the trail passes alongside a large meadow and arrives at the Foresthill Road in less than 0.3 of a mile. There is a small dirt parking area on Foresthill Road which some use as a shuttle parking area. Located a few hundred yards down Foresthill Road towards Auburn there is a fee parking and staging area for the Divide Loop Trail. At the intersection, the Loop continues for another 8 miles, crossing Foresthill Road again near Drivers Flat Road, eventually returning to complete the loop at the Grizzly Bear House site trailhead.

Geologist Laird Thompson, Ph.D., displays a replica skull of a saber-toothed cat. Fossil bones of the saber-toothed were found in Hawver Cave which is part of the same limestone formations as Lime Rock.

HISTORICAL SNAPSHOT:

Robbers Roost

Lime Rock found a place in local legend as Robbers Roost. When Foresthill was a still a booming gold mining site, a local band of outlaws, the Gassaway Gang, is reported to have used the rock as a strategic lookout point to signal gang members across the canyon on the Foresthill Divide wagon road when the stagecoach was en route from Foresthill to Auburn.

In January 1905, Pacific Lime and Plaster Company began operations in Clipper Gap to extract limestone from the Lime Rock area and transport it to their dehydration kilns in Benicia, Solano County.

TRAIL AT-A-GLANCE:

Lake Clementine Access Trail

DISTANCE: 1½ miles one way; ¾ hours (hiking)

DIFFICULTY: Easy down, moderate up

ELEVATION CHANGE: +/- 750’

LAKE CLEMENTINE ACCESS TRAIL

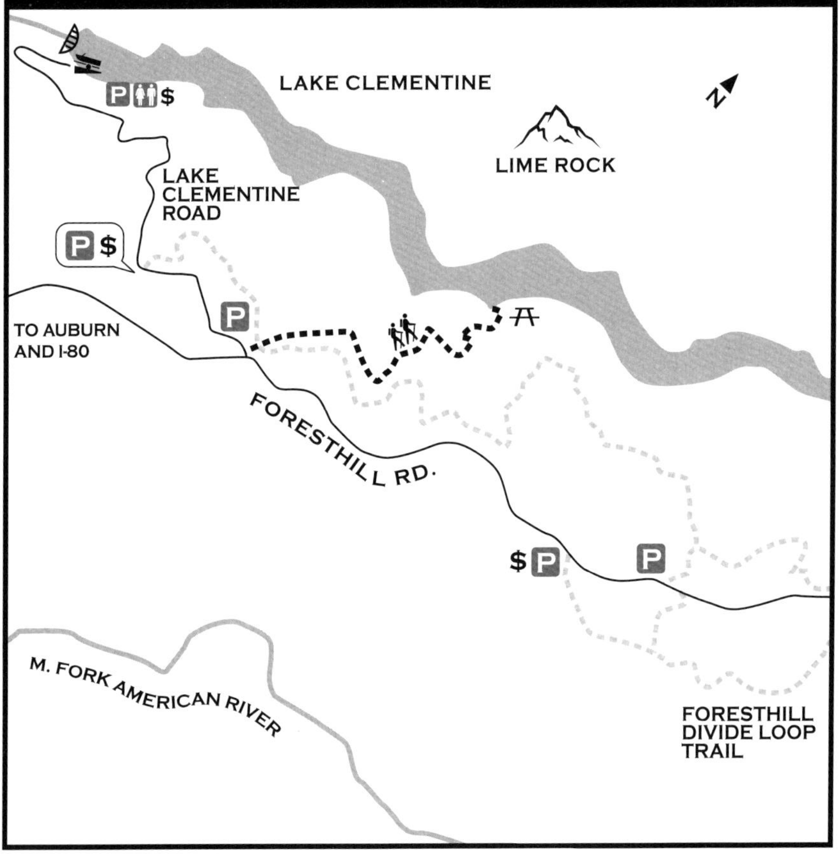

Lake Clementine Access Trail

Trail Snapshot

This is a good year-round trail due to its gentle gradient and alternating stretches of sun and shade. This wide, pleasant trail traverses typical foothills woodland while providing superb views of Lake Clementine and Lime Rock. It is the only trail that goes down to the lake above the dam and below the Upper Lake Clementine day use area.

Trailhead Parking *(N38-56.107; W121-00.254)*

The trailhead is on Lake Clementine Road off Foresthill Road. Take I-80 to the Foresthill exit. From the Foresthill Road and Lincoln Way intersection stoplight, proceed towards Foresthill for approximately 3.2 miles. Turn left on Lake Clementine Road. Just after turning, the parking area is on the right. The trailhead is behind the green gate (#115), about 200 feet back up the road.

Above is a juvenile peregrine falcon with brown markings. Adults have a blue back, white upper chest and yellowish claws.

Lake Clementine Access Trail

The Lake Clementine Access Trail begins behind the green gate, (#115), just 200 feet back towards the Foresthill Road. The trail goes straight down the hill behind the green gate. Do not take the unsigned Lakeview Connector Trail *(see page 69)* that crosses the Lake Clementine Access Trail going left and right, parallel to Foresthill Road.

This nicely graded service road offers an enjoyable hike down to the edge of Lake Clementine, past bay, canyon oak, ponderosa and foothill pine and stands of manzanita and madrone, whose smooth reddish trunks always feel cool to the touch. Occasionally, flocks of gray band-tailed pigeons can be observed roosting in the pines. There is a nice display of maidenhair and bracken ferns along the side of the trail about half way down in the wetter months.

The trail ends in a small clearing at the edge of Lake Clementine where a small stream bubbles over moss covered rocks in this shady riparian creek area. Trees overhang the area and provide welcome shade on sunny days. In summer, this is a nice place to picnic, fish or swim in the lake.

Lake Clementine and Lime Rock, seasonal home to peregrine falcons *(see sidebar below)*, are quite visible as you hike down. The Lime Rock outcrop on the opposite side of the canyon are a continuation of the same type of hard limestone deposits mined for commercial use since the 1880s at the Mountain Quarry located on the Middle Fork American River.

WILDLIFE SNAPSHOT:

Peregrine Falcons

Lime Rock is a seasonally protected home to Peregrine Falcons. Using good bird watching binoculars, the mated pair, Rawlie and Zeina, as the locals affectionately know them, can be observed roosting on the limerock ledges and soaring overhead in aerial courtship flights that include figure 8s and rapid dives around February. They also hunt swallows and other birds, catching them in mid-air in their yellow talons. When mature, these exceptionally fast, grayish falcons are about the size of a crow. They can often be seen rapidly beating their wings as they fly. Narrow-tails, pointed-wings and rapid wing beats are characteristic of peregrines in flight.

Lime Rock is private property with no public access, During the nesting season from March to July, access is strictly prohibited.

TRAIL AT-A-GLANCE:

Applegate-Long Point to Lake Clementine Trail

DISTANCE: 2½ miles to river one way; 1 hour down, 2 hours up (hiking)

DIFFICULTY: Easy down, bottom 1/3 moderately steep and not as well graded

ELEVATION CHANGE: +/- 1,050'

APPLEGATE-LONG POINT TO LAKE CLEMENTINE TRAIL

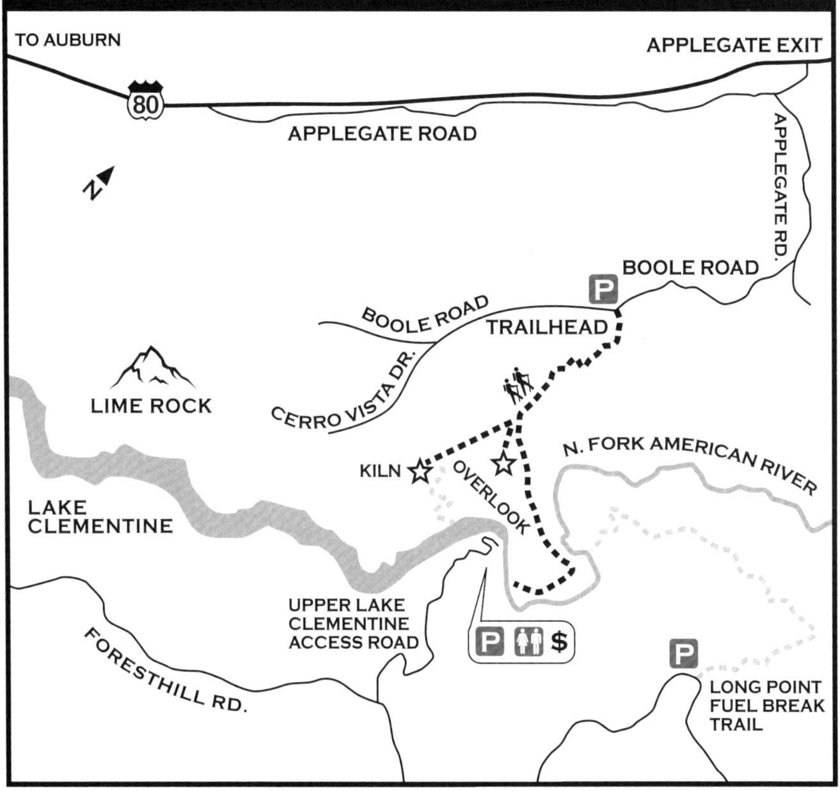

Applegate-Long Point to Lake Clementine Trail

Trail Snapshot

This old road, first built to bring limestone from the river to the Central Pacific Railroad, provides a wide, easy route from Applegate to the river and Upper Lake Clementine and a historic limekiln (see sidebar below). Much of the trail is in the shade of conifers and oaks. It offers a bird's eye view of Lake Clementine and scenic views up the North Fork American River bars.

The Limestone Kiln is located on private property. It is a protected historic site.

Historical Snapshot:

The limestone kiln, circa 1906, is a remnant of the expansive limestone quarry boom that took place in Placer and El Dorado Counties in the late 1800s and early 1900s. The kiln appears to have never been used to refine limestone into dehydrated lime for use in cement and plaster. Instead the limestone was hauled out of the canyon by wagon to a Central Pacific Railroad connection near the villages of Applegate and Clipper Gap to be processed elsewhere by the Pacific Lime and Plaster Company.

Trailhead Parking

(N38-58.998; W120-59.078)

Parking is on Boole Road 1.6 miles off I-80. From Auburn take the Applegate Exit off I-80. Turn right onto Crother Road towards the canyon. Turn left at Applegate Road. Go east for 0.3 of a mile. Just after the concrete railroad overpass turn right onto Boole Road. Go south for 1.3 miles, passing a retreat center, Hilltop Court and Roland Drive. The trailhead is an old dirt road on the left, with 4 cement posts across it, near a big black oak. There is very limited parking along Boole Road. There is another gated turnout and parking area on the left near Cerro Vista. This adds approximately ¼ mile more to the hike through the shaded fuel break connector trail.

Applegate-Long Point to Lake Clementine Trail

The Applegate-Long Point to Upper Lake Clementine Trail starts at the cement posts by the black oak on Boole Road. In less than 300 feet the dirt road crosses through a small clearing. Continue straight through the clearing to the trail proper, which is now a wide, graded fire break road that drops gently down the hillside to the North Fork American River. The trail alternates between sun and shade, with occasional glimpses of the river through the trees.

At approximately 1½ miles, a wide opening is reached where 3 trails meet. The main trail continues downhill on the left. The trail that enters at a 90 degree angle on the right meanders downhill to an old limekiln. Just before the limekiln, the original road continued down to the river to a limestone deposit. A side trip to the limekiln adds 2 miles round trip.

The middle trail brings you to a rock outcropping. From atop this beautiful overlook, views of the sandbars in the river below and the Long Point Fuel Break Trail on the opposite ridge can be seen. The river is about 450 feet below and about a mile away. The large gravel beach below, where the main trail ends, and the Upper Lake Clementine beach across the North Fork are both visible.

Back on the main trail, continue steeply down to the

beach and river. Take time to relax and go for a swim, or even scramble up river to cool pools in the summer before starting the steep hike back to the trailhead. In mid and late summer, the river is easy to ford. Be very careful during the spring run-off.

Historical Snapshot:

Lake Clementine *(below)*

Lake Clementine is used exclusively for public recreation. It was created by the North Fork Dam, completed in 1938. The dam was designed and built by the Army Corps of Engineers in order to collect sedimentation from upriver hydraulic mining, but mining interests were unable to overturn the California State Courts 1884 ban on hydraulic mining.

North Fork Dam *(right)*

The North Fork Dam creates a spectacular waterfall in the spring.

TRAIL AT-A-GLANCE:

Codfish Falls Trail

DISTANCE: 1.7 miles to falls one way; ¾ hours

DIFFICULTY: Easy, but trail is narrow at times with steep drop-offs to river

ELEVATION CHANGE: Minimal

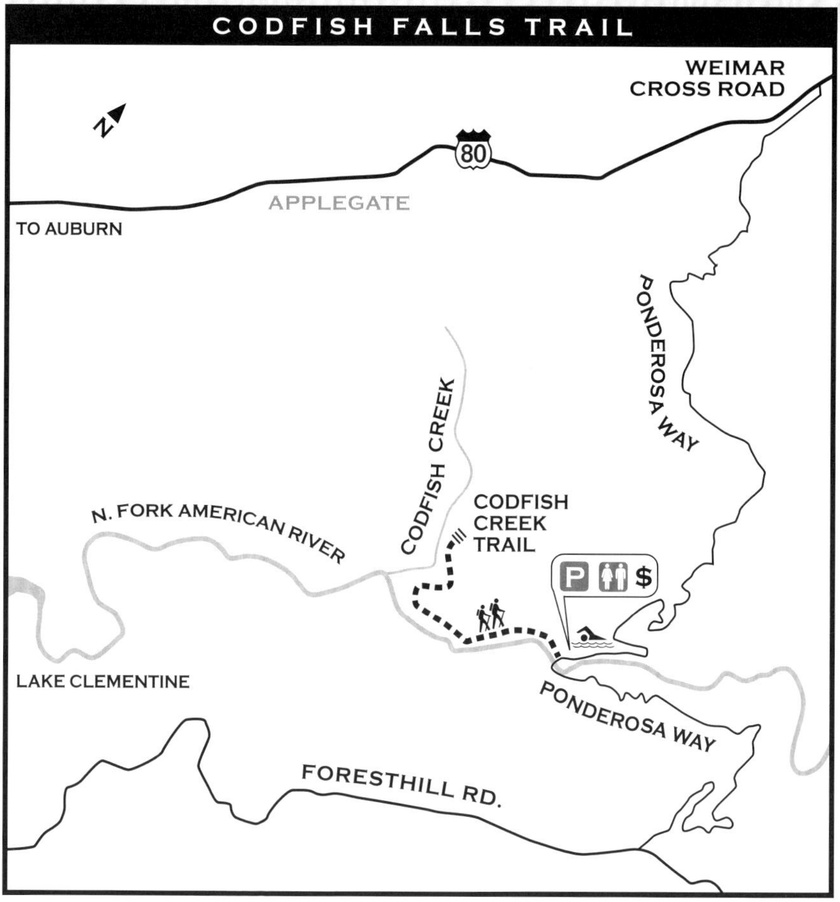

Codfish Falls Trail

TRAIL SNAPSHOT

This easy trail provides beautiful views of the North Fork of the American River and leads to an impressive 40' waterfall. An excellent brochure details the flora and fauna on this trail and is available online at www.parc-auburn.org. The pamphlet was written and illustrated by Heather Mehl and edited by PARC's Eric Peach for Heather's 2001 Colfax High School Senior Project.

Fee Trailhead Parking

(N38-59.995; W120-56.420)

Trailhead is on Ponderosa Way, 6 miles south of Weimar. From Auburn, take I-80 east to the second Weimar exit (Weimar Cross Road) and turn right at the bottom of the off-ramp at the stop sign onto Ponderosa Way and follow it down to the river. The road becomes dirt after about 1 mile. Park near the bridge. The trail begins across the sandy beach on river right. Caution: Ponderosa Way is recommended for sturdy vehicles with clearance. Winter rains can add to the driving adventure.

Popular Codfish Falls in the spring

CODFISH FALLS TRAIL

Codfish Falls Trail provides an excellent opportunity to experience some beautiful river canyon scenery. In the spring, a stunning array of wildflower blooms cut loose along the trail and a profusion of pipevine and tiger swallowtail butterflies enjoying the cool, moist morning air. In the summer, the falls dry up considerably and the trail is hot in the afternoon, so morning hikes are recommended. Bring a picnic lunch to enjoy at the falls or by the river.

The trail starts at the parking area where Ponderosa

Way crosses the bridge over North Fork American River. It parallels the river downstream (river-right) for the first mile and then heads up Codfish Creek to the falls. The first mile is relatively flat, and there are many side trails down to the river for those interested in cooling off on hot summer afternoons. If you look closely, you may spot dippers (also known as water ouzels) in the river. They are small, brownish-gray birds about the size of a robin, and they can often be seen bobbing up and down, and then suddenly diving below the water. Merganser ducks are commonly seen in the river, diving for fish and insects.

Illustration by LeeAnn Bigley and Laurel Mathe

American dipper birds nesting behind a waterfall.

Many species of plants native to a riparian woodland ecosystem can be seen on this trail. Look for three species of oak: canyon live oak, interior live oak, and black oak. Redbud blooms purplish red in the spring. The red berries of toyon are a sure sign of fall. Many fine examples of ponderosa pine, grey pine (also known as foothill, ghost or whispering pine), and Douglas fir grow along the trail.

The North Fork was commercially dredged for gold well into the 20th century. Large mounds of dredged cobble tailings are on the opposite side of the river.

Shortly after the trail leaves the river to follow Codfish Creek there is a short side trail that leads out to a gravel bar where Codfish Creek meets the North Fork. This is a good year-round place to picnic or swim in the summer. Across the river, tucked in the bedrock by a deep swimming pool, there are Indian bedrock mortars.

The trail to the falls continues on another ¼ mile through the forest woodlands emerging at a lush cascading waterfall bordered by ferns.

Common merganser

Illustration by Heather Mehl

Wildlife Snapshot:

Pipevine and the Pipevine Butterfly

The Codfish Creek Trail pipevines are host to the Pipevine Swallowtail butterfly. The vine often climbs bay or other canyon shrubs. Its bloom resembles a pale green pipe. The adult butterfly lays its eggs on the vine leaves. The eggs hatch into orange and black caterpillars that eat the pipevine leaves. An iridescent blue adult pipevine swallowtail brings nature to our fingertips.

Pipevine bloom

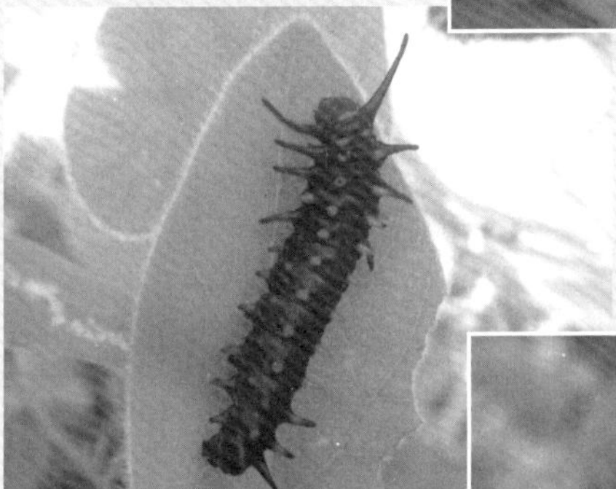

Pipevine caterpillar and pipevine swallowtail

TRAIL AT-A-GLANCE:

INDIAN CREEK TRAIL

DISTANCE: 2 miles one-way; 1 hour hiking each direction (hiking)

DIFFICULTY: Easy, but the trail is narrow and has rocky stretches and steep drop-offs to the river; high spring run-off may prohibit Shirttail crossing

ELEVATION CHANGE: +/- 50'

INDIAN CREEK TRAIL

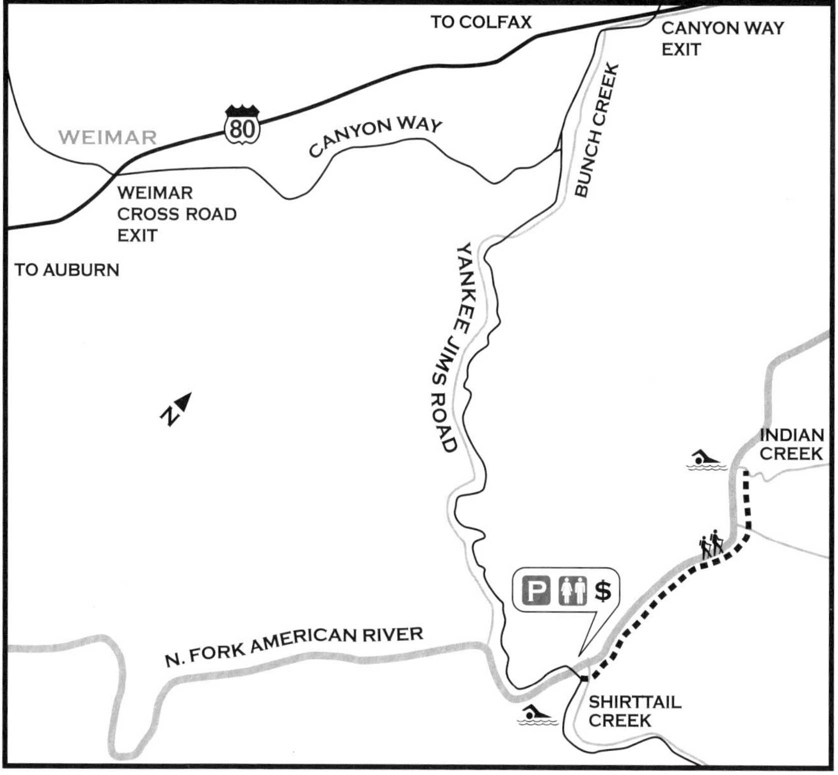

Indian Creek Trail

Trail Snapshot

This easy trail offers exciting seasonal hikes. It allows you to enjoy the American River Canyon without the steep canyon climb or descent. The trail follows a contour, providing great views up and down the canyon as well as many opportunities to take a dip. Oaks, bay laurel and pine trees keep much of the trail in the shade, which is welcome in summer. Hikers are seldom out of sight or sound of the river.

Above: Summer dipper

Below: Indian rhubarb plants on Indian Creek

Fee Trailhead Parking

(N39-02.410; W120-54.189)

Trailhead is off Yankee Jim's Road on the North Fork American River near Shirttail Creek. Take I-80 towards Colfax. Take the Canyon Way/Placer Hills Rd. exit and turn right (west) onto Canyon Way. After approximately 0.8 of a mile, turn left (south) onto Yankee Jim's Road. The road becomes gravel. Yankee Jim's Road is a narrow, twisting, former Gold Rush supply wagon road. In some places there is not enough room for two vehicles to pass. It descends rapidly to the North Fork of the American River. Drive slowly. Hikers, rafters and miners frequently use the road, and visibility around the narrow curves is limited. For passengers, there are some exceptional views of Bunch Creek waterfalls and the river. At the river, there is limited parking on either side of the single-lane cable suspension bridge built in 1930.

After crossing the bridge, take the wooden stairs down to the rock steps and on to the gravel bar where Shirttail Creek meets the North Fork.

Indian Creek Trail

The Indian Creek Trail is on the upriver side of Shirttail Creek. Depending on water level, wade or boulder hop across Shirttail Creek. During high spring runoff it may be too dangerous to attempt to cross. Once across Shirttail Creek, look for a large flat rock overlooking the river where there are small Indian grinding rock mortars and a *metate slick*. The trail goes from Shirttail Creek to Indian Creek. This narrow but easy trail is cut into the hillside above the south bank of the North Fork American River. While there are many ups and downs, there is little significant elevation gain or loss.

Several side trails drop down to the river along the way. Whenever there is a choice, on your way to Indian Creek, always choose the right or uphill fork since the downhill choice always leads to the river. Wildflowers are abundant in the spring.

The trail crosses Salvation Ravine with its year-round water flow, and gigantic parasol leafed Indian rhubarb plants about ¼ mile before arriving at lush Indian Creek. Long deep swimming pools, (bring goggles or a mask), diving rocks and a sandy beach on the opposite bank are all appealing attractions to the Indian Creek area. A short, challenging scramble up Indian Creek leads to a large pool fed by an enchanting series of waterfalls. Water ouzels, or dipper birds, often nest behind the falls.

Note: The Indian Creek trail continues on upriver to Windy Point. It is being restored by volunteers but has some very rough transitions and is not generally recommended for the casual hiker at this writing.

FIRE ECOLOGY SNAPSHOT:

The Robbers Fire

In the summer of 2012 the Robbers Fire burned along this canyon trail from Shirttail to Indian Creek. Most canyon plants, shrubs and trees are fire adapted and vigorous growth can be observed sprouting at the base of the burned canyon flora. The burnt ash-charcoal odor of the fire-charred canyons is being replaced by the aromatic menthol scent of bay laurel. Hikers will be able to observe first hand the natural restorative cycle fire ecology has in the canyons for many years to come. Bring loppers and handsaws to help clear the deadfall across the trail from the fire. Fortunately, the river riparian zone and Indian Creek were relatively unaffected by the fire.

Yankee Jim's Bridge

Shirttail Creek - Devil's Falls

Shirttail Canyon is an enchanting, beautiful canyon whose link to the gold rush and year-round creek make it a favorite recreation destination. Hopefully the transition period will not be too tough as it gradually springs back to life from the ashes of the Robbers Fire that started on its banks in the summer of 2012. Swimming, fishing, gold panning and scrambling are favorite activities on Shirttail creek. Devil's Falls, about a mile up from Yankee Jim's Bridge, is a natural spot for a cool shower on hot summer days. Walking Yankee Jim's road from the bridge to Devil's Falls reveals wagon wheel ruts in the bedrock road bed cut in by steel rimmed wagon wheels during the bustling Gold Rush boom times. For the adventurous combine a walk up the road to Devil's Falls, hike down to the creek on the trail just before the falls and scramble-swim back down the creek to the North Fork for a satisfying challenging adventure. Be alert, the North Fork Shirttail Dam at Sugarpine Reservoir controls the flow on Shirttail Creek, which can fluctuate. Rattlesnakes are found along Shirttail Creek.

Stage stops in front of Devil's Falls.

TRAIL AT-A-GLANCE:

WINDY POINT TRAIL

DISTANCE: 1½ miles one-way; ¾ hours (hiking)

DIFFICULTY: Moderate to difficult. Trail is narrow, with loose rock and steep drop-offs.

ELEVATION CHANGE: +/- 550'

WINDY POINT TRAIL

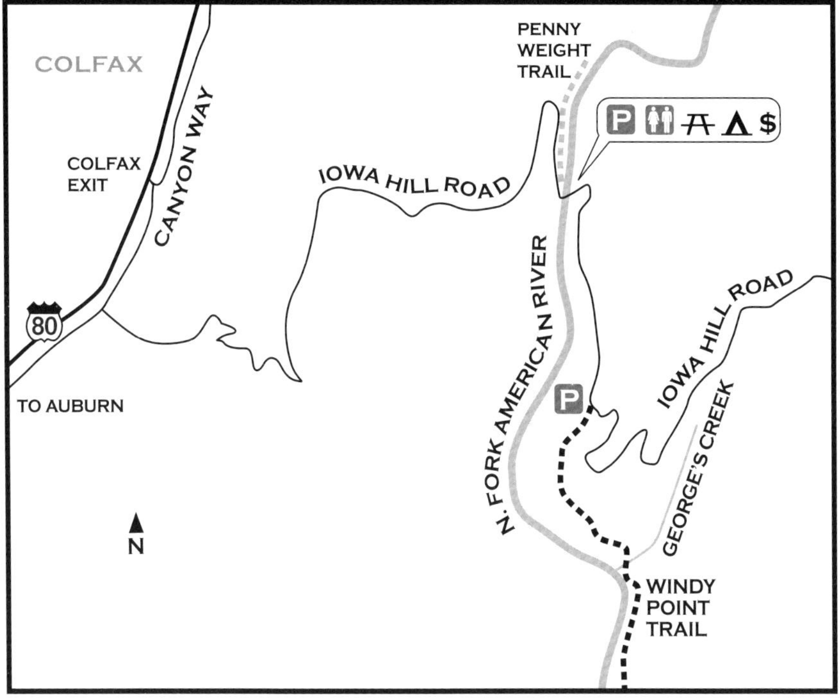

Windy Point Trail

Trail Snapshot

This short but challenging trail offers aerial views of the North Fork Canyon and when timing is right a stunning wildflower display. The trail traverses sections where the whole hillside is carpeted with blue, yellow, purple, and gold wildflowers highlighted against a blue sky and green canyons dominated by oaks and gray pine. In spring, it is a photographer's and wildflower lover's delight. Caution: watch for poison oak, as it thrives along the trail.

Trailhead Parking

(N39-05.420; W120-55.259)

Trailhead is on Iowa Hill Road. From Auburn, take I-80 east to Colfax. Exit at the Colfax, Grass Valley, Hwy. 174 exit. Go right at the exit onto Canyon Way. In approximately 0.3 of a mile turn left on Iowa Hill Road. Drive approximately 3.1 miles down Iowa Hill Road and across the North Fork American River. After crossing the bridge continue for approximately 0.8 of a mile through the small camping area and up the road towards Iowa Hill. Several large boulders and a very small sign that simply says "trailhead" mark the trail. There is limited parking on the right shoulder just before and at the trailhead as the road bends to the left and away from the river.

Harlequin lupine at Windy Point meadow

Caution: Iowa Hill is a narrow paved road with no guardrail. Drive slowly and watch for approaching vehicles since some places are not wide enough for two vehicles to pass.

Windy Point Trail

The Windy Point Trail provides access to some beautiful and steep river canyon scenery. This old miner's trail is a narrow single file path cut into a steep slope above the North Fork of the American River. It has some sharp drop-offs and lots of loose shale and rock, which make it a challenge. Plan on spending as much time enjoying the scenery and wildflowers as hiking. Near the start, after leaving the woodlands, as the trail narrows and the views open up look back and north across the canyon to the famous "Cape Horn" section of the first Transcontinental Railroad, which is still in use. Its completion was one of the extraordinary engineering and construction feats of the 1860s.

Jim's Ferris, cofounder of the ASRA Canyon Keepers and coauthor of American River Canyon Hikes, *at Windy Point meadow*

The trail starts out fairly wide and level in a shaded woodland filled with larkspur and buttercups in the spring. It soon narrows as it crosses a steep slope above the river gorge. The river below is heard well before it is seen. In the spring after a rainstorm outstanding waterfalls cascade down the canyon on the opposite side. Remember to watch your footing while soaking in the colorful wildflower displays of monkey and popcorn flowers, butter and eggs, and brodiaea along the trail in the many small clearings.

Kayaks and rafts may be visible in the river below as they exit Chamberlain Falls and prepare to enter Tongue and Groove on this class III-IV section of the river.

A vibrant palette of wildflowers cascades from the rock terraces above the trail. The large open Windy Point Meadow in full bloom overflows with goldfields, poppies, meadow foam and the less common purple and yellow harlequin lupine as the meadow merges with the rapidly flowing river below.

The trail leaves the meadow in a short steep decent to cross George Creek filled with aquatic insects, newts and an occasional fleck of gold. Caution: The creek may be too hazardous to cross in high water.

After crossing the creek look for the scarlet fritillary (brown bell) hidden along the path. Continuing on about 1/4 mile a spur trail leads to a lunch spot on the riverbank. Close by, huge woodwardia ferns grow in a grotto while California sister butterflies drink from the moist sand that is filled with the footprints of raccoons.

The hike back to the trailhead is steep and can be hot. Be sure to carry enough water and snacks especially if children are along for the adventure.

Evan Jones, trail guide, trail blazer and coauthor of Take A Hike, *at "Portrait Rock"*

Note: The main trail continues on and eventually connects to Indian Creek Trail and Yankee Jim's Road. Trail repairs are in progress but it is still very rough in sections and is not recommended for casual hikers.

North Fork Gorge Scramble

For Wild and Scenic river adventurers, there is no better way to spend a hot summer day than a scramble down the north fork gorge from Windy Point to Yankee Jim's Bridge. Shorten the scramble by taking the trail on river left at Indian Creek. Swimming the deep cool pools, wading the riffles and scrambling over the rocks past sandy beaches, lush fern grottos and button willow scented river banks is the reward for this simple but rigorous river immersion experience.

All the gear that is needed is a small daypack or a paddler's dry bag with shoulder straps. When using a daypack wrap and double wrap perishable and non-waterproof items in plastic bags. Essentials include food, water swimming goggles, sunscreen, headlamp or flashlight and a first aid kit. Wear running shoes or sturdy river sandals

When walking across slippery areas it is best to have a sturdy stick to balance with. Allow plenty time to appreciate the beauty and explore the nature of the river. *Scrambling the river is much slower than hiking the trails and extra time is also needed to drop off a shuttle vehicle. Be safe, don't gorge scramble alone.*

Tom Petersen, author of Georgetown Trails Guide

The water ouzel, also known as the American dipper, dives and submerges itself under water to search for aquatic insects to eat.

TRAIL AT-A-GLANCE:

STEVENS TRAIL FROM COLFAX

DISTANCE: 3.2 miles to river; 1½ hours down, 2½ hours up (hiking)

DIFFICULTY: Easy down, moderate up

ELEVATION CHANGE: +/- 1,150’

STEVENS TRAIL FROM COLFAX

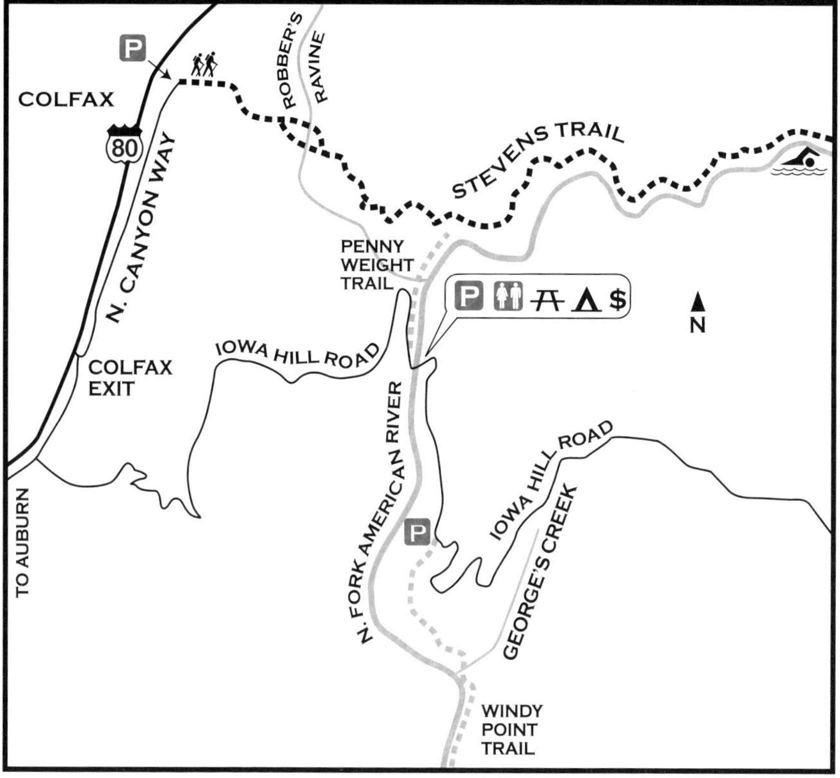

Stevens Trail from Colfax

TRAIL SNAPSHOT

This very well maintained trail is one of the most popular historic hiking trails to the Wild & Scenic North Fork American River, in part because of its easy access from Colfax and mild gradient. The river views, spectacular wildflower display in the spring and cool swimming pools in the summer make it a very appealing destination. Take plenty of water and use caution, as the trail is hot during summer months and moderately steep at times with narrow passages and sheer cliffs.

Breath-taking view of the Wild and Scenic North Fork looking upriver from the Stevens Trail

Trailhead Parking

(N39-06.376; W120-56.837)

Parking is on N. Canyon Way in Colfax. From Auburn, take I-80 east to Colfax. Exit at the Colfax, Grass Valley, Hwy. 174 exit. Go left at the exit onto N. Canyon Way. Continue 0.6 of a mile; turn left into a small parking area. Look for 'trail' sign marking the trailhead.

STEVENS TRAIL FROM COLFAX

The Stevens Trail starts at the Bureau of Land Management parking area on N. Canyon Way just north of Colfax. After a short distance, the trail crosses streams, the last stream has a bridge and a road; turn right on this dirt road. At the ¾ mile point, the trail intersects another firebreak road; bear to the left and look for a metal 'trail' sign. Shortly the trail forks again at a sign directing hikers to the left and bikers and horses to the right for a less rocky crossing of Robbers Ravine. Hikers cross Robbers Ravine at a lush rocky waterfall area. Soon the two trails rejoin.

Shortly after the waterfall, the trail encounters an immense bed of shale cascading down the steep mountainside and the remains of a mineshaft, abandoned long ago. In fact, there is evidence of widespread mining activity all along this trail. Above the bed of shale is the Cape Horn section of the first Transcontinental

Railroad. Here the railroad bed was originally cut into the steep canyon wall by Chinese laborers suspended on ropes down the steep sides. During the early days of train travel passenger trains would stop at Cape Horn for the "American River View".

From this point on, the trail enters the steep North Fork American River canyon and traverses the canyon upriver. This part of the trail offers magnificent views of the river and wildflowers in the spring. The Iowa Hill Bridge can be seen downstream. In places the trail is built on hand stacked rock retaining walls, an indication of the large amount of work required to build this trail *(see sidebar below)*.

The trail meets the river at Secret Ravine, where more signs of mining are evident. The foundation of an old suspension bridge and a few rusting cables are all that remains of the cable suspension bridge that used to cross the river here. Take time to enjoy the river before hiking back out.

HISTORICAL SNAPSHOT:

Stevens Toll Trail

The Stevens Toll Trail was originally completed by Truman Allen Stevens and partner John Rutherford. A trail with a gentle gradient suitable for pack animals was urgently needed to serve the growing needs of the gold mining enterprises on the south side of the North Fork. Once completed Stevens, who operated a ranch in Iowa Hill and a livery stable in Colfax, ran the toll trail. By 1871 a cable suspension bridge crossed the river. The toll was 25 cents per person, 50 cents for rider and horse, 40 cents per stock animal. The trail's main years of use were 1870 to 1895.

Although the trail can be found on a 1900s era USGS topographic map, it wasn't popular among locals until Boy Scout Eric Kiel charted it in 1969. In 2002 the trail was listed in the National Register of Historic Places, due largely to the efforts of Jay Shuttleworth. The trail is maintained by volunteers with assistance from the Bureau of Land Management.

TRAIL AT-A-GLANCE:
STEVENS TRAIL FROM IOWA HILL

DISTANCE: 3.7 miles each way; 2 hours down to the river, 2½ hours from the river back to Iowa Hill (hiking)

DIFFICULTY: Moderately strenuous

ELEVATION CHANGE: +/- 1,600'

STEVENS TRAIL FROM IOWA HILL

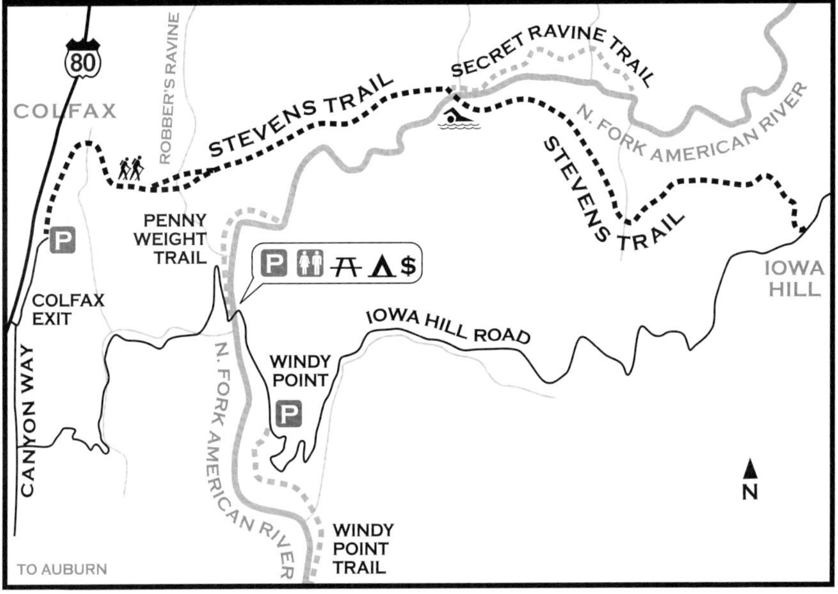

HISTORICAL SNAPSHOT:

Hydraulic Mining

The most destructive form of gold rush mining took place at Iowa Hill. Water cannons were trained on the hillsides washing away the soil and light gravels into sluice ditches that were built to catch the heavy gold. The North Fork was turned into a turbid, filthy mess, suffocating the aquatic life, as the ditches emptied sediment and debris into creeks that drained into the river. Fortunately, the California courts stopped hydraulic mining in 1864. Modern suction dredging also has detrimental effects on aquatic life.

Stevens Trail from Iowa Hill

Leopard lily

Trailhead Parking

(N39-06.417; W120-51.632)

Trailhead is on Iowa Hill Road. From Auburn, take I-80 east to Colfax. Exit at the Colfax, Grass Valley, Hwy. 174 exit. Stay right at the exit then continue straight on Canyon Way. In approximately 0.3 miles turn left on Iowa Hill Road. Drive 9 miles down Iowa Hill Road and across the North Fork American River to historic Iowa Hill. Park across from the store. The signed trailhead begins behind the historic Iowa Hill Store and Bar. Friendly advice and provisions are available.

STEVENS TRAIL FROM IOWA HILL

The shaded Iowa Hill side of the Stevens Trail has a fairly gentle gradient down to the North Fork descending approximately 1,600 feet in about 4 miles. After leaving the store and hiking a short distance through thick woods, it opens up into the deeply scarred remains of a hydraulic mining pit. The trail winds through rock piles grown over with stunted manzanita and pines.

Breaking away from the hydraulic mining pit wound, the vast majority of the trail continues on beneath a shaded canopy that can, in the height of the spring-bloom, host a variety of shade loving wildflowers including globe & leopard lilies. The trail, supported by hand stacked rocks in many spots, eventually opens up to views of the North Fork ending its gradual descent at the cable suspension bridge site. **Warning:** The trail can be overgrown with poison oak if not recently pruned.

HISTORICAL SNAPSHOT:

Gold Rush Cemetery

The history of Iowa Hill is best told in the gold rush vintage cemetery about a ½ mile beyond town on Iowa Hill Road. The graceful stone markers and wrought iron work combined with the census registry at the entrance to the cemetery offer a glimpse into the diverse group of people that rushed to the American River goldfields and the harsh reality of a short life in pursuit of precious gold.

Historical Snapshot:

Pennyweight Trail *(N39-06.024; W120-55.535)*

Pennyweight, a British unit of weight measurement in use since the Middle Ages, found popular use in the California Gold Rush by miners, gold traders and jewelers. Very small amounts of fine gold less than a troy ounce can be weighed and given a monetary value. There are 20 pennyweights in an ounce of gold. On All Souls Day, November 2, 2012, a pennyweight of 24 karat gold would fetch $84. An ounce would tip the scales at $1680. Although there is little gold to be found after over 150 years of continuous prospecting, panning and dredging, the legendary, romantic attraction of the American River and gold persists.

The Pennyweight Trailhead is on the left side of Colfax-Iowa Hill Road just a few hundred yards before Mineral Bar, the site of the historic and modern Colfax-Iowa Hill Bridges. The value of the pennyweight and the lure of the river make this a popular river trail. Meandering up-river there are several spur trails that lead to fine swimming, panning and fishing spots. To reach the big gravel and sand bar at the end of the mile long trail take the upper trail at the first intersection. Cross the small delicate pools at Robbers Ravine and continue past the old cabin sites eventually reaching the river at a big gravel bar. A faint trail continues another ¼ mile up-river across the bedrock bar. Hikers on the popular Stevens trail can often be seen crossing the slope directly above.

Auburn State Recreation Area's Mineral Bar Campground

The campground on the terrace next to the Iowa Hill Bridge has many nice campsites for out-of-the-area visitors from which to launch river and canyon adventures. For a fee, the campground has the basic amenities; toilets, picnic tables and campfire rings.

Western States Trail: Auburn to Foresthill

History of the Western States Trail

By Vince Haughey

Tevis Cup Rider in the last leg of the Tahoe to Auburn 100 mile race.

The earliest trails were established by Paiute, Washoe and Nisenan Maidu Indians hunting and trading in the Sierra. The legendary Western States Trail that passes through the canyons on a patchwork of Indian, mining and logging trails, is best known for the ultimate endurance challenge it provides for ultra-marathon equestrians and runners. Silver buckles are awarded to those finishing the Tevis Cup Horseback Ride and Western States Endurance Run in 24 hours or less from Squaw Valley to Auburn. Approximately 30 of the 100 race miles from Foresthill to Auburn are in the Auburn SRA. They were designated a National Recreational Trail in 1974. The well-maintained Western States Trail offers the adventure hiker the opportunity to access and experience one of the last remnants of astonishing wilderness, from ridge top to the river, that our area has to offer.

Following the river on the south side (El Dorado County), and gradually descending, the trail passes the site of the miles-long Grand Flume operation, photographed by pioneer photographer Charles Weed in 1858. From there the trail rises sharply out of the canyon, crossing Highway 49, meandering through a series of oak wooded knolls and tributary streams, dropping into the canyon for the final time, and crossing the river into Auburn on the arched concrete Mountain Quarries Bridge (also called No Hands Bridge). The competitors loop around Robie

Point, returning to present-day civilization after re-creating a route of migration, adventure, and commerce that served the early pioneers and gave California horses and riders the highest reputation from 1852 on.

The modern endurance ride was directed for three decades by Wendell Robie, who was born in Auburn in 1895. The Tevis Cup was established as a perpetual trophy of the "Western States 100 Miles in One Day Ride" by Will, Gordon, and Lloyd Tevis in honor of their grandfather Lloyd Tevis, who was president of Wells Fargo & Co. from 1872 to 1892. The Wells Fargo express empire had taken over the Pony Express operation, rescuing it from financial ruin, at the beginning of the Civil War.

The first Tevis endurance ride was held on August 7, 1955. From that race until 1960 each ride transported the U.S. mail and the beginning and ending times were recorded by the Post Office cancellations in Tahoe City and Auburn, respectively. Later the ride began at Squaw Valley, and occasional route changes have been made to accommodate the intrusions of modern roads or other changes such as the destruction by flood of the bridge at Oregon Bar in 1964.

Concern for the condition of the horses is emphasized by riders and organizers of the race, and a veterinary committee monitors the condition of the horses along the way. In addition to the Tevis Cup for the winner, the finisher among the first ten whose horse is judged to be in superior condition is awarded the Haggin Cup in honor of James B. Haggin. Haggin was a horse breeder and a friend and business partner of the elder Lloyd Tevis, having come with him to Sacramento in 1849.

For more information contact The Western States Trail Foundation at 1216 High St., Suite C, Auburn CA 95603. Visit their website at www.teviscup.org or call 530-823-7282.

An excerpt from their brochure reads:

"Mostly it travels a wilderness route. At the full of the Riding Moon, each year, the trail climbs through Squaw Pass to the Emigrant Trail Monument, placed there by Robert Watson (in 1931) for the crest of the Sierra Nevada, where the dawn of the morning displays in every direction an unforgettable scene of grandeur and color. Peerless in this world, as you look below for the following riders, is the sweeping breath inspiring view of matchless Lake Tahoe in a sapphire setting under snow-crowned peaks and rugged mountains.

To the west, from the far north to the far south, are mighty eye-reaching timbered slopes of great river watersheds and deep canyons. As centuries pass, we can believe other riders have felt and will feel as you do, a throb of feeling and confidence that somewhere in the beautiful blue haze mantle of far-off distance is your destination. Before then, you will have made a companion of the worn trail under the hooves of your horse while riding long westerly ridges that point to far away low country and even to other mountains that border the ocean of the setting sun."

THE TEVIS CUP

The image of a rider on a horse is central to western lore. Match this image with the eternal grandeur of the Sierra Nevada–the great barrier and challenge to early pioneers in California–and one can understand the lure of the Tevis Cup Ride, a one-day competition held each year during the "Riding Moon" of mid-summer.

The event calls for rider and horse to begin before dawn in the Lake Tahoe Basin and to traverse "roughly" a hundred miles along sections of the old Pony Express route which once connected the silver fields of Nevada to the gold fields of California. Ending after nightfall at the Placer County Fairgrounds in Auburn, the trail riders will have climbed an aggregate of two vertical miles and descended another three vertical miles over a course of sawtooth crests, ridges, and steep river valleys–encountering along the way the headwaters of the Middle Fork American River, later passing along the main street of Foresthill.

From Foresthill the trail drops into the Middle Fork Canyon via Dardanelles Creek and passes through the vast panorama of river bars once thronging with speculative humanity seeking gold. Once along the river the trail approximates the prospector's route from bar to bar, passing through Ford's Bar and Oregon Bar, where Middle Fork riches were first discovered in 1848. The trail crosses the river at Poverty Bar, a couple of miles downstream.

TRAIL AT-A-GLANCE:

WST: Overlook Park Staging Area to the Confluence

DISTANCE: 5.1 miles one way; 2½ hours each way (hiking)

DIFFICULTY: Easy to moderate down. Moderate up.

ELEVATION CHANGE: +/- 550 ft.

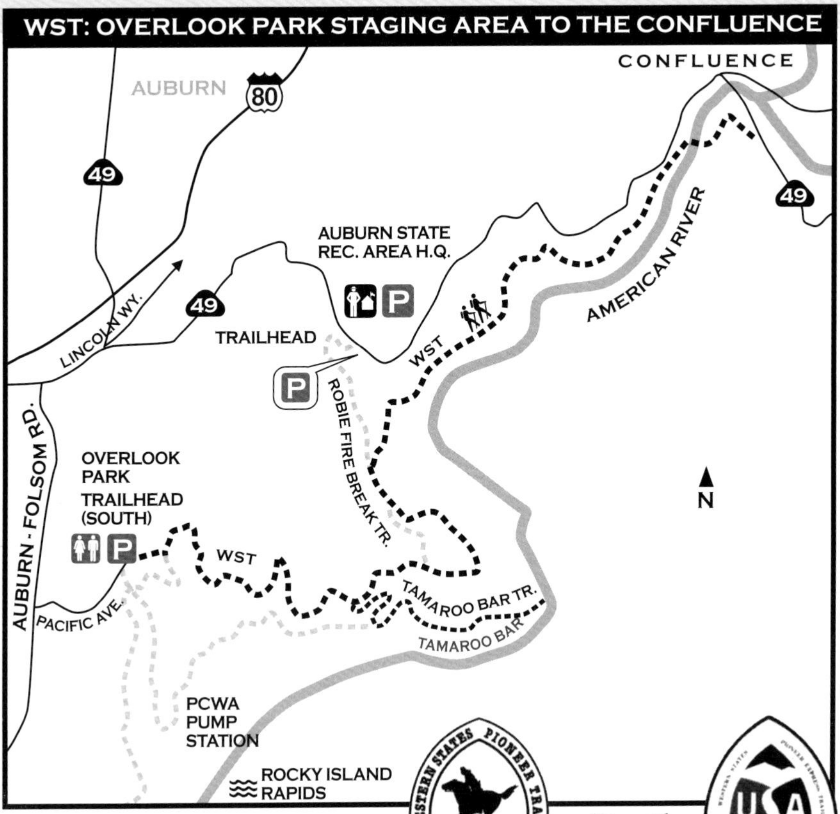

Commonly found trail signs along the Western States Trail

WESTERN STATES TRAIL:

Western States Trail from Auburn to Foresthill

TRAIL SNAPSHOT

For convenience, the trail segments are listed in reverse order that they are used by the endurance athletes and equestrians. They are equally challenging and satisfying when biked or ridden in either direction. Due to the remoteness and inaccessibility of many stretches of the WST in the Auburn SRA and beyond in the Tahoe National Forest adequate mental and physical preparation are very important, for the deep canyons although beautiful, are relentless in their challenge and unforgiving to the ill-prepared. With few exceptions no bikes are allowed on the WST in the Auburn SRA.

Trailhead Parking

(N38-53.358; W121-04.131)

The Western States Trailhead is at the Overlook Park behind the Gold Country Fairgrounds. Take Hwy. 49 to Lincoln Way through Auburn then left onto Auburn-Folsom Road, go past the fairgrounds and turn left on Pacific Avenue. Turn right after 0.5 of a mile into the Overlook Park area. For a fee, equestrians can park in the gravel staging area next to the Overlook parking area.

WESTERN STATES TRAIL

The WST trail begins at the horse watering trough, gently descending downhill across a shaded creek area eventually opening up to aerial views of the Placer County Water Agency's pump station and the restored China Bar River Park Area completed in 2008 when the diversion tunnel was closed *(see page 186 for*

TAMAROO BAR SIDE TRAIL

About 1.4 miles out, there is a junction for the Tamaroo Bar Trail that leads to a rapid at the top of the bar, a huge plunge pool and gravel island. The Tamaroo Trail crosses a flat wide terrace before it narrows and descends to the river. Occasionally, river otters are seen diving for crayfish. Button Willow that blooms in the summer along the banks attracts Tiger Swallowtail butterflies. The side trail near the rapid leads to the very obscure Pardners Rock Trail.

photos). Scars from the Auburn Dam project, halted over 35 years ago, are beginning to naturalize where the canyon walls were terraced and the foundation was cut to bedrock. They are a stark reminder of how close the American River canyons came to being flooded by a 700 foot high concrete eggshell dam. The WST continues around the canyon edge with several Auburn neighborhood and firebreak trails entering from the ridge. Brown carsonite markers designate the WST.

Raccoon tracks

The WST stays high on the Robie Point Firebreak trail/road for approximately 1 mile to a clearly marked right turn down into a steep canopied ravine that crosses a creek and comes out on the old Mountain Quarries Railroad grade. Concrete trestle footings can be seen to the right. The trail takes a left here past the timber remains of the water tank used to fill the boilers of the oil-fueled steam engines that hauled limestone from the quarry to the main railroad line in Auburn. The trail alternates between wide graded railroad bed and deep ravines that were once bridged by trestles. One of the more prominent ravines passes beneath a waterfall named by the horseback riders the "Black Hole of Calcutta". It's a good spot to cool off in the summer but can be difficult to cross in the winter after a heavy rain. The trail picks up the railroad grade once again passing many spur trails that lead down to swimming holes and sandy beaches along the river. On the Auburn side of the Mountain Quarries Railroad Bridge history plaques offer a glimpse into its storied past. It was nicknamed No Hands Bridge by a horseback rider who rode across on her stead reinless, hands held high over her head, before a railing was installed. Flocks of swallows hunt insects near the river and make mud nests on the bridge in the spring. Immediately after crossing the bridge, the WST makes a short climb on the right to a switchback just above, and parallel to, Highway 49.

River otter tracks

TRAIL AT-A-GLANCE:
WST: Confluence through 49 crossing to Quarry Road Trail

DISTANCE: 3½ miles one way, 1½ hour one way (hiking)

DIFFICULTY: Moderate to strenuous

ELEVATION CHANGE: +/- 600' to 1230'

WST: CONFLUENCE TO QUARRY ROAD TRAIL

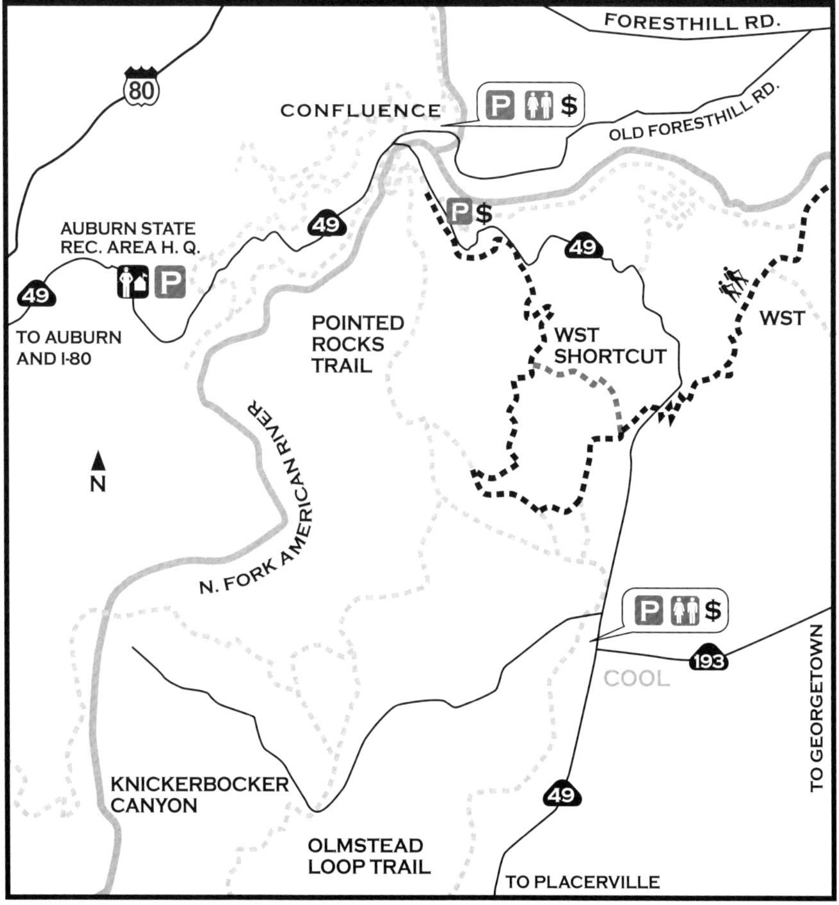

WST Confluence through Highway 49 crossing to Quarry Road Trail

Trailhead Parking *(N38-54.895; W121-02.393)*

Free parking along Hwy. 49 south of the bridge crossing to Cool, or fee parking at the Quarry Road Trailhead parking area.

Dogface butterfly and chrysalis. The host plant for the butterfly is false indigo.

WST CONFLUENCE: HWY. 49 TO QUARRY ROAD

In the spring small bright yellow California dogface butterflies, our state insect, can be observed along the trail, near the creek crossings and the Pig Farm Trail cutoff. As the trail reaches the flat ridge and skirts the oak woodland edge of Knickerbocker Flats stay left following WST or Robie Trail signs. Descend gradually again to the Hwy. 49 crossing at the Limestone Quarry office. From here the trail drops steeply through a rocky, rutted area alongside the quarry tailings to the Quarry Road. An optional left here loops 2 miles back to the Quarry Road Trailhead at Highway 49.

The Tevis WST continues along the Quarry Road Trail near the river for another 3 miles to Maine Bar or 4 miles to the Poverty Bar wet-river crossing where the horseback riders ford the river. Runners climb up Brown's Ravine from Quarry Road to the upper WST. *(See also Poverty Bar Trail description on page 127.)* A few spur trails provide access to the river along the rolling Quarry Road Trail. There is a picnic area on the historic Maine Bar knoll. Maine Bar was the site of a significant gold rush village called "Craniwell's Claime" of hastily built structures including a "fandango" dance hall, dinner house and St. Nicholas Hotel that served the miners. The 49ers displaced the Indians who used this area as a seasonal river campsite. Grinding rocks can be found on the rocky outcrop at Maine Bar and downriver.

TRAIL AT-A-GLANCE:

WST: Brown's Ravine at Quarry Road Trail to American Canyon Trail

DISTANCE: 8.7 miles one way; 4 hours one way, 5 hours when including the trails that link this segment of the WST to the trailheads (hiking)

DIFFICULTY: Moderate climb up

ELEVATION CHANGE: +/- 1,000' to 1,800'

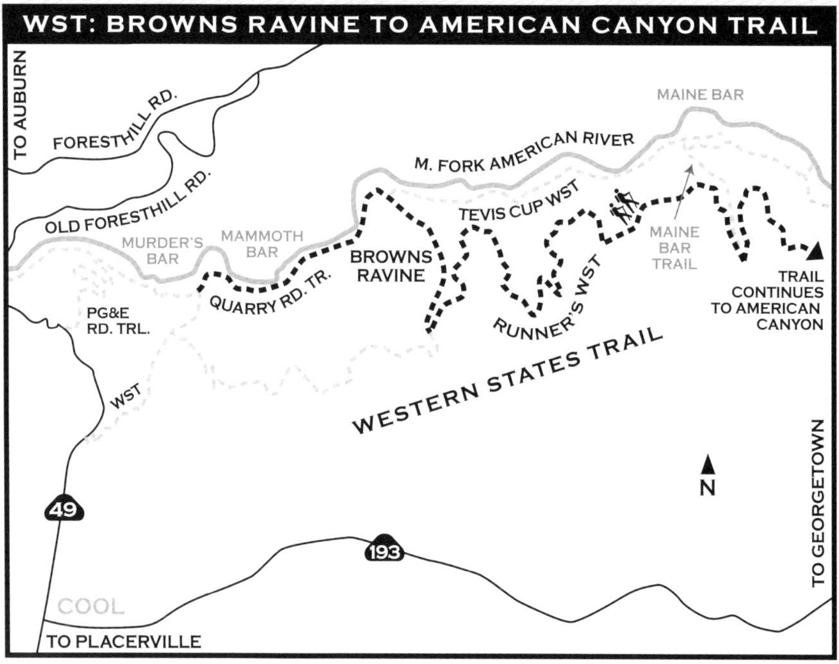

Charles Weed's 1858 glass-plate negative was the source of this photo of "Craniwell's Claime" at Maine Bar.

WESTERN STATES TRAIL:

Brown's Bar at Quarry Road Trail to American Canyon Trail

Barbara Schoener Fieldstone Memorial bench and wild garden area, planted with bulbs and rosemary, is a tribute to a courageous woman and runner who loved running the wild American River Canyon trails.

The runners upper WST splits at the Brown's Bar intersection on the right one mile after the WST connects to the Quarry Road.

The runners continue on up Brown's Ravine crossing the creek a couple of times. The final crossing is on a bridge less than a mile from the Quarry Road intersection. This long stretch of WST below Auburn Lake Trails winds in and out of canyon ravines through thick oak pine and fir forest with occasional aerial views of the river and intersects with the American Canyon Trail in 7½ miles. At 4½ miles take the left fork following WST markers near a gravel road intersection. This road goes up into the Auburn Lake Trails subdivision.

About 2 miles before the trail intersects the American Canyon junction there is a beautiful fieldstone memorial bench and wild garden area, planted with bulbs and rosemary. This bench is dedicated to the memory of Barbara Schoener, the runner who was attacked and killed by a female mountain lion in April of 1994. She is survived by her husband and two children. The lion that killed Barbara Schoener was hunted down, treed and shot by Fish and Game trappers. The lion's cub that was discovered in the forest was spared and placed in the Folsom Zoo. Official figures indicate that well over 2,000 lions have been killed under permit in California since 1972. Take a moment to rest here enjoy the view and reflect on the human relationship with the beautiful wild side of the canyons. It's best to hike with a friend and avoid prey behavior in any encounter with cougars.

TRAIL AT-A-GLANCE:

WST: American Canyon to Ruck-A-Chucky Crossing

DISTANCE: 5.7 miles; 3 hours one way (hiking)

DIFFICULTY: Easy to moderate

ELEVATION CHANGE: +/- 1455' to 800'

WST: AMERICAN CANYON TO RUCK-A-CHUCKY

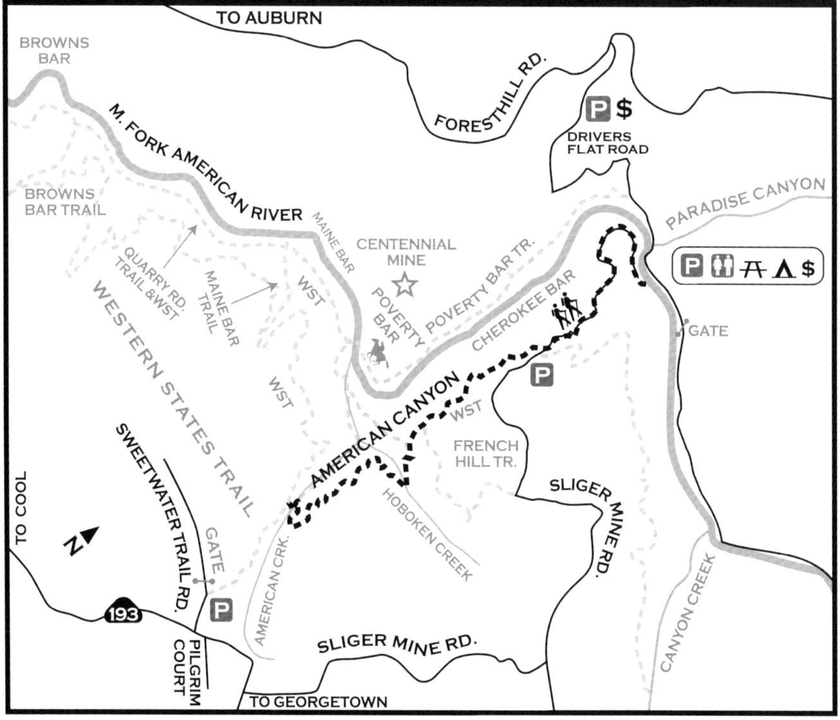

Note: Local equestrians and hikers maintain the French Hill Trail as a shortcut between the WST and Sliger Mine Road.

WESTERN STATES TRAIL:

American Canyon to Ruck-A-Chucky Crossing

About 2 miles from the Schoener memorial the WST intersects with the American Canyon Trail. The American Canyon Trailhead is on Sweetwater Trail Road just before the 3rd gate entrance to Auburn Lake Trails. This is a convenient place to access the WST and other trails for the loop and upriver or downriver hikes. *(See also the American Canyon Trail description on page 121.)* To stay on the WST catch the American Canyon trail for a short distance and then bear to the right dropping down rapidly through thick Douglas fir forest to the wet American Canyon and Hoboken Creek crossings. The climb out eventually catches a sunny contour weaving in and out of Hoboken Creek Ravine.

The trail continues on past Dead Truck Trail intersection to pass just above the Sliger Mine concrete artifacts being reclaimed by the temperate oak woodland forest. At first glance they resemble mossy temple ruins in Central America. From here it is a short distance to Sliger Mine Road where the Robie-Canyon Creek Trail intersects at the green gate. The WST gradually descends on Sliger Mine Road above Cherokee Bar. Bear to the right at Cherokee Bar and continue down to the old Greenwood Bridge river crossing site. The bridge washed out in 1964. Runners wade across the river holding onto a rope stretched across the river for the race or, in years of high water, they are ferried across in a raft.

TRAIL AT-A-GLANCE:

WST: Greenwood Bridge/ Ruck-A-Chucky Campground to Fords Bar

DISTANCE: 5.2 miles one way, 2½ hours one way (hiking)

DIFFICULTY: Moderate

ELEVATION CHANGE: +/- 800' to 1,100'

WST: RUCK-A-CHUCKY TO FORDS BAR

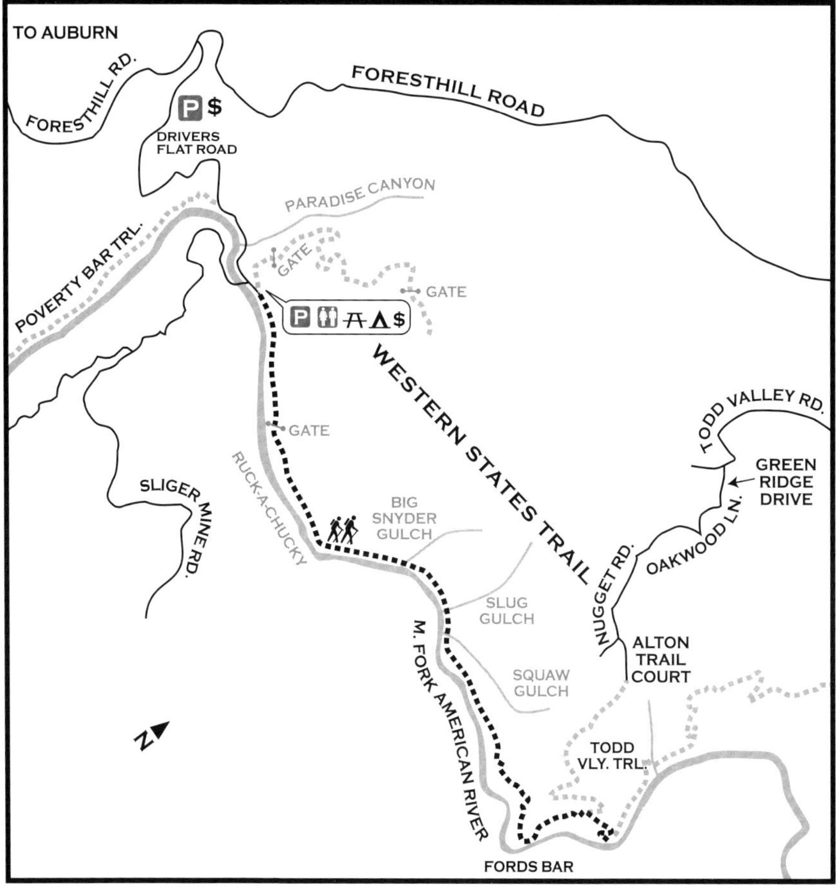

Greenwood Bridge/Ruck-A-Chucky Campground to Fords Bar

100 mile runners at the Greenwood Bridge ford on the Middle Fork.

Fee Trailhead Parking

(N38-57.897; W120-56.205)

Fee horse trailer parking area at top of Drivers Flat Road. Fee parking and camping at Ruck-A-Chucky.

From I-80 Foresthill exit and drive 8 miles on the Foresthill Divide Road to Driver's Flat Road, turn right and drive the 3 miles down the dirt road to the river.

WST: GREENWOOD/RUCK-A-CHUCKY TO FORD'S BAR

The Tevis horseback trail crossed to the north side of the river 3½ miles back onto the Poverty Bar Trail that intersects with Drivers Flat Road *(see page 127)*. Both segments of the WST merge here at the Ruck-A-Chucky Campground. The equestrians make a short deter around the campground through Gas Canyon to Francisco's for a vet check. From here the runners' trail follows an old road that climbs gradually upriver to the spectacular rolling thunder of Ruck-A-Chucky falls, an awesome river-wide jumble of boulders. This is also the site of a failed 1930s attempt by the Army Corps of Engineers to build a silt debris dam.

Common horsetail

Above Rucky-A-Chucky falls across from Canyon Creek the trail veers to the left on single track trail staying close to the river through moist streams at Big Snyder and Slug Gulches. Look for the segmented scouring rush and horsetail fern (*Equisetum arvense*), possibly the oldest plant genus on earth. Natural field rock walls dotted with dudleya succulents, host plant to the Sonoran blue butterfly, border the trail. The trail climbs steeply through mid-canyon meadow blooms of lupine and poppies in the spring, dropping down to river level again at Fords Bar's spacious, warm, sandy beaches below Todds Valley. From Todd Valley a trail/road at the end of Alton Trail Road leads to the WST and Ford's Bar.

Trail At-A-Glance:

WST: Fords Bar to Foresthill at Mosquito Ridge Road

DISTANCE: 10.6 miles one way, 6 hours one way (hiking)

DIFFICULTY: Steep to moderate

ELEVATION CHANGE: +/- 1,000' to 3,200'

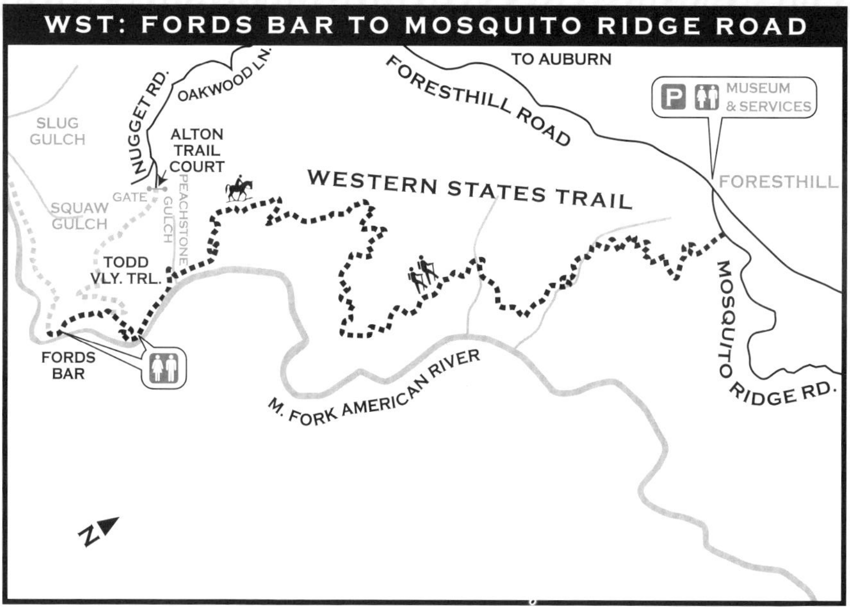

Historical Snapshot:

Todd Valley

Todd Valley was first settled by Dr. Todd who built a log house for a store and hotel at the site of his residence, which also included a corral for horses, in 1849. The town commenced to grow after 1852 when rich diggings were discovered on the flat and nearby Poker Hill. In 1859 much of the town was destroyed by a conflagration but it was gradually rebuilt and expanded. Today the valley has been subdivided into residences.

Western States Trail:

Fords Bar to Foresthill at Mosquito Ridge Road

Trailhead Parking *(N38-58.418; W120-52.228)*

Access to this last long, remote section of trail is through the Todd Valley Subdivision. From the I-80 Auburn-Foresthill exit, drive 13.8 miles to the first Todd Valley Road, turn-off on the right. Take this right and continue for 1 mile to Green Ridge Drive, turn right onto Green Ridge. Go 0.1 of a mile and turn left on Oakwood Lane. Go 0.4 of a mile to Nugget Road, turn left at Nugget Road and travel 0.5 of a mile to Alton Trail, turn left on Alton Trail go 0.3 of a mile to the trailhead, a large open area, at the end of the street. The trail to the river is a dirt road that starts at the left side of the clearing. Hike 2+ miles, partially through private property. The last mile to intersect with the WST and Fords Bar is steep.

Illustration by Diane Kragy

WST: Fords Bar to Foresthill at Mosquito Ridge Road

The trail climbs gradually and then steeply for the first 2.3 miles through Peachstone Gulch. This long, remote stretch of trail offers solitude and stays high on the slope with panoramic views of the mystical layered canyon ridges and distant shimmering ribbon of American River far below. A circular stone trough catches water for the horses at an unnamed creek. The trail switches in and out of the side canyons crossing Pond and Dardanelles Creeks. Pipes, still visible, were laid between these creeks for the historic Eagle Creek Hydroelectric Project that once supplied power for several mines. The hydroelectric project was rediscovered by Tevis riders looking for a missing link to the WST in the 1980s and subsequently rebuilt.

The trail continues through deep forest before the scenery gradually opens up as the trail crosses a road. Make a left on the road for a few hundred yards and then right onto the trail as it climbs through chalky, bleached terrain past the Baltimore Mine to Mosquito Ridge Road and Foresthill. There are trailhead signs and a small turnout area at Mosquito Ridge Road. The trail can also be accessed through the historic residential area of Foresthill. There is limited parking at Mosquito Ridge turnout *(N39-1.056; W120-49.256)*.

FOREST HILL DIVIDE MUSEUM

The Forest Hill Divide Museum features exhibits and artifacts from the Forest Hill Divide's rich mining, timber and Native American history.

Hours: Open weekends noon to 4:00 pm
Season: From May to October
Address: 24601 Harrison Street, Foresthill, CA 95631
Phone: 530-367-3988
To schedule a group tour: 530-889-6500

Western States Endurance Run

By Vince Haughey

If all the trails in this book are too tame for you, try the Western States Endurance Run, 100 grueling miles across the rugged Sierra, Squaw Valley to Auburn. This "crown jewel" of ultra-distance footracing tests the absolute limits of human stamina and will.

The run was founded in 1974–after finishing the equestrian Tevis Cup Ride over the Western States Trail in 1971 and '72, Gordon Ainsleigh, who had given his good horse Rebel away to a girlfriend and when his 1973 replacement horse went lame, decided to try the 1974 100 mile trek on foot. Gordy trained himself the way he trained his horses, running the last 40 miles of the trail in brutal 100° heat time and again during the 6 weeks prior to the race. On race day Gordy pushed through 107° heat and finished in Auburn in 23 hours and 42 minutes.

Western States Endurance Run

Address: P.O. Box 99
Auburn, CA 95604
Website: www.wser.org

Held in June, near the full moon, over 400 runners enter this ultra-distance footrace, with hundreds more turned away. Over half reach the finish line in Auburn. Timothy Olson set the course record time of 14:46:44 hours in 2012. Ellie Greenwood set the female record time of 16:47:19 hours in 2012.

Just finishing–despite the 100-degree-plus heat, vertical climbs, rough and rocky trails and rattlesnakes–is an incredible achievement. According to Ainsleigh, the key to success is to keep "the internal environment as constant as possible." John Demorest, veteran of several races, once said, "In these ultra races, every 5 miles after the halfway point is harder than the first 50."

The technology of nutrition and electrolyte-replacement drinks has come a long way since Ainsleigh's near-suicidal run in 1974, when he took in an estimated 54 pounds of fluid and lost considerably more. The practices of wearing a light-colored shirt, keeping it wet, some-times putting ice cubes under one's hat, and placing aid stations every few miles–all have helped improve times and enhanced the survivability of the endurance runner. But none of this explains the ultra-joggers' enthusiasm for the punishment of the annual 100 mile run.

Mountain lion tracks

From the Squaw Valley starting line, runners climb to the crest of the Sierra Range. At one time, the runners crossed the tiny head-waters of the Middle Fork in the beautiful Little American (Picayune) Valley. Now the trail has been relocated up on the mountainside to mitigate erosion damage. For the next 40 miles, the runners pace themselves along the ridge tops of the Foresthill Divide and Red Star Ridge.

The torture of canyon crossings marks the middle 20 miles of the race. Near the Last Chance Mine site, the trail drops 1,800 feet into the North Fork of the Middle Fork, then up the other side. The El Dorado Creek canyon is a 2,100 foot drop and climb with a few smaller canyons along the way.

Runners on a 24 hour pace reach the hottest part of the day at mile 65. Running along the contour of the Middle Fork corridor, they face the extreme harsh, hot, dry, dusty conditions of the south-facing slope, always with an eye out for rattlers!

Night falls and runners that have not dropped out continue by flashlight. After wading across the Middle Fork near Ruck-A-Chucky Falls, they arrive on the El Dorado County side in the coolness of big trees. Midnight passes; dawn approaches. Ainsleigh found this stretch of the trail to be "supportive". But he reports that biochemical changes cause many runners to go through their most extreme emotions here–desperate exhaustion or an uplifting surge of willpower.

Crossing 'No Hands Bridge' at the confluence of the North and Middle Forks of the American River, the runners have to climb one more ridge to reach the finish line in Auburn.

Gordon Ainsleigh philosophizes, "Life is just too easy. Society is so cushioned, we have no opportunity for struggle. People are bred to struggle. We need to express that or else be incomplete." So it was a natural that Ainsleigh would make the Western States Trail into a footrace. It is fitting that our modern need for struggle can be expressed, once again, in the setting where hunter-gatherers thrived for thousands of years.

TRAIL AT-A-GLANCE:

QUARRY ROAD TRAIL TO MAINE BAR

DISTANCE: 5.6 miles one way; 2¼ hours each way (hiking)

DIFFICULTY: Easy

ELEVATION CHANGE: +/- 210'

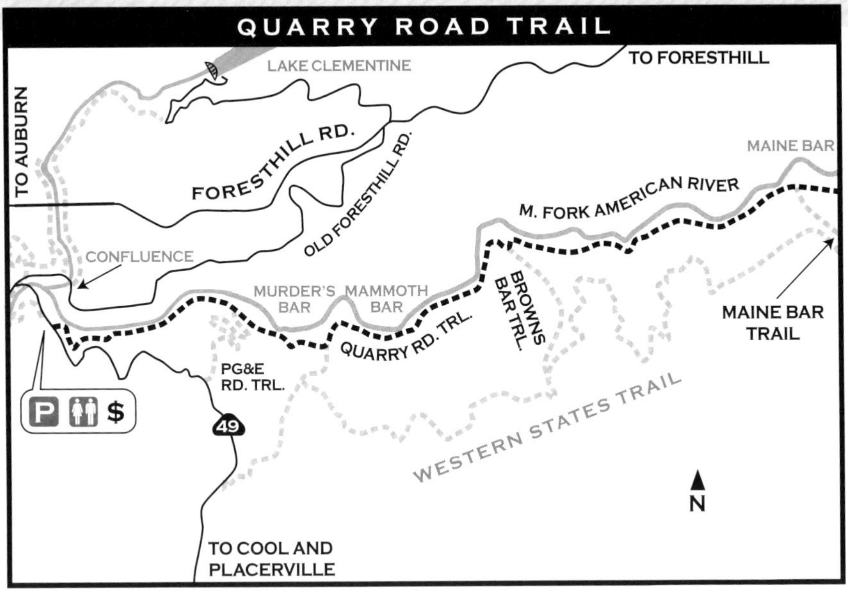

Note: Bicycles are allowed on the Quarry Road Trail from the Hwy. 49 trailhead to Poverty Bar, although the last 4 miles of this trail is WST.

Quarry Road Trail

TRAIL SNAPSHOT

The Quarry Road Trail popular with bikers, mountain bikers and horseback riders takes in expansive views and interesting mining history along the Middle Fork. The popular Hawver Cave, Limestone Quarry picnic area and Cave Valley rock climbing area are just a little over a mile from the trailhead. Maine Bar less than 6 miles from the trailhead was at the heart of the 1850s Grand Flume–a 13 mile long wood and canvas flume built by private mining companies to control river flows so miners could pick and shovel gold from the river bed. The trail has moderate climbs and drops, but stays close to the river for blackberry picking and swims on hot summer days.

Ringtail cat tracks

Fee Trailhead Parking *(N38-54.713; W121-02.095)*

Trailhead is 2 miles south of ASRA Park Headquarters. Take Hwy. 49 south from Auburn, turn right across the American River towards Cool. Turn left on a small dirt road ¼ mile south of the river crossing. Trailhead is beyond the fee parking area at green gate #151.

Canyon wren

QUARRY ROAD TRAIL

The Mountain Quarries Railroad used the first 1¼ miles of this road-trail in the early 1900s to transport limestone from the quarry up to Auburn. After 1¼ miles, the trail bears right up a short hill above the picnic area. Remnants of a large limestone-loading platform for the rail cars can still be seen on the left. At the top of the hill, a separate unmarked trail, known as the PG&E Road Trail, takes off uphill from just above the ruins of the limestone-loading platform.

The PG&E Road Side Trail *(hikers and bikers only)*

This trail offers fascinating views into the now abandoned quarry. A short uphill trek and a couple of switchbacks bring you to an open amphitheater in the quarry–well worth the

C.R.A.G.S.:

In 2012 Climbing Resource Advocates of Sacramento, CRAGS, put in the successful bid to reopen the Cave Valley Rock Climbing Area. The area has spectacular vertical limestone rock faces left over from the continuous limestone mining operations that originally began in the late 1800s. Currently it is open for year-round climbing Friday, Saturday and Sunday.

detour. For those with enough stamina to take this 1¼ mile trail to the top, it offers some awesome viewing spots of the river canyon and quarry. It comes out at a gate and tiny parking area on Hwy. 49 at the top *(N38-54.628; W121-01.114)*.

Returning to the Quarry Road Trail and continuing upriver, the trail meets the historic Western States Trail (WST) at the 2 mile point. In the river below, you can hear the Murderer's Bar Rapids, named for a deadly skirmish between miners and Native Americans that occurred here in 1849. Mammoth Bar Off-Highway Vehicle Area is just beyond Murderer's Bar across the river.

At the 3½ mile point, the trail intersects with Brown's Bar Trail, which heads uphill to the runners WST. The Quarry Road Trail continues parallel to the Middle Fork American River for another 2 miles. Just before reaching Maine Bar, the trail intersects with Maine Bar Trail. Like the earlier Brown's Bar Trail, this too heads very steep uphill along a creek and intersects at the top with the higher WST. The Quarry Road Trail ends one mile upriver at Poverty Bar where the horseback riders ford the river in the Tevis Cup.

Historical Snapshot:

Hawver Cave or Mountain Quarries Mine

The Mountain Quarries Mine, that contains some remnants of Hawver Cave, is readily visible just off the Quarry Trail. It is just beyond the tall concrete remains, about 1¼ miles from the trailhead.

The cave was named after Auburn dentist and amateur paleontologist, Dr. J. Hawver, who brought the cave's importance to light. Between 1906 and 1912, Hawver with the assistance of U.C. archaeologists, found and preserved many remains from the cave.

These included 10,000-year-old fossils of the dire wolf, saber-toothed cat, a giant ground sloth, glyptodon, woolly mammoth and other prehistoric animals. The limestone mining operation, which started in 1911, eventually destroyed all but a few tiny remnants of the original Hawver Cave.

The limestone formed from coral reef 250 to 300 million years ago. Over time the reef metamorphosed into limestone. 150 million years ago the meta-sedimentary rock surrounding the limestone turned into greenstone. When the tectonic plates shifted over millions of years formations of limestone and greenstone became a part of California's geology.

It is anticipated that the underground portions of the mine will be open to public tours. There are two local displays featuring Hawver Cave, one at the Placer County Courthouse Museum and the other at the Sierra College Library. State Parks Resource Specialist, Caveman Gene Lorance, has been surveying the mine/cave for several years. His web site hawvercave.org has the latest information about the cave's geology, paleontology and history *(see page 225)*.

Hawver Cave or Mountain Quarries Mine entrance. State Parks plans to open the cave to public tours in the future.

Auburn dentist and amateur paleontologist, Dr. J. Hawver

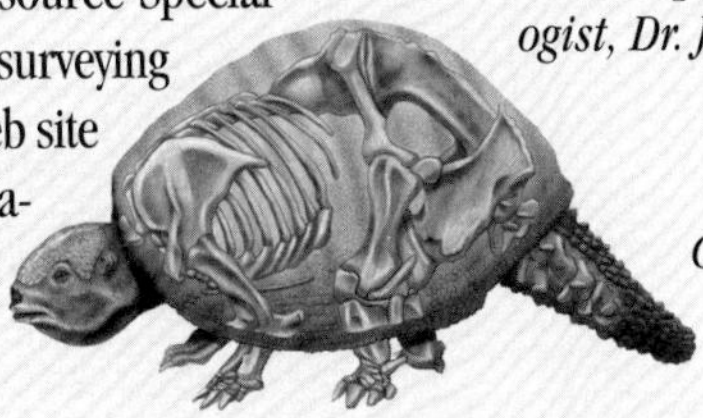

Glyptodon

TRAIL AT-A-GLANCE:

THE AMERICAN CANYON TRAIL

DISTANCE: 2.4 miles to river, 1½ hours down,
Alternate American Canyon Loop
5 miles round trip; 2½ hours (hiking)

DIFFICULTY: First 1.7 miles, easy down, moderate up
Last 0.7 of a mile, moderate down, strenuous up

ELEVATION CHANGE: +/- 1,100'

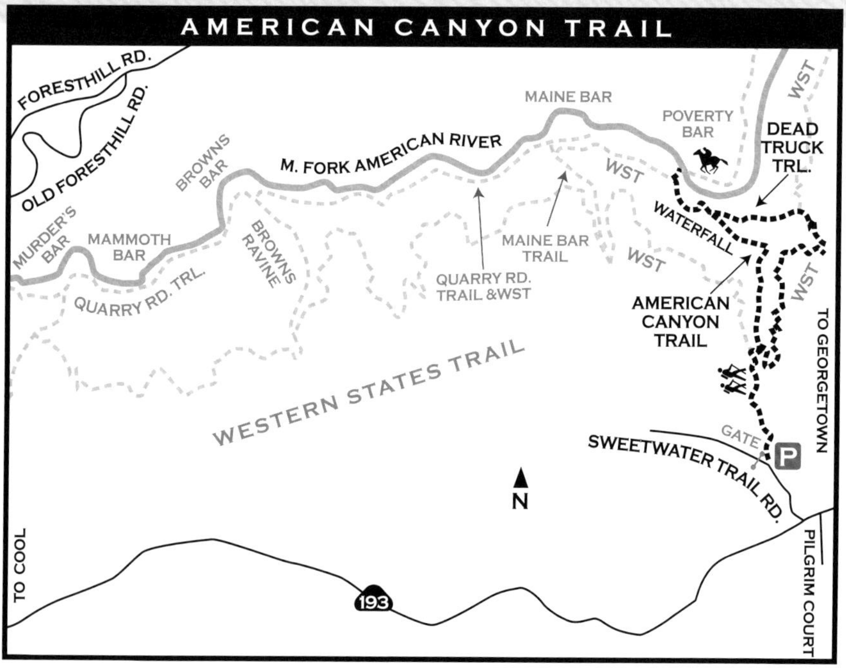

The American Canyon Trail

TRAIL SNAPSHOT

This steep trail has everything needed for a great day of exploration: rugged mountain canyons, a beautiful stream with waterfalls, a wide variety of plant and unique animal life, gold rush era history and panoramic views of the Middle Fork American River. Remember your binoculars, camera, sunscreen, water and a lunch to enjoy while you soak up the scenery.

Tiger swallowtail butterfly and California poppies

Trailhead Parking *(N38-54.809; W120-55.624)*

Trailhead is on Sweetwater Trail Road east of Cool. Take Hwy. 49 south to Cool. Turn left on Hwy. 193 at flashing red light and drive 5.7 miles. Turn left on Sweetwater Trail Road across from Pilgrim Court and look for trailhead on right side just before the gated entrance to Auburn Lake Trails. Curbside parking is available along Sweetwater Trail Road.

AMERICAN CANYON TRAIL

The American Canyon Trail is a densely treed forest of fir, pine and oak for the first mile. Bay laurel, blackberry bushes and poison oak can also be found along most of the trail.

About ¾ miles from the trailhead, the trail joins the historic Western States Trail (WST) for a short distance. Take a right at the first trail intersection with the WST, and go straight at the next intersection to stay on the American Canyon Trail.

Just past the 1 mile point, the trail crosses American Canyon Creek and Hoboken Creek. The confluence of these creeks, just downstream from the trail, offers a beautiful place to cool off. Look for California newts, also known as firebellies, on the trail and in the pools.

Continuing on the main trail, if you look closely, you may spot a 30 foot high hand-stacked rock dam built by gold rush miners on trail right, partially hidden behind a pile of rock mining tailings. About 1¾ miles from the trailhead, a small, very steep

California Newts, with their bright orange underbellies, move from their moist forest hiding spots in the spring to gather into mating balls in foothill river tributary streams. The females' eggs are fertilized and the young hatch with primitive gills that develop into lungs. Although it may be tempting to pick them up, it is best not to handle these newts. This species is extremely toxic to predators when ingested.

unmarked side trail on the left leads down to a hidden waterfall and a deep bedrock pool where you can escape the heat on hot summer days. Please use caution while climbing on the wet, slippery rocks. The side trail that leads to the waterfalls is a few feet before the intersection with Dead Truck Trail on the right.

After the intersection with Dead Truck Trail, the path becomes very steep, dropping 600 feet in less than ¾ miles past a mining era homestead and vineyard that supplied wine to miners. The trail crosses American Canyon Creek again and reaches the Middle Fork at Poverty Bar, not far from the ford where the Tevis riders cross the river.

American Canyon, Dead Truck, WST Loop

For a brisk loop, take a right at Dead Truck Trail up a short steep climb to the WST. Make another right at the WST intersection climbing then descending into Hoboken and American Canyon Creeks respectively. The final steep switchback climb out of American Canyon intersects American Canyon Trail. Stay left and return to the trailhead at Sweetwater Trail Road.

TRAIL AT-A-GLANCE:

Robie-Canyon Creek Trail

DISTANCE: 4 miles to Canyon Creek; 2 hours out and 2 hours back

DIFFICULTY: Steep climb to earthen flume trail then moderate

ELEVATION CHANGE: +/- 490'

ROBIE-CANYON CREEK TRAIL

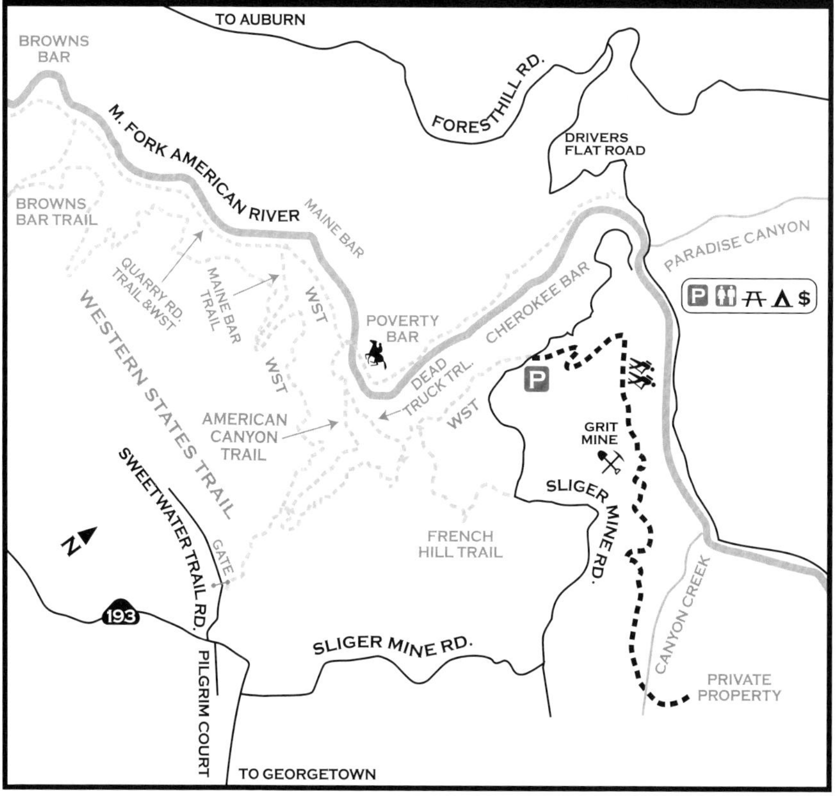

Robie-Canyon Creek Trail

TRAIL SNAPSHOT

Hiking upriver, this 8 mile round trip trail begins at a series of short steep switchbacks that level out as it picks up an old earthen flume which carried water from the tributary streams to the mines. High on the canyon wall the trail offers aerial views of the Ruck-A-Chucky rapids area. Bring binoculars and a camera.

Trailhead Parking *(N38-56.997; W120-55.847)*

Take Highway 49 south to Cool. Turn left at the flashing stoplight onto Highway 193 towards Greenwood and Georgetown. Six miles from Cool before entering Greenwood, turn left on Sliger Mine Road. The road passes through a rural area. After 2 miles stay left at the first 'Y'. At mile 4 stay right just past the solitary cemetery dating back to the Gold Rush. Continue another mile on the bumpy Cherokee Bar dirt road to the trailhead marked on the right, almost directly across from a road that intersects on the left. The main road continues on to Cherokee Bar and Ruck-A-Chucky. The Greenwood Bridge that crossed the river at Ruck-A-Chucky washed out in 1964. Trailhead turnout on Sliger Mine Road has space for a few cars to park.

ROBIE-CANYON CREEK TRAIL

Climbing steeply, the trail reaches the level contour of the mining-era ditch. From here the trail flows like water under your feet. It meanders past aromatic fir and bay. During the Spring nesting season look for junco bird nests with pinkish blue eggs tucked into the mossy trail banks. Ruck-A-Chucky rapids roar far below and, occasionally in the summer, rafters can be heard hooting as they paddle their way past the boulders and through the rocky drops in the river.

The miners built wooden flumes for the water to cross the tributaries, but those have long since rotted away. About half way in, after side-stepping multiple piles of bear scat, a remarkable dry-stacked rock wall appears. Standing about

3 feet high, its serpentine shape anchors the trails edge for a few hundred yards. Each stone has been laid with such accurate precision there is hardly room for a leaf to pass between the stones. The "not-so-true" Grit Mine, a yawning hard-rock mine shaft and rock source for the wall, greets hikers. The Grit yielded the 22 oz. "Fricott" nugget on display at Golden Gate State Park.

The rest of the trail to Canyon Creek meanders to the creek crossing, a good place to have lunch. The creek is canopied by big leaf maple and alder trees, the trail connects to Power House and Bottle Hill Roads via a detour built around private property that is posted and blocked. For the very adventurous, Canyon Creek is large enough to scramble down to the Middle Fork.

Dark-eyed Junco

The trail was built with a generous grant from the Wendall T. Robie Foundation to link the communities of Greenwood and Georgetown with the American River canyons.

About half way to Canyon Creek a remarkable hand-stacked stone wall appears. Standing over two feet high, Its serpentine shape anchors the trails edge for a few hundred yards.

TRAIL AT-A-GLANCE:

POVERTY BAR TRAIL

DISTANCE: 2.3 miles one way; 1 hour (hiking)
Winter: Due to Drivers Flat Rd. closure, add approx. 2 miles each way

DIFFICULTY: Easy

ELEVATION CHANGE: +/- 100'

POVERTY BAR TRAIL

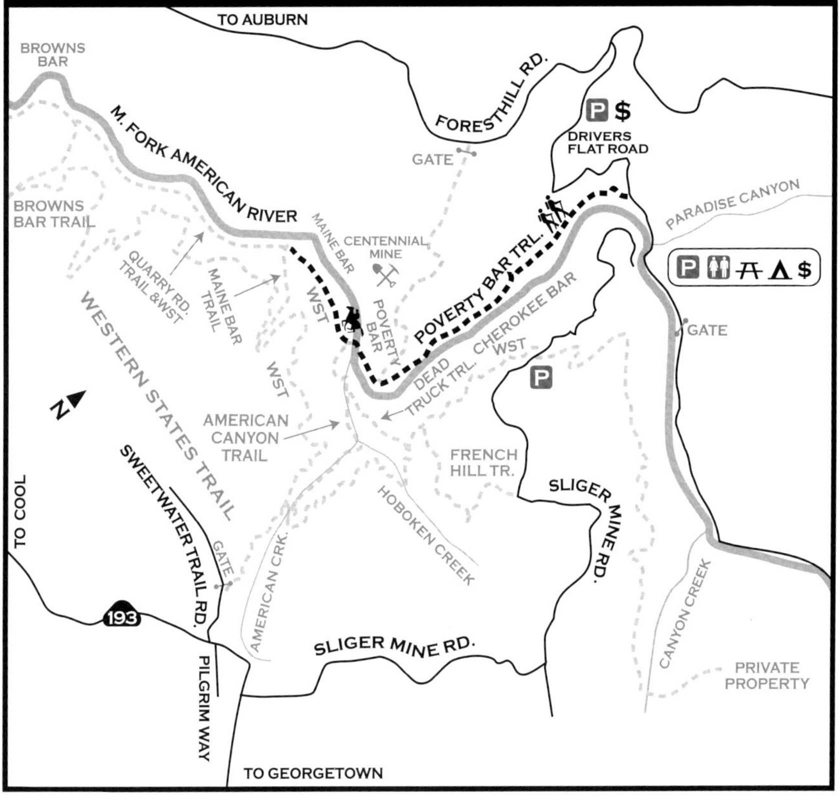

Poverty Bar Trail

TRAIL SNAPSHOT

This well-maintained trail is used by Tevis Cup equestrians who cross the river on race day at Poverty Bar. Drivers Flat Road is closed in the winter, adding approximately 2 miles each way.

Trailhead Parking

(N38-57.897; W120-56.205)

From Auburn take the Foresthill exit drive 8 miles to Drivers Flat Road on right. Drive 2.2 miles to trailhead marked by a pipe sign on the right There are small turnouts on both sides of the road for parking at the trailhead.

POVERTY BAR TRAIL

Juvenile Red Tailed Hawk

The Poverty Bar Trail meanders in and out of tributary stream ravines that feature cascading waterfalls in the spring. The middle section of the trail that burned in the 2006 wildfire offers hikers the opportunity to experience the fire adapted ecology of the canyons. Wildflowers, grasses and pipevine fill in where once thick forests grew. The trail crisscrosses ruins of gold mining camps through shady forests lined with blackberries and wild grape. A massive wild fig dominates the river bar just past the mining ruins. There are several places to access the river for swimming along Poverty Bar. The sandy beach and willow are on private property at the end of the bar where the Tevis riders ford the river here *(N38-56.197; W120-56.688)* at low water. The Poverty Bar trail continues to Maine Bar where it connects to the Quarry Road Trail.

TRAIL AT-A-GLANCE:

Roanoke Mine and Cock Robin Point Trail

DISTANCE:	4+ miles round trip to Otter Creek at Fords Bar; 2 hours down to river, 3 hours back (hiking)
DIFFICULTY:	Very steep, strenuous
ELEVATION CHANGE:	+/- 2,200 feet in 2 miles!

ROANOKE MINE & COCK ROBIN POINT TRAIL

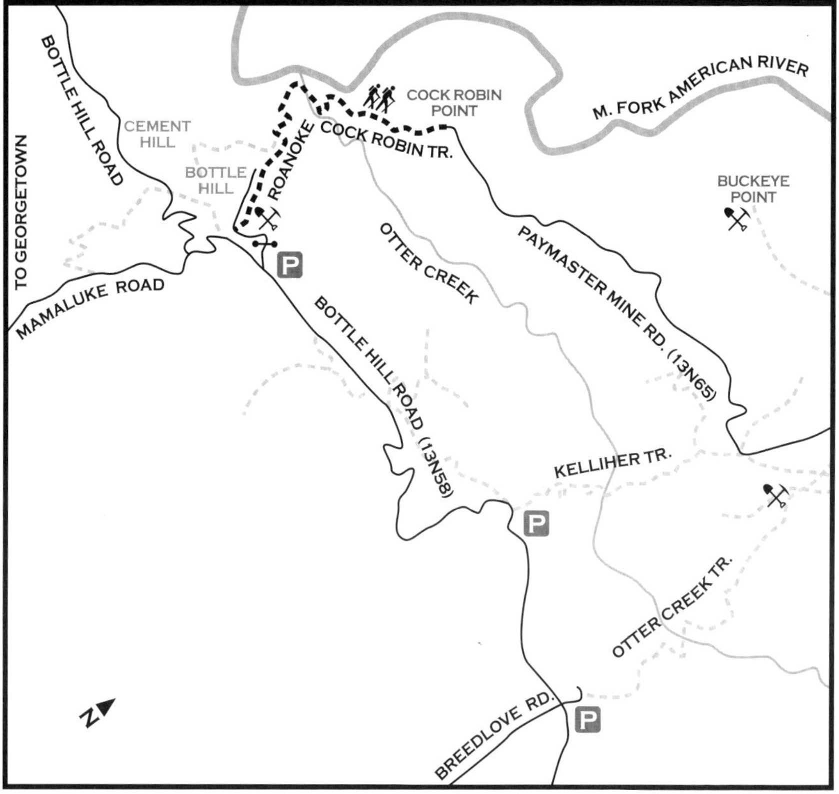

Roanoke Mine and Cock Robin Point Trail

Black-headed grosbeak

TRAIL SNAPSHOT

This very steep trail, named for the mine it passes by, was an early connection from Georgetown that crossed the Middle Fork at Fords Bar passing through Todd Valley and then on to Foresthill.

Trailhead Parking *(N38-56.790; W120-50.693)*

From Auburn, take Hwy. 49 south to Cool. Turn left at the stop light onto Hwy. 193. At 12.2 miles in Georgetown turn left at Church St. onto Mamaluke Rd. Drive 1½ miles and cross Canyon Creek bridge. Continue about ½ mile and turn right at Bottle Hill Road, also signed 13N58. Continue on for 1½ miles to an open flat area on the left. Park off the road and walk 0.3 of a mile down the dirt road to the hairpin turn where the obscure, overgrown unmarked trailhead is on the right.

ROANOKE MINE AND COCK ROBIN POINT TRAIL

The trail begins parallel to a creek past the Roanoke Mine on the right *(N38-56.789; W120-50.893)*. Don't even think about entering this mine. David Frasier spent Christmas holidays in the mine in 1888 after his candle went out. Friends were able to find and rescue him after 10 days but declared his mind had gone astray in the ordeal. The trail switches back and forth steeply, quickly reaching the river near a cobble bar below the sandy beach areas at Otter Creek. In the spring black-headed grosbeaks with their striking ochre-brown upper chest and back feathers are heard singing their loose, fluid robin-like song from the treetops along the river. There is a pleasant swimming hole about a half-mile scramble up Otter Creek.

The very steep, faint, obscure, unmarked mining era Cock Robin Point Trail begins its steep ascent of the canyon at Otter Creek. Cross the creek and walk upstream looking for the trail on the left. It reaches the canyon rim at forest service road *(13N65)*.

HISTORICAL SNAPSHOT:

In his daily journal 49er miner and shareholder, Stephen Wing, tells of using this route from Uniontown (Lotus) to Big Spring Mine in Todd Valley and then on to Foresthill.

September 22, 1857: "Got an early breakfast and started anew for Foresthill. Stopped in Georgetown about an hour to talk with Mr. Knox and get directions for my route. Passed through Mamaluke and Bottle Hill, down to Fords Bar on the Middle Fork then up the opposite side to Todd's Valley and then to Forest House where I arrived a short time before dinner."

TRAIL AT-A-GLANCE:

OTTER CREEK-PAYMASTER MINE TRAIL

DISTANCE: 4 miles round trip; 2½ hours (hiking)

DIFFICULTY: Moderate to steep to strenuous

ELEVATION CHANGE: +/- 1900'

OTTER CREEK-PAYMASTER MINE TRAIL

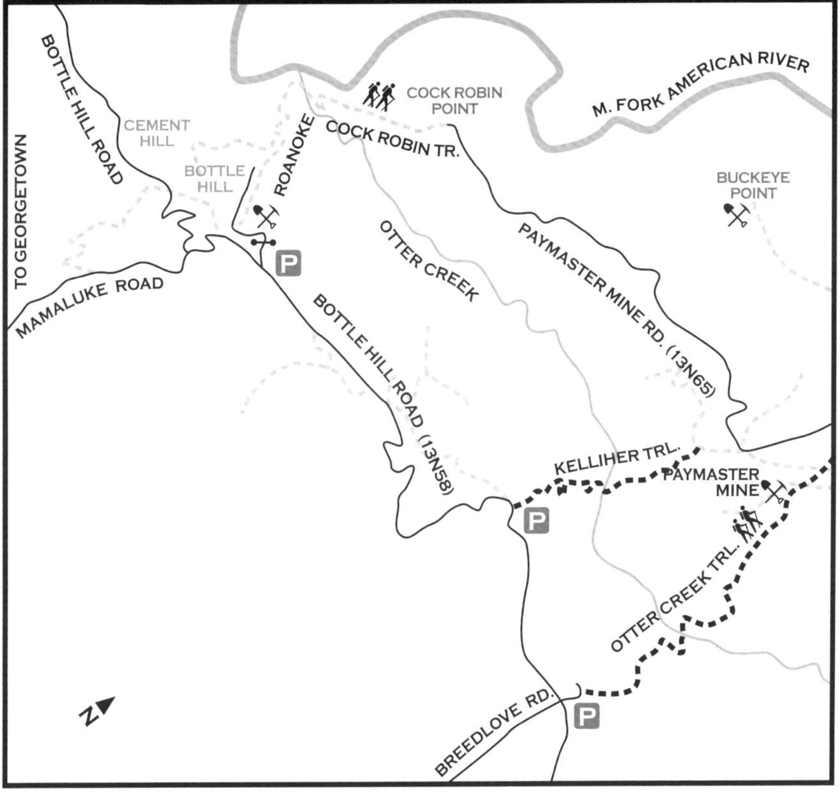

Otter Creek-Paymaster Mine Trail

TRAIL SNAPSHOT

This trail is also known as the Paymaster Mine Trail. It switches back and forth eventually crossing Otter Creek and then climbs out on the Volcanoville side to the mine located about a mile or so after crossing Otter Creek. The trail bears to the left as a single track at the signed trailhead.

Trailhead Parking *(N38-56.953; W120-46.738)*

From Auburn take Hwy. 49 south to Cool. Turn left at the stop light onto Hwy. 193. At 12.3 miles turn left at the stop sign in Georgetown onto Main Street/Wentworth Springs Road. At 3 miles turn left on Breedlove Road. Continue straight 2.8 miles crossing Canyon Creek in 1 mile and Bottle Hill Road (an off-center intersection) in 2.4 miles. Continue on 0.4 of a mile to a 'T' where the trail begins as a road on the right. Park well off the road.

OTTER CREEK-PAYMASTER MINE TRAIL

A botanist's delight this trail *(N38-57.265; W120-46.768)* is a popular Georgetown favorite. Hiking down through the switchbacks over a historic mining ditch, past old growth forest, the trail offers good views of the canyon. Look closely for historic candlestick trail blaze marks on the trees, a tall vertical slash candle topped by a short vertical flame. Trillium and fawn lilies can be found along the trail. The trail crosses enchanting Otter Creek sprinkled with leopard lilies and red columbine near its confluence with Missouri Creek. Bedrock mortars and petroglyphs can be seen near the confluence by the keen hiker. When Otter Creek is low enough look a little downstream for the creek crossing and climb the switchbacks about a mile up to the Paymaster Mine spur trail on the left marked by a post. The Paymaster is slowly crumbling into oblivion, vanishing with time.

KELLIHER TRAIL

(N36-57.126; W120-48.177)

A nearby option for those longing for more Otter Creek and gold rush mining sites. At Bottle Hill Road (not always signed), turn left for 1.4 miles to park at a clearing on the right near the power lines. Trailhead is marked 11E08. The first few hundred yards of rutted trail transitions into better trail where lush oak forest gives way to serpentine soils, scrubby growth and knobcone pine trees. The Jone's Ditch side trail has been cleared to the left and is well worth 0.5 of a mile side hike.

The short, steep Kelliher Trail drops down to Otter Creek near its confluence with Quartz Creek in less than a mile. Cross the creek to reach the Kelliher's homestead that featured a south facing terraced vegetable garden watered from nearby Quartz Creek. Mrs. Kelliher sold fresh produce to local miners. There are remnants of extensive gold prospecting scattered about the entire area. The trail continues faintly on up to the Paymaster Mine Road making a loop hike possible.

TRAIL AT-A-GLANCE:

North Fork of Middle Fork Trail

DISTANCE: 1½ miles to confluence with El Dorado Creek; 45 minutes one way (hiking)

DIFFICULTY: Easy

ELEVATION CHANGE: +/- 1,100'

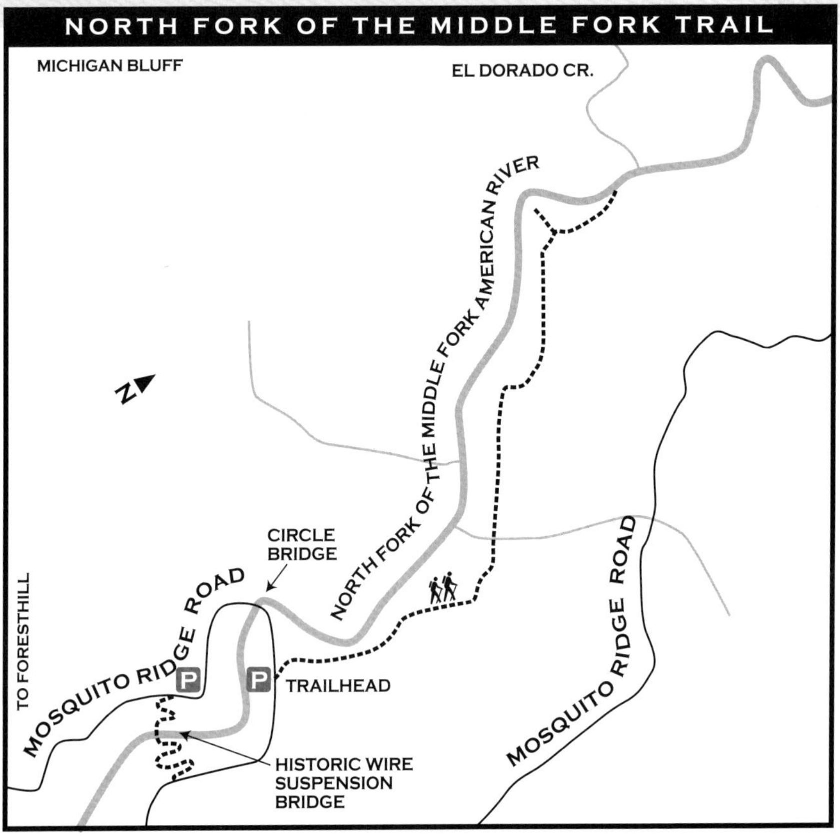

North Fork of Middle Fork Trail

Trail Snapshot

The north fork of the middle fork is entirely free of man-made obstacles flowing free and wild from its headwaters. The trail climbs steeply for the first few hundred feet from the road and then levels out to gradually follow the river upstream as a single track path. It features views of the steep rugged North Fork of Middle Fork canyon, spur trails to good fishing holes, wildflowers in the spring, rattlesnakes and mosquitoes. Gorge scramble options are possible.

Trailhead Parking *(N39-01.347; W120-43.224)*

From the Auburn-Foresthill exit at I-80 take the Foresthill Road 18 miles to the Mosquito Ridge Road junction in Foresthill. Make a right and continue 9.3 miles to the signed trailhead on the left just beyond the steel girder Circle Bridge that crosses the North Fork of the Middle Fork. Park in the turnout on the right.

North Fork of Middle Fork Trail

The North Fork of the Middle Fork trail climbs easily up the canyon past remnants of intense mining activity. During the spring months waterfalls pepper the canyon wall amid wildflower displays including wild iris, and globe lilies are abundant along this trail. Various spur trails popular with gold panners, fishermen and swimmers lead to the river's occasional deep emerald pools. The main trail continues through the 2001 Ralston Ridge Fire area that burned thousands of acres across the Middle Fork watershed.

Eventually the trail drops down to the river and becomes obscure. Follow the river closely to the trail's end at its confluence with El Dorado Creek. The mountain creek cascades down from the north below the historic town of Michigan Bluff located on the ridge high above. Most of the canyon above is inaccessible except by scrambling or taking the steep, rugged, faint trails that fork off the Western States Trail. Two of the obscure trails lead to the historic mining sites of Bogus Thunder and Bake Oven on the North Fork of the Middle Fork.

Andrew Hallidie "Wire Rope" Bridge crossing of the North Fork of the Middle Fork

At mile 9 on Mosquito Ridge Road there is a small turnout on the right before the Circle Bridge and the north fork of the middle fork trail. This short ½ mile trail starts at the turnout and switchbacks steeply down to the river. Take the first right fork near the top to easily access the steel wire cable bridge engineered by the renowned English engineer Andrew Smith Hallidie. A mechanical genius, Hallidie who perfected the San Francisco Cable Car transportation system, got his start in the Middle Fork gold mining operations. Hallidie patented his method of manufacturing flat wire braided into wire rope. The bridge, the last standing of its type in our area, was part of the Tillotson Trail–a pack animal trail that connected Michigan Bluff to Ralston Ridge. The wooden treads have rotted away and there is a big kink near the middle of the bridge making it unsafe to cross. The pebble beach and pool beneath the bridge invite hikers to linger and picnic, swim or fish. This is also a good place to begin a downstream scramble to the Middle Fork confluence.

Shelia Toner, Canyon Keeper, is a coauthor of The American River Canyon Hikes Guidebook.

Fly Fishing the North Fork of the Middle Fork

By Wild Bill Carnazzo

The many pools up and down the river from the Circle Bridge offer an almost infinite opportunity to experience the fine art of fly fishing on a gorgeous wild trout river. There are no restrictions to public access where spur trails off the main trail and rough streamside trails lead to pocket water and riffles that host mainly small rainbow trout and a few brown trout. For the adventurous, the impulsive swim or hike over a rocky outcrop to get to that hidden pool could be rewarded with explosive action.

In the spring, the most productive strategy is to fish subsurface with nymphs, using stonefly and mayfly imitations. As the water warms during late spring and summer, surface flies such as large stonefly patterns and mayfly imitations in sizes 14 and 16 will work well. Nymphs such as pheasant tails, prince nymphs, hare's ear nymphs and similar patterns will also take fish. During the summer, surface and subsurface caddis and yellow sally patterns in the same sizes work well. In the fall, smaller flies are required as flows drop water clarity increases and water temperature begins to drop. Small pheasant tail nymphs and blue wing olive flies work in the early afternoon, as do small caddis imitations. In the late fall midge patterns are the staple.

The late Bill Carnazzo, 1941-2013, fly fishing the Middle Fork.

Typical canyon creek equipment is necessary: a wading/hiking staff; sunscreen and bug repellent; plenty of water or a water filter; a compact first aid kit; good wading shoes; breathable waders for those times of the year when the air and water are cold, or neoprene wading socks for times when it is possible to wade "wet"; a 7' or 8' rod, equipped with a light reel and floating line; leaders tapered down to 4x with tippet spools of 4x, 5x, and 6x material; small split shot; and dry fly floatant. Be sure to crush hook barbs–it's easier on the fish and on the angler who accidentally buries a hook in a hand or elsewhere. Don't enter the canyon alone–there are many risks, all of which are manageable, but it is unwise to go solo here.

TRAIL AT-A-GLANCE:

CARDIAC TRAIL

DISTANCE: 1.4 miles to Oregon Bar from the Maidu Dr., gate #145 one way; .75 of an hour one way (hiking)

DIFFICULTY: Strenuous, steep and rutted
Passes through private property

ELEVATION CHANGE: +/- 780'

TRAIL AT-A-GLANCE:

CARDIAC BYPASS TRAIL

DISTANCE: 1.75 miles one way; 1 hour (hiking)

DIFFICULTY: Moderate, uses a combination of roads and trail

ELEVATION CHANGE: +/- 780'

TRAIL AT-A-GLANCE:

OREGON BAR TRAIL

DISTANCE: 0.8 of a mile one way; 20 minutes (hiking)

DIFFICULTY: Steep, strenuous

ELEVATION CHANGE: +/- 660'

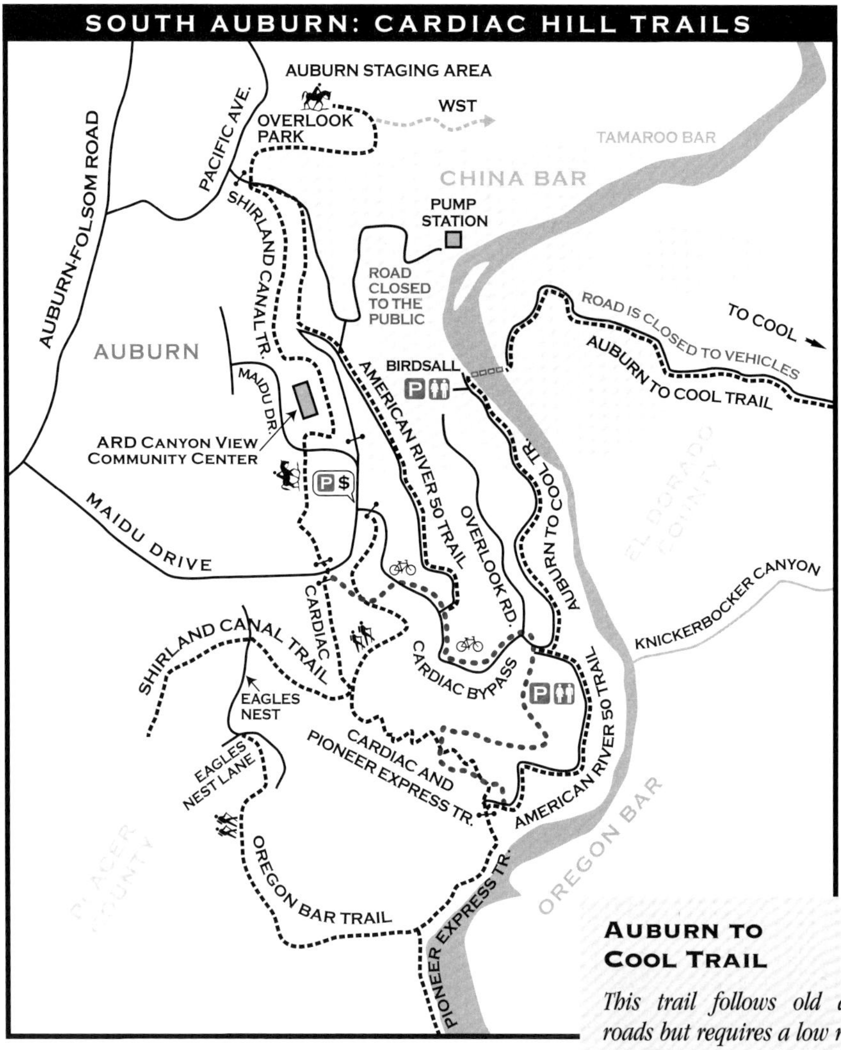

Auburn to Cool Trail

This trail follows old dam roads but requires a low river flow to cross at the Birdsall take-out area. Eventually a pedestrian bridge is planned to cross the river in this area to create an all-season trail for access to the Knickerbocker area trails and Cool.

South Auburn: Cardiac Hill Trails

The Cardiac Hill Area trails are popular steep trails in the south Auburn area that have historic connections to the Gold Rush and the abandoned Auburn Dam site. The trails can easily be linked at the top and the bottom to make interesting loop hikes and training runs and rides that include foothill scenery and views of the American River. There is easy access to the river for a refreshing swim, fishing or gold panning at historic Oregon Bar. Carry enough water in the summer months for the hot steep climb out.

Cardiac Trail

Trail Snapshot

This steep switch-backed trail was most likely established by miners for a quick access to Oregon Bar. As the trail descends to the river it zigzags in and out of private property. Please respect the private property signs and stay on the historic prescribed public trail.

Trailhead Parking

Same as Pioneer Express Trail directions on page 141.

Cardiac Trail

This 1.4 mile trail to Oregon Bar crosses through blue oak woodlands past abandoned mine shafts behind houses before it crosses the canal *(N38-52.115; W121-03.961)*, and turns into a steep narrow historic path used by many runners and athletes as a training hill to go in and out of the canyon quickly. All, including the casual hiker and equestrian, use Cardiac to link up with the other trails in the Cardiac Hill Area to form loop runs, rides and hikes of varying degrees of difficulty. Near the top, scenic glimpses of the North Fork come into view. This trail has many switchbacks and is deeply rutted in places. Always continue down the steep trail where other trails cross Cardiac. The trail ends at the Oregon Bar parking area *(N38-51.895; W121-03.580)*, near the river where other trails meet the road and parking. NOTE: at this time the Oregon Bar parking area is only accessible by car on weekends during the summer.

Cardiac Bypass Trail

Trail Snapshot

As the Auburn Dam site was abandoned Cardiac Bypass Trail was established deeper in the bowels of the dam site to provide a slightly longer more gradual 1.75 miles access to Oregon Bar. It utilizes paths, paved road and an abandoned dirt road to accomplish this objective.

Trailhead Parking

Same as Pioneer Express Trail on page 141.

Cardiac Bypass Trail

As its name implies the Bypass veers off to the left of Cardiac almost immediately taking the left ventricle at Maidu gate #145 as it descends down and crosses the Shirland Canal. Shortly after the crossing the canal it intersects and follows the main dam site paved road. Just after a fenced Bureau of Reclamation storage area, the trail turns abruptly to the left down a dirt road. The trail intersects the main road again crossing the Oregon Hill parking area and picking up a path that intersects Cardiac trail. Cardiac Bypass crosses back and forth many times taking the more gradual route down to the Oregon Bar parking area.

Oregon Bar Trail

TRAIL SNAPSHOT

This steep 0.8 of a mile trail to the Pioneer Express Trail was partially destroyed by the Canyon Rim development but luckily a Placer Land Trust public trailhead easement remains..

Trailhead Parking

(N38-51.908; W121-04.203)

Same as Pioneer Express directions to Maidu Drive. Once on Maidu Drive turn right at the first stop sign onto Burlin Way. Take the second left onto Peregrine Way. Take the first right onto Eagles Nest into the Canyon Rim subdivision. The trailhead is at the intersection of Eagles Nest and Eagles Nest Lane. Park along Eagles Nest.

OREGON BAR TRAIL

This is the steepest most direct trail to the river of the three trails in the Cardiac Hill area. It begins a couple of hundred feet below the Shirland Canal. The trail follows a seasonal stream that provides cool relief when making the steep climb out. It passes through a canyon wildfire zone where shrubs and trees are restoring themselves naturally by stump sprouting. In the spring wildflowers dot the trail. A couple of other trails intersect this trail but they eventually lead to posted private property. Left at the bottom *(N38-51.604; W121-03.828)*, leads a short distance to Oregon Bar; right leads downriver about 6 miles to Rattlesnake Bar on the Pioneer Express Trail.

Ron Gould, North Fork Trails Guidebook *author, and friends walk the Shirland Canal Trail.*

SHIRLAND CANAL TRAIL

The Shirland Canal Trail runs through Auburn below the Skyridge and Falcons Point subdivisions. The canal provides agricultural water to Western Placer County. The Cardiac Hill Area trails can be combined at the top with the Shirland Canal Trail and near the river with the Pioneer Express Trail to make loop hikes an easy option. The canal trail also links to the Auburn Staging area at Overlook Park. The canal has a very gentle gradient is mostly shaded by oaks. In spring California newts can be seen in the canal. This is a favorite trail for locals. Be courteous and respect the private property along the trail. Best to keep dogs on leash out of the canal. Use caution not to fall in as the water is swift and the banks are steep.

TRAIL AT-A-GLANCE:
Pioneer Express Trail

DISTANCE: 7.4 miles from Oregon Hill parking one way; 3½ hours (hiking)

DIFFICULTY: Easy

ELEVATION CHANGE: +/- 150

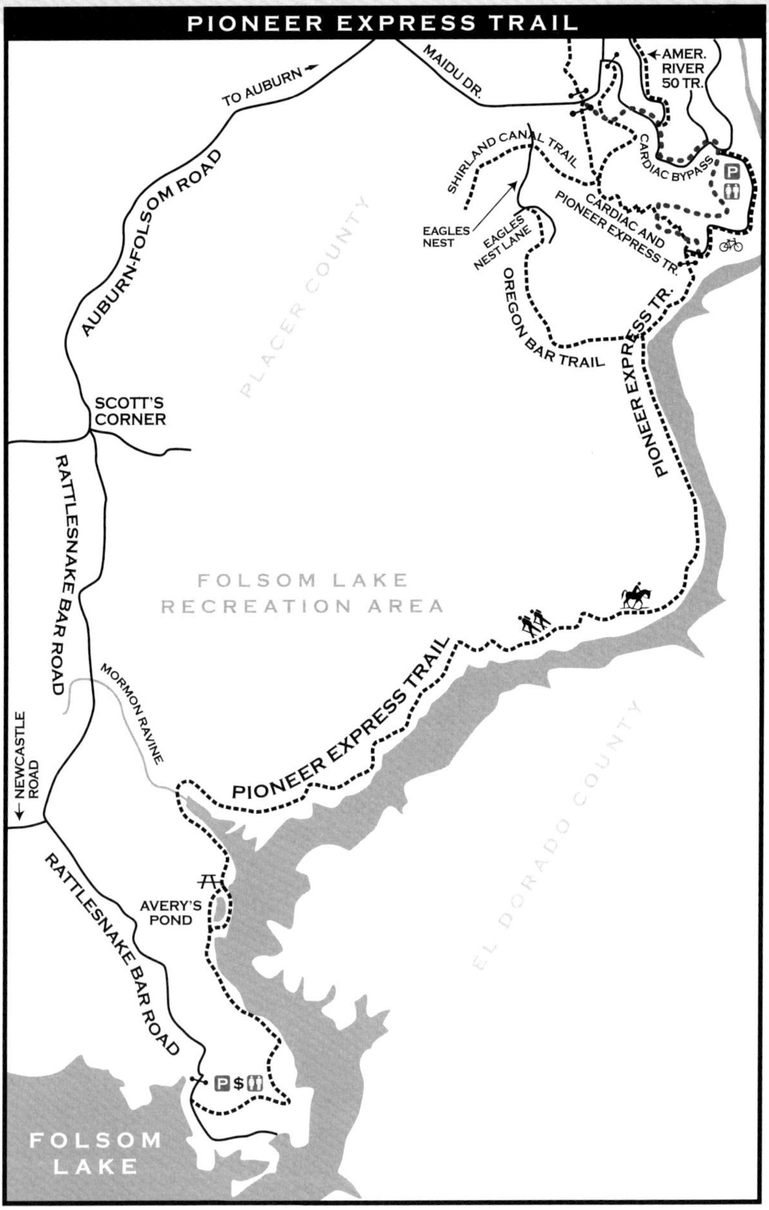

Pioneer Express Trail

Trail Snapshot

The scenic 8.5 mile Pioneer Express Trail from Auburn follows the steep Cardiac Trail down to the river near Oregon Bar where it connects to the well-maintained path to Rattlesnake Bar. Once at the river this easy fairly level downriver path parallels the historic North Fork Ditch. Expect wildflowers in the spring and some oak woodland shade in the summer.

Trailhead Parking *(N38-52.374; W121-05.044)*

The trailhead is on the right at gate #145 on Maidu Drive. From Auburn take Auburn-Folsom Road at the Lincoln Way (Courthouse) intersection towards Folsom 1.5 miles. Turn left at the Maidu Drive stoplight intersection with Auburn-Folsom Road near the fire station. After the second stop sign, look for gate #145, at 0.8 of a mile, where the trailhead begins on the right. Follow the Cardiac/Pioneer Express trail signs to cross the canal and then down Cardiac Trail *(see page 138)*. An alternate fee parking area is at the China Bar entrance area *(N38-52.509; W121-03.927)*. From here take the Shirland Canal Trail to the west where it intersects with the Cardiac Trail.

Pioneer Express Trail from Oregon Bar

Eager gold miners established a path along the North Fork of the American River traveling on foot and by horse searching for gold deposits in the foothills. Their path became known as the Pioneer Express Trail–the most express route from Sacramento to Auburn and the gold rich river bars and dry diggings along the American River. The American River 50 mile foot race celebrates this trail.

The Pioneer Express Trail section from Oregon Bar to Rattlesnake Bar *(N38-51.895; W121-03.580)*, generally parallels and uses the 19th century North Fork Ditch, as it meanders above the river along the edge of the canyon cliffs through oak woodlands, meadows and deep ravines for about 7 miles. Seasonally in late winter and spring stored water in Folsom Lake fills in the North Fork forming a long finger of the lake up to Oregon Bar. As the lake lowers in the summer, the river resurfaces. Spur trails that lead to sandy beaches and the water's edge cross the fading, overgrown ditch.

In the spring spider web fragments float in the air and the well maintained trail is a cornucopia of wildflowers that include shooting stars, hounds tongue, baby blue eyes, sierra blue iris, buttercups and many more. Deep blue iridescent pipevine swallowtail butterflies dazzle with their over and under courtship flight. Occasionally, untended fruit trees, the last living remnants of earlier homesteads are seen along the trail.

Mormon Ravine, the deepest ravine the trail passes through, has been developed to incorporate a small PG&E

The North Fork Ditch began at the Birdsall Dam and ran 25 miles downstream to Orangevale and Fair Oaks.

Historical Snapshot:

The North Fork Ditch, completed in 1856, was conceived by the American River Mining and Water Company as a means to deliver water to over 40 gold mining districts and for agricultural use in rural Sacramento communities. The ditch was built using a combination of construction techniques. Originally hand dug, it was anchored to rocky cliffs in steep areas and timber flumes were built across ravines. Other areas were supported by stacked, cemented rock along the steep cliffs. Later cement was used to line the ditch.

In 1898 the Birdsall Dam was added to the North Fork Ditch to store water for release into the ditch. Located near the diversion tunnel outlet of the abandoned Auburn Dam site, the dam was 18' thick at the base, 283 feet long, 16' high.

hydroelectric power plant. A bridge makes for an easy stream crossing here. Avery's Pond, possibly used to regulate North Fork Ditch flows, offers picnic tables and sometimes interesting waterfowl to observe.

Near the Rattlesnake Bar boat launch area a spur trail on the left leads to the equestrian staging and trailhead parking area *(N38-50.684; W121-04.537)*. The Pioneer Express Trail continues on around Folsom Lake, through Granite Bay, connecting to the American River Parkway Trail near Folsom and eventually ends at Discovery Park in Sacramento.

AMERICAN RIVER
50 MILE ENDURANCE RUN

American River 50 Trail through the Auburn Damsite

The American River 50 Mile Endurance Run Trail connects the Pioneer Express Trail at Oregon Bar *(N38-151.895; W121-03.580)*, with Overlook Park where the Sacramento to Auburn race finishes. From Oregon Bar parking area continue up the dirt road past Knickerbocker canyon on the right. (The Knickerbocker waterfalls are spectacular in the spring and worth the hike to view them.) The road trail comes out at the intersection with the Cardiac Bypass Trail and Oregon Hill parking area. Take the bypass trail uphill to the paved road, then go through the gate *(N38-52.263; W121-03.682)*, on the paved road to the right. Follow this road across the top of the abandoned Auburn Dam concrete foundation–a surreal experience to see how close we came to devastating 48 miles of river canyon. Continue on up the paved road staying left at the intersections. At the top, before the bridge, follow the road to the right to the trail intersection which skirts the edge of Overlook Park and loops back through the Auburn Staging Area to finish at the Overlook Park.

Recommended Trail Guide Reading

See page 415 for suggested trail guides on hiking the American River Canyons.

The Mammoth Bar OHV area offers a wide range of trails in a beautiful canyon setting adjacent to the Middle Fork of the American River.

Open for OHV schedule:

October 1st to March 31st:
Sunday, Monday, Thursday and Friday
8:00 am to 5:00 pm

April 1st to September 30th:
Sunday, Monday and Thursday
8:00 am to one-half hour after sunset

Open every day for non-motorized recreational use including hiking, mountain biking and horseback riding. However, to avoid user conflicts, non-motorized users should choose a day when motorcycles and OHVs are not allowed. During wet weather the park area may be temporarily closed.

Riding is allowed only on designated trails and the motocross track. Please observe all regulations and "Tread Lightly".

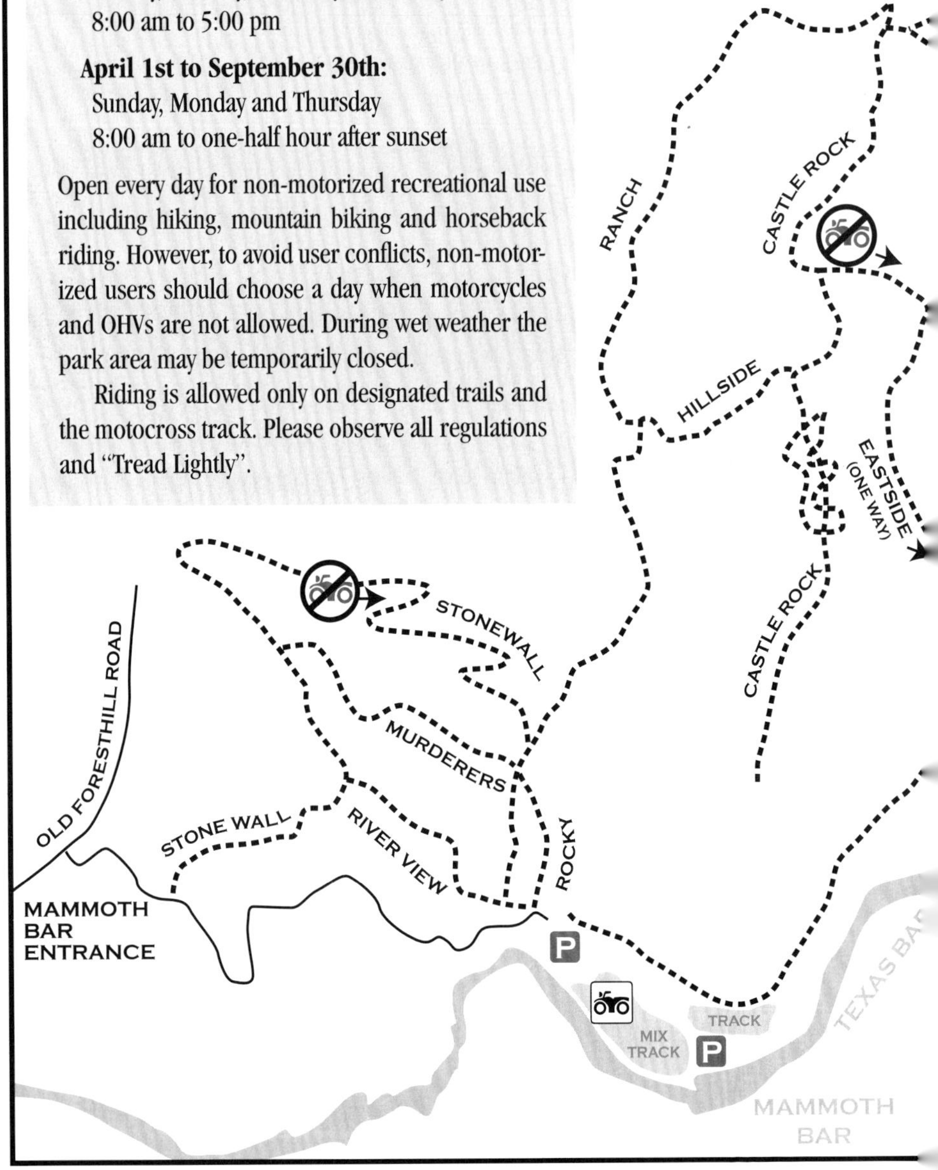

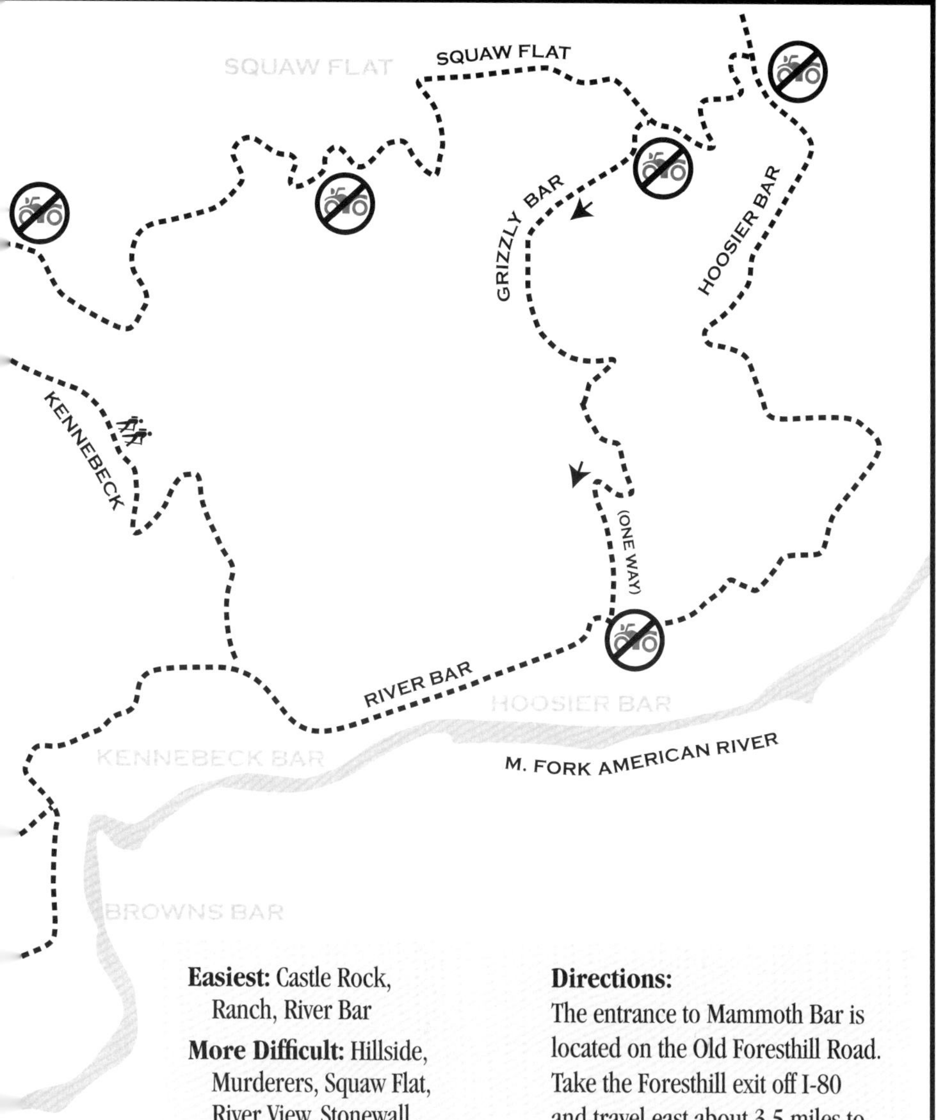

Easiest: Castle Rock, Ranch, River Bar

More Difficult: Hillside, Murderers, Squaw Flat, River View, Stonewall

Most Difficult: Eastside, Grizzly, Hoosier, Kennebeck & Rocky

No Quads Allowed: Grizzly Bear, Hoosier Bar, Squaw Flat, Eastside, Stonewall

One-Way Trails: Grizzly Bear, Eastside, Stonewall, Squaw Flat

Directions:
The entrance to Mammoth Bar is located on the Old Foresthill Road. Take the Foresthill exit off I-80 and travel east about 3.5 miles to the Old Foresthill Road. Turn right and the entrance is about 1.5 miles down the road on the left.

River Sisters

They become wild and erotic near rivers,
be it torrent or trickle

It must be–something to do with survival,
aliveness, a creature looking.

I have seen them,
women who hug mud.
They wrap themselves,
roll in it, then hug each other,
squeezing the river within.

I particularly like them in various shades of plateau,
mesa colors where rocks, rivers, mud and women
are denominated by red.

Some spend hours by granite wall,
watching waterfalls.

Consumer culture wilderness supply corporations,
see them as substrate,
youthful and sexy in graphic wild.

Lingering in pools, river stillness,
something of them flows to the sea.
Yet they are always new water
offering new eyes.

Some have gray hair
Some walk close to death with age or disease,
still wanting to be near rivers.
And when defending a watershed,
they fight like mothers.

- Roger Groghan

CHAPTER TWO

The American River:
Introduction to the Whitewater of the North, Middle and South Forks

The three forks of the American River described in this guidebook offer a wide variety of boating opportunities. The lower segments of the North and Middle Forks, and the Middle Section of the South Fork, from Coloma to Greenwood, are good for novices and family river trips. The upper segments of all three forks, and the gorge section of the South Fork are best suited for intermediate to advanced boaters.

All three forks originate from the Sierra Nevada snowpack. The North Fork has a smaller and lower elevation snowpack without storage dams, resulting in a shorter spring season run. It offers outstanding wilderness scenery and solitude. The Middle and South Forks have much larger watersheds with upstream reservoirs, which allow for summertime flows from hydroelectric releases.

Whitewater guide author, Tony DeRiggi rafting the Middle Fork of the American River.

Quietly floating the river offers the opportunity to experience the lush riparian (riverside) habitat and to view wildlife up close, including river otters, turtles, and many species of birds from the small water ouzel to the great blue heron.

All three forks run through the heart of the legendary Gold Rush Mother Lode, flowing past historic mining sites such as Sutter's Mill, where gold was first discovered. The keen observer may find Maidu/Nisenan grinding rocks that have been used for grinding acorns for thousands of years. Friendship, exciting rapids, historic sites, dramatic scenery and wildlife viewing are some of the rewards for whitewater river boaters.

River Safety

The Forks of the American River described in this section offer boaters a wide variety of quality whitewater runs. However, this guidebook is not a "How-To-Run Whitewater" guide and it does not recommend that any person should run the river.

Running rivers is hazardous, with risks that include serious injury or death. Do not run the river unless you have the requisite whitewater skills and experience. Do not rely only on the descriptions in this book, as rapids frequently change unexpectedly due to natural events such as high flows and rockslides, and the book does not include every rapid or hazard. River flows may change suddenly, increasing the difficulty of a rapid. New dangers, such as fallen trees, may appear at any time.

Always use extreme caution and scout any unfamiliar rapid. Do not go whitewater boating alone. Drugs and alcohol impair your judgment and increase risk of hypothermia. It is highly recommended that you learn whitewater rescue and first aid skills before running whitewater.

Be aware of the risks of swimming whitewater if you fall out of the boat:

- Float downstream feet-first for protection from rocks
- Never stand up in swift water to avoid foot entrapment
- Actively swim clear of strainers in the river, such as trees and brush, which can be a deadly hazard.

Gear for a safe river experience includes:

- Snug-fitting quality (class III or V rating) lifejacket. Correct fit essential for children.
- Helmets for class III and above
- Protection from cold water exposure, such as a wetsuit or dry suit, and whitewater footwear.
- Quality inflatable boat with multiple air chambers, spare paddles or oars, repair kit, rescue ropes, and first aid kit.

Leave No Trace: Help Preserve The River

Remember that other living things, both plants and animals, are dependent on a healthy river ecosystem, and that you share the use of the river with them. Please take care to minimize your impact:

- Do not litter. Pack out all your trash and properly dispose of it. Young fish, snakes, and lizards can become trapped and die inside pop-top cans. Otters and raccoons can get paws caught or cut in empty food cans. Ducks and other birds can become entangled in plastic loops of 6-pack carriers.
- Do not use soap or detergent in the river. These are harmful to fish and amphibians.
- Do not disturb the soil and vegetation along the river. This damages fragile riparian habitat, adds sediments to the river, and accelerates erosion.
- Use toilets provided by State Parks and marked on maps in this guide. If not available, properly dispose of human waste, which can harm water quality.

A Guide to the Difficulty Ratings of the Rapids

Class I: Flat moving water or small riffles with no obstacles

Class II: Waves are present, but no obstacles. This should be the limit for runs by most open canoes and novice boaters.

Class III: Longer rapids, with bigger waves, stronger currents and an obstacle such as a rock or hole that requires a maneuver during the rapid. Requires intermediate whitewater experience and skills.

Class IV: Steeper, longer, faster currents, big waves and holes, and possibly several obstacles that require turning and lateral movement of the boat in the rapid. Scouting recommended. Experienced boaters with advanced skills only.

Class V: More dangerous in every way than a class IV, usually has waves or holes that will flip boats, difficult to avoid undercut or wrap rocks, and steep vertical drops. Always scouted and usually portaged.

Class VI: Not Runnable. Even more dangerous than Class V due to huge waterfalls or unavoidable boulder sieves. High risk of serious injury or death.

Disclaimer

The authors and publisher assume no liability or responsibility for any injury, loss or damage that occurs while boating the river runs found in this guidebook. Your safety on the river is your responsibility.

Recommended Reading

For a guide to some of the class V (expert only) whitewater runs in the upper American River Canyons, which are not covered in this book, please see:

Books:

California Whitewater, 3rd Edition
By Jim Cassady and Fryar Calhoun, 1995. Contains Guide for Giant Gap run.

Field Guide to California Rivers
By Tim Palmer, 2012. Concise guide to upper sections of the North Fork above Giant Gap, the Rubicon River, which is the largest tributary to the Middle Fork, and three runnable tributaries of the South Fork, including Silver Creek, Pyramid Creek, and the Silver Fork.

Websites:

California Creeks Website
www.cacreeks.com
For description of Giant Gap along with the class 4-5 Kyburz to Peavine Road run of the South Fork.

Dreamflows Website
www.dreamflows.com
Provides up to date information on river flows, along with a valuable forum where boaters can learn about access issues, new hazards, river events, etc.

THE RUN AT-A-GLANCE:

Colfax-Iowa Hill Bridge to Yankee Jim's Bridge

DIFFICULTY:	Class IV+ for rock entrapment hazards, more difficult above 2,000 cfs
LENGTH:	5 miles to Yankee Jim's or 9½ miles to Ponderosa Way Bridge take-out
SEASON:	February to mid-June depending on snowpack
GRADIENT:	41 feet per mile, pool and drop
RUNNABLE FLOWS:	900-3000 cfs; small rafts and kayaks OK above 500 cfs; IKs above 400 cfs with possible portages
FLOW INFO:	Inflow gauge at Lake Clementine (North Fork Dam) www.dreamflows.com or www.cdec.water.ca.gov/river/americanStages.html
PUT-IN:	Auburn SRA Mineral Bar campground along Colfax-Iowa Hill Road, elev. 1110'. Parking fee
TAKE-OUT:	Yankee Jim's Bridge at Shirttail Canyon 900' or Ponderosa Way Bridge, parking fee
SHUTTLE:	Boaters often meet at the Weimar Crossroads exit Park and Ride lot. Shuttle from Colfax/Iowa Hill bridge to Yankee Jim's 12 miles (40 minutes) one-way, partly dirt road. To Ponderosa Way Bridge 21 miles (60 minutes) one-way, partly dirt road.
OUTFITTERS:	www.parks.ca.gov; Go to Auburn SRA site click on whitewater link
WATER QUALITY:	Cold and clear, but purify before drinking
CAMPING:	Available at Mineral Bar Campground at put-in. 17 sites with tables, fire pits and toilets. No drinking water. Camping fee. For camping on the river a permit is required.
EMERGENCIES:	Placer County Sheriff (Auburn): 911, California State Parks Dispatch: (916) 358-1300. Auburn SRA 530-885-4527

The Upper North Fork of the American River

Whitewater guide by Otis Wollan, updated by Tony DeRiggi, John Donovan and Eric Peach. Geology by Terry Wright, Ph.D.

The Colfax-Iowa Hill Bridge to Yankee Jim's Bridge Run

Old prospector on his way to the Diggins.

The North Fork American, with no dams upstream, is truly a wild river. This is a popular Class IV+ run for rafts, kayaks or whitewater canoes primarily in winter and spring, when water levels exceed 500, or 900 cfs for large rafts. The North Fork is a dangerous river to boat at both low and high flows. Drownings and injuries have occurred at high and low flows due to underwater entrapment hazards. At flows from 1,100 to 2,000 cfs most dangerous rocks are covered, passages are wider, and maneuvering is much easier. Rafting is not recommended at flows above 3,000 cfs, as hydraulic intensity increases markedly and eddies and rescue options decrease. It should only be attempted by very experienced whitewater boaters. A mile-by-mile guide cannot replace the responsible judgement of each individual boater. Boaters often continue another 4½ miles on the Class II-III Shirttail Creek to Ponderosa Bridge section.

UPPER NORTH FORK PUT-IN & TAKE-OUT SHUTTLES

To Colfax-Iowa Hill Bridge Put-In:

Take the Colfax exit off Interstate 80. Turn right on the frontage road, go 1/4 mile and turn left at the Maidu Indian Cemetery on to Colfax-Iowa Hill Road. Take the paved road 3 miles to the put-in

across the river, on the south side, in the campground area.

Colfax-Iowa Hill Road is a remnant of a Gold Rush wagon road, and has many hairpin turns and switchbacks. The last long easterly switchback has a spectacular view of Cape Horn, a huge rock monolith which marks the lower gateway into the Wild & Scenic portion of the North Fork.

Commercial North Fork raft trip begins in swift current at the Colfax-Iowa Hill Bridge put-in. Class III-V white water action begins at the first river bend, with little time to train the crew. Private boaters put-in at the calm water just upstream of the historic suspension bridge.

SHUTTLE FOR TAKE-OUT AT YANKEE JIM'S BRIDGE:

Take the Weimar Cross Road exit off I-80. Take Canyon Way towards Colfax to Yankee Jim's Road, and then turn right. (This road is also marked by a "Foresthill 13 miles" road sign.) The paved road becomes a dirt road cliff hanger, which follows Bunch Canyon Creek, a pretty tributary stream to the North Fork full of Indian rhubarb and waterfalls. If you get out of your car and inspect the bedrock, you may find old wagon wheel ruts in this old stagecoach road.

Park either side of the suspension bridge. Across the bridge on river left there is a good trail leading to the beach just downstream of where Shirttail Creek enters the river. Return to Canyon Way, take a right and continue to Colfax-Iowa Hill Road, and turn right to reach the put-in.

MILE BY MILE GUIDE

COLFAX-IOWA HILL BRIDGE TO YANKEE JIM'S BRIDGE

Colfax-Iowa Hill Bridge Put-In

This is the jumping-off spot for river trips on this exciting Class IV wild river run. It is also the take-out for the expert Class V Giant Gap run. A fee use campground and parking area is on the east bank (river left), and a short path from there leads to a put-in spot beneath the shade of black locust trees planted by miners. Another put-in, used by commercial trips, is on the opposite side of the river downstream of the new bridge. Put-in can be busy on weekend mornings during rafting season (April to mid-June).

Foothill Rocks

The geology of this area is typical of Sierra foothill canyons. The steep-walled gorge was cut into hard bedrock by the river. The Sierra was a low rolling plain about 10 million years ago; today's mountains formed when this plain uplifted like a trap door with hinges in the valley and opened to the east. Steep faults on the east side caused the uplift.

The western slope is a low angle surface and the eastern slope is steep as a result. Rushing rivers cut into the west slope to form the present canyons. The river carries hard cobbles and granite gravel from the heart of the range which act like teeth grinding into solid bedrock. These can be seen scattered about the shore at put-in.

Gold & Quartz

The ancient bedrock is black slate here; the 350 million-year old Calaveras complex of mud and sandstone formed on the ocean floor and was changed by heat and pressure. The change process (metamorphism) caused the foliated or bladed structure of this rock. Snow-white quartz veins, formed by intrusion of hot fluids into cracks, lace the black slate. Gold also traveled with these hot fluids, and is found with the quartz in hard rock mines.

Gold also eroded with the bedrock during canyon formation and is found mingled with dark heavy sand and caught between

North Fork American River Gauge at Iowa Hill Bridge

Approximate Discharge in Cubic Feet per Second

Gauge Height	.00'	.50'
1.3	510	539
1.4	568	598
1.5	628	659
1.6	691	722
1.7	754	787
1.8	820	853
1.9	886	920
2.0	954	988
2.1	1022	1057
2.2	1093	1129
2.3	1165	1201
2.4	1238	1275
2.5	1312	1350
2.6	1389	1428
2.7	1467	1507
2.8	1547	1587
2.9	1628	1669
3.0	1710	1752
3.1	1794	1836
3.2	1879	1922
3.3	1965	2008
3.4	2052	2096
3.5	2141	2185
3.6	2230	2276
3.7	2321	2367
3.8	2413	2459
3.9	2506	2553
4.0	2600	2647
4.1	2693	2741
4.2	2788	2836
4.3	2883	2931
4.4	2980	3028
4.5	3077	3126
4.6	3175	3225
4.7	3275	3324
4.8	3375	3425
4.9	3476	3526
5.0	3578	3629

Data based on field measurements taken by Western Hydrologics Systems for California State Parks, Auburn State Recreation Area (Revised 03/2006)

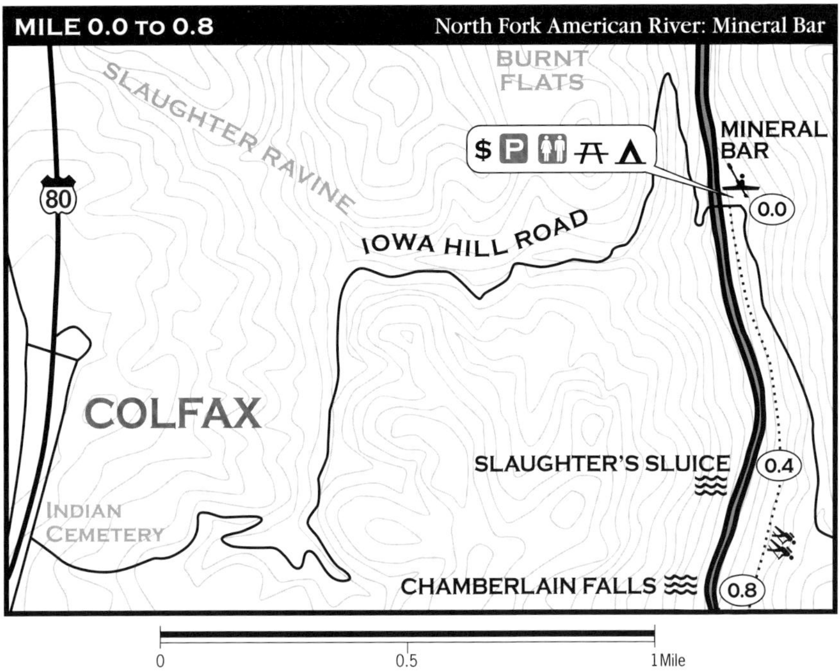

bladed ribs of slate in the river bed. Cobble mounds in the campground were heaped by miners in hot pursuit of this placer gold. Miners still swish dark sand concentrate in pans to find gold flakes and nuggets carried by the winter floods.

The river canyon is straight at this put-in spot because landslides and erosion follow the weak planes of foliation, or layering, in the slates.

Cobbles on shore are from rock types upstream. Light speckled granite cobbles come from the large area of plutonic igneous rocks which form the core of the Sierra and the walls of Yosemite. White quartz and gold flakes also come from the granite. Metamorphosed volcanic rocks are green with dark angular fragments, indicating an explosive volcanic origin. Light green banded rocks are metamorphosed volcanic ash. Light gray hard chert was formed on the deep ocean floor. Green shiny rock is serpentine, formed by the reaction of water with peridotite, a rock formed deep under the surface of the earth.

Bedrock

These rocks and recent geologic studies done in the Sierra indicate that there are two sets of bedrock types. The older rocks are originally sedimentary, volcanic and plutonic rocks which originally formed on the ocean floor 300-160 million years ago. These rocks traveled on the ocean floor until it plunged under the edge of the continent. The continent acted like a huge bulldozer and caught up these pieces of ocean floor, plastering them to the edge of the continent. This was accomplished by about 160 million years ago, when molten granite and quartz veins intruded and metamorphosed the ocean floor rocks. A huge mountain range, the "ancestral Sierra," was formed of the granite and deformed metamorphosed ocean rocks about 140 million years ago.

LEGEND

- PAVED ROADS
- DIRT ROADS
- TRAILS
- RIVER
- CREEKS
- PRIMITIVE TRAILS
- PUT-IN & TAKE-OUTS
- (0.0) MILE MARKERS
- RAPIDS
- P PARKING AREAS
- TOILETS
- PICNIC & CAMPING
- HORSE ROUTES
- HIKING ROUTES
- BIKE ROUTES
- $ FEE AREAS
- GATE

Mile 0.0-0.4 Put-in

Under the newer bridge at the put-in on river right, you can check the current flow at the gauge attached to the bridge footing *(see table on page 153)*. There is an eddy on your river right after the first turn from which you can see the entrance to Slaughter's Sluice. *The first stretch of river is straight, following the foliation of the slate deposits. Downstream you can see the sheer, pale-green cliffs of the gorge.*

Mile 0.4-0.8 Slaughter's Sluice (Class IV)

The usual entrance is just to the right of the house-sized boulder through churning whitewater to begin this tortuous boulder slalom around car-sized rocks which requires quick and precise maneuvering over a series of sharp ledge drops. At high flows it is possible to enter on the left side of the house rock. Avoid the rock sieve on the far right.

After the Sluice there are constant rapids to the small pool above Chamberlain Falls. There is a small eddy on the left where you can scout the falls. Watch carefully for the tell-tale river horizon line as no major features designate exactly where the falls are. At flows below 1,500 cfs, the top of a boulder can

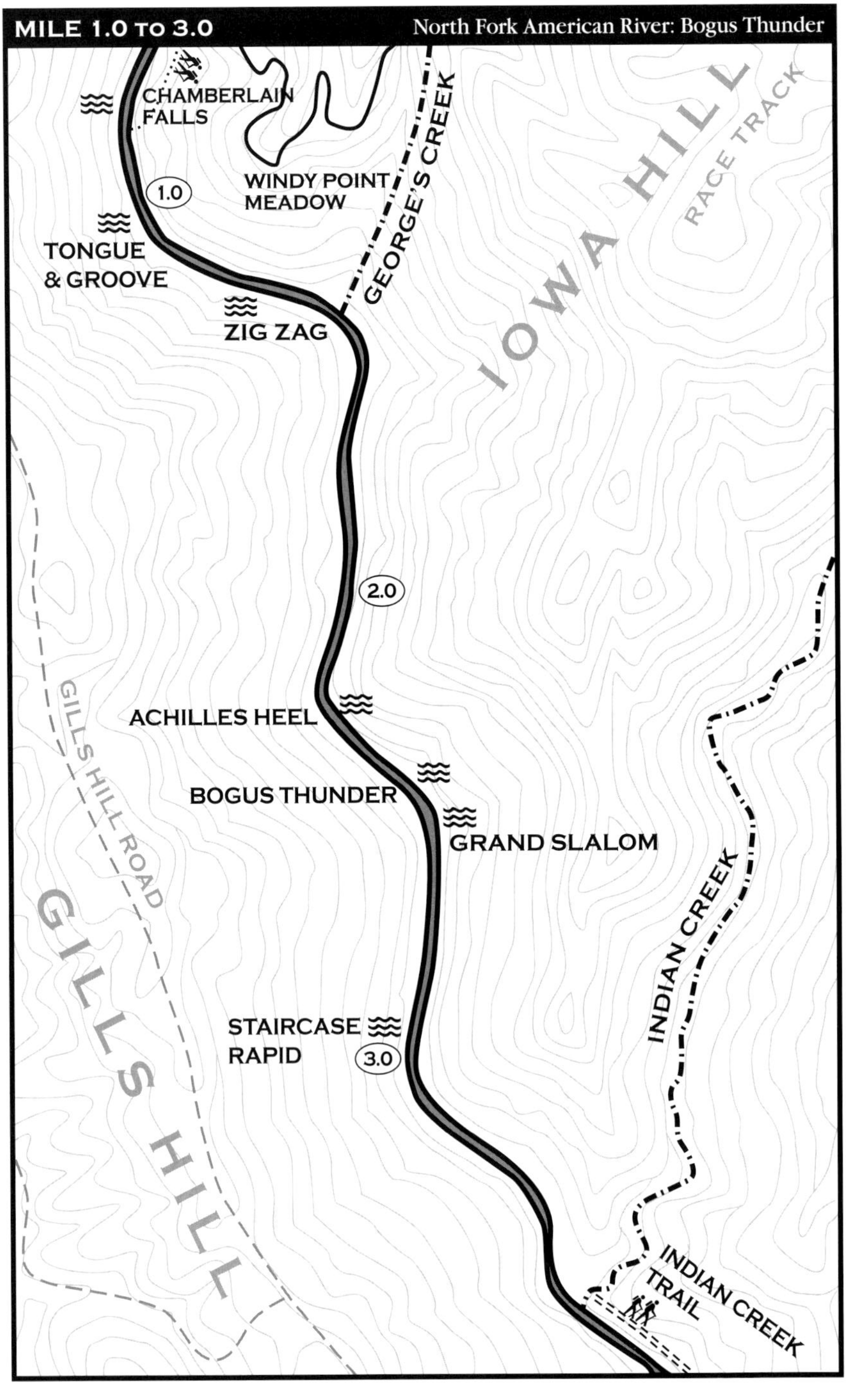
MILE 1.0 TO 3.0
North Fork American River: Bogus Thunder
CHAMBERLAIN FALLS
WINDY POINT MEADOW
GEORGE'S CREEK
IOWA HILL
RACE TRACK
1.0
TONGUE & GROOVE
ZIG ZAG
2.0
ACHILLES HEEL
GILLS HILL ROAD
BOGUS THUNDER
GRAND SLALOM
GILLS HILL
INDIAN CREEK
STAIRCASE RAPID
3.0
INDIAN CREEK TRAIL
INDIAN CREEK

be seen in the middle of the entrance.

Most boulders are green metavolcanic rocks, which have been rolled downstream by floods and caught in the narrow, constricted canyon by ledges of hard bedrock.

Mile 0.8 Chamberlain Falls (Class IV)

The 6 foot falls are formed by a large midstream boulder in a constriction formed by slanting rocks from both riverbanks. Scouting is highly recommended. The chute along the right wall is the preferred route and the dangerous "keeper" eddy on the left center should be avoided. This strong eddy on the left can trap boats and people, and a drowning has occurred here. At flows below 900 cfs large rafts may get stuck and lining may be required.

Streaks of black in light green hard rock are alternating layers of silica-rich mudstone and volcanic ash which have been metamorphosed. The metamorphism process reforms silica to quartz crystals which have an interlocking texture and make the bedrock here very hard.

Mile 1.1 Tongue and Groove (Class IV)

A rocky horizon line marks this rapid which has two possible chutes. The narrow middle-left center groove is preferred at low flows when the wider far-left tongue becomes a rocky pour-over. Look out for surprise rocks at the bottom.

Windy Point Meadow

In the spring look left, mid-slope at the spectacular Windy Point canyon meadow filled with goldfield, meadow foam, poppy, monkeyflower and lupine wildflowers *(see also page 87)*.

Mile 1.6 Zig-Zag (Class IV)

A boulder slalom as the river turns left, and marked by a large mid-stream rock, necessitates quick and precise zig-zag maneuvering to avoid rocks and holes. Finish the rapid along the left or right wall to avoid sharp rocks in the center.

Mile 2.0 Fern Wall

Ledges and cliffs on river left shelter a green garden of maidenhair ferns and wildflowers on a smooth wall of foliated slate.

Mile 2.2 Achilles Heel (Class IV)

Easy to scout from the left. The river turns left into another challenging rock slalom through large boulders and narrow chutes.

The no-longer fearless rafters in these three photos show us how not to raft the North Fork. Their rubber-ducky quality boat is not adequate for this river's challenge and none of their gear is tied down. As they enter Chamberlain Falls, half the crew is swimming, and they are totally out-of-control. You can lose a lot more than your lunch on the North Fork.

Mile 2.3 Boulder Sieve (Class II)

House rocks block all but the far left channel here. Use caution as kayakers and swimmers have been swept under midstream boulders here.

Mile 2.4 Bogus Thunder (Class IV+)

Catch an eddy on the left to scout when you see the horizon line. This is a very challenging rapid. Rafts often wrap, flip or have swimmers here. At low flows there are entrapment rocks on the right, and large rafts may need to be lined. At flows around 1,000 cfs, the preferred route is to tuck behind the large boulder on the left and bump and grind down the far left narrow chute below. Advanced experts may try to enter center and make a difficult sharp left turn into the steep right to left diagonal slot. Above 1,500 cfs there is a chute down the middle to the right of a large, frothy dome called the "snowball". Avoid running too far right, where current forces boats into rocks along right wall.

White, silica-rich metamorphosed volcanic ash and broken fragments of breccia are present here. Boulders of

Bogus Thunder (Class IV) paddle raft running far left chute. The Snowball is visible on river right. Diagonal Slot run is seen on river right side of the raft

Inset shows raft stuck on the mid-river rock.

At mile 3.0, kayakers wait for their turn to ham it up at Nosestand Rapid just below Staircase.

this hard rock are scattered in the channel and form a constriction dam that causes this drop.

Inspired by a waterfall on the North Fork of the Middle Fork American River, historians Thompson and West wrote in 1888 of how "Bogus Thunder" waterfall was named:

"A fall in the river, a mile or more above the place, over which the waters of the stream plunge, and the sound of which reverberates throughout the gorge, fixes an impression upon the mind of a stranger who first visits the bar, that the noise he hears so distinctly is thunder. So thought the first explorers, until they finally located the cause and proclaimed the thunder bogus."

Mile 2.45 Flipper Wall (Class II)

At this drop just below Bogus the strong current can force boats into the wall on left. There is a nice lunch beach on right here.

Mile 2.5 Grand Slalom (Class III)

Run left through this boulder garden with tight passages, exit right of the house rock.

Mile 2.9 Staircase Rapid (Class IV)

Stop at the large eddy river right across from a cliff on the left and above the drop marked by flat-topped house boulders on river right. Hike downstream and scout from the top of the boulders on the right. There are three drops here. Enter left, but avoid the far left undercut boulder sieves where at low flows swimmers have been fatally entrapped. A large hole at the second drop is particularly nasty. To avoid it, after the first drop, you must run right of the large mid-river boulder pour-over and then avoid the undercut rock wall on the far right. The last drop has a ledge rock in the middle to avoid.

Nosestand Rapid

Just below the last stair-step, is a pool leading to a fantastic kayak play hole where kayakers like to go vertical.

Following Staircase, bedrock rapids are much fewer

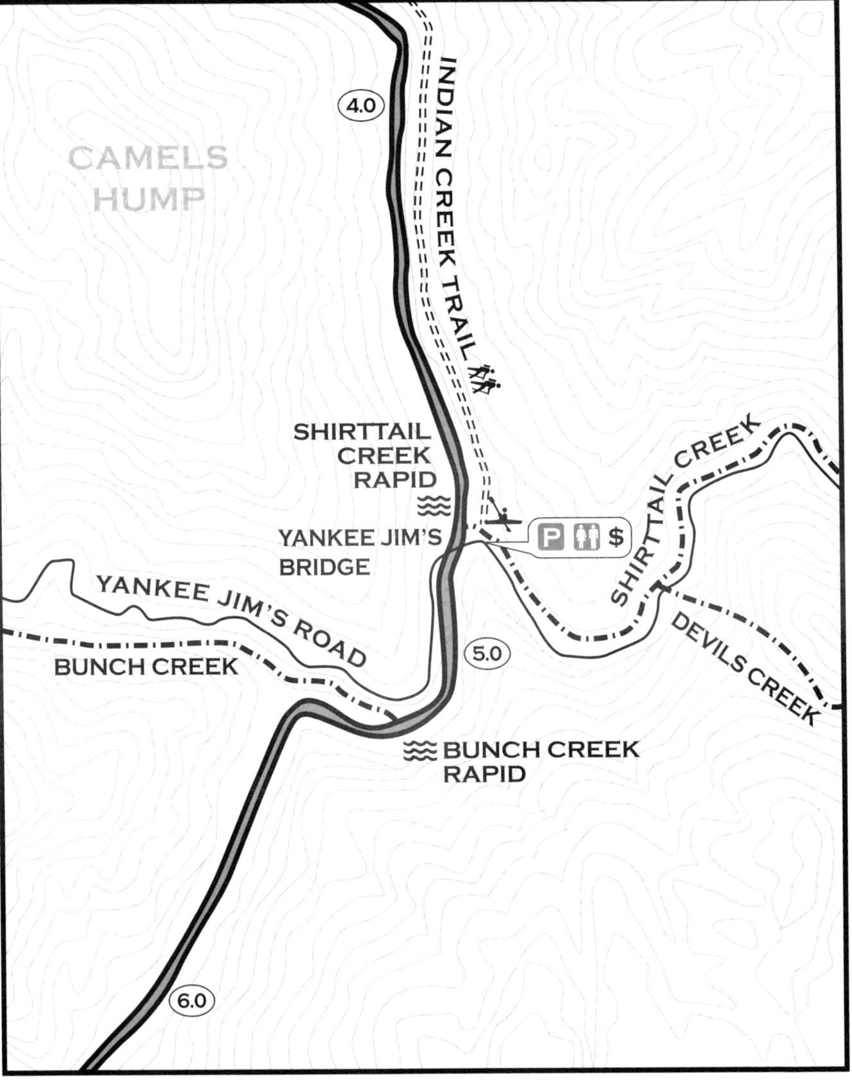

and gravel bars are the rule; time to lunch and relax. Dark, high ledges on both banks are hard accumulations of lava with pillow structures, indicating that they were formed on the ocean floor 350 million years ago.

Mile 3.8 Indian Creek, *river left*

A popular lunch spot. For dessert scramble-hike about ¼ mile up this lush green garden of a side-canyon, lined with the umbrella sized leaves of the Indian rhubarb plant, for a swim in a spectacular springtime pool and waterfall.

Note: For emergencies or wilderness hiking, a trail on river left parallels the river from Indian Creek to Shirttail Creek, *(see page 83)*.

Mile 4.3

Broken rocks on the left are volcanic breccia-rock broken by being hurled out of a volcano by an explosive eruption.

Mile 4.8

Round cobbles high on the left bank are old river gravels, deposited as the river cut the canyon. Deposits such as these are called "pocket gravels" and are good places to look for placer gold.

Mile 5.0 Shirttail Rapid (Class II+) Shirttail Creek Canyon, *on left*

Avoid the rocks on the left as you enter the drop just before the take-out beach on river left. Shirttail Creek high flows roll big boulders into the river channel creating a fun challenging Class II drop just before take-out.

Shirttail Creek

By Harry C. Peterson

The unique name it bears was bestowed in the following manner: early in the summer of 1849 two men, one named Tuttle, formerly of the State of Connecticut, and the other Van Zandt, from Oregon, were prospecting upon Brushy Canyon and in that locality, and at the time supposed there was no one nearer to them than the people who were at work along the river bars. From Brushy they emerged into the valley of the larger stream into which it emptied. It was sultry and hot, and no sound but their own suppressed voices broke the silence of gorge. A bend in the creek a short distance below them obstructed the view, and they walked down the stream to overcome it.

Abruptly turning the point, they were astonished to see before them, but a little way, a solitary individual–whether white or red they could not at first determine–engaged in primitive mining operations, with crevicing spoon, and sheath-knife and pan. The apparition was perfectly nude, with the exception of a shirt, and that was not overly lengthy. The lone miner was in the edge of the water, and, happening to look up, saw the two men who had intruded upon his domain at about the same time that they discovered him.

Had this not been so, Tuttle and Van Zandt, as they declared afterward, would have stepped back, made some noise, and given the man a chance to don his overalls. As it was, the eyes of both parties met, and an involuntary "hello" came from all three mouths. "What in the devil's name do you call this place?" queried one of the intruders of the sans cullottes ["without pants" in French], who proved to be an American. He glanced at his bare legs, and from them to his questioners, took in at a moment the ludicrous appearance he made, and laughingly answered: "don't know any name for it yet, but we might as well call it Shirt-tail as anything else," and under that euphonious nomenclature has it since been known, and must thus go down to posterity. It is regretted that no record can be found of the name of the man in the shirt."

THE RUN AT-A-GLANCE:

YANKEE JIM'S BRIDGE TO UPPER LAKE CLEMENTINE

DIFFICULTY:	Class II-III
LENGTH:	4½ miles to Ponderosa Way Bridge 9 miles to Upper Lake Clementine day use area
SEASON:	February to June, depending on the snowpack
GRADIENT:	19 feet per mile
RUNNABLE FLOWS:	900-3000 cfs, small rafts and kayaks OK above 600 cfs, IKs above 400 cfs
FLOW INFO:	Inflow at Lake Clementine (North Fork Dam) www.dreamflows.com or www.cdec.water.ca.gov/river/americanStages.html
PUT-IN:	Yankee Jim's Bridge, elev. 900'. Parking fee area.
TAKE-OUT:	Ponderosa Way Bridge, elev. 800' or Upper- Lake Clementine day use area elev. 715' (usually closed until mid-April, call Auburn SRA 530-885-4527 for seasonal access information). Parking fee areas.
SHUTTLE:	10 miles (30 minutes) one-way to Ponderosa Way Bridge; 17 miles (40 minutes) one way to Upper-Lake Clementine
WATER QUALITY:	Purify before drinking.
EMERGENCIES:	Placer County Sheriff (Auburn): 911, California State Parks Dispatch: 916-358-1300, Auburn SRA: 530-885-4527

Yankee Jim's Bridge crosses the North Fork American just below the confluence with Shirttail Creek. This is a take-out and or put-in for private boaters and kayakers.

YANKEE JIM'S BRIDGE TO UPPER LAKE CLEMENTINE

Mile 5.0 Yankee Jim's Cable Suspension Bridge

The stone and timber steps built by the CCC in the 1990s have made this take-out for the upper run or put-in for the lower run much easier. The bedrock on the left contains oval-shaped volcanic pillow lava which was erupted on the ocean floor, (see side story about Shirttail Canyon on page 164).

Mimi finds the Class II-III stretch of the North Fork below Yankee Jim's Bridge a perfect place to kayak with her canine pals. Yankee Jim's to Ponderosa Way take-out is a good beginner-intermediate run.

Mile 5.5 Bunch Creek *on right*, Bunch Creek Rapid (Class II–III)

The river is split by an island, runnable either side, near the confluence of Bunch Creek which enters river right. The left chute is preferred by most, but strong, swift current can push boaters into the left rocky wall. Avoid the large hole right-center at the end of the rapid.

Mile 6.7

Mother Lode belt rocks are layered sandstones, pebbly conglomerates, and dark mud tones deposited 160 million years ago in an ocean trench next to an arc-shaped chain of volcanic islands. Pebbles in the conglomerates are the same rock as seen upstream; deposited on the eroded metamorphosed ash deposits. These rocks are softer than those upstream so the rapids here are mostly gravel bars.

Mile 7.5 Sore Finger Point, AKA 'Big Bend'

Large waves and holes can be found here at higher flows. This

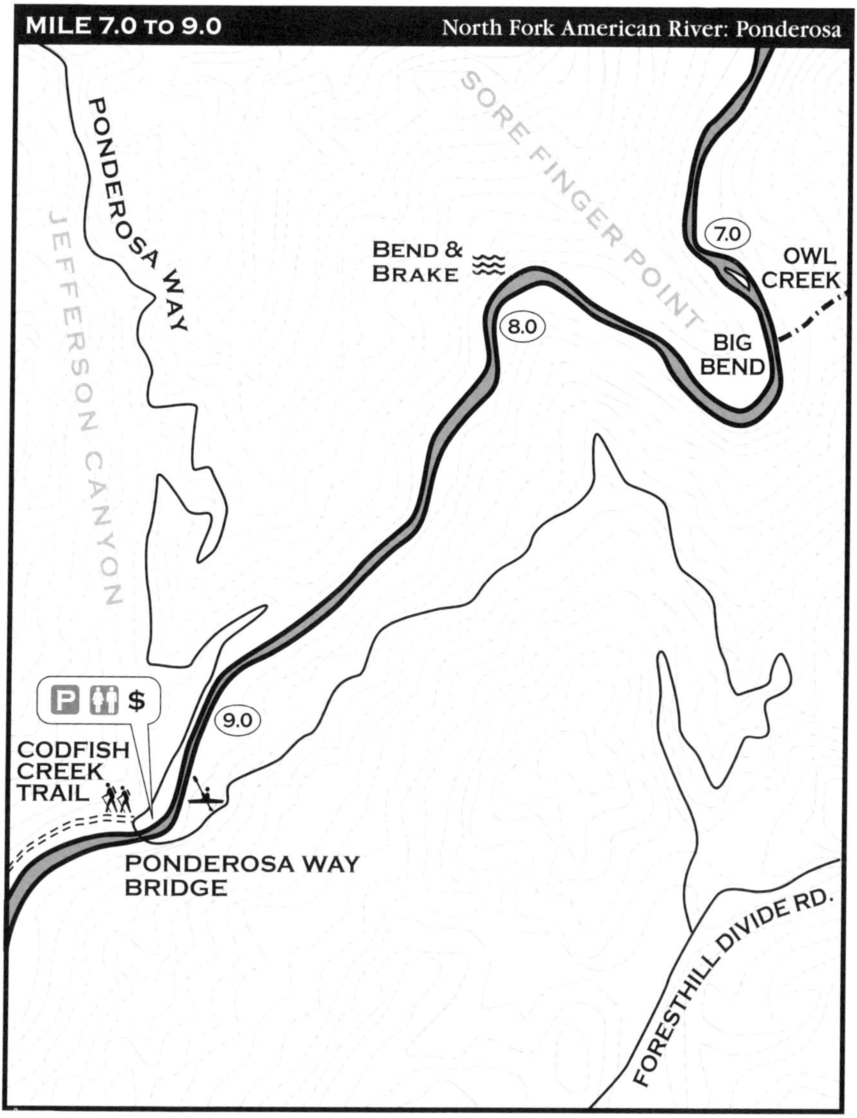

hard sandstone promontory sticks out like a sore finger and the river goes around a horseshoe bend. Surface gold mining on a large scale has altered the landscape on this private property.

Mile 7.8 to 8.4 Bend and Brake (Class II–III)

There are bends, slate ledges, and boulders, as an ever-changing river channel keeps this stretch full of surprises. Caution is advised here due to large waves and holes with hidden rocks.

NORTH FORK PUT-IN & TAKE-OUT SHUTTLES

SHUTTLE FOR TAKE-OUT OR PUT-IN AT PONDEROSA WAY:

Take the Weimar Crossroad exit off I-80. Turn right on Canyon Way and bear left onto Ponderosa Way at the railroad tracks and continue about 3 miles. Fee parking can be found along the road at the bridge. You might think about stashing snacks and dry clothes in the take-out vehicle(s). The drive is a scenic 20-30 minutes long on a combination paved/unpaved road.

SHUTTLE FOR TAKE-OUT AT UPPER LAKE CLEMENTINE:

From I-80 in Auburn, take the Foresthill exit. Continue towards Foresthill for 6 miles and turn left onto Upper Clementine Road, which is a fee use area. Continue on the dirt road to the parking area at the river.

MILE BY MILE GUIDE

PONDEROSA WAY BRIDGE TO UPPER LAKE CLEMENTINE

NOTE: Take-out at the upper Lake Clementine Day Use Area is generally closed from October to April. Take-out at the North Fork Dam Boat Launch Area requires a 4 mile flatwater paddle across the lake.

Gravel bars and occasional bedrock outcroppings characterize the run in this little explored part of the canyon. Cliffs of conglomerate pebbles make up the bedrock here. They originated from large-scale underwater landslides caused by volcanoes and uplifted sedimentary layers.

Mile 9.3 Ponderosa Way Bridge

The big sandy beach on river right is a popular sunbathing beach for families. It is also the take-out for the upper run or a put-in for the easy Class II wilderness run to Upper-Lake Clementine.

Mile 10
Big Dummy
(Class II)

Passing by small mountains of dredge tailings on the left and the Codfish Creek trail on the right the river encounters a river-wide slate ledge. Punch through the middle or sneak past on right. This is an excellent surfing ledge. The sedimentary slate deposits have been upturned here on river left forming springtime pools filled with aquatic animals.

The beauty of the North Fork is best enjoyed on the leisurely run between Yankee Jim's and Upper Lake Clementine take-out.

Mile 10.4
Codfish Creek

Bedrock mortars hidden on river left are a sharp contrast to a century of mining tailing gravels discharged into the river channel during high water from Codfish Creek on river right. Ever changing rapids and willow-alder strainers test your maneuvering skills.

NOTE: This is a nice place to stop before the rapid and hike ½ mile up to magnificent Codfish Creek Falls using the trail on the right side of the creek.

Mile 11 to 12 PARCland

PARC and the Placer Land Trust own approximately ½ mile of river and canyonlands in this serene stretch of river as part of our continuing commitment to the community for the conservation of the American River. Gentle rapids, with an

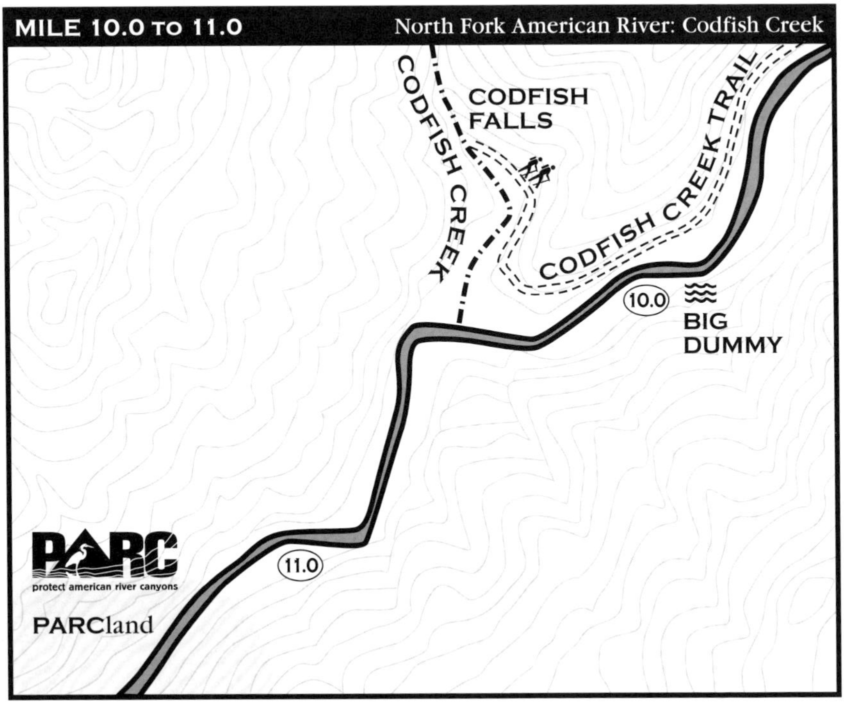

occasional boulder to dodge, set in beautiful canyon scenery loaded with opportunities to observe the great blue heron or other wildlife follow. All State Park rules apply here. No camping or fires are allowed!

Mile 13.6 Upper Lake Clementine Fee Day Use Area

The large gravel cobble bar on river left offers an easy take-out for whitewater boaters or a put-in for a paddle down the lake. Parking, picnic tables and portable toilets are provided. Currently, there is a day use fee.

Miles 14 to 18 Lake Clementine

The North Fork's 60 mile-long free flowing wild course is interrupted by tranquil Lake Clementine. Lake Clementine was created behind the 155 foot tall North Fork Dam built in 1939 by the Army Corps of Engineers for just one purpose; to hold silt and debris back from the flood plain in Sacramento. It currently generates no hydroelectric power, provides no irrigation water, and offers no flood control storage.

MILE 12.0 TO 15.0 North Fork American River: Upper Clementine

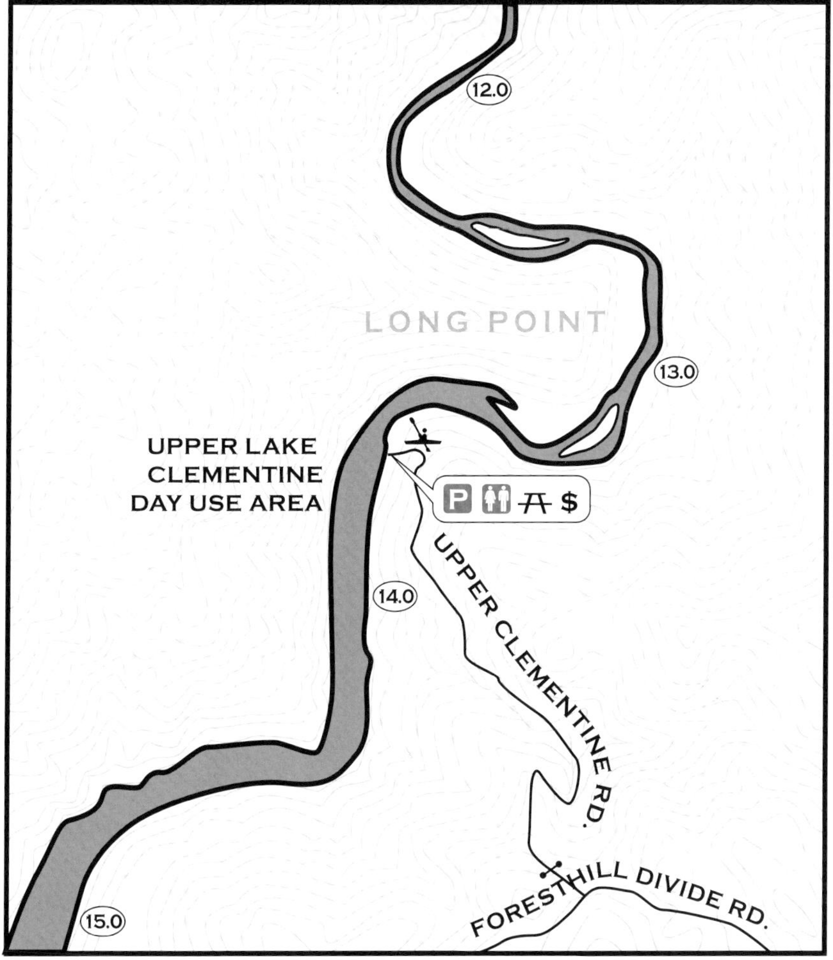

Thus, the reservoir's water level remains the same year round. Wildlife tucks itself into the quiet forested waters along the shore; riparian plant growth is thick and lush. There are precious few reservoirs in all California that have and hold their beauty like Clementine, whose stillness contrasts elegantly with the surging wild waters upstream.

Lake Clementine has become a very popular paddleboard destination.

Canoeing, stand-up paddleboarding, and flatwater kayaking are superb, particularly in the uppermost mile of the lake where motorboats are not allowed. In summer, the power boats and skiers easily dominate the narrow finger lake below upper Clementine. Jet skiing is not allowed.

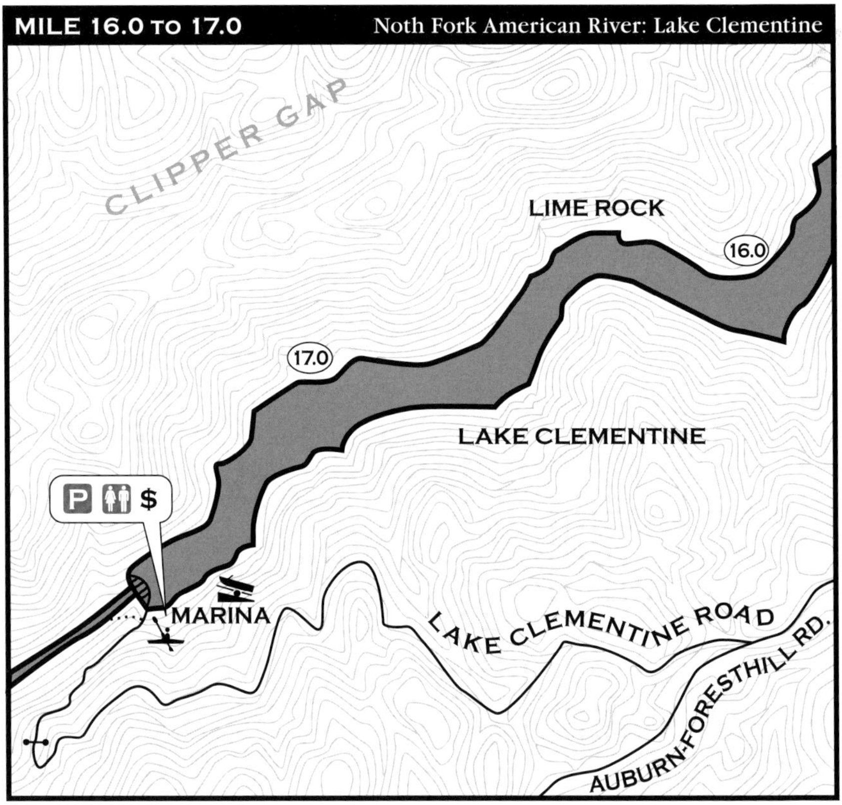

Facilities:

Lake Clementine features a boat launch ramp, marina and boat-in campsites. Launch fee is required. Along the upper end of the lake there are approximately 15 boat-in campsites at designated locations. Camping is primitive, chemical toilets are available, no drinking water, all sites have fire rings and some have tables. Reservations are available through Reserve America, 800-444-7275. NO DOGS are permitted in the campgrounds or on the lake.

Two well-marked roads lead to Clementine from Foresthill Road. The Lake Clementine road is paved. There is a small marina near the dam with permanent berths for a few boats. A concessionaire manages the marina berths for State Parks. Gas is available on weekends. The small parking lot has only enough room for 25 cars and trailers, and fills up quickly in the summer.

Lime Rock, or Robber's Roost: Mysterious Sentinel of the North Fork

The Rock and the Legend

By Marc Davis

According to an obscure Indian legend, eons before the arrival of humans a huge serpent slowly wound its way across the land and in the process created the American River canyons, exposing the towering rock formation now known as "Lime Rock". A celebrated local landmark, this spectacular outcrop of limestone soars more than a thousand feet above the river at a remote location north of Auburn.

Long after the advent of man, in more recent times, an ancient god came down from the heavens and retreated to Lime

Freighting on the Foresthill Divide

Rock, where he took up residence in one of the innermost caves, spending his remaining days in quiet seclusion, having been largely forgotten by the rest of the world. It was later said that if one listened closely, especially just before a storm, sometimes a low moaning sound could be heard coming from somewhere deep within the bowels of the rock, often rising to a howl as the fury of the storm increased--a mournful sound suggestive of a profound sadness long endured.

It was believed by some that this was the utterance of a for-

Lime Rock, or Robber's Roost, is the mysterious sentinel of the North Fork.

lorn spirit making its presence felt to those receptive enough to hear it; others contended that it was only the sound of the wind in the rock and nothing more. The Indians in the area are said to have used the promontory to send up smoke signals to neighboring tribes across the river and generally were attracted to the site, often camping in the vicinity to commune with the Spirit of the Rock.

Aside from the early Indians, a band of outlaws known locally as the Gassaway Gang once used Lime Rock as a strategic look-out and a convenient hide-out. The mysterious lady of legend who signaled fellow gang members from atop this vantage point when she spotted the stage approaching on the other side of the river was none other than Malinda Gassaway, the ring-leader's sister.

This elusive pair also operated a hotel and stage-stop in the nearby town of Clipper Gap, and apparently even resorted, on occasion, to robbing the very travelers who took lodging with them! Years later it was reported that the inside of the building was riddled with bullet holes. George W. Honn purchased the illustrious two-story house for $500 from the Gassaways on May 9, 1863, when it was known as the Golden Gate Hotel. Both the hotel and the gang have long since vanished without a trace, but the rock they immortalized in legend now also bears the name of "Robber's Roost".

Tales of booty hidden in one of its numerous caves have persisted for years, making Robber's Roost an explorer's delight. Moreover, the area continues to attract recreational hikers and climbing enthusiasts who make their pilgrimage here, lured by the scenic grandeur of the canyon and, of course, the rock itself. History buffs and students of geology have discovered much of interest as well.

The site has always held a strange fascination for local residents, and during the 1890s organized excursions to the rock were a common occurrence. One long-time resident of the area, now deceased, has vividly recalled how on clear, moonlit nights she and her sister would travel by horse and buggy to Lime Rock It appeared at those times like an apparition from another world, its whitish-gray surface almost luminous in the moonlight, the serpentine river shimmering in the mist far below, mystical and wondrously alive.

Besides attracting various kinds of human activity, Lime Rock is a favorite haunt of several species of birds, including the secretive canyon wren, which occasionally can be glimpsed as it furtively lurks among the rocky crevices, hunting for insects. More commonly heard than seen, its distinctive, cascading call echoes and rings from the sheer rock walls, a sound singularly appropriate to the setting. Red-tailed hawks and turkey vultures can frequently be observed roosting atop the out-cropping or, on quiet days, spiraling leisurely just above it. The golden eagle has been sighted on rare occasions near the rock

Besides the mice and other small rodents which inhabit the rock, another creature was once said to have been living in one of the caves. Perhaps it was only a bear, but no one ever knew for sure, it was never actually observed. But sometimes on especially stormy nights, if one listens intently, an eerie wailing or howling noise may be heard coming from deep inside the rock, bringing immediately to mind the old Indian legend.

North Fork Dam to Confluence

Mile 17.6 Angel's Run Put-in

The adventurous paddler is treated to gorge-like wilderness scenery and a string of Class II+ rapids in the Spring during flows of 600-2,000 cfs on the upper half of this seldom boated stretch. CAUTION: Be alert to the willow strainers all along this stretch.

Volunteers paddle out kayak loads of trash, including such items as shopping carts, tires and barricades tossed into the river from the Foresthill Bridge.

Just before arriving at the North Fork Dam on Lake Clementine Road, a ¼ mile steep, narrow trail suitable for carrying kayaks, (rafts not recommended), descends to the river across a bridge built by the CCC. The trail ends in a tough boulder scramble across the river bar to get to the pool above the first rapid. Paddle up close to the waterfall created by the 155 foot tall dam for a thrilling typhoon shower spray.

Mile 17.7 Yee Haw (Class II)

A series of boulders, possibly from the dam construction, form a long bouncy wave train.

Mile 18.1 Clipper Creek (Class II)

A series of tight drops with a fast running pool in the middle that marks Clipper Creek waterfalls. Water ouzel birds like to crevice nest in the big rock on the right guarding the falls.

Mile 18.9 Dipper's Rock (Class II)

Another series of boulders and overhanging willow branches to dodge in tight drops with a kayak flipping wave at the bottom.

Mile 18.8 Clark's Hole (Class I)

A rocky chute on river left is the easiest way to paddle out of this popular summer Auburn swimming hole.

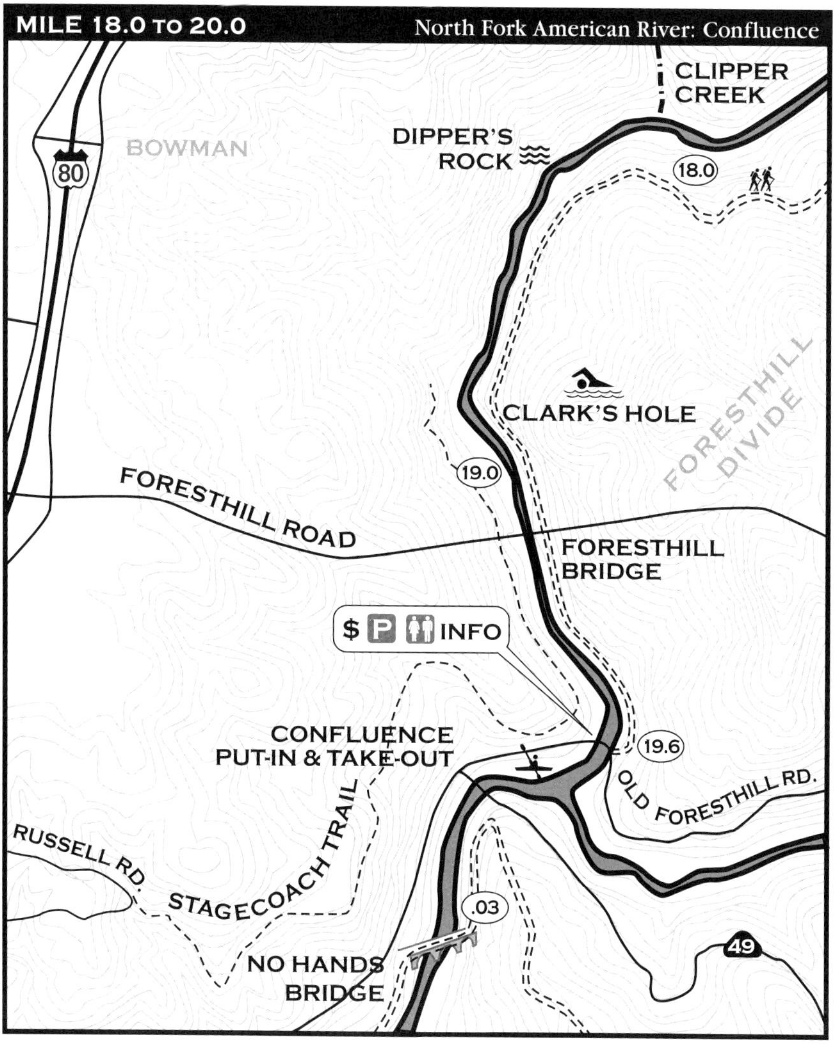

Mile 19.1 Auburn-Foresthill Bridge

Built in 1973, the 730' high Auburn-Foresthill bridge is the tallest in California. Another boulder field to navigate through. CAUTION: Careful here for cultural debris (sofas, motorcycles, computers, etc), dropped from the bridge into the river.

Mile 19.6 Curved Bridge Take-out or Put-in

This popular family swimming area beneath the Old Foresthill Road Bridge provides a take-out for the Clementine to Confluence run and is the preferred put-in for the Lower North Fork run.

THE RUN AT-A-GLANCE:

Confluence to China Bar or Rattlesnake Bar

DIFFICULTY:	Class II+ with one Class III (easily portaged)
LENGTH:	3.8 to China Bar; 5 to Oregon Bar or 9.8 miles to Rattlesnake Bar
SEASON:	All year. Check flows, Folsom Lake level and State Park access
GRADIENT:	16 feet per mile average, mostly pool and drop
RUNNABLE FLOWS:	600 - 3000 cfs, Class III above 2000 cfs
FLOW INFO:	Sum of (NFD) (2 miles, or about 40 minutes upstream) and release from Oxbow Powerhouse (OXB) (25 miles, or about 8 hours upstream) www.dreamflows.com or www.cdec.water.ca.gov/river/americanStages.html (FOL) Folsom Lake reservoir elevation http://cdec.water.ca.gov/river/res_FOL.html
PUT-IN:	North Fork below Old Foresthill Rd. Bridge, elev. 540'
TAKE-OUTS:	China Bar's Birdsall; or Oregon Bar or Rattlesnake Bar, elev. 370'
SHUTTLE:	7 miles (20 minutes) one-way to China Bar. 10 miles (30 minutes) one-way to Rattlesnake Bar
WATER QUALITY:	Cold and clear, but purify before drinking.
CAMPING:	A special river camping permit is required throughout the Auburn SRA except in designated camping areas. Call Auburn SRA headquarters at (530) 885-4527 for info.
EMERGENCIES:	Placer County Sheriff (Auburn): 911 California State Parks Dispatch: (916) 358-1300
ACCESS INFO:	Rattlesnake Bar, call Folsom SRA: (916) 988-0205; www.parks.gov.ca

The late Frank Olrich, 1943 to 1999, surfs the Tamaroo Rapid.

The Lower North Fork Below the Confluence

Geology by Laird Thompson Ph.D.
Whitewater by John Donovan, Tony DeRiggi and Eric Peach

The Lower North Fork, Confluence to China Bar or Rattlesnake Bar

The American River Confluence Parkway run was officially opened New Year's Day, 2008 after the diversion tunnel at the Auburn Dam Site was closed, and the river restored to its channel. The river goes through a beautiful canyon between the Confluence and the damsite, with foliated green walls of metamorphosed volcanic ash. There are many splendid beaches, swimming holes and trails below the Confluence.

A train crosses the Mountain Quarries Railroad Bridge with a load of limestone, circa 1912.

The Confluence to China Bar Birdsall takeout is a popular Class II-III run in the summer because of its easy access from Auburn. It contains many calm stretches, but culminates with the easily portaged Rocky Island Rapid, which is Class III at higher flows. Boaters can add over a mile of fun Class II-III

From No Hands Bridge to Tamaroo Bar Rapids the canyon takes on a wilderness feeling described here by Auburn writer Sandra Reeves:

"Enormous elegant arches frame the green canyon wall as we approach the imposing arches of No Hands Bridge heralding the entrance to dazzling ripples and rapids… clear cold water glides by, sparkling in the hot sun. Immense boulders and tall stately rock formations rise from the alder and willow greened banks…we bump over shiny, clean scoured cobbles. A water ouzel bird dips in a riffle for insects, hummingbird trumpet flowers seemingly bloom from solid rock, button willow fragrance drifts on the river and tall stands of cottonwood trees just beginning to yellow rustle in the breeze. Curious otters swim along the bank; a great blue heron sentry stands guard and a bald eagle roosts hidden behind a curtain of pine needles…all within a mile of Auburn."

rapids by continuing on to Oregon Bar takeout. This take-out requires a rigorous carry a few hundred yards uphill on a dirt road to vehicle access.

The Class II Oregon Bar to Rattlesnake Bar section is best run when the Folsom Lake level is below 395 feet to avoid a 1 mile flatwater paddle. Folsom Lake is usually highest in spring, and early summer. The flows below the Confluence are a combination of natural flows on the North Fork and dam releases on the Middle Fork. Check the flows on both forks and remember it takes 8 to 9 hours for the Middle Fork water release to reach the Confluence. However, since minimum flows are often enough for kayakers to paddle most of this run, it is possible to start your trip before the river comes up.

Geology of the Confluence Area

The greenish rocks are Jurassic mudstones that were deposited in a deep ocean setting about 180 million years ago. At the time, the edge of the continent was at the Nevada-California border, so these sediments were laid down about 80 miles offshore. With time and movement of the North American Plate Boundary, the sediments were hardened, heated, squeezed and ultimately pushed up vertically into their present position. They are greenish along the river where they have been polished by floodwaters, but the black rocks above are the same ones that are covered by black minerals (primarily manganese) due to chemical weathering. There is also intermixed lava along the river, called pillow basalts, that erupted onto the ocean floor 180 million years ago and are still seen as twisted, pillowy looking rocks.

LEGEND

- PAVED ROADS
- DIRT ROADS
- TRAILS
- RIVER
- CREEKS
- PRIMITIVE TRAILS
- PUT-IN & TAKE-OUTS
- (0.0) MILE MARKERS
- RAPIDS
- PARKING AREAS
- TOILETS
- PICNIC & CAMPING
- HORSE ROUTES
- HIKING ROUTES
- BIKE ROUTES
- $ FEE AREAS
- GATE

LOWER NORTH FORK PUT-IN & TAKE-OUT SHUTTLES

SHUTTLE FOR PUT-IN AT THE CONFLUENCE:

From Sacramento, take the Elm Avenue exit, turn left onto Elm Avenue and turn left again at the stoplight onto High Street/Highway 49. Proceed down into the canyon on Highway 49 to the curved bridge at the Confluence. Fee parking.

SHUTTLE FOR TAKE-OUT AT CHINA BAR:

China Bar access, including Birdsall and Oregon Bar, is from Maidu Dr., off Auburn Folsom Rd. Use fees are collected. Parking is available at the Birdsall take-out and the smaller Oregon Bar take-out. For entrance gate access information call Auburn SRA at 530-885-4527. Take the Highway 49 exit (South) from I-80. Turn right at High Street then turn left after 0.5 of a mile at Auburn-Folsom Road. Turn left after one mile at Maidu Drive then turn right in one mile at the China Bar entrance station. At the end of the paved road at the first parking lot, take the left fork to Birdsall take-out. For Oregon Bar, take the right fork to the parking area at the end of the road.

SHUTTLE FOR TAKE-OUT AT RATTLESNAKE BAR:

Take I-80 east from Sacramento to the Penryn exit and turn right at Penryn Rd. Follow for ½ of a mile, and turn left on King Road. After 2.4 miles, turn left at Auburn Folsom Rd. After 1.3 miles, turn right at Newcastle Rd. After 1.1 miles, turn right at Rattlesnake Rd. and enter Folsom SRA. Day-use fees are collected. This area is subject to seasonal closure, call Folsom SRA at 916-988-0205.

The Lower North Fork Confluence to China Bar or Rattlesnake Bar

Mile 0.0 Old Foresthill Bridge Put-in

This popular family swimming area beneath the curved Old Foresthill Road Bridge is the usual put-in for the Lower North Fork run. An alternate put-in is just upstream on the Middle Fork, where a trail leads from Old Foresthill Rd. down to a beach. Take care not to block gate or bathroom access when staging boats and please be courteous to picnickers and swimmers when putting in. At low summer flows the North Fork is shallow and rocky until you reach the Confluence.

Mile 0.2 Flip-Flop (Class II)

The pace quickens with Flip-Flop Rapid just below the Confluence. Strong current pushes paddlers towards a big rock on river left, Flip, then flows over a shallow riffle, onto rocks and then into an eddy pool on river right, Flop. A Class III above 1500 cfs.

Mile 0.2 Highway 49 Bridge

Emerald green pools flow past the ruins of the old Highway 49 bridge that washed out in 1964. Caution here, there are large iron girders, concrete and rebar below the surface.

Mile 0.3 Mountain Quarries Railroad Bridge

Down river the graceful arches of the Mountain Quarries Railroad Bridge completed in 1912 come into view. More commonly known as "No Hands Bridge", equestrians and hikers cross the river here on the Western State Trail. From April to September cliff swallows can be seen hunting insects and nesting beneath the bridge.

Mile 0.6 Condemn Bar (Class II)

Riffles followed by a left turn, then a small splashy wave train.

Mile 0.7-1.3 Full Moon Beaches

The river has a remote wilderness feel as it flows past polished rock formations, cobble bars filled with blooming blazing stars and sandy beaches popular with nude sunbathers.

Mile 1.5 Cathedral Cliffs

The rock walls of the canyon area are still the Jurassic mudstones, but in this area likely contain silts and some minor sands. Consequently, they are more resistant to erosion than at the confluence and form the high walls along the river.

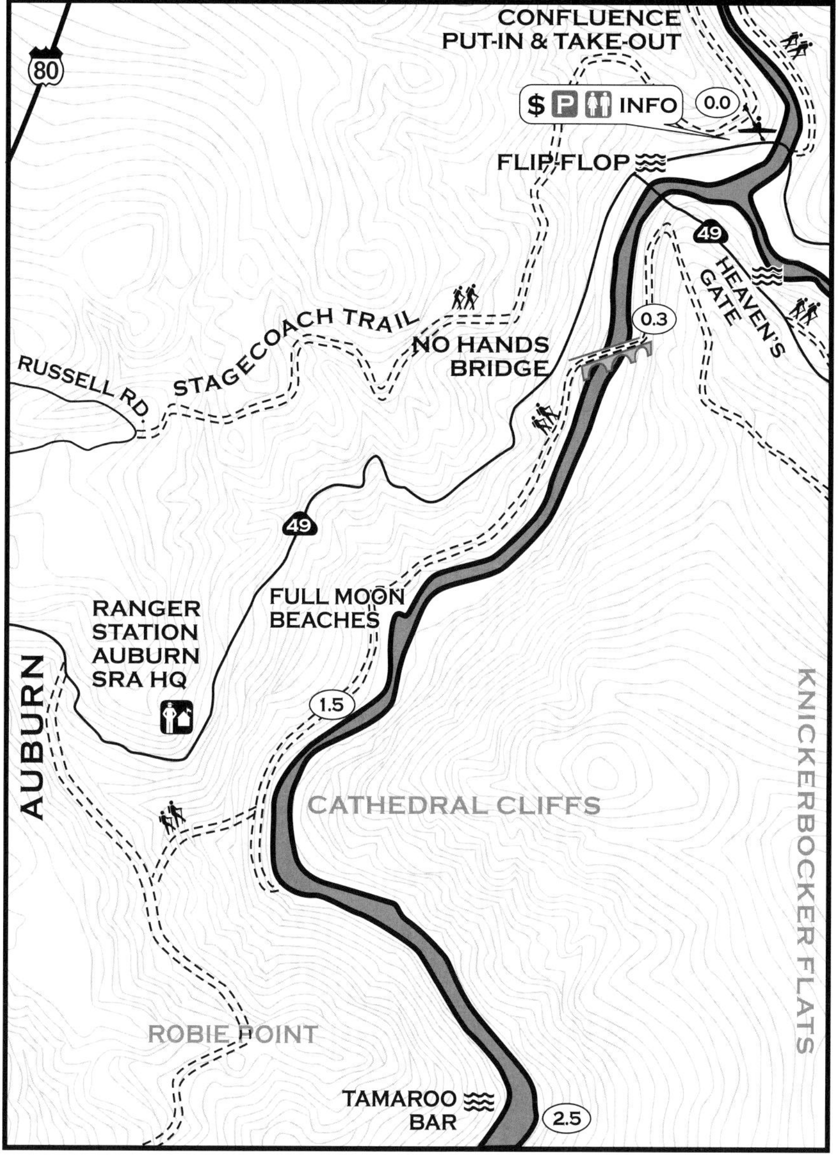

Mile 2.5 Tamaroo Bar Rapids (Class II)

A diagonal wave train along the right side, followed by a large recovery pool. Below the pool, the river is divided by a rocky island that once was Tamaroo Beach. Gold Rush era Tamaroo Bar was established in 1852 and named after the ship Tahamaroo which brought the first miners around Cape Horn to San Francisco in 1849.

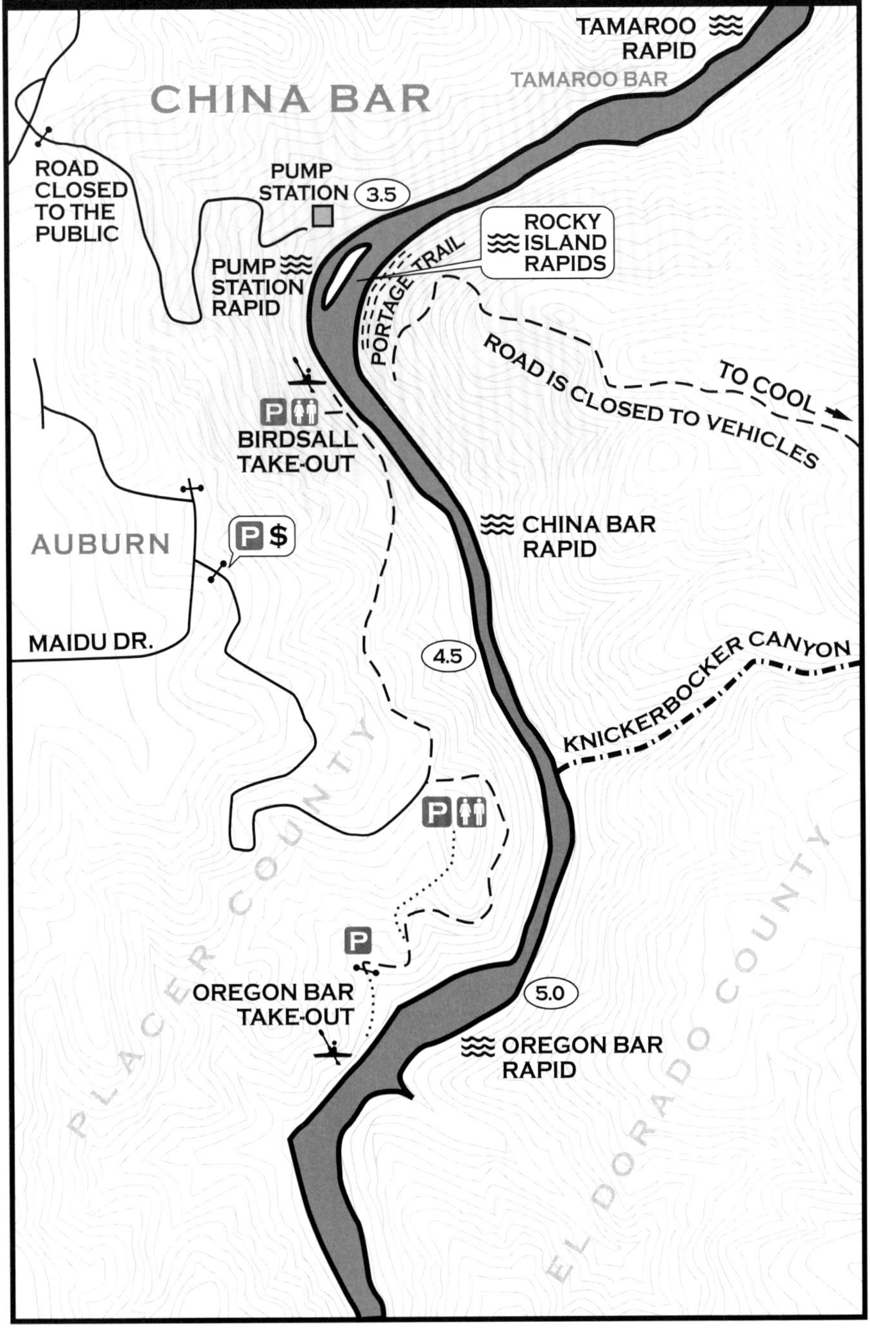
TAMAROO RAPID
TAMAROO BAR
CHINA BAR
ROAD CLOSED TO THE PUBLIC
PUMP STATION
3.5
ROCKY ISLAND RAPIDS
PUMP STATION RAPID
PORTAGE TRAIL
ROAD IS CLOSED TO VEHICLES
TO COOL
BIRDSALL TAKE-OUT
CHINA BAR RAPID
AUBURN
MAIDU DR.
4.5
KNICKERBOCKER CANYON
PLACER COUNTY
EL DORADO COUNTY
OREGON BAR TAKE-OUT
5.0
OREGON BAR RAPID

Mile 3.3 Auburn Dam Diversion Tunnel

The construction scars on the canyon walls from the 1970s Auburn Dam project can be seen here. On river left, the entrance to a 28 foot diameter diversion tunnel built as part of the abandoned Auburn Dam project is hidden behind a contoured pile of rocks and coffer dam dirt. For over 30 years the river was diverted though the mountain in this half-mile long tunnel. It was closed in 2007 when the State of California requested that the Federal Government restore the river to its natural channel and provide public access to the area *(see page 399 for the history of the Auburn Dam)*.

Mile 3.5 Rocky Island and Pump Station Rapids (Class II-III)

Large dam excavations and extensive construction roads on both sides of the canyon form the backdrop for this human-engineered rapid, consisting of two channels. The concrete walled channel on the right bank diverts water to the pump station. Portaging or scouting can be easily accomplished using the concrete walkway on river left, which also allows boaters to easily run the rapid more than once.

Run the left channel that consists of a continuous series of five man-made drops. The first two are easy, with the next ones becoming more difficult. At higher flows, the final rapids have strong reversals and it can be difficult to catch the eddy on the left to use the portage path. The difficulty of this rapid is flow dependent and is rated Class II up to 1,100 cfs, class III up to 2,500 cfs, and class IV at over 3,000 cfs.

Avoid the right chute, which flows over the smooth stainless steel intake screens for the pump station inlet. The chute design creates a dangerous, rocky reversal after the screens that can easily flip and hold swimmers and boats. It is divided from the rapid by the man-made rock island that is a good place to scout, eat lunch or photograph the action.

Geology of the Auburn Dam site area

There are numerous large boulders on the island that have been collected from around the former Auburn Dam site area. While none of them are in their original places, they show a lot of interesting variety. Look for green waxy rock surfaces–this is serpentine, a soft talc-like rock that

Pump Station Rapids under construction.

Closing of the diversion tunnel.

The river flow is restored to the channel.

Boaters carrying kayaks back on the trail to run it again.

Guy Cables spins the Hydro Bronc in the Pump Station Rapids at the 2nd Annual Really Cool-Auburn Festival in 2011.

is the California state rock. Look for rock fibers in the serpentine–these are crystals of asbestos. Where serpentine has been broken up for gravel and used to surface walking paths, this asbestos can get into the dust and be inhaled, causing lung disease. Look for white quartz veins in some of the rocks. These are the last minerals to precipitate out of a granite pluton as it is cooling–along with exotic minerals like gold. Prospectors still look for white quartz veins to follow when searching for gold. Some of the rock surfaces look like they have been highly polished. These are actually fault surfaces. The Foothills Fault Zone crosses the American River at the Auburn Dam site, and two inclined fault surfaces can be seen river right downstream from the pump station. This fault presence, along with a 5.7 magnitude earthquake at the Oroville Dam in 1975 caused the building of the Auburn Dam to cease.

Mile 3.8 China Bar's Birdsall Access Take-out/Put-in

Convenient river access road and parking area is on river right. Check with Auburn State Parks headquarters for hours of operation for the China Bar Area. Boaters can add over a mile of fun Class II-III rapids by continuing on to Oregon Bar takeout.

Mile 4.0 Auburn Dam Diversion Tunnel

The old tunnel exit is covered up by a pile of rocks on the left bank.

Mile 4.3 China Bar Rapid (Class II-III)

This half-mile long series of rapids resembles a Chinese Dragon twisting and turning in a Lunar New Year Parade. The river bends to the right and splits around the large boulder that divides the current. A bouncy wave train leads to a series of rocky drops and a sharp left turn at the bottom. Remnants of a concrete flume up on the right bank can be seen at the end of this rapid. Above 2000 cfs, this rapid becomes a continuous half-mile long class III.

Mile 4.8 Knickerbocker Falls

Knickerbocker Creek enters from the left. A series of cascades culminates in a remarkably beautiful 40 foot waterfall at the base of this mini gorge. A faint trail leads to the grotto pool at the base of the last waterfall.

You will notice that the fabric of the rocks has changed along here from those at the Confluence. In this area, the Jurassic sediments are a lot more thin-bedded and broken up. The reason is that the granites of the Oregon Bar pluton and the Penryn pluton are very close below you and when they intruded into the sediments, they caused the "country rock" to shatter. Knickerbocker Falls have formed in a narrow valley created along a fault. There are more faults through this area, as well as, at the Auburn Dam site. At full capacity Folsom Lake will reach here. (465 ft. elevation)

Mile 5.3 Oregon Bar Rapid (Class II+)

This rapid has a river wide ledge that splits the river into three channels. Run the middle channel which contains the most water. A number of rocks guard the middle entrance, forcing you to stay left and then make a sharp right turn. The middle channel has an eddy on the right half way down, before the last riffle. At high flows it is easiest to take out at this middle eddy in the rapid. After a short carry over the cobble island, paddle across the right channel to the take out.

The far left channel is shallow, narrow and rocky. The far right channel is not runnable at lower flows and contains a dangerous rocky Class IV drop at higher flows and must be scouted.

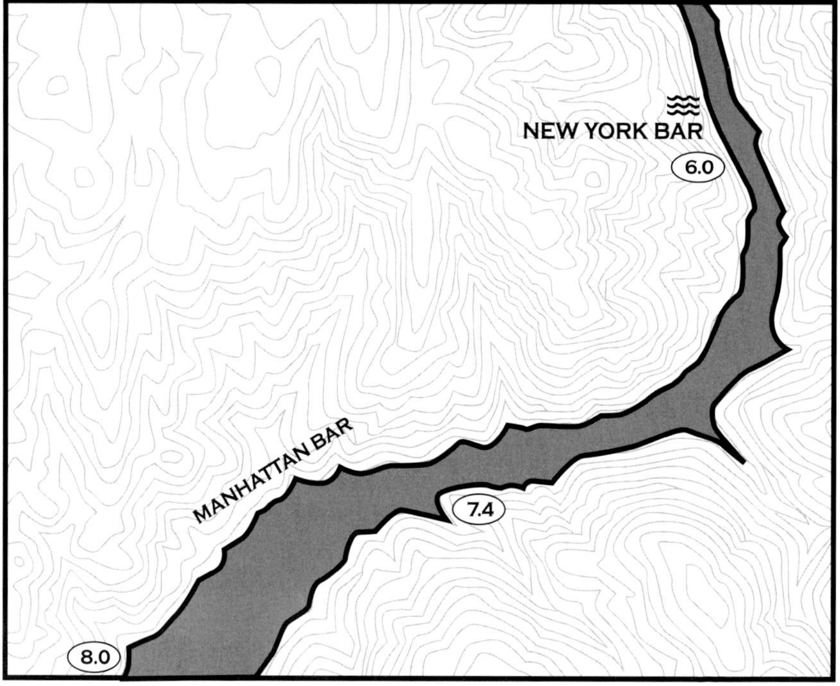

Mile 5.4 Oregon Bar Take-out and Parking

The Oregon Bar access point is on the right, but vehicle access may not be available year round. Take-out here is challenging. At this writing, it requires scrambling up the short, steep granite slope followed by a carry of about 300 yards up the road to the parking area. From here there is a trail, marked by a metal post on the left that leads to the alternate upper Oregon Hill parking area. Take care to select the correct trail as the Cardiac Trail to south Auburn and the Pioneer Express trail to Folsom intersect the take out trail.

The rocks at Oregon Bar are granite. If you stop and look at them, you can actually see the flow patterns created when the rock was molten, before it crystallized into rock. The plutons along here, the Oregon Bar pluton and the Penryn pluton, are about 125 million years old and probably crystallized into rock about 2 to 3 miles below the surface at that time. They have since been uplifted and exposed. From here on down to Folsom Lake, look for 3 things: 1) the Jurassic sediments, thin-bedded and splintery, 2) weird swooping patterns in the rock–flow patterns in the granite that were weak and formed faults with brecciated or broken rocks in them and 3) the decomposing granites down by Folsom Lake–rounded rock outcroppings that are chemically weathering into sands. These are often used for paths in landscaping projects.

Mile 5.5 Ohio Company (Class II)

Watch out for rocks in mid-channel.

Mile 6.0 New York Bar (Class II+)

The river enters a short, mini-gorge. Above 1500 cfs, holes develop along the right wall, and fast current to the left creates a strong eddy line down the middle.

Mile 7.4 Herons Roost

Steeper hills give way to rolling oak grasslands. The sharp limestone formations seen upstream transition to the round, light gray outcroppings of granite. Often herons are seen here roosting on the highest rocks. The river meanders past the long-gone gold camps at Manhattan Bar and Lacy's Bar.

Mile 8.7 Mormon Ravine (Class I or II-)

Mormon Ravine Creek enters from the right. The river is swift, winding its way between boulder clusters. The landscape is other worldly, devoid of vegetation and stacked up with all the silt and sand the river has carried into the lake since 1955. Lake surface elevation here is 395 foot.

MILE 8.1 TO 9.8 Lower North Fork American River: Rattlesnake Bar

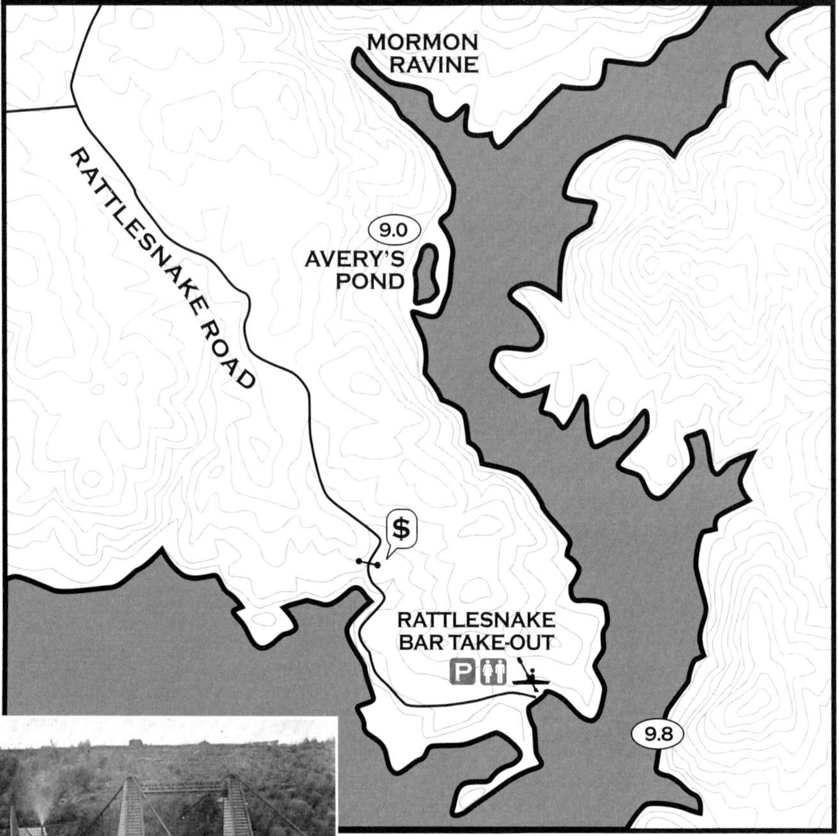

Rattlesnake Bar Bridge, photograph circa 1860s

Mile 9.0 Avery's Pond

A scenic spot with a picnic table on the right bank. Watch for buoys signaling the end of the no-wake zone.

Mile 9.7 Rattlesnake Rapid (Class II)

A good surf rapid when Folsom's water level is below 372 foot.

Mile 9.8 Rattlesnake Bar Boat Ramp Take-out

Summer hours 7:00 am to 8:00 pm. This take-out may be closed during the winter. Call 916-988-0205 at Folsom Lake SRA for current access information.

The Upper Middle Fork of the American River

By Tony DeRiggi, Eric Peach and Otis Wollan
Geology by Terry Wright Ph.D.

The Oxbow Powerhouse to Ruck-A-Chucky Campground Run

From Oxbow put-in, just below the Oxbow Reservoir, the river drops to the Confluence with the North Fork of the American some 24 miles down river, just above the Highway 49 bridge near Auburn. Rich with opportunity for exploration by boat, foot, or horse-back, the Middle Fork Canyon offers spectacular scenery, a remote wilderness experience and challenging whitewater. The river has eroded the canyon's walls, exposing a classic section of the ancient bedrock and concentrating gold placer deposits in the riverbed, some of the richest in the Sierra foothills.

This mile-by-mile guide is written for the boater, hiker or angler who is intrigued by the wildlife, geology and mining lore of the Middle Fork canyon.

Beauty and danger are the promises of the Middle Fork of the American River. The boating run that starts at the Oxbow Powerhouse includes the legendary Tunnel Chute Rapid and the formidable Ruck-A-Chucky Falls, a Class VI recommended portage. Travel light for an easier portage.

Rafting Ruck-A-Chucky Rapids on the Middle Fork of the American River.

This Oxbow to Greenwood run should only be attempted by experienced boaters who know the river and are ready for a strenuous and potentially dangerous river adventure.

THE RUN AT-A-GLANCE:

OXBOW POWERHOUSE TO THE RUCK-A-CHUCKY CAMPGROUND

IMPORTANT:	This is a remote wilderness run best done with advanced boaters.
DIFFICULTY:	Class IV with a Class IV+, (Tunnel Chute) and a difficult portage around Class VI Ruck-A-Chucky Falls
LENGTH:	15 miles to Ruck-A-Chucky campground, 1 or 2 days
SEASON:	May through September with reliable hydropower releases daily of 1,050 cfs in average water years
GRADIENT:	23 feet per mile
RUNNABLE FLOWS:	900 to 2,000 cfs. More difficult above 1,500 cfs
FLOW INFO:	www.dreamflows.com or www.cdec.water.ca.gov/river/americanStages.html
PUT-IN:	Oxbow Powerhouse, elevation 1080'
TAKE-OUT:	Ruck-A-Chucky Campground, elevation 700'
SHUTTLE:	25 miles, 1½ hours
OUTFITTERS:	One-day and 2 day trips; for a list of outfitters go to www.parks.ca.gov, select 'Gold Country', click on 'Auburn' then select 'Whitewater Rafting'
WATER QUALITY:	Cold and clear, but purify before drinking as microorganisms including giardia may be present.
CAMPING:	A special river camping permit is required throughout the Auburn SRA except in designated camping areas. Call Auburn SRA headquarters at (530) 885-4527 for info.
EMERGENCIES:	Placer County Sheriff (Auburn): 911, California State Department of Parks and Recreation Dispatch: (916) 358-1300

It is much more difficult, remote and longer than the South Fork American. Be sure to allow enough time and daylight to finish before dark.

During the May through September boating season in normal water years, a steady 1,050 cfs comes through the Oxbow powerhouse, usually starting between 8:00 am and 9:00 am–enough water for a great boating experience. In below normal water years, weekday flows may be limited. Be sure to check flows.

The occasional flood flows occur mainly from November to March. In February 1986 the Valentine's Day flood turned the walk-through tunnel at Horseshoe Bend into a giant water cannon which shot water some 200 foot through the air. The same flood overwhelmed and carried away the earth-filled 200 foot high coffer dam at the Auburn Dam site three miles below the North Fork confluence.

Helmets and high flotation PFDs are essential for Class IV rapids on the Middle and North Forks.

Geology at Oxbow Reservoir is similar to the North Fork American with the exception that the bedrock is slate and sandstone of the ancient Shoo Fly Complex. The Shoo Fly Complex is a sequence of sedimentary rocks that were originally deposited on the continental shelf approximately 400 million years ago. Subsequently they were metamorphosed (transformed by heat and pressure) and deformed by several mountain-building events, which formed the ancestral Sierra 160-90 million years ago.

The black slates are cut by gray bands of granite and white quartz veins, which intruded as molten rock during this period. Small square holes in the slate formed when iron pyrite crystals (fool's gold) weathered out and left their forms behind. Occasionally you can find brassy yellow cubes of pyrite in the rock. These crystals form from mineral-rich fluids associated with sulfur, which formed in a deep-ocean environment along with the rock.

UPPER MIDDLE FORK PUT-IN & TAKE-OUT SHUTTLE

To the Oxbow Powerhouse Put-in:

From Auburn take the Auburn-Foresthill Road 17 miles to Foresthill. Founded in 1850, the Gold Rush community of Foresthill has an interesting museum and many historic buildings. Turn right on Mosquito Ridge Road. Along Mosquito Ridge Road are several scenic vista points to view Horseshoe Bar and Tunnel Chute. Two miles

LEGEND

- PAVED ROADS
- DIRT ROADS
- TRAILS
- RIVER
- CREEKS
- PRIMITIVE TRAILS
- PUT-IN & TAKE-OUTS
- (0.0) MILE MARKERS
- RAPIDS
- P PARKING AREAS
- TOILETS
- PICNIC & CAMPING
- HORSE ROUTES
- HIKING ROUTES
- BIKE ROUTES
- $ FEE AREAS
- GATE

after crossing the Circle Bridge over the North Fork of the Middle Fork, turn right at the Oxbow Reservoir Road. Take the second right fork at the bottom down to the graded gravel bar put-in area, near the discharge outlet of the Oxbow Powerhouse.

Mosquito Ridge Road continues on to the Placer County Giant Sequoia Grove and French Meadows Reservoir.

To Ruck-A-Chucky Campground Take-out

Take the Foresthill exit off Interstate 80 in Auburn and drive east across the Auburn-Foresthill Bridge high above the north fork canyon. Continue 8 miles up Foresthill Road to Drivers Flat Road turnoff on the right. This road is paved the first half-mile, turning into steep dirt road the remaining 2 miles into the canyon with grand scenic views.

After the road reaches the river and crosses a side stream, continue onto the second fee parking area with the stone steps and gravel ramp for class II put-in. Park in a fee parking area. The first gravel lot by the river is a loading only take-out area for the upper class IV run. Drivers Flat Road was named for the teamsters who brought freight supply wagons to the many mining camps along the river.

MILE BY MILE GUIDE

Oxbow Powerhouse to Ruck-A-Chucky Campground

Mile 0.0 Indian Bar Put-in and Good Morning! Rapid (Class II)

The Oxbow Reservoir powerhouse, with its block concrete structure and high voltage lines, dominates the put-in site. Indian Bar has a large parking lot and toilets. A path leads to a narrow eddy put-in at the out-flow of the generating facility. Immediately below, a swift, cold, splashy whitewater chute is guaranteed to wake you up as it takes you to the calm pool where the North Fork of the Middle Fork enters on the right.

Round cobbles in the river bank at Indian Bar were deposited at high water caused by the melting of Pleistocene glaciers. Placer mining operations from the time of the 49ers to recent days de-

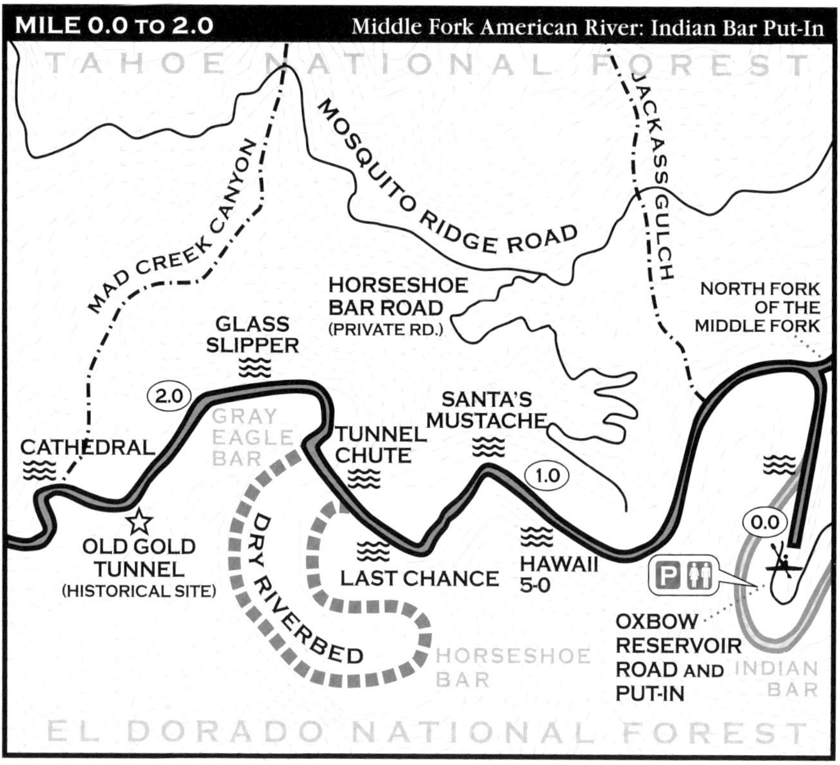

posited piles of cobbles on the left bank. Wreckage from a steam shovel and other machines were left by modern day argonauts.

Mile 0.2 North Fork of Middle Fork canyon

An alternate put-in for expert kayakers is the Circle Bridge where Mosquito Ridge Road crosses the North Fork of the Middle Fork canyon two miles upstream. There are great swimming holes up this canyon in the summer.

You can see bands of white quartz veins, light gray granite, and dark gray and black layers of alternating sandstone and mudstone now changed to slate. These layers were laid down 400 million years ago on the deep ocean floor by dense currents of sediment-laden water Subsequently, pressure and heat within the earth forced these layers into a vertical position, creating foliation.

Shiny white quartz veins cut into these vertical foliated rocks. Fluid when formed, the quartz was accompanied by gold when they crystallized at the same temperature from the cooling of molten granite. These events occurred over 100 million years ago, some 10 km below the surface. Uplift and erosion by the river created the present canyon rock.

Mile 0.5 Junkyard (Class II)

Avoid metal debris in the channel as the river turns right.

Mile 0.7 American Bar

American Bar on the right has been the scene of much modern placer mining. Large cobbles, rocks, and boulders were piled along the right side of the river at this site during the last mining operation. The rock piles, up to 30 foot high, were washed back into the river during the 1986 Valentine's Day flood.

Mile 0.9 Hawaii 5-0 Rapids (Class II-III)

The river turns right and drops into a rock garden with many surprises, including a left-center curling surf wave. Enter on river left.

Mile 1.1 Santa's Mustache (Class II)

A sharp left turn; watch out for the frothy whitewater cushion piling up on the river right wall at the bottom of this drop.

Mile 1.4 Last Chance Rapid (Class II)

Stop at the eddy on the right bank to scout Last Chance and Tunnel Chute Rapid. Be careful, after running the sandstone ledge reversal you must immediately set up for the entrance into the Tunnel Chute or paddle to the left bank above the Chute to portage.

Mile 1.5 Tunnel Chute (Class IV+)

There have been many injuries, damaged boats, and close calls in the Tunnel Chute. The utmost caution is advised and scouting is mandatory. There is road access to the Tunnel Chute over private land leased by anglers and miners who have been helpful in emergencies. Note: This area is private property.

Bedrock in the chute is black slate laced with white quartz veins. The platy aspect of the slate is metamorphic foliation, which results from the squeezing of mudstone deep in the earth. Blasting and chipping the foliated slate created the sharp blades of rock that can cut boats and people like knives. The river flows on as swift flat water below the chute through the tunnel and out into a large pool called Shangri-la.

Shoot the Chute:
Celebrating Over One Hundred Years of History since 1889

Tunnel Chute is a concentrated moment of rafting challenge and river history. Here, in the distance of a healthy stone's throw, the river drops eighteen foot in a roaring, violent whitewater rapid, a unique man-made rapid.

This rapid was created circa 1889 by miners who diverted the flow of the entire river through a tunnel they blasted and pick-axed through rock, allowing them access to a mile of dewatered river bed at Horseshoe Bar. The Chute was blasted out to guide the river's water down to the tunnel.

Entry maneuvers were successful. The rafters cheer as they are funneled into the top of the Chute. (First in a series of three photos.)

Here, in its natural state, the river once made a slowly moving mile-long loop, almost doubling back on itself, swirling around the narrow slate ridge through which rafters now float via the Tunnel.

The exaggeration of the river's curves around this bend evolved geologically through the action of erosion on the outside of a bend and by the deposition of sediment on the inside bend. This deposited material, at Boston Bar and Horseshoe Bar, became coveted for its gold content. Miners sought to divert the river to dry-up the riverbed around the loop to make it easier to mine the bars. In 1861, hundreds of miners rushed to the location of California's "first bedrock tunnel", but unseasonal rains washed away the diversion dam and camps. All that is left of this attempt is the five-foot-tall "walking" tunnel directly above the main tunnel.

The present Tunnel was built by the Horseshoe Bar Mining

Halfway down the Tunnel Chute, confident that their guide has it under control, these paddlers hang on.

Company. According to the state mineralogist's report of 1889, the lower tunnel (then 211 foot long) was built over the four prior years, and was "entirely satisfactory". The original inlet to this tunnel was a 30 foot vertical shaft in the riverbed. The Chute was built later. Labor being plentiful, most of the excavation was done by picks wielded by hand and a bit of dynamite. Horseshoe Bar proved to be one of the richest mining areas of the Middle Fork, and is still mined for gold.

Rafting the Chute

"After observing several attempts of this rapid (Tunnel Chute), the author is convinced it should not be run," wrote Charles Martin, a whitewater pioneer, in 1974. Today, some still agree, but most take the plunge. In 1982, Guy Cables, Jim Cassady and others began taking paddle boats through. The jagged walls and powerful hydraulics still cause an adrenaline surge, even in experienced boaters.

Boat captains gather their crews close around them to be heard above the rapid's roar while they explain the technique for running the Chute. Looking from face to face of their paddlers, the guide tells them that they must paddle hard in the strong current just above the Chute to make sure that they miss the rock walls then at the last instant they'll be commanded to "Drop!" or "Get Down!" in the bottom of the boat, ship their paddles and hold on.

Now, guide and crew walk back upstream to the eddy and board their raft. Concentration is intense. Guides repeat all the instructions and the "drop" maneuver. Timing is essential. Then they paddle out into the current and hover briefly upstream from the rocks that guard the entrance to the Chute.

The top part of the rapid acts exactly like a funnel, as the river's entire width is constricted into a channel narrow enough to spit across. The cold water current strengthens as it drops and is gathered into the bedrock-walled Chute. Rafters riding on a hydropower release of 1000 cfs experience the extreme funneling and turbulence, as one guide said, "of riding a high-volume river in a low-volume channel". Yahoo!

Floating down to this point the paddlers are exhorted to pull hard to keep the fast moving boat off the rock walls. A collision with the walls can rip a boat, cause a flip, or send paddlers flying. Now they must "Drop!", because falling out can cause serious injury.

Swimmers had better catch a deep breath, because buoyancy is reduced in the frothing whitewater. A swimmer in the final ten-foot drop is plunged completely to the depths of the "green room" before surfacing in the tunnel.

Rafters who have managed to stay on board down the Chute hit the big hole at the bottom where the whole raft momentarily disappears. Then there's laughter and cheers as the boat floats on into the swift flat current in the Tunnel.

Final triumph! Guide and crew begin to emerge from the frothy rapid, and float on into the tunnel. Yahoo!

It's mellow and cool and shady inside this mountain chamber and the light at the other side leads out to a large, deep, reflective pool. Shooting the Chute in a raft has felt like a quick run through the wash, rinse, and spin cycles in ice cold water.

Perhaps there is irony in this: the old miners carved a shortcut for the river through the bedrock because they were interested in the wealth that the river had left along its natural course. Today's river- runners gather to witness each other's runs down the Chute, to cheer each other on, to photograph for posterity this epitome of rafting adventures. Tall tales are swapped afterwards, and in the fine tradition of Mark Twain, become taller at the end of the

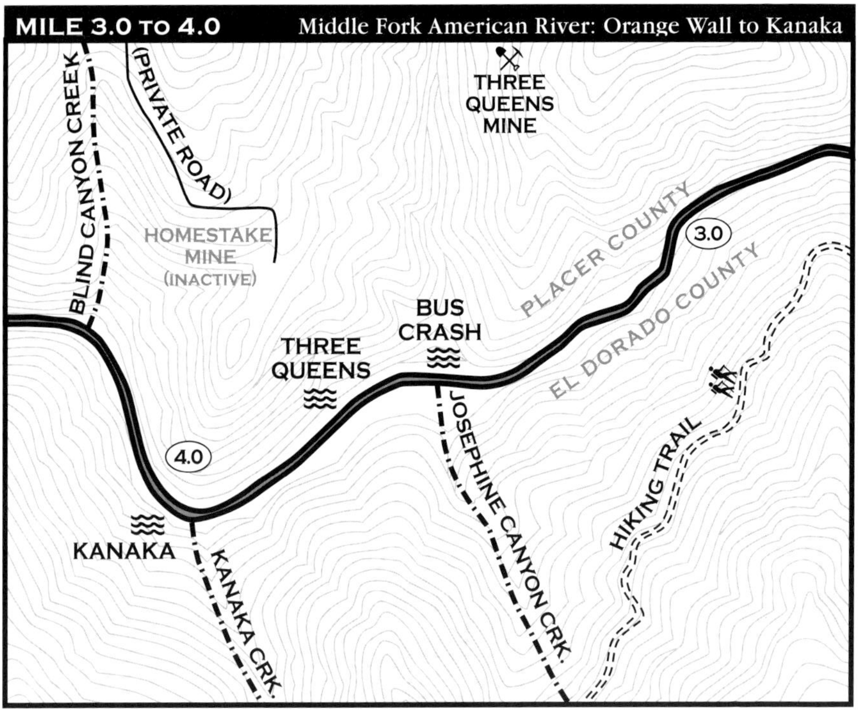

day's Middle Fork adventure. In time, our interest might again turn to consider the advantages of the river's natural course.

Could the old miners ever have dreamed of what goes on in their handiwork? Is it a coincidence that the width of the Chute is the bare minimum required for floating a raft through? By changing the river, during the gold rush, the miners created a wild whitewater rush for boaters to enjoy over a century later.

Mile 1.7 Glass Slipper Rapid (Class II)

Enter far right as you leave calm pool and avoid pour-over at the end on the right.

Mile 2.0 Mad Canyon and Ladies Canyon

Red cliffs on right are gashes left by a hydraulic placer mine. Cannon-like nozzles (called "monitors") played jets of water on the cliff face, and the gravel was channeled into a giant sluice to extract the gold. This method of mining was stopped by a ruling of the California Supreme Court in a lawsuit brought by Central Valley farmers whose lands were flooded when siltation clogged the river beds in the Delta. Siltation in the Delta had-caused major flooding in the farmlands in the late 1800s.

Mile 2.2 Old Gold Tunnel

A square dark hole in the low cliff on the left is the entrance to a unique tunnel, which goes through the slate and up to the surface 200 foot back from the river. This was a man-made sluice box. Boards were set on edge across the bottom of this tunnel at intervals and the gravels above were sluiced through by diverted river water. After draining the tunnel, men shoveled gold nuggets from behind the boards. This is a cool place to stop on a hot day for a hike through the tunnel and around to the boats downstream. Note: Private property.

Mile 2.3 Cathedral Rapid (Class II)

A gravel bar rapid which turns into a bedrock rapid at the bottom.

Mile 3.0 Crescent Moon (Class II)

A large rock hiding in the middle of a wave guards the middle of the river. This rock is difficult to avoid at low water and creates a "crescent moon" hole when the river is high.

Mile 3.5 Bus Crash, Orange Wall or Cannonball Rapid (Class III)

After a right turn, the river bends left and goes over a sharp, guide-launching drop, runnable either side. Avoid the large triangular rock on the left, after the drop called "The Catcher's Mitt". *The orange color on the right wall is from rusting (oxidation) of iron in serpentine.*

Mile 3.6 Green shiny serpentine, *river right*

Serpentine, the California state rock, comes from metamorphism of peridotite, an iron-rich rock present 20 km or more below the surface. When peridotite is faulted toward the surface, it combines with hot circulating water to form serpentine. The fault here is the Shoo Fly/Calaveras fault, which separates these two different rock units. The Shoo Fly complex includes the slates upstream and other sedimentary rocks laid down on the continental shelf and deep ocean 400 million years ago. The Shoo Fly complex may have originated in southern California, and coming by movement along faults to this area. The Calaveras complex, on the other hand, includes sedimentary and volcanic rocks that originated on the deep ocean floor about 350 million years ago.

Mile 3.7 Three Queens Rapid (Class III)

Rocky drop and big waves after a calm pool.

Mile 4.1 Kanaka Falls Rapid (Class IV)

The powerful water hydraulics at Kanaka liberates paddlers from this boat.

A sharp right turn in the canyon signals the rapid. Scout from the large eddy pool on river left. After the rocky entrance, work left to avoid the big keeper hole right center, which can flip boats. Be prepared to swim, since getting slammed in the hole and dunked in the river happens more easily than expected.

A hard cliff of serpentine on the right forms a stunning photogenic backdrop to Kanaka's maze of ledges, rocks and holes. Note: The river from here to Upper Ruck-A-Chucky is Class II.

Mile 4.3 Blind Canyon, *river right*, Fern Garden, on the cliff, *river left*

Bedrock is serpentine upstream of Blind Canyon and metamorphosed green foliated volcanic ash of the Calaveras Complex downstream. The fault contact between the serpentine and ash can be seen running up Blind Canyon. Look for water ouzel nests on river right, where there is a beautiful waterfall.

A short hike up Dardanelles Creek is a gorgeous, tiny canyon offering hidden pools and waterfalls.

Mile 5.0 Cache Bar & Rock, *river left*

There is rough, seasonal 4WD road access from Volcanoville. USFS primitive camp area.

Mile 5.9 Dardanelles Creek and Rapid

A trail starting on the left side of the creek leads to a series of small waterfalls.

The log building on the right is a small hydroelectric power plant which uses water diverted from the creek. The creek has cut into a beautiful sequence of folded layers of chert,

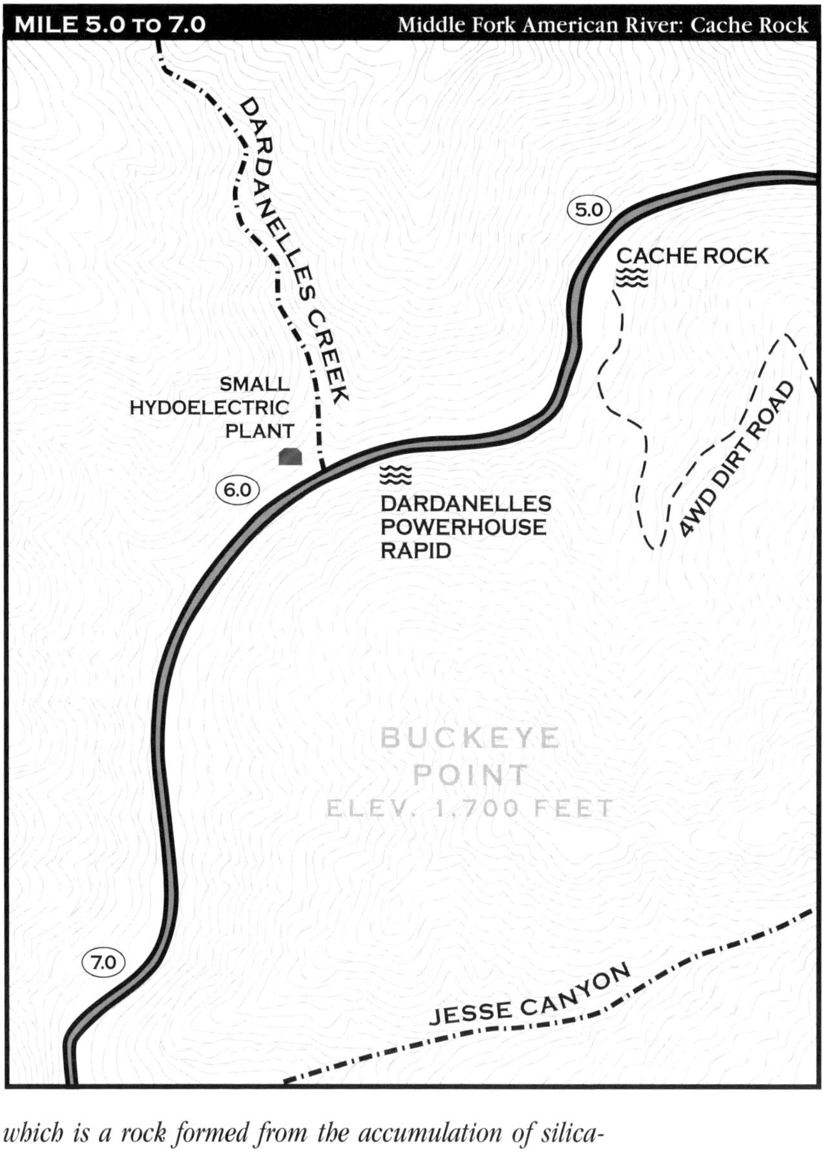

which is a rock formed from the accumulation of silica-bodied organisms on the deep ocean floor.

A narrow gorge and waterfalls are formed by the creek's erosion along these layers. If you look carefully, you can see hairpin folds in the layers from extreme directed pressure on these rocks. The chert is part of the Calaveras Complex; originally horizontal layers were pushed upward and intensely folded during mountain-building. Gray granite dikes cut across the layers.

This "Doodlebug" dredge was beached on a rocky bank of the Middle Fork in 1964 when Hell Hole Dam burst during construction on the Rubicon, a Middle Fork tributary.

Mile 7.4 Jesse Canyon

The river enters a right hand bend with several minor gravel bar rapids. *Green metamorphosed volcanic ash and slate from the Calaveras Complex are present here. Very few hard ledges occur in the river because the bedrock is fairly uniform and has been eroded for a long period of time.*

Mile 7.5 Doodlebug Line Bucket Dredge, *river right*

The dredge is not visible from the river. It is hidden in the vines and willows about halfway down this cobble bar. In 1964 this gold dredge, on its 100 foot long barge, was securely cabled to the shore at Dardanelles Creek, 2.2 miles upstream. When the Hell Hole Coffer Dam on the Rubicon River, a tributary of the Middle Fork, broke during construction, a wall of water 80 foot high ripped the barge and dredge from its moorings and eventually deposited it on this bar where it remains. Can you find the chime-like sound that one of the parts creates when struck with a rock?

A museum of different rocks is displayed here. Light speckled granites, dark serpentine, and volcanic rocks with large square black pyroxene crystals, creamy hard chert, and snow-white quartz create a mosaic of rock art.

Mile 7.6 Miner's Camp, *river right*

Beach with composting toilet and camping by permit.

Mile 10 to 10.5 Ford's Bar Campsites

The large sandbar on river right is a popular lunch spot and campsite with composting toilets on both upper and lower Ford's Bar. River camp permits required.

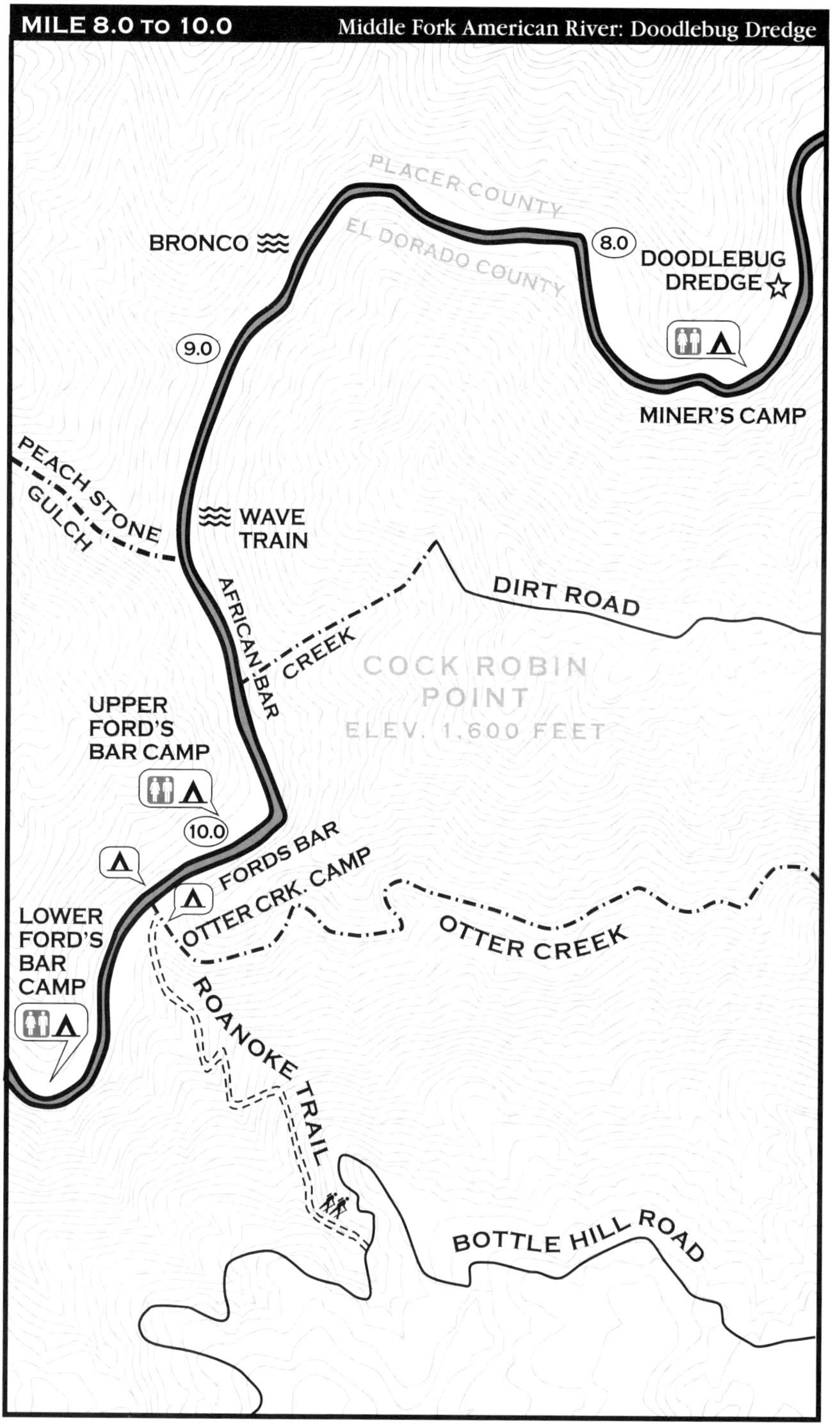
MILE 8.0 TO 10.0
Middle Fork American River: Doodlebug Dredge
PLACER COUNTY
EL DORADO COUNTY
BRONCO
8.0
DOODLEBUG
DREDGE
MINER'S CAMP
9.0
PEACH STONE
GULCH
WAVE
TRAIN
AFRICAN BAR
CREEK
DIRT ROAD
COCK ROBIN
POINT
ELEV. 1,600 FEET
UPPER
FORD'S
BAR CAMP
10.0
FORDS BAR
OTTER CRK. CAMP
OTTER CREEK
LOWER
FORD'S
BAR
CAMP
ROANOKE TRAIL
BOTTLE HILL ROAD

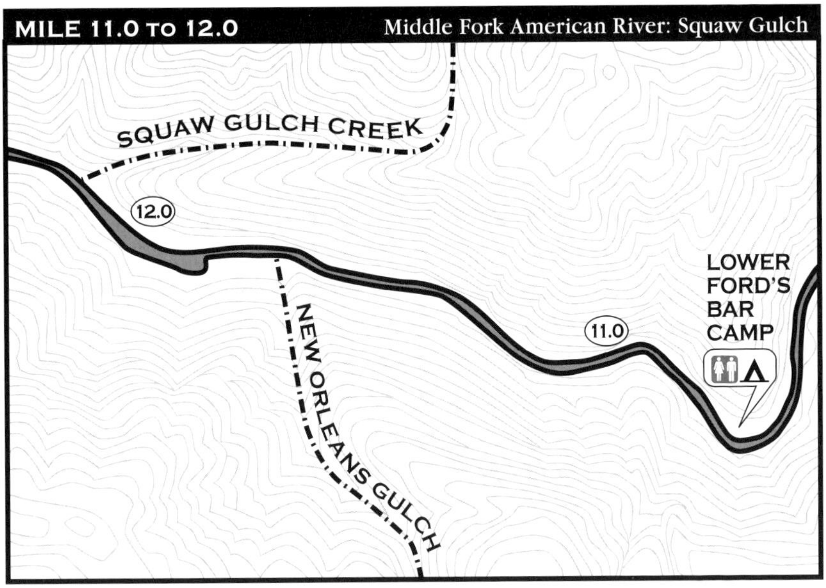

Mile 10.2 Otter Creek, *river left*

There is a campsite here, but no toilet. A hike and scramble one mile up Otter Creek leads to a swimming hole and ripe blackberries in mid-summer. Rock walls and a few building foundations are all that remain at the site of an old mining camp. The Cock Robin Point Trail leads up to Hornblende Ridge on the left. *Hornblende is a black rectangular mineral that is commonly found in granite.*

Mile 10.7 Lower Ford's Bar Camp, *river right*

Beach with campsites and composting toilet. A trail from here provides hiking access to Ruck-A-Chucky Falls 3 miles downstream. This trail is a section of the Tevis Cup horse race and the Western States 100 mile run.

Mile 12.2-12.4 Squaw, Slug and Big Snyder Gulches, *river right*

The sandy river bottom and lack of rapids here are caused by sediment trapped by the damming effect of Ruck-A-Chucky rapid. *The bedrock cliff on the left is hard green metamorphosed volcanic ash, a taste of things to come at Ruck-A-Chucky.*

Mile 13.1 Canyon Creek, *river left*
Emergency access road and toilets, *river right*

Power lines from a small hydroelectric plant can be seen here. A hike up Canyon Creek is well worth the effort. It is beautiful, shady,

At Chunder Rapid, a partially-submerged boulder in the center of the passage (this raft is just about to go over it) poses a danger to boaters.

and cool, with numerous smooth bedrock waterfalls and pools.

There are toilets above the sandy beach on the right. There is also a locked gated narrow road on river right which leads to the Ruck-A-Chucky campground take-out 3 miles downstream. This road is NOT used to portage Ruck-A-Chucky rapids.

Mile 13.2 Chunder Rapid or Upper Ruck-A-Chucky (Class IV)

The incredible roar of these falls warns boaters of the danger ahead. Scouting is strongly recommended here; scout on the right side and portage if necessary. This is a steep, sharp 8 foot drop over exposed rocks that must be run down the center chute just right of a pour-over rock hump. There is also a large boulder on the right to avoid just downstream of the drop.

This rapid is best run at full 1,000 cfs flow to avoid hitting partially submerged rock. Caution is vital here because the big falls are a scant 150 yards downstream across a pool. At high water, the strong current pulls swimmers towards the falls. After Chunder, stop at the sloping rock on the right bank before the falls to take out for the Ruck-A-Chucky portage.

Mile 13.3 Ruck-A-Chucky Falls (Class VI)

The first reaction standing on the top is awe. A thundering roar with spray shooting upward greets your eyes and ears. A jumble of house size rocks blocks the river and water forms cascades in narrow channels. The Army Corps of Engineer's failed attempt at building a dam here in 1939, which caused massive rock slides, created the waterfalls here.

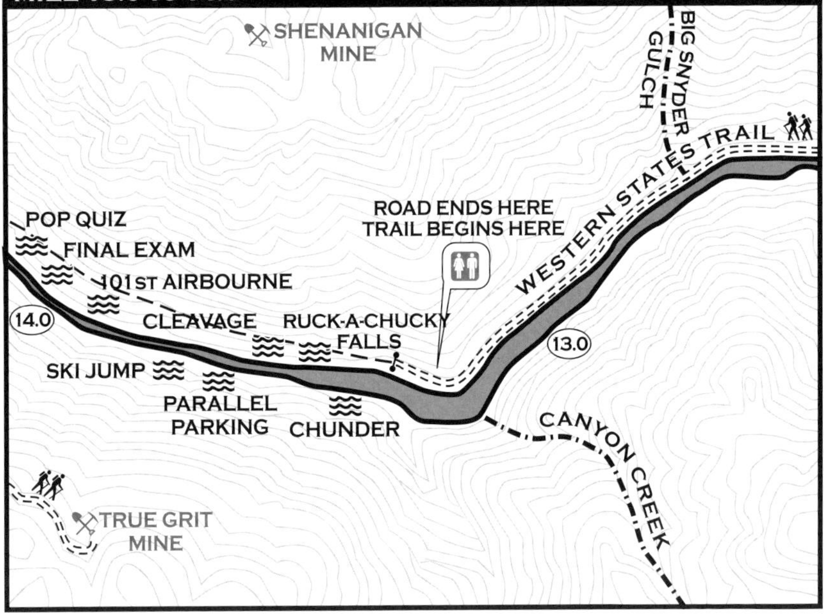

You have several choices of how to deal with this obstacle. It may come to mind to make a big pile of your equipment, burn it, and hike out. However, walking out involves difficult rock climbing and equipment is expensive, so most people find other ways.

Some outfitters have the guide make a dangerous solo run over the falls. Others push their empty boats over, but this requires the guide to make a dangerous jump from a midstream rock below the falls onto the moving boat to recover it. Boats can flip or wrap on rocks below the falls. Passengers walk around the falls on the portage trail.

California Conservation Corps (CCC) constructing the Ruck-A-Chucky portage trail.

Other boaters carry boats and gear using the trail on the right. This is a strenuous portage on a rocky, steep trail leading to a pool below the falls. Caution and planning are required to carry a raft over the large boulders at the end of the trail.

The Ruck-A-Chucky Portage Trail

California State Parks contracted with the California Conservation Corps to first build this portage trail, completed in 1989. It replaced an earlier

Commercial guides run Ruck-A-Chucky solo while passengers run portage trail.

Raft and guide emerge from bottom of Ruck-A-Chucky Falls.

cable system that washed out in 1986. The trail saves precious time and reduces the hazards of portaging.

The bedrock here is green, hard metamorphosed volcanic lava flows, ash tuffs, and broken breccias–the same as we see on the North Fork American River.

After a safe portage, with Ruck-A-Chucky Falls looming in the background, the rafters drop down "Cleavage" rapid.

Ruck-A-Chucky, the Middle Fork sharply drops several times at Class III-IV rapids

At Parallel Parking Rapid, this boat has successfully avoided the wrap-rock and safely made the lateral chute at river left; all are happy paddlers.

Mile 13.5 Cleavage Rapid (Class III-IV)

The next mile of falls and ledges are some of the best on the Middle Fork. After returning to the boats, get to the mid-stream quickly before this six foot drop. Avoid running too far right where there is a reversal because swimmers can be re-circulated or be swept into dangerous rocks at Parallel Parking.

Mile 13.7 Parallel Parking Rapid (Class IV)

Scout from the right bank to find the entrance slot between the boulders. Boats that miss the chute can flip or wrap on mid-stream boulders. After passing guard rocks center channel, there is a diagonal chute from center to left leading to a sharp drop between large boulders that sends boats up against a rock wall on river left.

Mile 13.8 Ski Jump (Class III)

Get ready quickly for this drop into big waves which can launch you airborne.

Mile 13.9 Guillotine Rapid (Class III)

Rocky drop with pour-overs to avoid, enter right then move left.

At the bottom of Parallel Parking Rapid these rafters move to the high side of the raft to keep it from flipping or wrapping.

Mile 14.1 The 101st Airborne meets Texas Chainsaw-Mama (Class III)

The river drops and bends to the left of a rocky island. The big rooster tail pour-over at the bottom of the rapid can easily eject passengers and guide and make them airborne. Avoid hitting the undercut rock ledge on the left after the rapid which can clip heads; it's a real Texas Chainsaw-Mama.

Mile 14.4 Final Exam or Deception (Class III)

Obstacles at the top must be cleared before the strong current, this time on river left, speeds you toward a house rock and a sleeper hole just left of this rock. Look out for an undercut slab on the left shore at the bottom of this rapid.

Mile 14.5 Pop Quiz (Class III)

For extra credit, this is a short, technical, "read and run" rapid. But you can't read it until you get real close. Enter far right then move left.

Mile 14.6 Paradise Canyon, *river right*

A gate here ends vehicle access on road.

Mile 14.9 Old Greenwood Bridge Site

In 1964, during construction of the Hell Hole Dam, heavy rains caused water to over-top the temporary coffer dam. A wall of water 80 foot high scoured the canyons and washed out the Old Greenwood Bridge and Highway 49 Bridge.

The bridge site also marks the location of another funda-

mental change in bedrock geology. We cross the Melones Fault Zone, marked by serpentine to the Calaveras Complex of ocean sediments and volcanics to vertical layers of the Mother Lode Terrane. These layers form outcrops and control the course of the river downstream

They were formed 160 million years ago as currents of sand and mud which flowed onto the deep ocean floor from volcanos. The layers were buried, then uplifted, compressed, tilted on end and metamorphosed to slates during mountain building. The bedrock makes a natural sluicebox for gold deposits.

The Greenwood Bridge (shown here) was wiped out in the 1964 flood caused by the Hell Hole Coffer Dam collapse. These early 1960s rafters fashion a triangular craft of inner tubes and wood. They accompany their "raft" on air mattresses.

Mile 15.1 Ruck-A-Chucky Campground, Oregon Bar take-out and fee use area

Take out on river right immediately below the rapid at the path that leads to the loading area. Campsites, toilets, picnic tables and parking are available here.

The Lower Middle Fork offers a Class II (easy rafting) run from the Greenwood Bridge site to Mammoth Bar.

THE RUN AT-A-GLANCE:

Ruck-A-Chucky Campground to Mammoth Bar

DIFFICULTY:	Class II+, Beware of willow strainers
LENGTH:	7 miles
SEASON:	April to October
GRADIENT:	12 feet per mile
RUNNABLE FLOWS:	600 to 3,000 cfs
FLOW INFO:	www.dreamflows.com or www.cdec.water.ca.gov/river/americanStages.html
PUT-IN:	Old Greenwood Bridge site, elevation 700' Note: Put-in is upstream of the gravel lot take-out by the river.
TAKE-OUT:	Mammoth Bar, elevation 580'
SHUTTLE:	12 miles, 30 minutes each way
OUTFITTERS:	One-day trips: For a list of outfitters go to www.parks.ca.gov select 'Gold Country', click on 'Auburn' then select "Whitewater Rafting'.
WATER QUALITY:	Cold and clear, but purify before drinking as microorganisms including giardia may be present.
CAMPING:	A special river camping permit is required throughout the Auburn SRA except in designated camping areas. Call Auburn SRA headquarters at (530) 885-4527 for info.
EMERGENCIES:	Placer County Sheriff (Auburn): 911, California State Department of Parks and Recreation Dispatch: (916) 358-1300.

The Lower Middle Fork of the American River

By Tony DeRiggi and Eric Peach
Geology by Terry Wright PhD.

Ruck-A-Chucky Campground to Mammoth Bar

This is a scenic Class II wilderness river run, ideal for beginners to intermediate boaters in rafts, kayaks or IKs. Experienced open canoeists will enjoy this run, which also has reliable flows and blackberries all summer. Make sure you know where to take-out. Immediately below Mammoth Bar is the Class V+ Murderer's Bar Rapid, a difficult portage with no trail over boulders.

When planning a trip check the flows, it takes up to 5-6 hours or more for the water release at Oxbow to reach the Ruck-A-Chucky Campground area for an early afternoon put-in. This stretch is well suited for long, hot summer afternoons.

Mammoth Bar take-out is a fee use area and also an OHV park, with toilets and picnic tables. Camping is not allowed here.

Kennebeck Bar in this 1857 photo boasts very intense mining activity. The population of the Middle Fork was estimated to be nearly 10,000 at its peak. The river was flumed, and "hurdy-gurdy" waterwheels operated siphon pumps and sawmills essential for mining the bars and sawing lumber for the miles of flume.

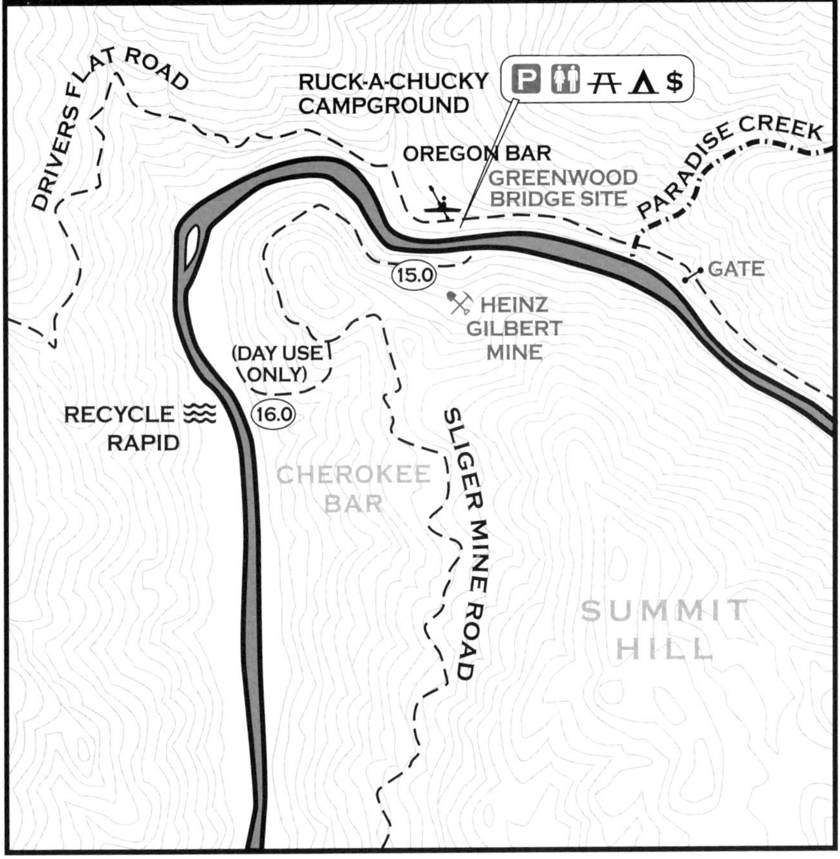

The bedrock geology begins with the Mother Lode Terrane (described at mile 14.9). The Terrane outcrops continue until the river sweeps right around Poverty Bar and cuts into the Sierra Foothills Melange. Melanges are formed most by mixing along faults or by underwater landsliding where ocean crust is sinking under the edge of the continent.

Melanges are a mixture of many different kinds of oceanic rocks; sedimentary, igneous and metamorphic. These rocks are suspended in a matrix of serpentine or sheared mudstone. Awesome Murderer's Bar is a band of melange with very hard metavolcanic and plutonic igneous rocks. J-turn rapid is formed around a 40 foot wide block of volcanic ash that slid down a submarine slope. The mélange, which may be between 180 to 300 million years old, became part of the continent 160 million years ago and was uplifted and eroded to the present canyons in the last 9 million years.

LOWER MIDDLE FORK PUT-IN & TAKE-OUT SHUTTLE

TO MAMMOTH BAR TAKE-OUT

Take the Foresthill exit from I-80 in Auburn. Drive east 3 miles on Foresthill Road. Turn right on Old Foresthill Road, after 1½ miles turn left into Mammoth Bar OHV Park, a fee area. Drive past the OHV track. Stay on the left side of the cobble bar to reach the parking area near the take-out pool at the upper end of the cobble bar. Check the gate closure time at the entrance to avoid being locked in.

TO RUCK-A-CHUCKY CAMPGROUND. TAKE-OUT FOR THE UPPER MIDDLE FORK & PUT-IN FOR THE LOWER MIDDLE FORK

Take the Foresthill Exit off I-80 in Auburn and drive east across the Auburn-Foresthill Bridge high above the north fork canyon. Continue 8 miles up Foresthill Road to Drivers Flat Road turnoff on the right. This road is paved the first half-mile, turning into steep dirt road the remaining 2 miles into the canyon with grand scenic views.

After the road reaches the river it crosses a side stream. Continue on to the second fee parking area, with the rock stairs and gravel ramp, for the class II put-in. The lower gravel parking lot by the river, opposite camp 5, is the loading area for the upper Middle Fork, class IV run take-out.

Kennebeck Bar from a similar vantage point is shown here in 1989. Inflatable kayaks are an exhilarating way to enjoy the natural beauty and wildlife found on the Lower Middle Fork. It is encouraging when comparing to the photo on page 217 to see how well the river and the canyons have recovered from the gold rush.

MILE BY MILE GUIDE

RUCK-A-CHUCKY CAMPGROUND TO MAMMOTH BAR

Mile 15.1 Ruck-A-Chucky Campground put-in

Put-in at the gravel ramp by the picnic table by the oak tree.

Mile 15.5 Cherokee Bar Rapid (Class II)

Finny ledges form on hard layers and foliation in bedrock.

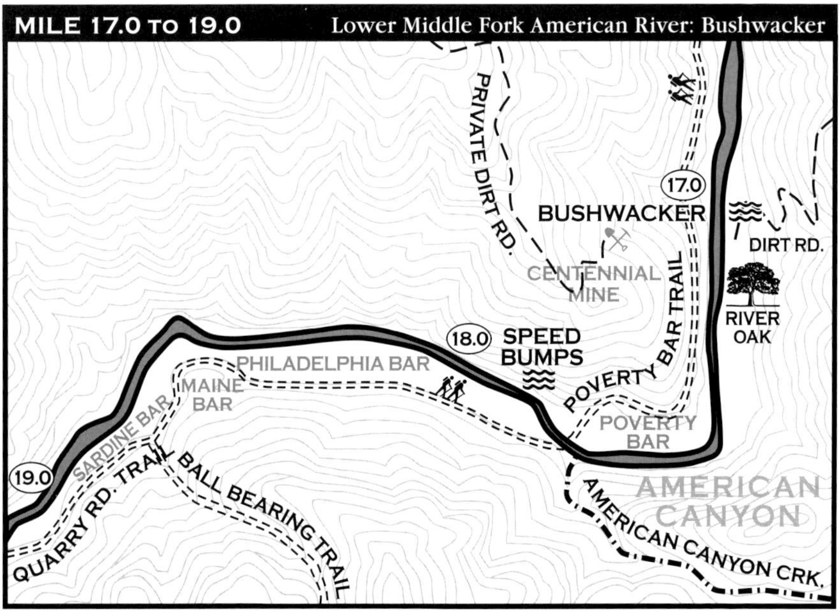

Mile 15.8 Cherokee Bar, *river left*

Sliger Mine Road access from Greenwood makes this large beach a popular day use area. *This long, straight reach of the river follows the natural plane of geologic weakness parallel to layering and foliation in the Mother Lode Terrane.*

Mile 16 Recycle Rapid (Class II+)

The lower Middle Fork is an exceptional run for beginning kayakers.

The river turns right and drops over ledges. Avoid midstream boulders at the bottom of the rapid. This rapid has an exciting river surfing hole. Catch the eddy on the left at the bottom to return upriver and practice your river surfing skills!

Mile 16.8 Sliger Mine & Stamp Mill

Remains of the Sliger Mine foundations can be seen mid-way up the canyon wall to the left.

Mile 17.1 Bushwhacker Rapid

At the end of the mile long pool lined with blackberries the river divides around an island. Run the narrow tongue down the cobble bar on the left side of the island to avoid the dangerous brush strainers along the right bank.

Woohoo! But be careful, rock jumping can result in serious injury and death.

Mile 17.5 Poverty Bar, *river right*

Poverty bar was a beehive of mining activity with thousands of miners working gold bearing placer deposits in the river. This stretch of river was diverted into the Middle Fork's Grand Flume in the late 1850s.

Mile 17.7 American Canyon Creek, *river left*

Be alert or you will miss this gorgeous side canyon. It is difficult to catch the small eddy, on river left, in the middle of this swift rapid. A short hike up American Canyon will reward you with an Elve's chasm of falls, pools, and ferns. Blackberries are abundant here in season. The fig trees in the canyon were probably planted by Chinese miners who worked in this area after constructing the Transcontinental Railroad in the late 1800s.

A shady American canyon creek, with its waterfalls and pools, becomes a paradise of a lunch stop.

The green serpentine bedrock ledges are blocks of metamorphosed volcanic rock and chert from the melange.

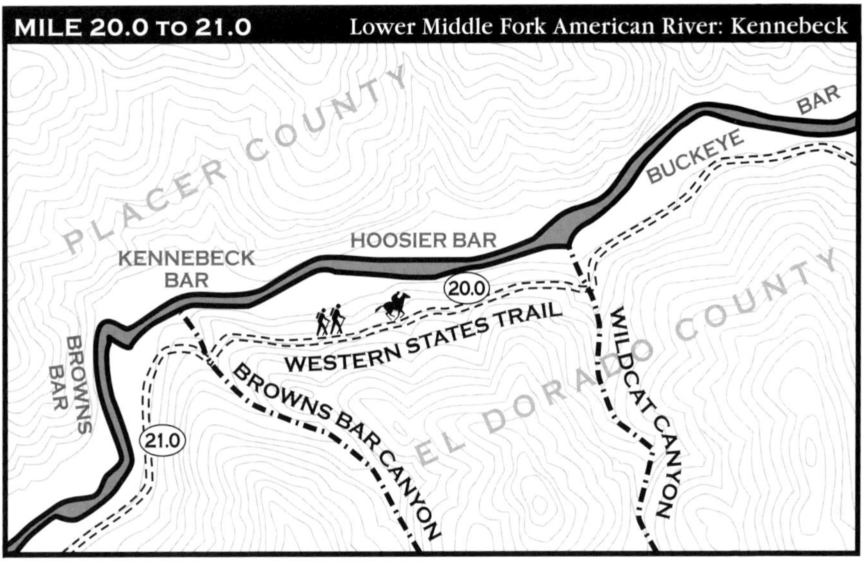

LEGEND

- PAVED ROADS
- DIRT ROADS
- TRAILS
- RIVER
- CREEKS
- PRIMITIVE TRAILS
- PUT-IN & TAKE-OUTS
- (0.0) MILE MARKERS
- RAPIDS
- PARKING AREAS
- TOILETS
- PICNIC & CAMPING
- HORSE ROUTES
- HIKING ROUTES
- BIKE ROUTES
- $ FEE AREAS
- GATE

Mile 17.8 Speed Bumps or Fuzzy Bunny (Class II+)

At the end of Poverty Bar the river turns to the left and drops over ledges that form splashy waves and reversals.

Mile 17.9 Philadelphia Bar, *river left*

Many river bars were named after the homes of the prospectors that toiled for gold on them. *Below here, blocks of hard rock are surrounded by sheared mudstone matrix in the melange.*

Mile 18.5 Maine Bar Rapid (Class II)

Take the main tongue right center over this rocky ledge. The knoll on the left was once the site of a thriving mining village.

Mile 19.0 Buckeye Bar

An erratic stark white "tooth" of chert, that resembles a profile of George Washington, sticks up from the river bed on right.

Mile 20.2 Kennebeck Bar, *river right*

Enjoy cool deep pools for a swim before take-out.

MILE 22.0 TO 23.0 Lower Middle Fork American River: Murderer's Bar

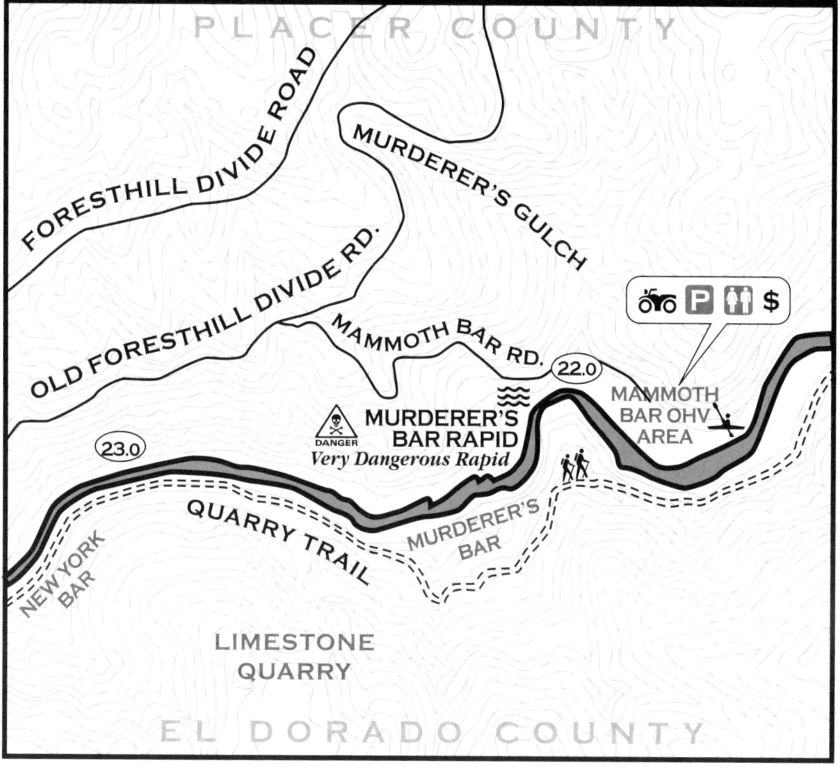

Mile 21.6 Mammoth Bar take-out

A sign on river right marks the take-out at the calm pool at the top of Mammoth Bar. Take-out here to avoid the treacherous Class V+ Murderer's Bar Rapid, which is not only extremely dangerous to run but very difficult to portage.

Mile 22.0 Murderer's Bar Rapid (Class VI)

Do not run this rapid, deaths have occurred here! Cliffs above a small gravel bar on the left; and a jumble of boulders on the right serve as recognition. Be sure to take out on the right, well above the rapid, to portage because the entrance has a strong, swift current. A narrow chute sends the full force of the river directly onto a large rock which splits the current. River right is a deadly boulder sieve and running left of the large rock is extremely difficult. Because there is no trail, the strenuous and dangerous portage requires carrying boats and gear over huge boulders on river right.

Close-up of Grand Flume operation at Poverty Bar, 1857. Private mining companies joined together to build a 13-mile-long wood and canvas flume annually; its story is told in the history section of this book.

NOTE: This area was named after the first bloody conflict between miners and Native Americans that occurred here. *(See Gold Rush History.) The hard rocks here are pieces of dark course grained gabbro, metamorphosed lava flows, and other iron-rich igneous rocks which occur as a zone in the melange with serpentine matrix.*

Mile 22.6 Limestone Ridge, *river right*

This quarry on the left ridge and blue-gray outcropping on the right are made up of unusually pure limestone. *Limestone usually forms as a coral reef in warm, shallow seas teeming with life. The limestone here is found mixed with deep ocean sedimentary and volcanic rock.*

Hawver Cave

By Vince Haughey

Caves sometimes act as natural museums or time capsules, collecting fossils and artifacts and preserving them from the surface elements for later discovery. Such a place was Hawver Cave, an extensive and complex cavern situated in a limestone lens of the Calaveras formation on a knoll at 1,300 feet above sea level just southwest of Murderer's Bar.

Dr. Hawver

The cave had been known as "Quarry Cave" or "Lake Cave," and from the 1880s had helped supply lime for the kiln at the Pioneer Mine, near Ophir. One of the earliest recorded visitors was miner Stephen Wing. The following is an entry from his daily journal. The date was August 29, 1859:

"Monday: Left Uniontown on Friday morning last for Todd's Valley. Started at 3 o'clock - before daybreak Went up with W. Hughes on a fruit wagon–by way of Murderers Bar–Middle Fork. Stopped at Knickerbocker Ranch and took breakfast about 7 o'clock. Stopped at Cave Valley and visited the cave, which is quite a curiosity. It contains three apartments, the first is about 10 ft. below the surface of the ground and is nearly circular in shape. It has a good board floor on the edge of which all around is a row of seats for the accommodation of visitors. Religious services are often performed there and it is occasionally used for a ballroom The second apartment is somewhat smaller and higher than the first. The third connects with the outer world by an aperture in the top and a flight of stairs. The rock is a species of Limestone and there are several lime kilns in the vicinity."

The cave eventually became well known to paleontologists for its abundant Pleistocene fossils, after first being reported

Hawver cave was located in the limestone dike above Murderers Bar. The limestone became valuable for cement, and the cave area was quarried and destroyed. The quarry was founded by the Pacific Portland Cement Company. A railroad carried the limestone down the river, across what is now called "No Hands Bridge," and up the canyon. The old railroad grade forms much of the trail that leads downstream from the Confluence at the Route 49 Bridge to Full Moon Beach. The quarry is still active; the limestone is used for road base and cement.

in 1906 by Dr. J. C. Hawver of Auburn. Bones found protruding from cave deposits proved to belong to extinct animal species. Twenty-four vertebrate types were identified, including the ancient ground sloth, mastodon, horse, bison, cougar and several smaller carnivores and rodents.

E. L. Furlong of the University of California recorded in 1907 that *"The bones are in a perfect state of preservation. The remains have every appearance of being gradually accumulated in the fissure by falling and washing in from the surface, probably in part through the agency of rivulets ... the animals probably used hollows or large crevices in the rocks as retreats and places in which to eat their prey. Numerous bones were*

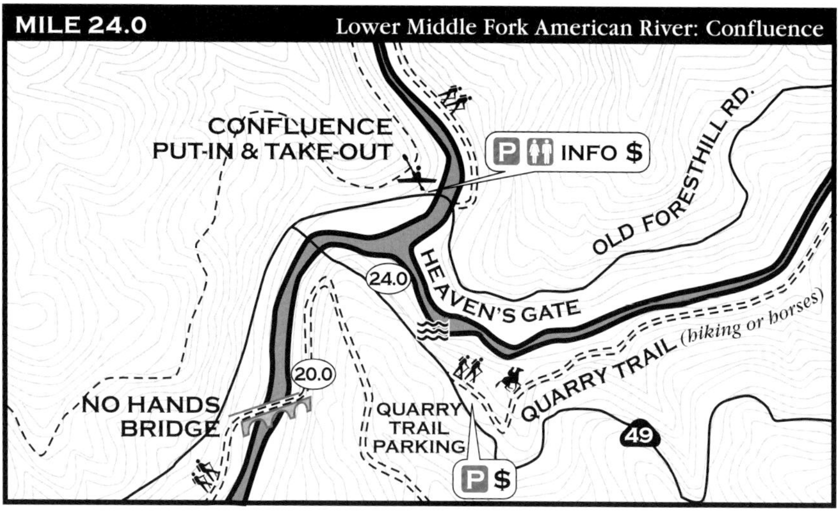

accumulated in this manner, and were in an excellent situation to be entombed in the crevices of the limestone."

A few remains were removed to the University Museum in Berkeley, but investigation of the cave was often difficult owing to the constant presence of pools of water and slow flowing streams in the numerous grottoes of the cavern. Air mattress rafts were used by investigators to paddle from wall to wall. The action of this water was responsible for the dynamic nature of the cave, on the one hand creating the openings and fissures through the dissolution of soil and limestone, and on the other hand cementing up former fissures through the deposition of a breccia (cemented deposits) consisting of carbonated lime. It is in this breccia that the bones were found.

In 1908, human bones were uncovered at the lower end of the main cave. Since the cave was ill-suited for human habitation, it was assumed that the Indians had used the vertical shaft as a burial vault. Accompanying the human remains, perhaps as burial offerings, were found complete specimens of basalt, slate, and limestone projectile points (which pre-dated the use of obsidian) along with other various tools made of stone or animal bone. This evidence has been estimated to be over four thousand years old. The exploration of Hawver Cave continued for several subsequent years, but eventually the quarrying operation completely destroyed the cave. *(See page 119 for more information.)*

Wallace, William J. and Lathrap, Donald W., "Early Implement Assemblage from a Limestone Cave in California," *1952.*

Furlong, Ed, "Reconnaissance of a Recently Discovered Quaternary Cave Deposit Near Auburn, CA," *1907; Science, n.s. vol. 25, pp. 392-4; Lancaster.*

Gernes, Phyllis Lindert, "The Daily Journal of Stephen Wing," *Garden Valley, 1982.*

The Mountain Quarries Railroad Bridge celebrated its 100 year anniversary in 2012. MQRR Engine 202, although inoperable, returned to the bridge in September 2012. The 202 is currently on display at ASRA Park Headquarters.

Mile 23.7 Heaven's Gate or J-Turn (Class III)

At the downstream end of a gravel bar on river right a huge rock island almost blocks the river. Scout from the right bank to find your route through the maze of bedrock slots boulders and ledges. This rapid was made more difficult when a huge rockslide occurred here on February 18, 1986. Water soaked hillsides gave way when the Auburn coffer dam collapsed, suddenly draining the temporary 200 feet deep lake that was backed up here. The fast currents draining the lake scoured the river canyon, downed trees and closed Highway 49 to Cool for three months while the damage was repaired. *The big rock is a block of hard, metamorphosed volcanic ash that slid off of a volcano into the deep ocean.*

Mile 24.0 Confluence take-out, *river right*

Below J-Turn take out at the beach on river right just before the Confluence with the North Fork. A path leads up to the parking area on the Old Foresthill Road.

See the *'Confluence to China Bar'* section of the Lower North Fork for 4 more miles of Class II and III rapids.

The South Fork of the American River

By John Cassidy, Maureen Daley-Hutter, Updated by Tony DeRiggi and Eric Peach
Geology by Terry Wright, Ph.D.

Chili Bar to Salmon Falls Bridge

The South Fork American is one of the country's premier recreational and historical rivers. Known as the most popular commercially rafted river in the West, the South Fork has natural beauty and whitewater for almost everyone.

Hot air balloons dip their baskets in the whitewater rapids of the South Fork in early morning when canyon winds are gentle.

While it is popular, the South Fork is not recommended for inexperienced boaters or inner-tubers, with the exception of the Coloma to Greenwood Creek section. Even at lower flows of approximately 1,000 to 2,000 cubic feet per second, the South Fork is Class III with some challenging and potentially dangerous rapids. The river gradient is a steep, 30 feet per mile in the upper gorge below Chili Bar, easing to 9 feet per mile through the Coloma Valley, increasing to 33 feet per mile through the lower Gorge. The run ends at Folsom Reservoir.

Rafting the South Fork of the American River

Water levels are controlled by SMUD and PG&E at Chili Bar and White Rock dams, which make scheduled releases of water for river recreation. The hydro-electric plants on the South Fork provide electricity for the Sacramento region. The water stored in Folsom Reservoir is used to maintain water quality for the Delta and is distributed for city and agricultural use.

The South Fork American has a significant amount of privately owned land along the river. Homeowners, commercial outfitters, private boaters, ranchers, anglers, hikers and picnickers all share this beautiful river. Rafters may stop on public lands along the river, which are marked by signs.

El Dorado County is the South Fork's managing agency, and policies are guided by a River Management Advisory Committee. To respect the rights of property owners a quiet zone is marked by signs in the Coloma to Lotus area. .

Private boater permit tags, required by county ordinance, should be displayed on all water craft. Available free of charge at Henningsen-Lotus Park, Coloma State Park, Camp Lotus, and Chili Bar put-ins, these tags contain information about health and safety guidelines, and include a river map showing public and private lands, toilet locations, campgrounds, and quiet zone boundaries.

Slate Quarry Plant

Just upstream from the Chili Bar bridge, on the south side, is the old Slate Quarry Plant, established in 1886. The quarry produces slate used in roof shingles, walkways and other products. Originally known as "Buck's Quarry", the slate it produced then was not crushed, but hand cut into shingle or board slate, from which counters, coffins and chalk boards were made.

During the height of the Cold War the extensive tunneling attracted the attention of the federal government and the Campbell Soup Co. One was on the lookout for a bomb shelter site; the other was interested in raising mushrooms.

In 1979, Placerville Industries Inc. acquired the property, erected a new plant on slightly higher ground, and sold as scrap the mills, Pelton wheels, and generators that had been in use for over 60 years. The new plant remains the oldest continuously running slate quarry in the state.

Geology

Chili Bar is composed of vertical layers of black slate and volcanic rocks formed in an oceanic setting as horizontal layers during Jurassic time (about 160 million years ago) and compressed, heated, and uplifted to their present position during the Nevadan mountain building event about 140 million years ago. These rocks were intruded by molten granite, which is exposed in the Coloma area, about 130 million years ago. Downstream from Coloma, the river cuts through an ancient ocean floor complex, which has been highly faulted, now called the Sierra Foothills Melange. The river cuts through the Bear Mountains Fault zone at the head of the gorge, which exposes very hard dark rocks of amphibolite, heated and changed ocean floor lava.

The terrain is typical of the Sierran Foothills river

Chili Bar rafting put-in on a summer Sunday morning is busy. Hundreds of whitewater rafters put-in here every weekend.

Mark Leder-Adams, Rapid Shooters

THE RUN AT-A-GLANCE:

CHILI BAR TO SALMON FALLS BRIDGE

DIFFICULTY:	Class III. Class IV above 6,000 cfs
LENGTH:	6 miles to Marshall Gold Discovery State Historic Park. 8 miles to Henningsen-Lotus County Park; 11.5 to Greenwood Creek; 20.5 to Salmon Falls Bridge. Coloma Marshall Gold Discovery Park to Greenwood, Class II, 5.6 miles. One or two day trips.
SEASON:	Year round depending on water supply and hydroelectric demand.
GRADIENT:	Upper run 30' feet per mile; Coloma Valley 9 feet per mile; lower run 21 feet per mile
RUNNABLE FLOWS:	1,000 cfs to 6,000 cfs. Kayaks OK above 800 cfs
FLOW INFO:	Gauge at Chili Bar Dam: www.dreamflows.com or www.cdec.water.ca.gov/river/Americanstages.html. A monthly calendar of scheduled releases is available on www.dreamflows.com. (It takes 2 hours for the water to reach Coloma and 3 hours for the water to reach Camp Lotus.)
PUT-INS:	Chili Bar (elevation 930' feet), for upper run. Marshall Gold Discovery State Historic Park. Henningsen-Lotus Park or Camp Lotus for Class II Greenwood Creek Run or Class III Gorge Run. Greenwood Creek for Gorge Run only.
TAKE-OUTS:	Marshall Gold Discovery State Historic Park, Henningsen-Lotus Park, Camp Lotus or Greenwood Creek for upper run. Salmon Falls Bridge, (elevation 440' feet), for Lower Run.
SHUTTLE:	25 miles, 1 hour each way for entire river run. ½ hour each way for upper or lower run only. For shuttle, contact colomashuttle.com, 530-303-2404.
OUTFITTERS:	www.theamericanriver.com for a list of commercial outfitters
WATER QUALITY:	Cold and clear, but purify before drinking.
CAMPING:	Private Campgrounds: Camp Lotus 530-622-8672, American River Resort, Coloma Resort, and Ponderosa Park. Camping on river at BLM public land river right mile 12.2 with toilet facility.
EMERGENCIES:	911: El Dorado County Sheriff, 530-626-4911. California State Parks Dispatch: 916-358-1300.

canyons. A 1,500 to 2,000 foot deep canyon has been incised into a gently rolling upland surface. This surface was formed by erosion of the Sierra Nevada during the period 130 to 50 million years ago. River gravels and lava flows were formed on this surface, and the area looked like the Central Valley today. Nine million years ago, the area was uplifted, and the present river canyons were formed.

Rapids are mostly rock gardens, where boulders are stranded by flood or rockslide on hard bedrock ledges. In the lower gorge, ledges of hard amphibolite and gabbro form formidable bedrock obstacles, especially at Satan's Cesspool rapid.

Chili Bar Bridge

About 200 feet upriver from the present bridge, a stretch of shallow water provided a fording spot to travellers between Placerville and the gold mines of the Georgetown Divide. From 1851 until 1853, a cable-operated ferry connected the two shores when the water was high. In 1854, the first bridge was built. Eight years later, though, the bridge, and tollhouse were carried away by high water in the historic 1862 flood. A concrete arch bridge was built in 1922 and replaced in 1993 by the modern bridge that stands at the site today.

SOUTH FORK PUT-IN & TAKE-OUT SHUTTLE

To the Chili Bar Put-in

To get to Chili Bar from Highway 49 turn north on Highway 193 about 1 mile north of Placerville. After 3 miles on a winding road, cross the bridge then immediately turn left into the Chili Bar River Access fee area operated by the non-profit American River Conservancy. Contact ARC at 530-642-1667 for information. Season pass available. No overnight camping.

Coloma or Lotus River Access

From put-in at Chili Bar, take Highway 193 south. Make a sharp right turn onto Highway 49. In 8 miles, Marshall Gold Discovery S.H.P. has river access. For Henningsen-Lotus access, go left on Lotus Road and drive a ½ mile to the park. No overnight parking here. For Camp Lotus, go 1 mile, turn right on Bassi Road, go one mile to Camp Lotus on the right. Nice grassy camp sites under cottonwood trees. Camp Lotus, run by Bill and Robin Center, also offers showers, food, supplies and often fresh baked treats. Camping reservations are recommended.

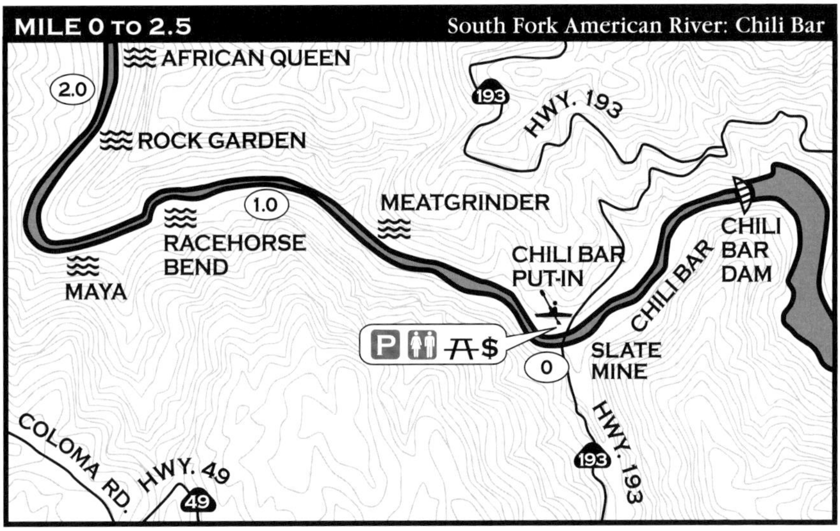

Greenwood Creek River Access

The take-out for class II run from Coloma, or put-in for Gorge run. Greenwood Creek River Access is on Highway 49, 3 miles north of Lotus Road. Good for kayaks but the parking lot is some distance from the river so it is a long carry for rafts on the trail.

Salmon Falls Bridge Take-Out

From Coloma, go north on Highway 49 about eight miles. At the top of a grade, just before the town of Pilot Hill, turn left on Salmon Falls Road and left again. You're still on Salmon Falls Road, which winds about seven miles down to the bridge. Skunk Hollow and Darrington Trailhead take-out fee use area before the bridge has parking lots on both sides of the road. Across the bridge, fee parking at Salmon Falls is generally used by commercial outfitters.

From Highway 50 exit at El Dorado Hills Blvd. Drive north and cross Green Valley Road onto Salmon Falls Road and continue to Salmon Falls Bridge.

Mile by Mile Guide

Chili Bar to Salmon Falls Bridge

Mile 0.0 Chili Bar Put-In

Although American history has fully adopted the California Gold Rush, in 1848 and early 1849 a "Californian" was a native-Spanish speaker and the Gold Rush itself could be considered a chapter in Mexican and South American history. Some of the best miners came from Chile, where mining had been a way of life since the days of the Spanish conquistadors. A group of these Chileans arrived in the South Fork area and first mined in Garden Valley and Johntown. Trouble arose when the foreigners were accused of panning other miners' tailings at night. Fights followed, and a vigilante group formed to escort the South Americans across the river, from where they were instructed never to come back.

It turned out to be unnecessary advice. The next morning, the Chileans found their new home by the river to be excellent diggings and they stayed there for years. A smallpox epidemic in 1886 wiped out the last of those that hadn't returned home. Evidence of their graves, marked with slate headstones, can still be found on the hillsides nearby.

The White Water Rodeo Competition at the American River Festival celebrated its 31st year in 2012.

Geology

The river cuts through a spectacular steep, wooded canyon at Chili Bar. The high level of the gravel terrace indicates that it was formed during high water flows of the glacial period which ended 10,000 years ago. The high precipitation and melting of the glaciers contributed to flood flows up to 100,000 cfs along the Sierran rivers. These flows moved huge amounts of material and probably contributed substantially to the cutting of the canyons. The put-in at Chili Bar is on a low river terrace which is flooded frequently during the spring melt runoff.

The bedrock at Chili Bar is black, platy slate. The platy nature is called foliation, which is caused by metamorphism (squeezing of rock under high temperature and pressure). The squeezing causes the rock, which was originally a mud and volcanic deposit on the ocean floor, to be tilted up on end and grows parallel mica (flat) minerals. These parallel minerals allow the rock to split along parallel planes, forming slate. Marina fossils from the Jurassic Period about 150 million years ago can be found in the slate.

Mile 0.4 The Greenhorn or Coloma-Lotus Ranch Ditch

On the left bank of the river, some twenty feet above the water, lies the beginning of the Greenhorn or Coloma-Lotus Ranch Ditch. Built between 1850 and 1854, the system was designed to deliver water to downstream mining operations at the same time it provided power to waterwheels along the way. The wheels drove pumps to empty the river of whatever flow had bypassed the dam.

The system took the water the length of its 13 miles with less than a 200 foot drop from its starting point at Chili Bar to its terminus just below Lotus. Plagued by constant repairs and money problems, the owners gave over the maintenance and accounting of the ditch to the El Dorado Irrigation District in 1960.

The ditch was damaged so heavily in the 1997 flood that the segment from Chili Bar to Coloma was abandoned and large pumps were placed at the upper end of American River Resort in the Coloma Valley to pump water up to the canal.

Mile 0.5 Meatgrinder Scouting Beach

BLM public land from here to the end of the Triple Threat Rapids. This beach on river right is a good opportunity to look at the rocks and hike down the old carriage road to scout Meatgrinder Rapid.

The light-colored granite causes the resistant bedrock ribs of the rapid. The granite was originally molten and oozed its way up through the volcanic rocks while they were still deep underground. The granite cooled slowly and formed large crystals of quartz (gray) and feldspar (white). Kelsey Creek is a beautiful spot 0.1 of a mile downstream.

Mile 0.6 Meatgrinder (Class III+)

The canyon curves right as you enter a long, quarter-mile, rough rock garden with big waves and a hidden boulder at the bottom. Enter right of center, move left to avoid rocks on the right. Mid-rapid move right to avoid the partially submerged wrap rocks mid-channel and finally avoid Rhino Rock on the right at the end of the rapid.

Mile 0.8 Tramway Remains

Visible at the top of the left ridge are the remains of the tramway run by the Eureka Slate Quarry over 100 years ago. The Quarry used towers and cables to support 500 pound slabs of slate as they were pulleyed high over the gorge.

Tower No. 15 Eureka Slate Company. One of the more ambitious engineering schemes hatched in the South Fork canyon around the turn of the century, the tram hauled 500 lb. slabs of slate. Power to the whole operation came from a Pelton wheel in Slatington (Kelsey) more than 2 miles away. Although the slate miners were never too successful with their scheme, the El Dorado Lumber Company ran a similar operation for 30 years, hauling more than 25 billion board feet of milled lumber from Georgetown Divide.

The power for the tram was provided by water taken out of the Loon Lake Reservoir and ditched to the town of Kelsey, then known as Slatington, some 40 miles away. The system was abandoned in 1919 and shortly thereafter most of the towers were destroyed by fire. The steel cables, though, or at least parts of them, can still be found on the southern hillside.

Mile 1.0 Quartz Mines

The Chapparel, the Champion and the Excelsior were quartz mines that were located a short distance below Chili Bar. They were worked quite extensively, employing a ten-stamp mill run by water power.

Mile 1.3 Racehorse Bend Rapid (Class II+)

A sharp left bend pushes boats through waves and rocks toward the right slate wall.

Mile 1.5 Maya (Class II-III)

Easier at low water, but at high flows over 3,500 cfs big, dangerous holes appear in the channel. Possible to sneak far right. The ledges are a good kayak play spot at normal summer flows.

Mile 1.7 Long Point

The river makes an abrupt turn to the north, around Long Point. On the right, across from Live Oak Bar, are some beautiful exposures of slate, sandstone, and siltstone.

A close look at the layering in the sandstone reveals its marine origin; the grains of sand in the bottom layers are biggest, those at the top are smaller and lighter. These layers are typical of turbidites, layers which form from underwater dense clods of sediment swept down the sides of marine volcanoes into deep marine basins. These currents can move at 60 miles per hour. The change in grain size in the layers occurs when the current slows down to deposit the sediment cloud in a layer. The larger, heavier grains settle out first and the smaller, light grains (silt and clay) follow. The river cuts through similar bedrock for the next 3 miles.

Mile 1.8 Rock Garden (Class II)

Enter right and work through a maze of rocks.

Mile 2.0 African Queen (Class II+)

Several willow covered islands usually run on river right and then returning left to main channel, ending in a mid-river ledge drop. There is a BLM beach on the left under pine trees after the rapid.

Kayaker plunges through First Threat. The trough and wave of this rapid is one of the finest kayak surfing spots on the river.

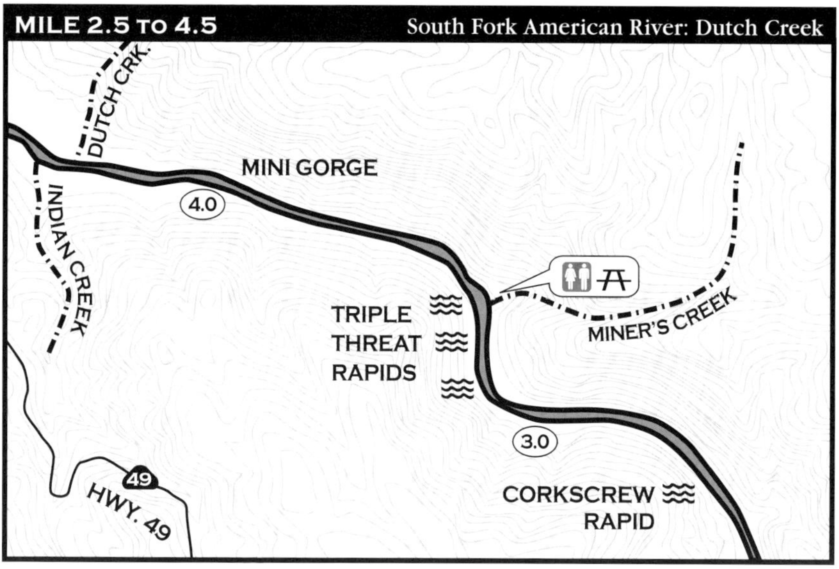

Mile 3.1 Miner's Creek and Triple Threat Rapid (Class III)

A series of big, fun drops begins here. The river enters a rock garden then turns right into the First Threat, which has a popular kayak play hole that can flip a raft. The second threat can be a swimmer's rapid ending in a large eddy on the right. A popular lunch spot with composting toilet is on the right at Miner's Creek on BLM land. Enter the Third Threat mid-channel to avoid the shallow rock bar on right.

Mile 4.0 Mini Gorge/360° (Class II+)

The river speeds up into a fun wave train where the swift current helps guides spin 360° turns.

The mini-gorge slate bedrock gives way here to a body of rock known as the Coloma Granite. This mass of rock originally intruded into the slate more than 5 miles beneath the surface of the earth, where temperatures are high enough to turn granite into a semi-fluid. These 5 miles of material eventually eroded away and undoubtedly helped create the rich bottomland of the San Joaquin River/Sacramento River Delta.

The country opens up here into low-rolling hills, a marked contrast to the steep-walled canyon upstream, due to the composition of the bedrock. The granite here is mostly quartz- free and, in comparison to the slate, sandstone, and volcanic rocks upstream, weathers fairly easily. The hills are spotted with ex-

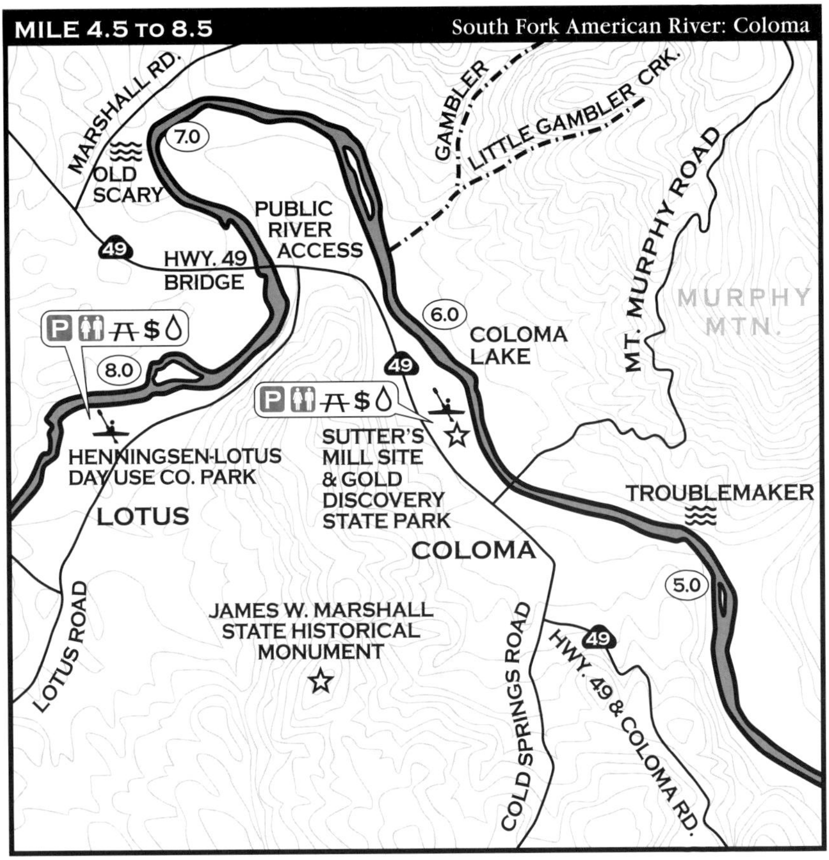

posed granite outcroppings, due to the fact that granite chemically decomposes when in contact with moist earth, but is much more resistant to pure rainwater.

Mile 4.2 Clement's Gardens

Louis Clement and his wife built the terraces back from the bank in the 1850s. Their flower gardens were reputed to be lush producers of imported roses and shrubbery where elegant dinners were served by Chinese lantern light. Today, it is still possible to identify some of their imported shrubs now intermixed with the native vegetation.

The Clements were the first winemakers in the Coloma area. They used mulberries and other fruits which they cultivated.

Mile 4.4 Indian Creek

The first gold quartz mine in the state was located just above Indian Creek, seen entering on the left. In 1851 the stamp mill there was a primitive apparatus using wooden shafts fixed with iron "shoes." It was eventually improved to a 12-stamp operation which finally went out of business in 1858. At Indian Creek a sawmill was also in operation during the earliest days of the Gold Rush.

Private homes and campgrounds begin to appear here. El Dorado County asks boaters to observe a "quiet zone" from here to mile 11.5.

Mile 4.5 Pleasant Flat

Some of the richest claims on the river were found on the south bank here in 1852. In 1860, the bar was hydraulically mined. Today the giant mounds of tailings are the only evidence remaining.

Mile 5.0 Tooth Rock or Raft-Eater (Class III)

After leaving a large pool, the channel on the right side of the island leads to a sharp wrap-rock to avoid.

Mile 5.1 Dutch Creek

Dutch Creek enters on the right. "Dutch", a Forty-niner's term for any Northern European, was probably applied to a German miner called "Dutch John" who explored and mined the ravine in 1848. The confluence was the site of an 1853 sawmill, operated by the Agnews family.

An 1850 Long Tom Operation. One of the earliest photographs to show Chinese laborers, this daguerreotype was taken in the Pleasant Flat area and has become a "classic" Gold Rush photo.

Troublemaker at very low water (unraftable fish flows of less than 300 cfs). At normal rafting flows, water pours over the rocks, here exposed, to form the famous Troublemaker Hole.

Troublemaker once again earns its reputation.

Mile 5.2 Troublemaker Rapid (Class III+)

The biggest rapid so far, a river-wide ledge strewn with boulders, is almost always run on the far left. Scout when you see the campground on the left. Avoid walking through private campsites. At flows above 3,000 cfs Troublemaker can easily flip rafts.

The river goes under a powerline, around the right side of a low rock island before dropping into the S-turn along the left, which has diagonal waves and holes. Finish either side of Gunsight Rock which blocks the middle of the exit. **WARNING:** Swimmers must avoid the mid-stream rocks in the fast current at the end of the rapid due to potential foot entrapment hazard.

Mile 5.3 Mt. Murphy

The steeply-sloped peak visible on the right is Mt. Murphy, named for Patrick O'Brien Murphy, an Irishman whose fear of Indians led him to construct a fortress on the top of the mountain in the 1850s. When it finally became clear that the Maidu weren't going to storm the hill, Murphy began using the cannon he hauled up to signal the approach of the Sacramento stagecoach. It was removed and mounted in front of the Coloma Community Grange Hall.

Mile 5.6 Coloma Bridge & Grange Hall

The one-lane crossing structure installed by the County in 1917 at Coloma, is the tenth bridge that has spanned the site. Originally a shallow fording spot, and then for a short time a ferry, the first bridge was completed in 1850 by Ed Raun who reportedly collected up to $250 per day in tolls.

Just below the bridge on the left stands the Coloma Community Grange Hall. The property was originally donated to the townspeople by James H. Gallagher in 1930. During the Great Depression, the money was raised within the little community and the structure was built over a two month period.

Mile 5.7 Sutter's Mill & Coloma

A replica of Sutter's Mill erected by the State stands on the left bank. The actual location of the original sawmill is about one quarter mile downstream and is marked by a stone monument.

John A. Sutter was a Swiss immigrant who arrived in California in 1839 with ambitious plans. Looking around, he saw in the little bayside village of Yerba Buena plenty of opportunity for a man with energy and vision. So thinking, he set about finding ways to provide some of the necessities of growth for the new American territory.

In 1847, Sutter was involved in the construction of a flour mill at Natomo, but a shortage of lumber had stalled the project. It was just at this fortuitous juncture that James Marshall arrived, with his offer to build a sawmill in the mountains. A partnership was soon formed, the Coloma site located, and by the end of that year prospects for success must have looked excellent.

While the new discovery meant riches for many, Sutter comments on his fate in 1857: *"What a great misfortune was this sudden gold discovery for me! All my great plans were destroyed. Had I succeeded with my mills and manufactories for a few years before the gold was discovered, I should have been the richest citizen on the Pacific shore; but it had to be different. Instead of being rich, I am ruined."*

He himself made a brief effort at mining but "the expedition proved to be a heavy loss." Following this experience, he decided to have no more to do with this gold affair.

The town of Coloma sits by the South Fork in a broad, flat valley. The name, whose meaning is a matter of dispute, is of Maidu origin. There are indications that it once applied to a village in the area. Coloma is, of course, the site of Marshall's gold discovery, and what remains of the historic town is now a state park.

In Marshall's later years he became something of a public, even controversial figure. He was called upon a number of times to authenticate his claim as the original "discoverer", and on one occasion set down his version of the events in this way:

"Being a millwright by trade, as there was a ready cash sale for lumber, I concluded to seek a location in the mountains and erect a mill, to supply the valley with lumber. Some time in April, 1847, I visited New Helvetia, commonly known as the "Fort", where I made my resolution known to John A. Sutter,

Sutter's Mill, 1851. Marshall's discovery of gold was on January 19, 1848.

James Wilson Marshall

James Marshall was born in Hunterton County, New Jersey in 1810. As a boy he received a practical education, learning from his father the trade of wheelwright and carpenter. The journey that would eventually land him in California started in 1840 when he decided to seek fame and fortune in the far west. Initially, he settled down near Fort Leavenworth, Kansas, on the Platte Purchase, where he began to homestead a few acres. But over a period of several years his health worsened and, on the advice of a physician, he abandoned his home and joined an emigrant party bound for Oregon. That winter, in the year of 1844, Marshall spent at Fort Hall, on the Snake River. The following year he made his way to Oregon and thence California where July 1845 found him at Sutter's Fort.

Marshall's industry and skills soon enabled him to gather together the beginnings of another homestead some livestock, tools, and acreage in Butte Country. But the Bear Flag Revolution broke out in 1846 and Marshall joined up with Fremont's California Battalion. That year he was a member of the rescue party that marched to Kearny's relief after the battle of San Pasqual.

In 1847 Marshall mustered out of the service in San Diego and made his way by foot back to Sutter's Fort where he discovered that his meager holdings had vanished in the revolution's turmoil. Consequently, Sutter's offer of partnership in a mill-building enterprise found in him a ready listener.

Marshall's later years were filled with frustration; his claims to the original gold discovery site were swept aside; his government pension was revoked; his health problems re-surfaced. He became something of a misanthropic recluse, working as a gardener in the Coloma valley area, until his death in 1880.

Sen., and requested of him an Indian boy, to act as an interpreter to the mountain Indians in the vicinity of the American River–or Rio de los Americanos, as it was then called.

On the 16th of May, having completed my work for Capt. Sutter, I started, with an Indian boy, Treador, and W. A. Graves. On the 18th of May we entered the valley of Culluma; and on the 20th, Gingery joined our company. We then traveled up the stream now called Weber Creek, the Indian name for which is Pul-pul-Full, to the head of the creek; thence higher in the mountains until we arrived at the South Fork of the American River, where it divides into two branches of about equal size, from whence we returned by Sly Park and Pleasant Valley to the Fort."

Johann August Sutter

Johann Sutter was born in Kandern, Baden in February of 1803. The facts regarding his ancestry and early life are obscure, at least partially owing to the fact that his own statements are contradictory and frequently misleading. Amidst the confusion, it seems certain that in 1826 he married Anna Dubeld by whom he had three sons and a daughter, and, after a number of "escapades", took his abrupt leave from Berne in the spring of 1834, eventually arriving in St. Louis. The following three or four years were spent drifting about the West, joining an emigrant party to Oregon and sailing to Honolulu, Sitka, and finally arriving in San Francisco in 1839. Shortly thereafter Sutter received a grant to begin his colony "New Helvetia" in the Sacramento Valley.

Sutter's energy and ambition were soon rewarded by the early success of his new Californian estate. Land was cleared, irrigating ditches were dug, grain was sown, orchards and vineyards were planted and a fortified 'post" was soon erected. Sutter was a delegate to the convention which drafted the first state constitution, and was a candidate for the governorship in the state's first election.

The discovery of gold, however, began a decline in Sutter's fortunes. He left his Sacramento fort for Hocks Farm in Yuba County where he began a long, and ultimately unsuccessful, campaign to receive compensation for the loss of his land grants. He died in 1881 in Lancaster County, Pennsylvania, frustrated in his dealings with the government but remembered by history for his important, but unwilling role in the California Gold Rush.

Marshall goes on to describe the months spent constructing the mill and the difficulties they had provisioning it. The moment of discovery is put in these words:

"... we were in the habit at night of turning the water through the tail race we had dug for the purpose of widening and deepening the race. I used to go down in the morning to see what had been done by the water through the night; and about half past seven o'clock on or about the 19th of January - I am not quite certain to a day, but it was between the 18th and the 20th of that month - 1848, I went down as usual, and after shutting off the water from the race I stepped into it, near the lower end, and there, upon the rock, about six inches beneath the surface of the water, I discovered the gold. I was entirely alone at the time.

I picked up one or two pieces and examined them attentively; and having some general knowledge of minerals, I could not call to mind more than two which in any way resembled this sulphuret of iron, very bright and brittle; and gold, bright, yet malleable; I then tried it between two rocks, and found that it could be beaten into a different shape, but not broken. I then collected four or five pieces and went up to Mr. Scott (who was working at the carpenter's bench making the mill wheel) with the pieces and said, "I have found it."

"What is it?", inquired Scott.

"Gold", I answered.

"Oh! No", returned Scott, "that can't be."

I replied positively, "I know it to be nothing else."

Within a year of this portentous event, the lonely sawmill site became home to: bakeries, blacksmith shops, livery stables, meat markets, restaurants, bath houses, banks, hardware stores, law offices, a court house, a theatre, newspaper office, an art gallery, gunsmith's, post office, fire house, 13 hotels, 2 breweries, and a growing number of gambling halls, saloons, and bordellos.

One consequence of being the first place invaded by the Forty-Niners was becoming evident by the late 1850s when Coloma gained the less noteworthy distinction of being one of the first abandoned by them. By 1883 the population had dwindled from a high of 10,000 transients to a more stable 2000, nearly all of them settlers.

Historic painting of Coloma Valley by John Little.

Dredging has turned the river out of its old bed many times (note extensive tailings). The arrow indicates the original mill site.

Quite apart from its mineral wealth, the Coloma Valley was blessed with the more lasting qualities of fine soil and a long growing season, and it was these that the new Colomans meant to exploit.

James Henry Gallagher, born in 1865 on a ranch near Dutch Creek, began an orchard on his homestead at the base of Mt. Murphy in 1904. He married Louisa Veerkamp, daughter of a well-known pioneer family, and had three sons, Melvin, Raymond, and Frank.

Frank and Raymond share their remembrances of Coloma from 1905 to 1930: "... *We spent a lot of our time caring for the orchards and vineyards. There was the spraying and pruning, all the irrigating in the summer ... and then the picking and loading. We grew pears and all kinds of plums and sent them by railroad to New York and Boston ... the Freestone peaches went to San Francisco, and the lady apples, they used to be quite popular. Folks would use them as Christmas decorations. We had to polish each one before we packed them in shelf paper.*

When our dad went to school in Coloma, there were over a hundred kids. There were six when I went. Every day when we came home from school, we used to have to hike all over Mount Murphy to get the cows and bring them down to milk ...

We had lots of work to do. But we used to take Sunday afternoon off and go down to the swimming hole and sand bar ..."

In 1970 the State acquired a large portion of the Gallagher property for the Marshall Gold Discovery Site Park and removed the 60 year old buildings and orchards.

Mile 5.9 Coloma Lake Marshall Gold Discovery Park, *river access*

There is river access at the downstream end of the Marshall Gold Discovery Park at North Beach for a fee. There are picnic tables, potable water, BBQs, public toilets and fee parking.

John Nicholson, one of the discoverers of the Last Chance Mine, shared in the $90,000 worth of gold that was first found here in 1862. The story goes that three miners were ready to give up on the place when a Sacramento firm staked them with supplies. They resumed mining, struck it rich, and called the claim, appropriately enough, "Last Chance".

Mile 6.1 Tunnel Bend

The river begins a turn to the left here and then cuts back on itself in an oxbow about 1 and ½ miles long. To the miners looking for ways to divert the water out of its bed the turn suggested an ambitious plan; and, in July, 1850, a group of them banded together to form the South Fork Tunnel Company, headed by John T. Little. One hundred men labored for almost a year cutting a water level shaft–6 feet wide, 7 feet high–through the granite hill below Coloma.

When the men were finally able to turn the river out of its bed, the diggings turned out to be an expensive disappointment and a flood soon caused the South Fork Tunnel Co. to close up operations.

Dredging

The Depression era brought a resurgence of interest in placer gold mining. Wages and material costs were down, new extraction technology existed, and people were out of work. The three factors combined to create a mini-rush back to the Mother Lode for a look at what the 49ers had left.

One of this new breed of miners formed a dredging operation that worked up and down the river from Coloma to Lotus. The dredge was described as a "Doodlebug Line Bucket Dredge", a barge with a generator powered sluice box that was floated within a man-made reservoir scooped out of the river bottom and attached by cable to the banks.

Another type of dredge, the dragline-operated bucket dredge, collected and deposited gravel loads into a hopper that sorted out the gold. The entire operation was moved from time to time as the gravel played out.

The Forty-niners pick and shovel was replaced in one generation by massive "doodle-bug" dredges.

For six years one company, known as the General Land and Mining Co., worked this stretch of river. Whether they ever struck it rich or not is a matter for speculation. Landowners of the period report that the dredgers would never let on how they were doing.

Mile 6.4 and 6.5 Little Gambler and Gambler Creeks

The extent to which this section of the river was originally inhabited by the Forty-niners is evident in the profusion of names given to nearly every creek and gulch.

Mile 7.0 Old Scary (Class II)

Once this was the most difficult rapid on the Coloma-Lotus run, but was rearranged by high water in 1982. Usually run in the deeper channel, right of the island, but avoid rocks far right at end.

Originally the river's course was more direct, gradually bending over a quarter of a mile, but the Forty-niners diverted it into an artificial channel where the river still flows today.

Mile 7.4 Highway 49 Bridge

Undeveloped river access under bridge.

Mile 7.7 Cemetery

A Chinese burial ground once existed on the hill above the road. The graves were emptied and the remains taken back to China when the last of the Asian miners left for their homeland.

Mile 7.8 Sawmill Site

On the left is the former site of the Stearns and Chapman Co. sawmill, next to Sutter's, is the oldest in the area. The demand for lumber outstripped production in the early 1850s.

Mile 7.9 Old Lotus Bridge Site

Portions of cement piers and steel bar are the only evidence of the old Lotus Bridge that was first erected in 1850. From 1881 to 1917 it was the only wagon crossing between Salmon Falls and Placerville. In the mid-1960s Highway 49 was realigned and the old Lotus Bridge was demolished by Caltrans.

Mile 8.0 Henningsen-Lotus Park, *River Access*

This 22 acre gravel quarry was donated to El Dorado County for conversion to a multi-purpose county park. It is a popular fee river access beach with toilets and grass picnic area. Overnight parking is not allowed.

Mile 8.2 Lotus

The town of Lotus sits back from the left bank. "Marshall" was the name originally given to the mining camp that sprang up here in 1850. Later that was changed to "Uniontown" to honor California's admission as the 31st state, but when the townspeople applied for a Post Office in 1881, it was discovered that the name was already taken. George E. Gallaner, the first postmaster, suggested "Lotus" because it seemed to him the inhabitants of the town were about as easy-going as Homer's fabled "lotus-eaters".

Today's gold is a recreational rush when the water comes up at Beaver Point.

The Chinese in the Gold Fields

Unquestionably the most distinctive of the foreign groups to work the California gold fields were the Chinese. Understanding how and why they arrived in such number (20, 000 through San Francisco in 1852) is helped by a little familiarity with conditions in China at the time.

In 1850, China was a vast collection of separately governed districts. The political picture was an ever shifting pattern of alliances made and broken between districts, resulting in a great deal of economic hardship for a large percentage of the population. In addition, a revolutionary movement was gathering strength against the Manchu dynasty, who for 200 years had ruled over the political patchwork of China.

Against this background of political turmoil and economic hardship, the news of gold and good wages in America excited a great deal of interest. Particularly in the Pearl River Delta, the area around Canton where sea voyages were nothing extraordinary. There were many who looked upon a sojourn to California as an adventure and a good opportunity to better their status at home.

Untitled. 1875. Unknown artist. Gelatin silver print. Collection of Oakland Museum of California. Gift of the estate of Anne Protopopoff.

Such an attitude reflects the major difference between the Chinese and many of the other ethnic groups that came to make their fortunes. The Chinese never really left home; they took it with them. They organized dozens of little "Chinatowns" throughout the Motherlode where they kept their language, appearance and customs intact. Their intention was not to settle down, but rather to work hard, gather up some savings, and finally to return home to family and motherland. And for the vast majority of them, that's exactly what happened.

Note: One mile south of Coloma on Cold Springs Road is the Wakamatsu Tea and Silk Farm Colony, founded by Japanese emigrants in 1869, now listed in the National Register of Historical Sites.

Lotus went through the same precipitous rise and fall as did Coloma, from a peak of 2,000 transients in 1850 to a steady 20 families or so by 1900. The Bassi, Wagner and Herzig families, all of whom grew up by the little riverside village, share their memories in this excerpt: *"Everyone raised their own vegetables and all their fruit. We just bought our staples, like flour and sugar, at the stores. We made our own cheese and butter, salami, sauerkraut and wine ...we packed meat in lard and smoked all our ham and bacon in the smokehouse. We had beef cattle and milk cows. We hunted for deer, rabbit, squirrels, and sometimes we went fishing for suckers and pike at old Chesapeake.*

Mostly we went to school and worked when we got home. The chores were lined up and that's all there was to do. In the summer, we put bells on all the cows and herded them up to our property in the Sierra. There were all kinds of meadows for the animals to graze. And when we left in the fall, we stocked food in the cabins and left the places open, just in case hunters or travellers got caught in a storm.

Entertainment? Well, we played baseball at the ballfield in Lotus. We had picnics on Mother's Day, May Day and the Fourth of July. Everybody in town who wanted to come was invited. There weren't any phones or telegraphs then. We went to dances with our parents at Schultz's (Sierra Nevada House II), and danced the fox trot and waltz to the orchestra music."

Mile 8.5 Lotus Ledge

Was a popular kayak surfing hole, until it was washed out by high water in 1997.

Mile 9.0 Camp Lotus

William H. Valentine first homesteaded the property now known as Camp Lotus in December 1868, when President Andrew Johnson was in office. Valentine planted his 160 acre piece in grapes, pears and peaches. He sold a portion of it to Albert Herzig in 1907.

In 1939, the General Land and Mining Co. contracted with Albert for mineral rights to his riverbank. They proceeded to dredge the area for two years, leaving thirty foot piles of rock on Herzig's riverbank.

The El Dorado County Department of Roads removed most of the tailings in 1961 and levelled the remainder into a private access road. "That's when our troubles started," Herzig remembers, "with a good road down to a nice picnic spot, you couldn't keep the public out."

Herbert and Marcella Herzig, who had inherited the 55 acre

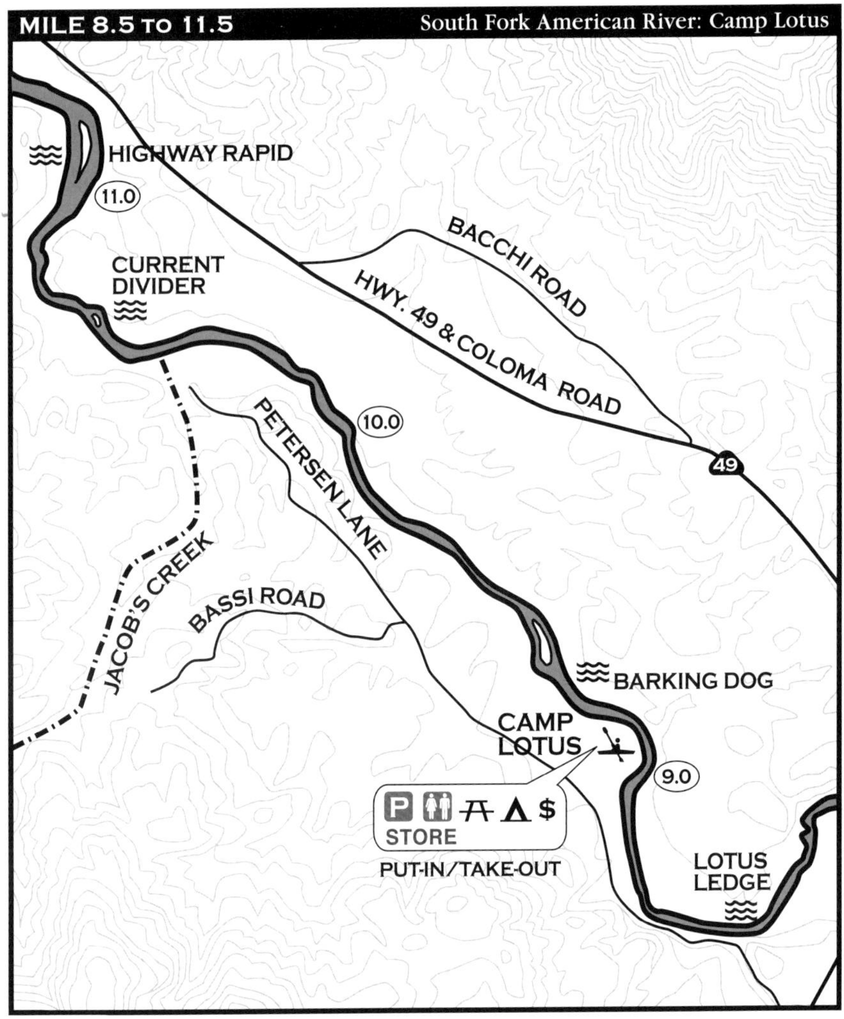

ranch, applied for the Riverview Park Campground permit in the late 1960s. The property was purchased by the Bill & Robin Center family in 1976 to become present-day Camp Lotus.

Camp Lotus has long been a favorite meeting place for river runners on the South Fork and a popular overnight spot for two-day trips. Shaded campsites, store, hot showers, toilets. Reserve in advance 530-622-8672.

Mile 9.2 Barking Dog Rapid (Class II+)

The river bends right into a very popular kayak play hole. Please respect the private land ownership on both sides of the river by not trespassing.

Mile 9.4 – 11.0 Bacchi Land

The riverfront acreage here is owned by the Bacchi family, one of the largest landholders in the valley. The ranch was started by William Bacchi, a Swiss immigrant who came with the original wave of gold seekers in 1849, but like many of the Forty-niners, he soon turned to other pursuits, less colorful, but a bit more reliable than gold panning.

William Bacchi

By 1861 Bacchi had winter pasture for a herd of dairy cattle in the South Fork valley and had homesteaded summer range in the Sierra. A son, Henry, was born to him in 1879, and the younger Bacchi carried on the family business. Grandson Francis recalls what early ranching was like along the South Fork: *"We cleared thousands and thousands of acres of land. We girdled a lot of trees. We used a pole ax to chop all the bark off the base of the tree. When the trees died a year later, we cut them all down, and the roots rotted. We ran over five hundred goats in there to eat back any suckers. This way we made winter pasture for our cows, but we never planted any grass. We just got the shade off the ground and let the sun hit it and nature took over. The filaree, burr clover, and soft chess stem grass grew tall..."*

In 1952 the Bacchi ranch totalled some 13,000 acres between Salmon Falls and the Sierra. Since then, however, government projects at Folsom and Stumpy Meadows have reduced their holdings. Now in the fifth generation, Bacchis continue raising cattle on lands acquired by their forefathers. Bacchi lands along the river are being used by rafting companies for overnight camps and lunch stops.

Mile 9.7 – 9.9 BLM Public Land

BLM public land and Dave Moore Nature Area on right.

Mile 10.0 Wagner Ranch

The Jessie Franklin Wagner Ranch used to front the river on the left here. Its nineteen hundred acres included nearly a mile of riverfront and was partially bought with the profits of a quartz mine that Frank and John Wagner first discovered in 1885.

Frank's son George remembers the early days: *"It was a four-foot wide ledge of quartz that came out of the ground. There was a steam-powered engine to work the machinery and they just followed this ledge into the hillside. They only had candles for lights, but they found $10,000 worth of gold in six months!*

Bacchi ranch is the backdrop to Turtle Pond, a lazy stretch of river.

They never worked the mine on a steady basis, though. Then in 1913, my father took a notion to go back into it. He sunk another shaft 80 feet deep with an 80 foot horizontal drift off it. It was a lot of work to hoist all that rock out of the shaft using a gas engine for power. By golly, though, within six months of starting to mine in 1913, my dad and uncle struck it rich! They made over $10,000! I remember one brick that weighed thirteen pounds. That was a lot of money back then."

Mile 10.6 Current Divider (Class II+)

A rocky island that is usually run to the right returning to center at the end.

Mile 11.2 Highway Rapid (Class II+)

A long rock garden usually entered left center. Avoid the many rocks in the channel, exit on the tongue to the right at the bottom.

Mile 11.4 Swimmers Rapid (Class II)

Popular swimmers rapid wave train that ends in a large eddy.

Mile 11.5 Greenwood Creek, *river access*

The BLM provides parking for free river access on river right, off Hwy. 49, primarily suitable for kayaks and small boats as there is about a quarter of a mile long trail between the parking lot and the river. BLM public lands on right until mile 13.4.

Mile 11.9 Turtle Pond

A shallow area here was once called Hawk's Ford. Western Pond Turtles warm themselves on logs along the shoreline.

Mile 12.0 Cable Crossing Rapid (Class II)

Wave train at the end of Turtle Pond. Cable and car are now gone.

Mile 12.3 The Melange

The river enters a new geologic zone called the "Sierra Foothills Melange." "Melange" means, literally, "a mixture". Rocks with lots of faults are typical of melange, which is thought to originate from large-scale faulting of the ocean floor under the continental margin.

The open country gives way to more hilly topography as the river passes Clark Mountain (on left). On close inspection, the rocks in the small rapid here are not granite. Each outcrop

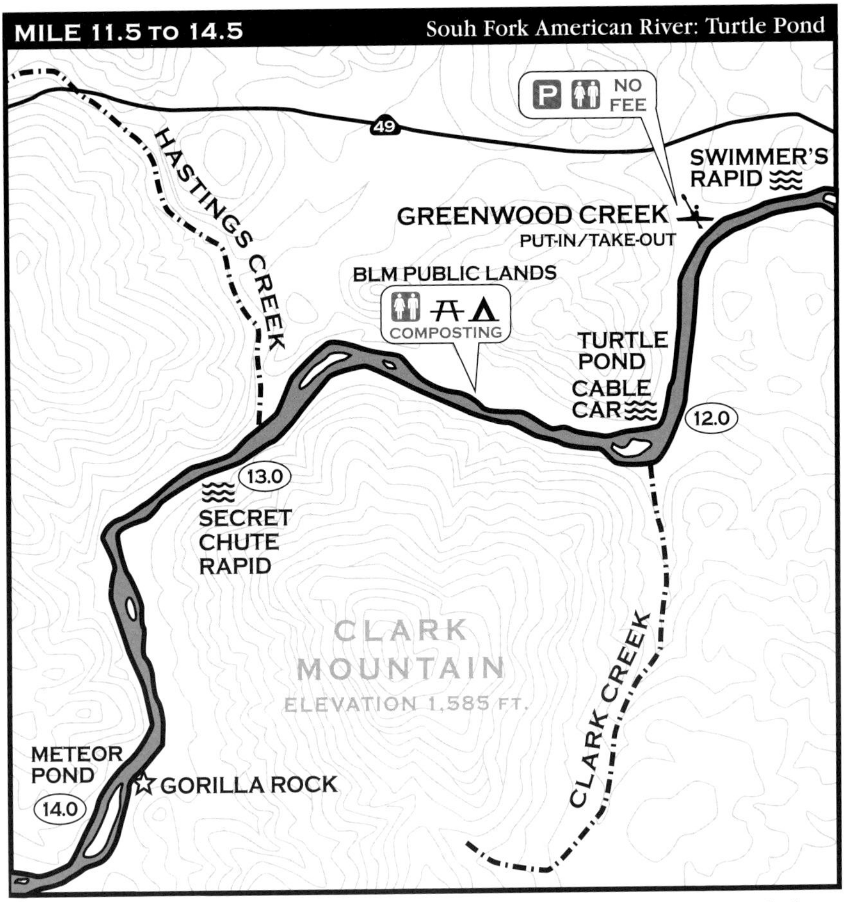

is a different type of rock: smooth white fine-grained chert, dark green greenstone and dark speckled gabbro. This is the upstream edge of a large slab of ocean basement rocks. Downstream, these rocks display pillow structure, typical of lava formed on the ocean floor. Clark Mountain and the ridge directly downstream are all one intact slab of ocean floor rocks. These rocks have been metamorphosed under heat and pressure. They have also been highly faulted and sheared on a small and large scale. The downstream boundary of this slab is a fault with serpentinite.

Mile 12.2-12.6 Campsites and Toilets

Popular large BLM beach on river right with multiple campsites/picnic areas and a composting toilet. Access can be made by foot as well from Greenwood Creek and Magnolia Ranch parking areas.

Mile 12.8 Hastings Creek

The flat on the right was formerly known as Dutch Bar. BLM public lands here.

Mile 12.9

One F. C. Nigley arrived at the South Fork placer diggings in August, 1849, and, after a variety of experiences, joined together with a group of other miners to dam and divert the river at this point. Mr. Nigley, a native of Pittsburgh, Pennsylvania, kept a remarkable journal of his days in California, from which the following section is excerpted:

August 9, 1849
This town is now called Coloma and is the County Seat of El Dorado County ... found here an immense no. of miners, among them two Polish Mssrs. who got here yesterday. Quite a smart town here. Nearly every house is a store. The prices are at present: Flour, 50 cts. per 1 lb., Bacon 1 dollar and all other things in proportion. Boarding $28 per week.

August 10
Dug and washed all day and only got 2(c) dollars worth. Not enough to board one.

August 11
Today two others with myself bought a washer or rocker. Paid 4 oz. for it and went to washing out gold with it. Got about $16 worth. It costs at least 2 (c) per day to buy your provision and cook it yourself and sleep under the trees.

August 12
Worked out a little better than yesterday, not much. August 14 today got $8 worth each. On last Sunday 11th wrote to my wife.

August 15
Worked hard and only got about $1 worth each and became a good deal discouraged.

August 16
Today got $22 of dust for 3.

September 15
Prospected down the River and found a place to dam the river 7 miles down that I think is far better than the other one up the river, but on discussing the matter over, came to the conclusion, that it was too late in the fall to dam the river this year, so wrote

out and posted notices of our claim to this portion of the river and decided to look for a place in the Dry Diggins, where we could work during the winter and then put in our dam when the river was low enough in the summer.

July 1st, 1850

Left the others working our claim and took Patterson and went to work in another claim up to the 16th. Done very well-averaged $33 per day. But the river has fallen low enough, so that we should commence our dam. We cleaned our claim. Put what property we did not take down with us into the cabin. Went seven miles to Coloma and down the South Fork 7 miles to our bar and we named it Butter Bar. Other companies were trying to jump our damming claim so often that we had to send two men to maintain possession, and it cost us considerable. The name of the Co. going into the dam, F. G. Wegely, I. 0. Patterson, P. Bergan, J. Beiber, M. Herson, S. S. Beatty, Wm. J. Stewart, M. Mechling, John Chamberlain, Frank Gerbode, Thos. L. Tadbrook. I had bought the interest of the 12th man, Greib, out, so that I had two shares, hiring a man to work for me.

August 1st

Spent all the last part of July working on the dam or rather the race for the dam and during all the month of Aug. continued ourselves and hired all the hands that we could get at $6 per day on the race and getting out for the dam on the 10th.

August – September

All the last part of this month we worked at our dam and finished it on the 17th of Sept. 1850. From that day to the 24th had seven good days work in the bed of the river. The first days yield was $364 worth of gold. 2nd day $624. 3rd day, $990. 4th day, $1516. 5th day, $2511. Sixth day $4250. Seventh day $6600. Total takeout of our damming claim was $16,855 and our total expenses were for wages, provision ... and all other was $11, 460, leaving a profit of $5,855. Being 12 shares made per share $448 clear profit and as I had two weeks previously bought out Gerbode and Tadbrook I held 4 shares. All agreed to defer the reputting in of our dam until next summer and that we would go back to the dry diggings for the winter and come back and put the dam in again next summer. But as had promised my wife that I would not stay away more than 2 years concluded to start for Pgh. (Pittsburgh).

Our dam held the longest against the flood but about 2 o'clock the large logs of the dam at Dutch bar which was built on the same place as ours, came down. Stuck ours and took it away. Some very bad language was used about that time.

September 25, 1850
Started for Penn. fully intending to bring my wife back with me to be a putting in the dam again next spring ...

Mile 13.1 Secret Chute (Class II)

Take far left channel into the chute.

Mile 13.8 Old Chesapeake/ Meteor Pond

Forty-niners blasted channels all through this area, turned the river from its course, and washed the riverbed gravel through sluice and rocker box. Known as "Old Chesapeake," the deep holes became the favorite swimming spots of the Jessie Franklin Wagner family at the turn of the century.

Mile 13.9 Gorilla Rock

On river left is a popular jumping rock.

Mile 13.9 Convict Rock

The huge granite outcropping high on the hill just downstream of Gorilla Rock on the left bank was named "Convict Rock" in July 1903 when Lotus storekeeper Chris Ulhenkamp spotted the clothes of 13 Folsom Prison escapees spread all over it.

Catching some air while jumping into Gorilla Pond!

At the time, the National Guard, which had been called out in the hunt for the thirteen, was only a few miles away at the Wagner place. George Wagner, who was only four at the time, remembers: *"Blue uniforms with big white stripes down the side of the pants ... and brass on their caps. They marched up to the house and stacked their guns. You know how they pile their guns, like a teepee. They left one man to guard them, while my mother fixed food for all of them. She sent my sister and I down to the chicken house and told us to get every egg we could find. They ate everything!"*

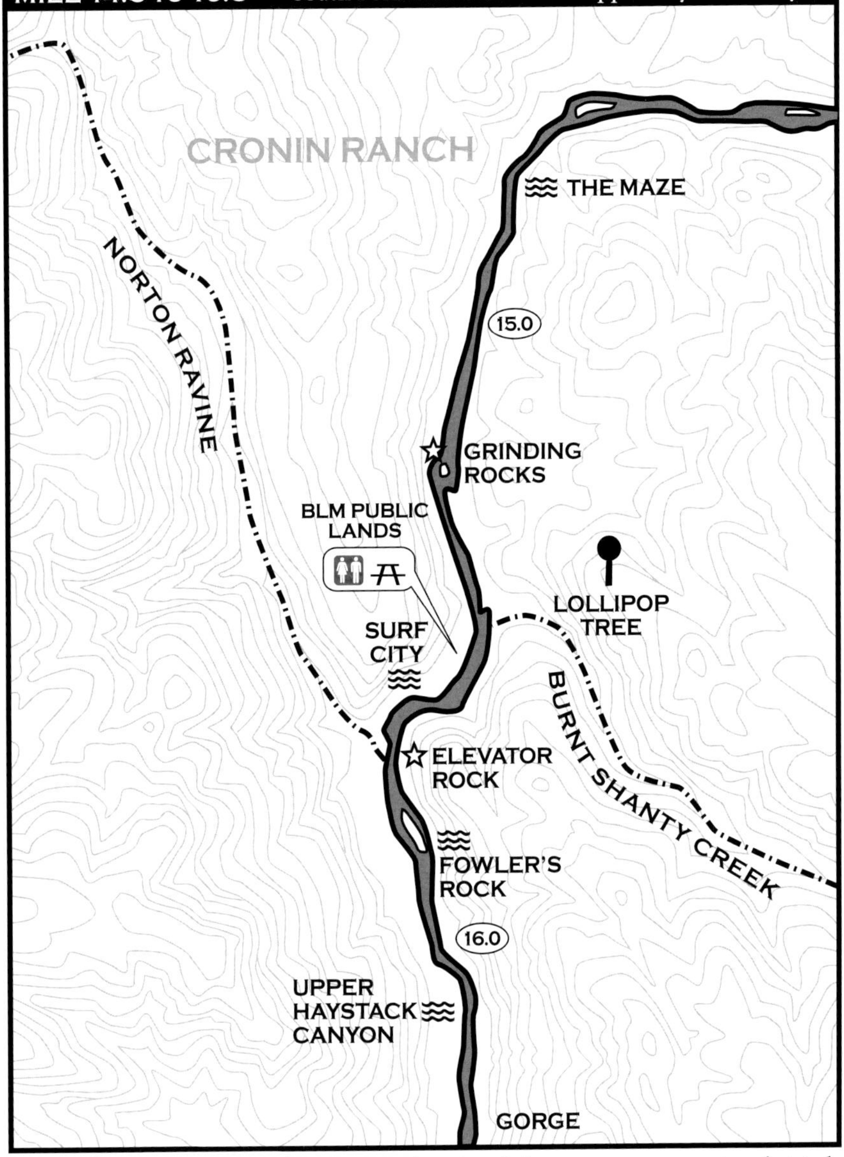

Within six months, six of the men were recaptured, tried, and convicted of killing a guard – a crime for which all six were hung. The gang leader, "Red Shirt" Gordon, together with the other six, was never found.

Mile 14.0 Outcrops of Greenschist

Green outcroppings in the river bed and banks were originally volcanic ash falls mixed with fine-grained sediment which accumulated on the ocean floor. The layers were metamorphosed to greenschist, so named because of the schistose, or platy-banded nature of the rocks. Many small folds are visible in these outcrops. This rock type is consistent downstream to the gorge. The bedrock here does not have any melange features. It is probably another large intact slab of ocean floor because it is surrounded by serpentinite.

Mile 15.0 Lollipop Tree/Grinding Rocks

This signal for the approach of the lower gorge is visible on a downstream hilltop. Indian grinding holes are found atop the large boulder island on the right of the main channel.

Mile 15.3 BLM Cronin Ranch Day Use Area

Beach on river right with picnic tables and toilets.

Mile 15.5 Elevator Rock or Car Crash

A large rock that slopes into the water on river left. Norton Ravine follows a major fault called the Bear Mountains Fault Zone.

Mile 15.8 Fowler's Rock (Class III)

Scout from the gravel bar on river left. The Lollipop tree on the mountain behind Fowler's Rock signals the beginning of the gorge. Fowler's Rock is the first of the big rapids in the gorge. The river curves left around a gravel bar then flows between a cliff on the left and a large house rock on the right. Avoid the ledge hole next to the house rock. The usual run is to the right of Fowler's Rock, the wrap rock in the center. This rapid requires a strong left-to-right move to avoid the rock. "Son of Fowler's" is a second sharp drop just downstream, usually run down a tongue left of the large boulder. At flows over 3,500 cfs some prefer to run to the left of Fowler's Rock. Named after Jeff Fowler, a boatman who once made a memorable, but unscheduled stop here.

Mile 16.0 Upper Haystack Canyon (Class II +)

The river begins to drop into a gorge with steep banks and a narrow channel that creates large standing waves.

The river cuts through the Bear Mountain fault zone and encounters the hardest rock yet: amphibolite and chert. The amphibolite is highly metamorphosed ocean bottom sediment, subjected to intense pressure and temperature.

Mile 16.0 The Gorge and the American River Land and Lumber Company

It was here during the years 1891 to 1899 that the American River Land and Lumber Company used tons of black powder in an effort to clear a channel for timber felled on the Georgetown Divide and floated downstream from a point several miles upstream of Chili Bar.

Their efforts were destined to fail, as one of the early workers commented: "... that river just couldn't be drove." But the ten years and one million dollars they expended in trying makes for a story worth retelling.

The Georgetown Divide is a ridge running westward from Lake Tahoe to the Central Valley, separating the drainage of the South Fork of the American from that of the Middle Fork. Around the turn of the century its outstanding forests began attracting the attention of lumbermen, one of whom called it: "The finest growth of sugar pine of any section of the state; trees growing up to eight and ten-feet diameter being quite common."

Unfortunately, the area is very rugged and at the time was a considerable distance above the nearest railway line. It was, as the journal "Pacific Coast Wood and Iron" put it in 1889, "quite inaccessible."

One man, however, thought he had the key. Horatio Gates Livermore was an immigrant from New England, where lumber companies had been driving timber down rivers for years, and with great success. There was no need to build expensive flumes or spur lines when nature provided a ready-made highway, Livermore felt.

Indian grinding holes are found at the finer river view points and capture the imagination.

An early survey of the river seemed to indicate no insurmountable problems, although a dam would have to be constructed near the town of Folsom to create a holding pond at the end of the run. In 1866 Livermore first began construction of a dam, but it wasn't until more than twenty years later, after he had arranged with the state to use prison labor, that real progress began. Between 1888 and 1893 the convicts put in 520,000 man-days building a dam 89 feet high and 450 feet across the top. It backed water up for a distance of four miles.

In addition, they constructed a granite canal around the dam designed to carry logs to the mill pond and water to an electricity generating plant. The same plant, incidentally, operated continuously from 1895 to 1952.

House rock at Fowler's with the Lollipop tree looming overhead. This unusual view is the slot to the right of house rock, a run used occasionally by kayakers.

Once the dam was well underway, Livermore began forming his timber company, the American River Land and Lumber Co., and set his sights on the Georgetown Divide.

Over the winter of 1891, the first cutting took place. The timber was transported with the help of immense cattle-powered trucks, and a temporary chute was constructed down Slab Creek, a tributary entering the South Fork upstream of Chili Bar.

Once into the water, the logs were "herded" downstream by river "drovers", most of whom came from Canada, "...fine men, all over six feet and tough. They were hard working, hard drinking men.

Ed Morton, one of those so described, talks about his experiences on the very first run: *"When the first boat started on the first log drive, I was in it at one oar, an Indian boy at another and a Swede at the back of the boat with a pike pole. The Swede got his pole caught between some rocks when the boat was right opposite the mouth of the log chute. The crazy Swede couldn't get the pole loose and wouldn't let go. I was pulling for all I was worth on the oar.*

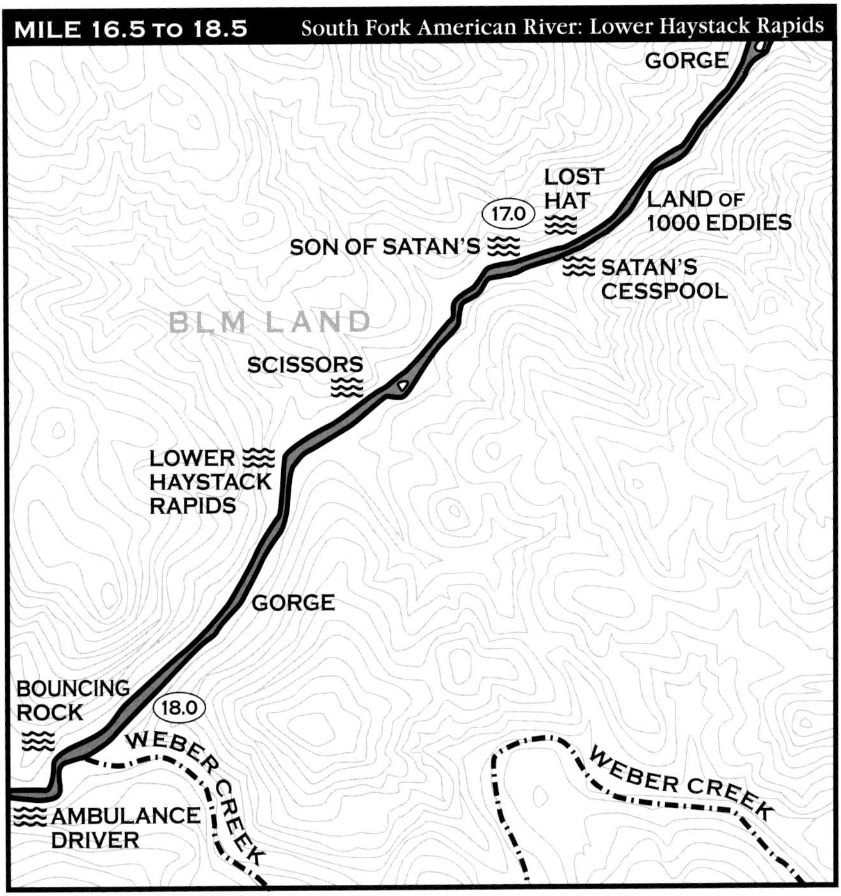

The Indian told me to be careful, that we'd be sunk if I broke an oar. I said, "Well, let me hit that crazy Swede over the head with it, then." About that time the current pulled the pole out of the Swede's hands and the boat went on down and we beached it. Just then a string of logs roared down the chute into the river.

They lost a lot of boats in that rocky river bed. Usually they took them down the narrow places with snub ropes handled by men on the shore. But one Indian from Canada was really handy with a boat. He got to drinking and took the boat down the rapids by the swinging bridge (at the site of the present Old Mosquito Road bridge) at flood stage without hitting a rock. All the time he was singing and shrieking at the top of his voice."

The trickiest section of the river was found at The Gorge and at Salmon Falls; not only did the falls themselves have to be negotiated, but a small diversion dam operated by the Natomas Water and Mining Co. as well.

That spring of 1891, the first year of operation, some 2,000,000 board feet of timber were started, but only 700,000 reached the holding dam. The rest were stranded at Salmon Falls and above. It was hardly an auspicious beginning, and in fact, there was talk of building a railway around the falls and gorge, or possibly a flume, but it remained only talk. Instead, boulders were blasted out of the narrows in an effort to open up the constrictions.

Meanwhile, at the head of the run, twelve miles of 3 foot gauge rail was brought from San Francisco to bring the logs from the interior out to the head of the chute. At the bottom a small "splash dam" was built to enable the men to send a sudden surge of water downstream to "splash" jammed logs over obstructions.

The supervisor, Colonel Cummins, announced enthusiastically in the summer of 1891: *"I am up to my ears in business; in fact, I am buried. There is timber enough to keep us logging for three or four years. This is good news and victory already perches on our Sugar Pine Banner."* Perhaps.

The next season started well enough. Warm rains in April raised the river enough to start the drive, and the Placerville Mountain Democrat reported: *"We get word that the river at Chili Bar is full of timber. The weather, however, has turned a little cooler and the rain ceasing may check the rise of water for some time, but the snow is in the mountains and must come down."*

It did, in fact, finally come down. But over the course of a very cool spring, and very slowly. Once again, most of the logs never made it past Salmon Falls. Those that did were trapped by the new boom built just above the holding dam. Constructed out of solid cement piers and steel cable, it was, in the words of the Sacramento Union, "...sufficient to support any strain that might be put upon it." One shouldn't always believe what one reads in the newspapers, though, and, in December of that year, the boom broke in the midst of a huge storm, sending hundreds of thousands of board feet over the top of the dam.

Whether or not Colonel Cummins ever got the chance to unbury himself is never made clear because shortly after this event, he was "superseded" as Superintendent of the American River Land and Lumber Co.

The Company's owners were not ones to give up easily, however. That summer each of the shareholders was assessed a $15 per share fee and a new, permanent chute was built on the hill above the mouth of Slab Creek at a cost of some $60,000. It stretched steeply down to the river for 2900 feet at a 30 degree incline.

One witness said, *"An engine (steam donkey) at the head of the chute hauls the logs by means of wire rope from the rollways in groups of five to eight, and as they reach the verge of the hill, their speed is considerably accelerated; and after passing 100 feet or so down the chute, they vanish in a cloud of smoke caused by their friction in the chute, a rumbling, whizzing sound following them for several seconds and the final plunge into the river being distinctly heard a distance of a mile back from the canyon."*

Canadian river drovers on the American River – "All over six feet and tough."

The drive of 1893-94 was another disappointment, but the following season was an especially high water year and a near success. Buoyed by this experience, the main mill at Folsom - the first all-electric sawmill in the world - was pushed to completion. Meanwhile, up on the Divide, the cutting continued unabated. After another mediocre floating season, the crews had accumulated 20 million board feet of prime sugar pine at the head of the Slab Creek chute, ready for the trip to Folsom.

The loggers waited anxiously for the winter rains to begin, and when they did, the first of the 20 million was started. The rains continued and the logs stranded from previous years floated free, over the falls and into the boom. The basin was filling fast and it appeared that the long gamble was finally paying off. Meanwhile it continued to rain ... and rain.

On March 25, 1899, the boom broke again, sending more than three million board feet over the dam and downstream–some as far as Rio Vista, more than 50 miles away.

It was the final blow. The American River Land and Lumber Co. was sold to its creditors. Horatio Gates Livermore never saw the end, having died in 1879, but his sons, to whom the enterprise had passed, managed to absorb the loss and indeed went on the help establish the Livermores as one of Northern California's foremost families.

Mile 16.8 Lost Hat (Class III-)

The river opens into a large pool from the narrow gorge, and then drops into large standing waves. The fast moving current continues to the left, entering Satan's Cesspool.

Mile 16.9 Satan's Cesspool (Class III +)

The most feared rapid in the gorge, and most photographed. It is possible to eddy out in the pool on the left above the drop to scout. As the river leaves Lost Hat it curves left into large diagonal waves and holes along the left rock wall. A rock above the final drop provides a good vantage point for photographers and spectators There is a small recovery eddy on the left immediately below the photographers rock .

At flows over 1700, there is an alternative class II route far right which can be entered by going right of the large rocks at the end of Lost Hat rapid.

Mile 17.0 Son of Satan's (Class II+)

Enter on right side of the tongue and avoid submerged rocks on the left center and the rock outcropping on the far right at the bottom. Swimmers from Satan's can be injured here if they cannot reach the small eddy on the left below Satan's and get swept down into the submerged rocks on the left.

Raft entering the big wave in Satan's Cesspool. Smile here for the photographer!

This rapid leads to a short gorge formed in amphibolite. Studies indicate that the original rocks were formed 300 million years ago and they were metamorphosed to amphibolite 190 million years ago. These dates are found by analyzing uranium and lead isotopes.

Mile 17.4 Scissors (Class III)

After a large pool, the river splits around an island, runnable either side, turns left and drops through large diagonal waves and ledges into a narrow exit between a house rock on right and rock wall on left.

Contact between gabbro (dark with light specks and streaks) and amphibolite. Gabbro was a large body intruded as a hot molten mass into the amphibolite. Dark and light bands formed in the gabbro as it crystallized. This is part of a large body called the Pine Hill Intrusive Complex. It extends downstream to take-out. The rock is extremely hard and forms a steep canyon here. Haystack Canyon rapid is formed by a twisting gorge in the gabbro. Banding in the gabbro is beautifully displayed here. White bands are quartz veins, intruded as a hot liquid along cracks after the gabbro crystallized.

Mile 17.6 Lower Haystack Canyon (Class II+, Class III above 4,000 cfs)

A narrow section of the gorge with large standing waves. A boat flipping hole appears at the end of the rapid during high flows. BLM public land until Weber creek on the left.

Mile 17.7 – 18.1 BLM Land

BLM land on both scenic banks provides good stopping places.

Mile 18.1 Weber Creek

This is a major drainage, on river left, reaching into the hills south and east of Placerville. Gravels here were worked by placer miners. There is a nice half-mile hike, up the creek, before you reach private property.

"Pinch'em Tight", site of an 1850 sawmill was operated by W. B. Skellinger. Actual gold dust became currency in 1848, a "pinch" supposedly equalling a dollar. Often the storekeeper, insisting on doing the pinching, would wet his thumb and forefinger, plunge his hand into the miner's pouch, and come up with a generous helping. The warning, "Pinch 'em tight" was heard coming out of Conrad Etzel's store so often that the camp located near Weber Creek soon became known by it.

Mile 18.2 Bouncing Rock (Class III)

The canyon once again becomes a steep gorge, created by the river slicing down through extremely hard gabbro. The river leaves the pool below Weber Creek. The gravel bar on the left pushes boats far right along a large rock outcrop of gabbro, and then the river drops into a large, but runnable hole that can flip boats. Easy to avoid by running left of the hole.

Mile 18.4 Ambulance Driver Run or Pre-Op (Class II+)

The river turns right and drops through a series of waves, ending in a pool with popular jumping rocks on the left. At high flows, avoid the big "Crystal Geyser" hole on river left.

Mile 18.6 Hospital Bar Rapids (Class III)

Named for a medical tent set up here in the Gold Rush. The last big drop in the Gorge, the river leaves the pool, drops through rocky waves and then turns left and drops into a huge series of diagonal waves to the right that can flip boats. Move right at the very end of the rapid to avoid the "Valet Parking" rock ledge on the left.

Weberville, an 1850 rendering.

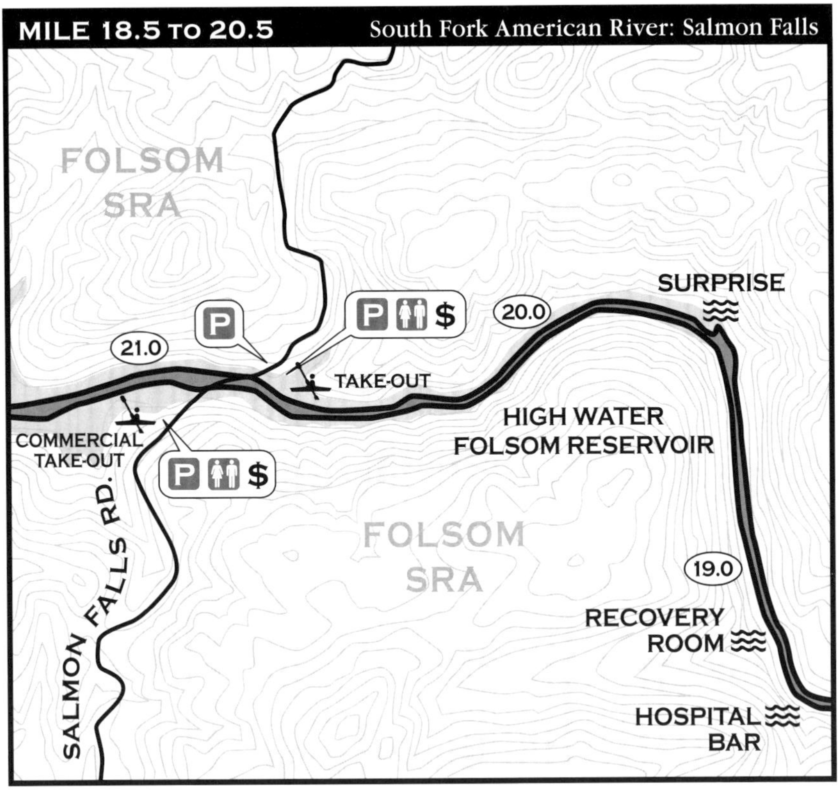

Mile 18.8 Recovery Room (Class II+)

The river drops through more big waves and holes. Avoid the large rock pour-over/hole on right. High water mark for Folsom Reservoir.

Mile 19.4 Surprise! (Class II+)

The river bends to the left and depending on the level of Folsom Reservoir, there is a surprise, the last big rapid of the South Fork. The main current runs down the center tongue into a boat stopping, guide launching hole. Easy to avoid on the right. When Folsom Reservoir is low, Class II rapids continue all the way to Salmon Falls Bridge.

Mile 19.6 Seldom Seen, or Bonus (Class II)

Move right to left through the boulders.

Mile 20.5 Skunk Hollow Take-out at Salmon Falls Bridge

The drainage on the right is Skunk Canyon. Take-out on river-right just before Salmon Falls Bridge. The paved ramp leads to 2 fee parking areas on both sides of Salmon Falls Road, with toilet and picnic tables at lower Skunk Hollow parking lot. The 'commercial' take-out and fee parking with toilets is on river-left downstream of the bridge at the Salmon Falls day use area parking lot.

Mile 23.0 Old Salmon Falls *(Under Reservoir)*

The settlement of Salmon Falls drew its name from a twenty foot falls a small ways downstream of the townsite. There was an effort at the turn of the century to blast the falls clear, to allow salmon to go further upstream to spawn, but the attempt failed.

Salmon Falls survived its tumultuous gold rush beginnings and eventually settled into small town respectability – a quiet, rural village with a one-room schoolhouse in 1935.

Lois Kelley, a former resident, recalls summertimes in the little town: *"We used to float in the Natomas flume, inside it. The ditch tender would walk on top and you always had to watch that he didn't catch you. It was really swift ... you couldn't stand up in it. You sort of got in it and whoosh! You were through!"*

In 1952 the Federal Government purchased the entire town as a part of the right of way for the soon-to-be-completed Folsom Dam. Lois Kelly's family re-settled in Brown's Ravine, near Folsom. Salmon Falls, was razed and flooded under the new reservoir, which was completed in 1956.

Terry Wright, Ph.D., (1943 to 2013), geologist and rafter, authored the geology descriptions in this guidebook.

Boats on the South Fork

Very likely the earliest boaters on the South Fork were the river drovers of the American River Land and Lumber Company of 1891 through 1899. Negotiating the South Fork gorge today may seem challenging; but herding thousands of logs through the same passages while poling a fifteen foot wooden scow was very likely a whole different experience.

With the introduction of inflatables and canvas covered foldboats after the Second World War, it was inevitable that a few whitewater pioneers would try the stretch of river from Chili Bar to Folsom in the new craft; and by 1951 there were a few early reports of just such attempts.

John Jastraub, of Sacramento, was another early river runner, and, along with Jim White, a part of a group called the Sacramento White Water Kayak Klub. The group sponsored trips on the Sacramento and lower forks of the

South Fork Boatmen of 1898.

American primarily in foldboats, but also in open canoes. Jastraub remembers running the Chili Bar to Coloma stretch as well as the "gorge" to Folsom, both in 1955. He used an open aluminum canoe and did occasional portages.

The South Fork continued to be run, although quite infrequently, through the late 1950s and up to 1961, when fiberglass kayaks began to make their appearance. In 1963, Bryce Whitmore ran the first commercial raft trip on the South Fork, and soon the Sierra Club River Touring Section was using the river regularly from Chili Bar down.

It wasn't until 1970s, however, that large numbers of people began to visit the river, mostly with the help of river trip outfitters.

Currently, the South Fork sees well over 100,000 visitors every summer and has become the most popular whitewater river in the West.

Threats to Boating on the South Fork

The South Fork of the American River has been navigated extensively for recreational purposes, and for commercial river trips, since the late 1960s. A rapid increase in the use of the river in the 1970s led to increasing conflict between the river-users, who believed they had the right to float down the 22 mile stretch of river, and land-owners, who believed that the fact that they owned the river bed gave them the right to stop rafting. In 1975, ARTA and several other rafting companies were sued by landowners, in an attempt to keep them from rafting on the South Fork of the American River. For a couple of years, tensions ran high, and there were quite a few incidents of conflict. Some were rather amusing, such as legal papers being served to rafters by a paunchy lawyer, wading and waving his way through the floating river traffic. Others, like staring down the barrel of a pointed rifle, and being harassed by cross-river "target practice" were less entertaining.

In this same period of time, El Dorado county was planning a series of dams on the South Fork between Chili Bar and Folsom Reservoir which would have drowned all but two miles of the river near Coloma.

In response to landowner pleas to regulate rafting, and perhaps due to the desire to dam the river, on August 10, 1976 the El Dorado County Board of Supervisors adopted Ordinance #1675, making it unlawful to "float, swim or travel in said waterway by any artificial means." Any such use of the South Fork from Chili Bar to Salmon Falls Bridge was to be a misdemeanor, except for fishing or swimming "in a lawful manner". However, even swimming in Coloma Lake while wearing a life-jacket would have subjected an individual to arrest.

There were two major points at issue in the legal battle. The first was whether the South Fork of the American River was navigable. While the State Constitution holds that, "If a river is navigable in fact, it is navigable in law", whitewater boating, involving only downstream navigation, was a right only recently affirmed a few years earlier by the courts. The case that the South Fork was a navigable river seemed quite strong in light of the fact that several hundred thousand people had successfully navigated it. Less certain was the question of whether a public governmental body, such as the Board of Supervisors, could restrict that right.

In 1975, the American River Recreation Association (ARRA) had been formed to protect the public's right to use and enjoy the American River, and ARRA had been closely following the legal case. Ten days after the county passed Ordinance #1675, Evelle Younger, California State Attorney General, represented by Jan Stevens, Assistant Attorney General, and Rick Frank, filed suit against El Dorado County to stop enforcement of the ordinance and have it declared invalid. The local court allowed ARRA to intervene, but refused the request for an injunction against the ordinance. However, the 3rd District Court of Appeals stayed enforcement of the ordinance pending a trial at the local court. This was a critical victory, for it allowed continued use of the river, and a means to raise money, while the legal battle continued. Unfortunately, nature was not so kind, and 1977 was so dry that there was no commercial use on the South Fork due to lack of water.

In April, 1978, the local court found that although the river was navigable, and therefore the public should have the legal right to use it, El Dorado County had the right to ban rafting as a reasonable regulation of use. The local court decision was appealed to the 3rd District Court. In August, 1979, that court reversed the lower court's decision.

The decision set the stage for El Dorado County to manage the river. The court recognized the difficulty of the task facing the county by saying "Reasonable regulation is in order; use prohibition is not. The problems of pollution and sanitation in our increasingly crowded state are difficult and complex, calling for imaginative and sophisticated solutions." Certainly the formation and evolution of El Dorado county's River Management Plan has been a difficult and complex process. This three year court fight cost ARRA over $100,000, money collected from outfitters and private boaters using the South Fork of the American River.

Like so many California Western Slope rivers in the 1970s, big dam projects were also proposed on the South Fork American that would have flooded the canyon destroying river habitat and boating opportunities. In 1976 El Dorado Irrigation District (EID) proposed the expansive South Fork of the American River (SOFAR) project, which initially included plans for Salmon Falls Reservoir, which would have flooded the entire Gorge, and Coloma Reservoir, which would have flooded upstream to Chili

American River Conservancy

Based in Coloma for more than 20 years the American River Conservancy, ARC, uses best available science, volunteers and partnerships to preserve rivers, land and the life they support. Through education and recreation, we inspire the care of natural landscapes for future generations.

Our uniquely integrated approach:

- Conserves the land forever
- Promotes education and recreational outings for young and old alike on these lands
- Builds a volunteer base to maintain the land and trails and restore habitat for a healthy future

Contact us at P.O. Box 562
or 348 HWY 49, Coloma, CA 95613
Phone: 530-621-1224

Website: www.arconservancy.org

AMERICAN RIVER CONSERVANCY

Preserving Rivers and Land for Life

Bar. Despite opposition and court challenges from environmental groups, permits for SOFAR were granted, but plans for the Salmon Falls and Coloma Dams were dropped in 1980 due in part to the positive economic benefit to the county from rafting. Ultimately SOFAR was not built due to EID's inability to find a financial backer.

To gain protection from future dam proposals, ARRA and FOR campaigned for, and were successful in 1982, when state legislation passed which prohibited dams from Chili Bar to Salmon Falls for 20 years. Despite strong efforts, the legislature has failed to renew and extend the dam moratorium since it expired in 2003.

Boating on the South Fork received a big boost in 2007. After a two year long campaign by FOR allied with other groups, SMUD signed a settlement agreement that significantly improved flows for fish and recreation on the South Fork as part of the federal re-licensing of SMUD's Upper American River Project, which is a network of eight dams and 11 powerhouses on the upper South Fork.

Current threats to the South Fork include a request by EID to divert water above Chili Bar which would reduce boating flows in the river, and a pending water rights application by San Joaquin County to take water from the proposed, but not yet built, Salmon Falls Dam.

This scratchboard illustration was created for PARC's American River Confluence Festival posters and t-shirts in 1998.

This book is dedicated to you!

PARC dedicates the following new and updated color ecology chapter to all who responsibly enjoy the river and canyons–especially those who fight to protect the wild and scenic values, lead outings, maintain the trails, clean-up the canyons, and provide for your safety. We want you to have the best most complete knowledge to appreciate all the beautiful and complex natural history the canyons have to offer. Please use the information and color illustrations in this chapter to enhance your recreational experience and that of your family and friends.

CHAPTER THREE

American River Ecology:
A Watershed Ecosystem

By Joe Medeiros, Professor Emeritus, Sierra College

A watershed is much more than the creeks and streams that flow through it. It is every piece of ground, every drop of water, and every living, dying, and decomposing thing that exists within the ridges that delineate it. Every watershed's biological story includes life, from the tiniest microbes within the soils, to the tallest trees and largest mammals–and all the interactions between them. Our watershed's physical story includes the rocks and soils, glaciers, snowfall and precipitation, floods and droughts, windstorms and firestorms, and many other physical attributes that have existed over millennia. Together, these physical and biological components have been tried and tested by time; they have evolved, relative to each other and to changing environmental conditions in the West. They continue to change and adapt today.

From barren rock in the high country through tens of thousands of acres of vegetated landscape, every snowflake and raindrop that falls within the watershed will eventually move downhill. Slowly but surely, through vertical and horizontal movement the water molecules collect, from the tiniest ephemeral rivulets to the largest year-around rivers. Some will evaporate en route and head back toward the clouds. Others will wet membranes and transport precious materials within the bodies of insects, fish, amphibians, reptiles, birds, and mammals. Water will cool the vessels of countless grass blades, shrub branches and tree trunks on its way to enable life-giving photosynthetic reactions–liberating oxygen from CO_2 and building sugars with released energy. Much of the water will pass from soil particle to fractured rock, eventually joining a waterway, whether small or large. It will carry its life-giving molecules, necessary nutrients, scouring particles and soil-enriching sediments downhill to become part of a grand cycle.

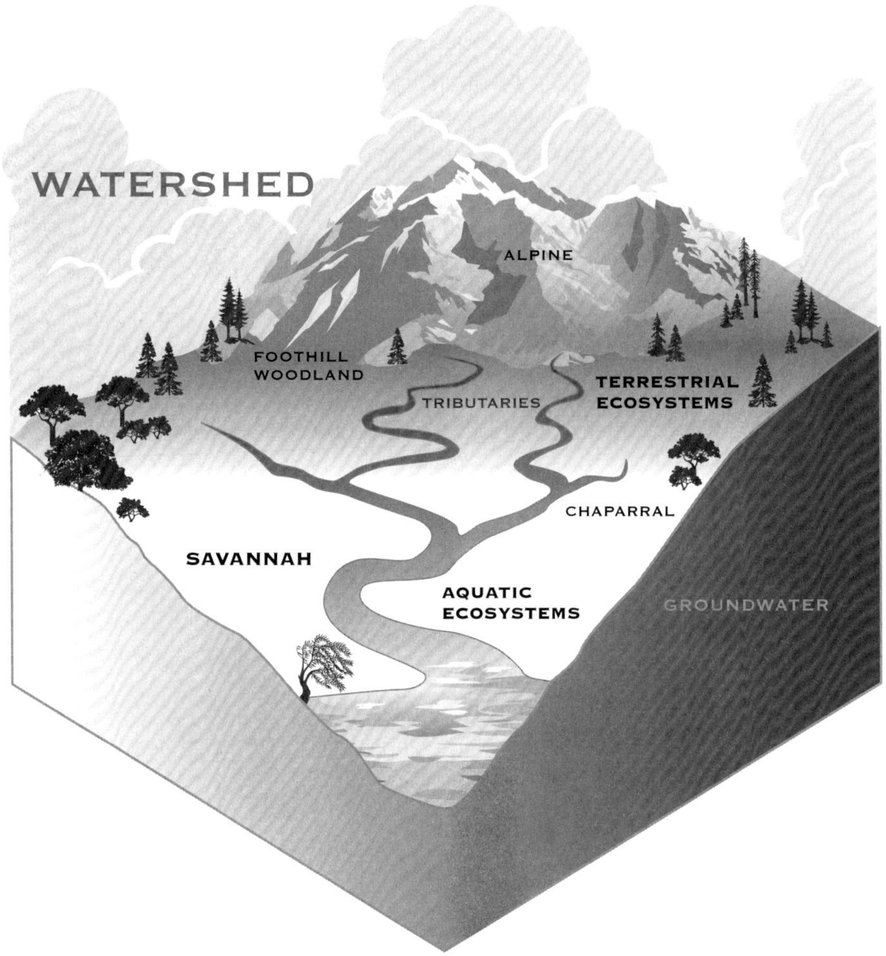

Aquatic Ecosystems

Lentic (Latin for "slow") systems include ponds, lakes and reservoirs. Lotic systems (*lotus* is Latin for "clear, rapid, where one can wash") include creeks, streams, and rivers. The steep-walled canyons of the American have created mostly fast-flowing lotic systems of energetic creeks and fast-flowing rivers. Our lentic systems are natural (glacier-carved tarns in the higher elevations and small lakes and ponds in mid-elevations) and man-made reservoirs. These all share the same ecological properties of being sun-driven and dependent upon photosynthesis. In every watery system algae (when provided with ample light and nutrients) support the ecological pyramid of primary consumers (plankton, microscopic protozoa, and smaller invertebrates). These feed the secondary consumers (primarily fish) which nourish the higher level consumers (snakes, turtles, birds, mammals). Turn over any rock in the river and you will find under it algae and invertebrates which represent important food chain components. Watch for dippers, kingfishers, mergansers, raccoons and river otters as they feast on the river's provisions. Sandpipers and killdeer work the shores. Herons and egrets stand patiently waiting to spear crayfish, fish, or frogs. Ospreys and bald eagles search the surface for prey. Long ago California grizzly hunted salmon–an important ecological component, now lost.

Joe Medeiros, Sierra College Professor, leads an American River ecology hike on the Quarry Road Trail.

Where ample water supply exists adjacent to terrestrial ecosystems, we regularly see wetlands or riparian ecosystems. Wetlands (marshes, backwaters, intermittent pools, etc.) often harbor species that enjoy features of both aquatic and terrestrial ecosystems. Here we'll find turtles, snakes, frogs, many birds and mammals. Riparian (*ripa* is Latin for "stream bank") vegetation lines the banks of larger streams and rivers. We find here shrubs like buttonbush and willows to tall trees like white alder, Fremont cottonwood and Oregon ash. Other intermediate ecosystems, like sandbars and gravel bars, enrich the ecological complexity of the American River watershed.

Like all other of Earth's grand ecosystems, our aquatic systems evolved flexibility to respond to changing environmental conditions. California's Mediterranean climate dictates a boom-and-bust water regime. Winter rains and spring snowmelt alternate with seasonal drought–prolonged rainless months accompanied by high temperatures and low humidity. Aquatic systems, especially lotic ones, have evolved strategies to tolerate, if not welcome, annual drought. From aquatic insects to foothill yellow-legged frogs and anadromous fish, seasonal responses were bred into water-dependent species.

Savannah

California is blessed with its own form of savannah–open woodlands wrapped with grassy wildflower fields. While a hike in the savannah is pleasing during any time of the year, the late winter and early spring promises luxuriant open fields of grasslands between the oaks and pines. Spectacular color accents the green grasslands as wildflowers abound. During fall and summer the golden remains of grassland stems blend with oak woodland backdrops–a unique and characteristic California landscape.

Micro-ecosystems

We often overlook tiny ecosystems and miniature communities. Everywhere we look we find Lilliputian communities are dominated by mosses, ferns, lichens, or even spike-moss, (a primitive relative of ferns that covers steep rocky slopes). Under rotting logs and rock piles are entire communities with highly complex diversity–ask any salamander!

Terrestrial Ecosystems

Steep and rocky ledges rise above 8000 feet in the headwaters of the American River. Downhill from these treeless alpine ecosystems, open forests of mountain hemlock, western white and whitebark pines struggle in deep snows to survive. Below this subalpine forest, a handsome, open forest of lodgepole pine and red fir grows, wrapped in deep snow during most winters. Below the lodgepole/red fir belt a mixed conifer/broadleaf forest flourishes. Here jeffrey and sugar pine grow along with white fir, incense-cedar, and Sierra juniper. Interspersed within the same forest are dogwoods, maples and oaks. Even lower in elevation lays an expansive ponderosa pine belt. Along with the dominant ponderosa grows Douglas-fir, black oak and other species that can tolerate lower rainfall and hot summers. Our lowest elevation forest is called the Foothill Woodland. Dominated by foothill pine and a variety of oaks (interior live, canyon live, blue, and black) this open woodland is complex and rich in biological diversity. Unfortunately, it is also in these same highly diverse foothills that the least protection is afforded to any region of the Sierra.

At these same lower elevations we also find chaparral, a regularly neglected but very important plant community. Existing within the same elevational band as the Foothill Woodland, the Chaparral is dominated by buckbrush, chamise, and manzanita species. Chaparral exists where fire or soil type (most often serpentine or volcanic) exclude intolerant species. It is a highly evolved, fire-climax community and is home for many rare species.

Each of these terrestrial communities are delineated using both physical (abiotic) and biological (biotic) attributes. Soils, climate, precipitation, fire, seasons and other abiotic features lay a framework within which biotic elements (biodiversity) can function. Time and evolutionary mechanisms join in to produce a dynamic equilibrium. We can identify the producers (photosynthesizers: grasses, mosses, herbs, shrubs, trees) and then list the consumers (herbivores, carnivores, omnivores, scavengers and decomposers) and name them by species. We can record and analyze the climate, precipitation, fire and flood intervals, and attempt to understand why each of our species lives where it does. But we will probably never fully understand the complexity and dynamism of ancient ecologic phenomena. Someone once said, "ecosystems are not only more complex than we think, they're more complex than we can think."

The hand of man is still palpable in the American River canyons. The ghosts of argonauts, timbermen, railroad builders, gunmen and thieves still haunt these canyons with artifacts, stories, and perhaps even spirits. But today, the canyons are filled with the voices of humans enjoying nature as well its valuable resources. They are studying, observing, rafting, fishing, swimming, photographing, biking, running, riding their horses, and appreciating their home watershed in newer, more enlightened ways.

They are incorporating history and land use into new management plans that are more sustainable. They have grown to appreciate the full spectrum of gifts, given to us free of charge, by this watershed.

Naturally functioning ecosystems are the lifeblood of our watersheds. When healthy, they stabilize our soils and protect against floods. Climate altering CO2 is sequestered in the healthy forest and abundant oxygen is released. Ecosystem resources provide food, shelter, clothing, medicines, pain relief and cures for disease. They also provide for us a genetic library of the past and for use in the future. We seek such places for recreation, for solace and healing–for spiritual and intellectual growth.

Watersheds continue to provide much more than our basic needs and we have historically failed to include these free "ecosystem services" into a true and honest balance sheet when we plan our developments and forest plans.

Thankfully, it appears that we humans are once again listening carefully to our living world. And we are finally beginning, just beginning, to learn how to give back.

Note: *The suggested human uses of the following plants have come from many sources. We cannot attest to the validity or safety of such uses – they are here for historical context only. As many California native plants are rare and endangered, we suggest that you don't use or eat any of our native beauties and that you defer to modern medicine and techniques if proven effective. Never use or eat any plant or fungus that you are not completely sure of (its name and its safety record).*

John Muir Laws:
A Gift of Illustrations

John Muir Laws the author and illustrator of *The Laws Field Guide to the Sierra Nevada* graciously allowed PARC to sample his illustrations featured in the following American River Ecology chapter. Our diverse sampling is an introduction to the invaluable collection of illustrations found in Law's field guide.

He accompanied PARC on several river trips to confirm our selection and created the button bush and toyon illustrations, not found in his book, especially for PARC. His field guide brings to life the astonishing natural diversity of the Sierra Nevada mountain range in a comprehensive 368 page guide book with 2,800 watercolor illustrations. Designed for quick and easy field use this richly illustrated guide covers Sierra trees, wildflowers, ferns, fungi, lichens, fish, reptiles, amphibians, birds, mammals, insects, other small animals, stars and weather. It is intuitively organized using color tabs and simple keys to assist in the quick identification of living things encountered along the trail. The book is the product of six years of intensive fieldwork, research, painting and field-testing in collaboration with the California Academy of Sciences, published by Heyday Books. For a listing of John Muir Laws workshops and presentations visit his website at www.johnmuirlaws.com.

John Muir Laws exploring and teaching.

The Laws guidebook is available through PARC's website at www.parc-auburn.org.

CONIFERS

Douglas-fir

Douglas-fir *(Pseudotsuga menziesii)*

Habitat: rocky soils of mountain or canyon slopes, in pure stands and mixed coniferous forests. *(Named for David Douglas, famed Scottish botanical explorer of Western North America.)*

The douglas-fir tree adapts to many soil and climatic conditions and co-occurs well with many species. Its thick bark helps it resist fire and drought. Its light-winged seeds are capable of traveling 1/4 of a mile in a moderate breeze. It regenerates vigorously and is often one of the first trees to germinate after a fire. The douglas-fir was used extensively by California Indians for houses, harpoon shafts, canoes, and other implements. The pliable roots were used in basketry and the cambium layer was utilized as an emergency food. A tea can be made from the fresh young needles and is purported to be high in vitamin C. One of the world's most important timber species, it ranks first in the U.S. in its total volume of timber, lumber production, and veneer for plywood. This can be credited to its yield of large old-growth logs with straight grain. It is also one of California's tallest trees. Squirrels, meadow mice, and song sparrows are just some of the Sierra fauna that feast on its seeds. Deer and grouse frequently nibble on its foliage.

Foothill or grey pine

Foothill or Grey Pine *(Pinus sabiniana)*

Habitat: dry slopes and ridges in foothills and low mountains, with oaks and other conifers, often in serpentine and chaparral.

This picturesque and delicate pine tree is the most common conifer in California. John Muir wrote: *"no other tree of my acquaintance is so substantial in body and yet in foliage so thin and pervious to light. The sunbeams sift through even the densest needled trees with scarcely any interruption."* Some of the first pioneers dubbed the Indians they met in the Central Valley "diggers" because roots and bulbs comprised much of their diet. Also, when these newcomers learned that Native Americans subsisted largely upon the rich seeds of a foothill pine they called the tree "digger pine." John Muir described the digger pine nut harvest as follows: *"The Indian men climb the tree like bears and beat off the cones with sticks while the women gather the big generous cones and roast them until the scales open sufficiently to allow the hard-shelled seeds to be beaten out. Then in the cool evenings men, women, and children form circles around campfires on the banks of the nearest stream and sit in easy independence cracking nuts and laughing like squirrels."* The Miwok Indians also boiled the twigs, needles, and bark into a strong tea to treat rheumatism. Seeds strung on thread made from wild iris fiber were used to decorate costumes worn in dance rituals. The pitch of the foothill and most pines was used for fastening arrowheads and feathers and for mending canoes. The nuts are also a staple food for squirrels, woodpeckers, jays, and other foothill birds. White settlers considered this tree to be rather worthless except for fuel because its wood is lightweight and not very durable. The unacceptable name "digger" pine is considered pejorative and racist. It illustrates our ignorance and misjudgment of the resourceful people who were here before us.

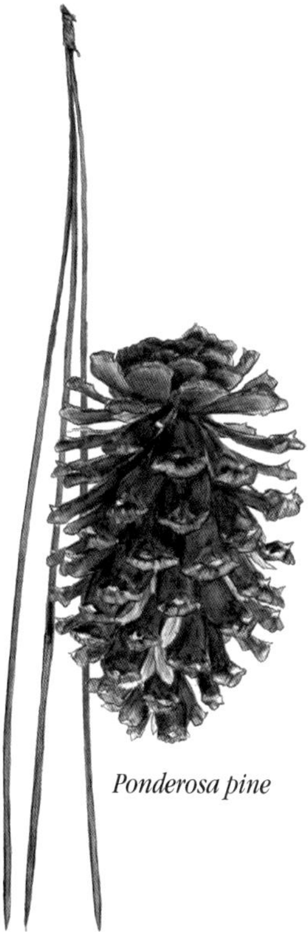
Ponderosa pine

Ponderosa Pine *(Pinus ponderosa)*

Habitat: west-slope foothills and mid-elevation mountain slopes.

The ponderosa pine occurs on nearly a million square miles in the western states, Canada, and Mexico, from near sea-level in the northwest to 10,000 feet in Arizona. The stately, fragrant pines are typical of somewhat arid mountain slopes above the broadleaf trees and below the alpine white pines. The first scientific explorer to note this plant was Meriwether Lewis, who collected cones in Idaho in 1800, but David Douglas suggested the name "ponderosa" some 30 years later after viewing some mammoth specimens. Naturalist-mountaineer John Muir loved this tree and wrote, *"of all pines, this one gives forth the finest music to the winds."* Unfortunately, not all take the tree in such a gentle fashion; indeed, it is the third most harvested tree in the United States.

Sugar pine

Sugar Pine *(Pinus lambertiana)*

Habitat: 2000-8000 feet in mixed conifer forests; usually visible on north-facing ridge tops.

The sugar pine is the monarch of pines and the fourth largest tree of North America. Unfortunately for this species, it has been over-cut for its great trunks, which are clear of lower branches. Blister rust has often prevented sugar pine from being successfully replanted. Sutter's Mill on the South Fork was built to exploit the straight-grained giant. The sap is sweet and was favored by mountain people, including John Muir. Sugar pines in age are great individualists with grand, asymmetrical tops much shaped by strong winter storms.

Knobcone pine

Knobcone Pine *(Pinus attentuata or tuberculata)*

Habitat: 2500-4000 feet on rocky serpentine slopes in small groups; usually less than 30 feet high.

This uncommon fire adapted pine produces small cones that grow in tight clusters around the trunk, remaining unopened for years until heated by fire.

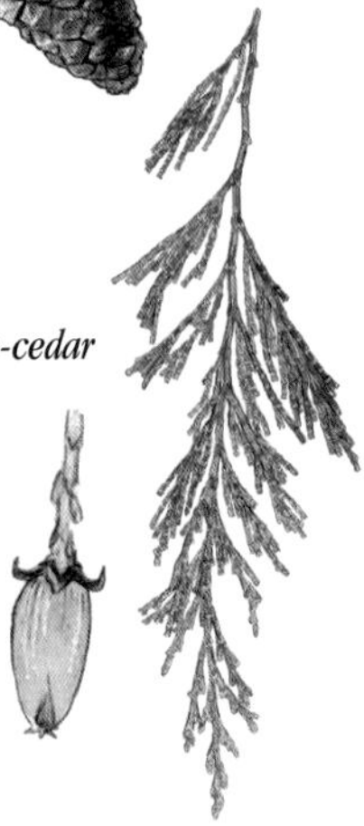
Incense-cedar

Incense-cedar *(Calocedars decurrens)*

Habitat: mountain slopes; in mixed coniferous forests.

Incense-cedar seldom forms pure stands, as its seedlings grow very slowly and other species tend to out-compete it. Often, it is found as an understory tree to younger and taller douglas-fir trees. Although it is drought-resistant, it is easily damaged by smog. Miwoks used the durable shreddy bark to make their huts called "oochums". Pioneers used the bark for roofing their cabins. Today the incense-cedar is of some commercial value as its wood is used for firewood and fencing. It also supplies more than 75 percent of the wood for the world's pencils because it is soft yet not splintery and can be sharpened in any direction with ease.

OAK HARDWOODS

Black oak

Black Oak *(Quercus kelloggii)*

Habitat: sandy, gravely, and rocky soils of foothills and mountains; often in pure stands or in mixed conifer forests.

The black oak is slow-growing, yet long-lived. Tree squirrels and some owls nest in rotted cavities of its trunks and limbs. Its summer foliage provides food and nesting for many birds. The California Indians prized this oak for fuel and for drying seeds, as it burns very slowly. The seeds were a primary staple food of mountain Indians. Deer relish the acorns and browse on the leaves of young trees. Although bitter, the black oak acorn is the favorite food of acorn woodpeckers, who store a cache of acorns for winter in hammered holes on the sides of trees and telephone poles. Today the black oak's primary commercial value is for fuel, furniture and flooring.

Blue oak

Blue Oak *(Quercus douglasii)*

Habitat: dry, loamy, rocky slopes; with other oaks and foothill pines.

Blue oak received its species name from David Douglas, a Scottish botanical explorer. The tree offers perches for many foothill birds and its abundant crop of acorns is eaten by livestock as well as by wildlife. It is used by people principally for fuel.

Valley oak

Valley Oak or California White Oak *(Quercus lobata)*

Habitat: valleys and slopes on rich loamy soils; forming groves in foothill woodlands.

The valley oak is the monarch among western deciduous oaks and a graceful shade tree. It receives its species name, lobata, from its deeply lobed leaves. It bears an abundant acorn crop, reputed to be the sweetest of all the oaks, but which are difficult to hull. This oak's copious mast of acorns also provides nourishment to acorn woodpeckers, deer, wood ducks, and flocks of band-tailed pigeons. Due to rapidly encroaching housing developments, over- grazing, and agriculture, this picturesque tree is gradually disappearing from the California landscape.

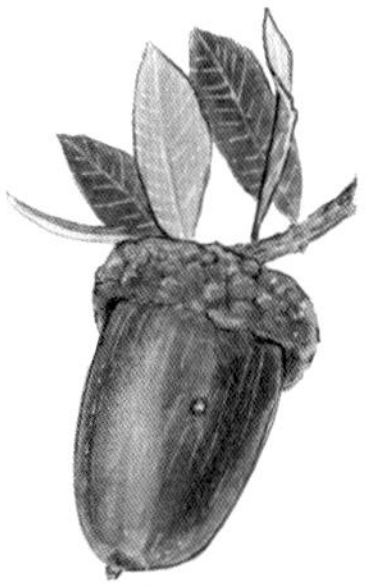

Canyon live oak

Canyon Live Oak or Gold Cup Oak *(Quercus chrysolepis)*

Habitat: sandy soils in canyons, rolling foothills, and rocky slopes; in pure stands and mixed forests.

The species Latin name means "golden-scale" and refers to its acorn cup, which is the canyon live oak's most distinguishing characteristic. This oak is slow-growing and long-lived. It has dense, straight wood that seasons well. It was used by early settlers for farm implements, wagon wheels, furniture, floors, and wedges for splitting redwood logs into railroad ties. It was favored by pioneers for the heads of mauls. Acorns and leaf insects of the canyon oak are food for many birds and tree-climbing mammals. Band tailed pigeons can swallow the entire acorn and let their powerful gizzards do the shelling. More than fifty types of gall-forming insects work on this oak.

Interior live oak

Interior Live Oak *(Quercus wislizenii)*

Habitat: slopes and ravines in foothill woodlands or near chaparral; with other oaks and Foothill pine.

The Interior Live Oak is slow-growing. Its dense, dark green foliage gives protected roosting places for valley quail and other birds. Insects found munching on its leaves are food sought by warblers, vireos, titmice, and other Sierra birds. Deer browse its young leaves, and its wood is used for fuel. It can resprout after burning.

DECIDUOUS TREES

Big leaf maple

Big leaf maple seed

Bigleaf Maple *(Acer macrophyllum)*

Habitat: wet soils along streams and canyons with alder, black cottonwood, willows, and oaks.

Both the common and scientific names refer to the large leaves of this beautiful shade tree, which is particularly showy in autumn. The California Indians made canoe paddles from the wood and maple syrup from the sap. They also used the bark of the maple for making rope, and the wood made excellent fires for smoking meat and fish. Split sapwood made basket sewing material. The seeds are food for mice, woodrats, squirrels, chipmunks, and some birds. The tender twigs and leaves from the young seedlings are important browse food for deer. The only western maple with wood of commercial value, it is used for veneer, furniture, handles, and woodenware, but because it rarely forms pure stands it is expensive to harvest. Delicious maple syrup can be made from the sap in winter.

Oregon ash

Oregon Ash *(Fraxinus latifolia)*

Habitat: wet soils along streams and canyons with alder, black cottonwood, willows, and oaks.

Oregon ash is the only ash native to the northwest. Its wood was used by the California Indians for canoe paddles and digging sticks. Indians believed that no poisonous snakes would live where the ash tree grew and that a stick made from its wood would make a rattlesnake retreat in fear. Also, a tea brewed from the bark was thought to cure worms. Today the wood of the Oregon ash is used for furniture, flooring, paneling, boxes, and fuel, but it is hard to harvest due to its scattered growth.

White alder

White Alder *(Alnus rhombifolia)*

Habitat: near stream banks in foothills and mid-elevation Sierra.

White alder is named for its pale green foliage and is a reliable indicator of running water, as it is usually confined to streams that run all summer. They are fast growers and have a short life span of about 80-100 years. Root nodules have micro-organisms which provide nitrogen to the tree. Its leaves drop when still green. The California Indians obtained a red dye from the bark by chewing it and using the colored spittle to dye stems of ferns for basketry. A tea made from the bark was used as a blood purifier, and to check diarrhea. Lumbermen consider it to be a "weed" tree.

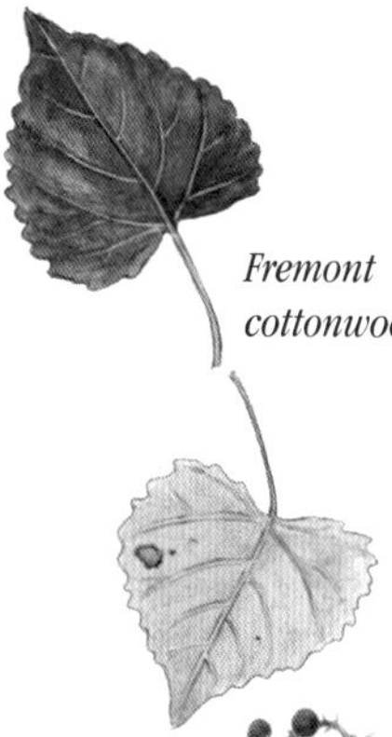

Fremont cottonwood

Fremont Cottonwood *(Populus fremontii)*

Habitat: moist soils around the Great Central Valley and Sierra Foothills.

Discovered by and named for western explorer John Charles Fremont, this whitish tree is a sure sign of water in a typically arid landscape. Mohave Indian women fabricated their skirts from the twisted inner bark fibers. Spanish settlers planted their plazas with cottonwoods and knew them as "alamos".

Pacific madrone

Pacific Madrone *(Arbutus menziesii)*

Habitat: upland slopes and canyons; in oak and coniferous forests; often an understory plant.

Its scientific name *menziesii*, honors its discoverer, Archibald Menzies, a Scottish physician and naturalist. The thin bark of the madrone makes it especially vulnerable to fires, but even if burned it readily stump-sprouts. California Indians ate the fruit raw and cooked; however, over-eating causes cramps. They also made a lotion from the leaves to treat sores and cuts. Charcoal from the madrone was employed by the early California settlers in the making of gunpowder. The wood of this tree is very brittle and not commercially developed, but can be used for making weaving shuttles and furniture.

Tree of heaven seeds

Tree of heaven

Tree Of Heaven non native *(Ailanthus altissima)*

Habitat: streambanks; widespread in waste places.

The scientific name of this tree comes from a Chinese phrase meaning "tall tree". This exotic was planted by the early Chinese miners of the Sierra Nevada foothills and has become widely naturalized. Chinese brought it with them to remind them of home. It grows very rapidly and is tolerant of crowded, dusty cities and smoggy, factory districts, often sprouting out of cracks in concrete.

California buckeye seed

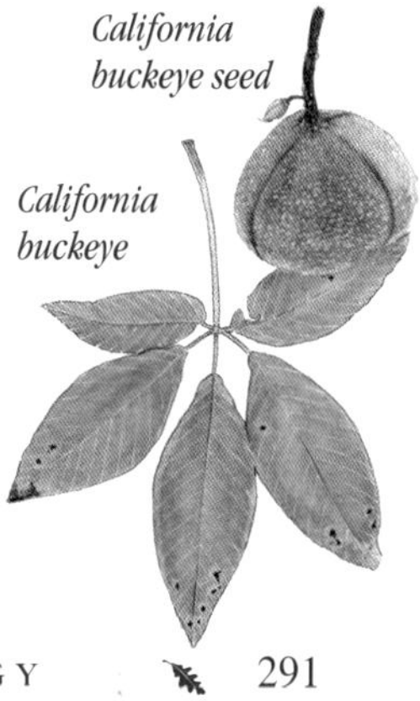

California buckeye

California Buckeye *(Aesculus californica)*

Habitat: moist soils of canyons and dry hillsides in chaparral and oak woodland.

The only native buckeye in the west, this species is sometimes grown as an ornamental. Indians used the buckeye fruits as seasonal food after leaching the toxins with boiling water. Miwoks and Maidus crushed the leaves to stupefy fish–the toxin did not affect those who ate the fish. Chipmunks and squirrels readily consume the seeds, but some honey bees are poisoned by the pollen.

SHRUBS AND VINES

California bay or California laurel

California Bay or California Laurel

(Umbellularia californica)

Habitat: moist soils, especially in mountain canyons and valleys; mixed forests.

The California bay tree requires damp soil and is found growing along streams in shade. Its volatile leaf oils induce perspiration and were employed by both the California Indians and pioneers in steam baths and as a rubbing compound for rheumatism, to repel fleas and to get rid of lice. The Miwoks made hunting bows from the bay and often bound the leaf to their foreheads to cure a headache. The leaves were also crushed and sniffed to clear stuffy sinuses (too much though can induce a headache). The trappers of the Hudson Bay Company brewed the leaves into a medicinal tea. The tree has an attractive, light brown wood that takes a beautiful finish and is used for paneling, veneer, bowls, boxes, and other wooden ware, commercially marked as Oregon myrtle in that state. Its leaves can be used as a seasoning but are much stronger than the commercial European bay or grecian laurel.

Blue elderberry

Blue Elderberry *(Sambucus nigra subsp. caeerulea)*

Habitat: commonly on stream slopes to 5400 ft.

Their large quantities of tart bluish berries are relished by birds and humans. They are excellent for baking and the crushed fermented berries are used to make fine homemade wine. Care must be taken to remove poisonous stems leaves and all other material. Called the "music plant" by the Maidu the smaller branches were hollowed out, carved and tuned with hot pine pitch to make dance whistles. The larger hollowed out branches are still used for clacker sticks.

One of the five willow variety

Willows *(Salix spp.)*

Habitat: wet soils along streams or gullies in valleys, foothills, and mountains; often in pure stands or with cottonwoods.

***Note:** There are about five different species of willows along the rivers of the Sierra Foothills. Rather than describe each of them in detail, they will be dealt with as a genus.*

The willow's name is derived form the Celtic *sal*, meaning "near", and *lis*, meaning "water". Willow species are quick-growing with a short life span. Their thickly-matted root systems are valuable in preventing soil erosion along stream banks, and consequently help to stabilize watersheds. California Indians wove strips of the willow bark together for twine and the twigs were widely used in weaving baskets. They also boiled the bark and used the strong tea to remedy sore throats and tuberculosis. Powdered willow bark was also used as aspirin and as a poultice for burns. Beavers use willows for food almost exclusively. Willows are the domain of many small birds.

Button bush or button willow

Button Bush or Button Willow *(Cephalanthus occidentalis)*

Habitat: riparian-wet soils bordering streams and lakes.

The distinctive fragrant globular flowers of this 5 to 20 feet high shrub fill the river with a sweet scent from July through the summer. The flowers also produce large amounts of nectar making them attractive to butterflies and bees. Ducks and other water and shore birds consume the seeds. The glossy poisonous foliage of this abundant species is unpalatable to livestock.

Wild grape

Wild Grape *(Vitis californica)*

Habitat: foothill belt on trees near streams.

Wild grape vines climb shrubs, trees and grow along the ground. Their dense foliage provides excellent wildlife habitat but can kill trees and shrubs by excluding the sunlight. The grapes are sweet but do have large seeds. Indians used the leaves to wrap food for roasting food and the stringy bark for twine.

Blackberry California blackberry *(Rubus ursines)* or Himalayan blackberry *(Rubus armeniacus)*

Habitat: streams and moist soils; shady woodlands, fields, and empty lots. Himalayan blackberry is a very weedy-bramble introduction from Eurasia.

Himalayan blackberry

The Latin word *rubus* means bramble and relates to the thickets that blackberries form. The berries are sweet and very delicious. They can be prepared in many ways: jams, jellies in pancakes, in muffins, or just eaten fresh off the vine. The California Indians dried the berries and pounded them to form cakes or mixed them with dry meat and fat to make pemmican. Tea made from the roots was the most frequently used remedy for diarrhea and for sore throats. The leaves also make a good tea. Blackberries rank at the top of the list of summer foods for much of the Sierra's wildlife, particularly birds and wood rats. The stems and foliage are browsed by mule deer and the dense thickets provide great nesting sites for birds and protective cover for many small mammals.

California blackberry

Mock-orange

Redbud

Toyon or Christmas berry

Manzanita with berries

Manzanita with flowers

Sierra coffeeberry

Mock-orange *(Philadelphus lewisii)*

Habitat: canyon slopes and moist river flats.

Wild Mock-orange is a beautiful flowering sight of our canyons and fills its vicinity with a fine fragrance during late spring to early summer. Indian peoples used the straight young shoots for hunting implements.

Redbud *(Cercis occidentalis)*

Habitat: canyons and slopes of foothills and mountains.

California Indians used the wood for bows and the strong pliable bark for patterns in baskets. The bark is also very astringent and, when made into a tea, provides a remedy for dysentery. Deer browse on its young foliage.

Toyon or Christmas Berry *(Heteromeles arbutifolia)*

Habitat: on dry slopes of chaparral and oak woodland zones.

Toyon is very showy in autumn and winter with evergreen leaves and abundant red berries, popular for Christmas decorations. It is a pioneer plant in eroded soil and sprouts vigorously after fire or cutting. The berries were prized by the California Indians, who ate them boiled, baked, or dried and ground into meal. A tea was also made by crushing the berries and pouring boiling water over them. A tea from the bark and leaves relieved stomach aches. Berries are winter food for robins and waxwings, among others.

Whiteleaf Manzanita *(Arctostaphylos viscida)*

Habitat: dry slopes of mountain canyons, chaparral foothills and oak woodlands.

Manzanita is Spanish for "little apple", referring to its small berries. The California Indians and, later, Spanish settlers, made the ripe berries into a cider. They also ate large quantities fresh or dried for flour. The dried seeds were beaten to a fine flour and made into mush or thin cakes that were baked in ashes. The attractive reddish-brown branches of the manzanita become twisted into odd shapes which are trimmed into collectors' items called "mountain driftwood".

Sierra Coffeeberry *(Frangula californica subsp. tomentella)*

Habitat: chaparral and understory of foothill woodland.

The California coffeeberry received its common name from the two seeds which superficially resemble coffee beans. The attractive fruits are feasted upon by fox, coyote, raccoons and numerous birds. Like its relative cascara, coffeeberry contains a strong laxative in its bark, a good remedy for bloat.

Poison-oak *(Toxicodendron diversilobum)*

Habitat: moist soils of streams, through foothill belt to lower mountain slopes and valleys.

Poison-oak is the most widespread California shrub and has one of the largest gene pools, allowing for a great variance in its form, ranging from a small, woody plant to a massive vine or dense shrub. Many people have allergic reactions to Poison-oak ranging from a slight itch to a massive rash with blisters and severe swelling. Immunity to poison-oak is erratic and may come and go. It is best to always exercise caution after coming in contact with this plant. Wash the skin with cool water and soap, preferably Fels-Naptha. The product Tecnu is a well-know successful soap remedy, (used before or after contact).

Poison-oak

Chamise *(Adenostoma fasciculatum)*

Habitat: most common plant of the chaparral community; from the lower foothills up to the ponderosa pines; often in pure stands, especially on serpentine soil.

Chamise often grows in thickets that are almost impenetrable to people and pack animals but afford favorable shelter for many mammals such as deer, rabbits, and rodents. It stump sprouts abundantly after a fire. A tea made from the leaves was considered by the California Indians to be valuable for colds, cramps, and lockjaw. The oil from the stem was used in healing sores and infections, and an infusion from the leaves and bark was also said to be useful in treating syphilis.

Chamise

Buckbrush *(Ceanothus cuneatus)*

Habitat: dry chaparral slopes in foothill belt.

The leaves and stems are favorites with the deer, giving the plant its common name. The California Indians made a tea from the bark and roots to aid in digestion. Some tribes used the reddish roots for a dye. The flowers make a good, lathery soap when crushed and mixed with water. Several other species of ceanothus occur in the Sierra.

Buckbrush

Yerba santa

Yerba Santa *(Eriodictyon californicum)*

Habitat: open, dry, rocky slopes and ridges; especially prevalent in chaparral communities.

The common name of this plant, meaning "saintly herb", was given to it by a Spanish missionary who learned of its many medicinal properties from the California Indians. The Miwoks boiled a leaf tea for colds, coughs, and sore throats. A poultice of fresh leaves was applied to promote healing of wounds and put over fractures to reduce the swelling. The dried leaves were the principal ingredient in a pleasant smoking mixture. This herb entered the U.S. pharmacopoeia in 1894 and has been employed as a tonic and to relieve coughs, colds, stomach aches, diarrhea, and asthma. To make a tea, tear up 2 to 3 leaves and pour boiling water over them, cover, and let steep. Chewing the fresh leaves produces a refreshing taste after the initial bitterness dissipates.

BROAD LEAFED HERBS

Monkey flowers

Monkeyflowers *(Mimulus species)*

Habitat: wet places from sea level to high mountains; frequently along stream banks.

There are approximately 100 different species of monkeyflower in California with colors ranging from yellow to purple. The very common seep-spring monkeyflower *(mimulus guttatus)*, is illustrated here. The reddish-scarlet monkeyflower *(mimulus cardinalis)* is a common creekside plant.

Yarrow

Yarrow *(Achillea millefolium)*

Habitat: occurs in open areas in a vast variety of habitats from the coast to high mountain altitudes.

The genus name of yarrow, achillea, refers to Achilles, who in the legendary siege of Troy revealed the healing powers of this herb in treating the wounds his warriors received in battle. A tea from the leaves and flowers mixed with equal parts of mint has been used in treating fevers and colds. It is reputed to have anesthetic properties and the powdered root may be inserted in the hollow of a decaying tooth to relieve the pain, or applied to deep bodily wounds. Yarrow was greatly esteemed by English herbalists for stomach cramps and to stimulate the appetite. An old legend says that an ounce of yarrow placed under the pillow before going to sleep will bring vision of a future husband or wife. Dried yarrow stalks were tossed to read the I-Ching in China.

Lupine *(Lupinus spp.)*

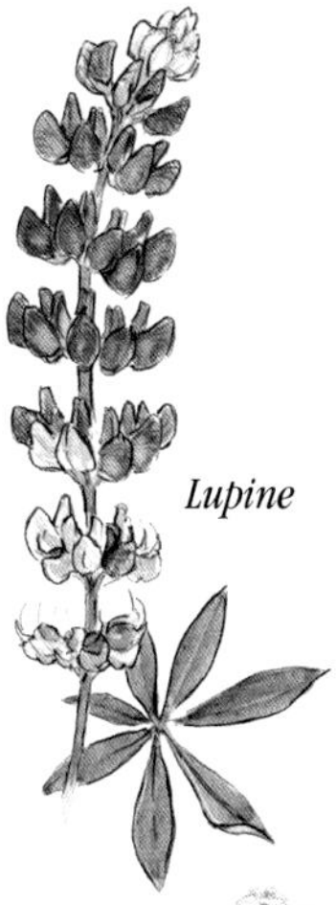
Lupine

Habitat: open, grassy meadows to rocky slopes.

Push the flower petals back to reveal a wolf's claw hidden inside. The genus name *lupinus* means wolf, and refers to the folk notion that the lupine is wolf-like in character, devouring nutrients from the soil. Actually this is far from the truth, as they enrich the soil with nitrogen. Their thin, deep roots help to stabilize sandy soil and were planted on the sand dunes upon which Golden Gate Park was built. In 1967 Arctic lupine seeds were discovered frozen in a lemming burrow. They were estimated to be 10,000 years old, and when planted, germinated in 48 hours. As their pods mature and dry, their walls become elastic and burst open, instantly throwing the seeds a long distance. On sunny, warm afternoons they can be heard softly popping like muffled popcorn. Many species are toxic to livestock.

Miner's Lettuce *(Claytonia perfoliata)*

Miner's lettuce

Habitat: loose, moist soil in shady places; frequently near streams.

Miner's lettuce is one of the few native plants from this country that has been introduced into Europe. It was a popular salad herb for the California Indians, who also made a laxative tea from it. The miners, who had little fresh food, used it to stave off scurvy. Miner's lettuce makes a tasty, nutritional salad and can also be steamed like spinach. Its black, tiny seeds are an important source of food for small songbirds.

Canyon Dudleya *(Dudleya cymosa)*

Canyon dudleya

Habitat: hot, dry, rocky cliffs at lower elevations.

There is only one species of this genus in our canyons, *(dudleya cymosa)* by there are many succulents in this genus and family. Canyon dudleya is also called liverforever or stonecrop. They were considered a delicacy by some California Indian tribes and the fleshy leaves were eaten raw but many plants in the genus dudleya are rare or endangered species and should not be taken for casual food.

California Poppy *(Eschscholzia californica)*

California poppy

Habitat: open meadows to grassy slopes.

The genus *eschscholzia,* was named by Chamisso, a German naturalist who found the California poppy on San Francisco's sand dunes in 1816 and named it after his expedition's surgeon, Eschscholz. The California Indians used the poppy's narcotic qualities as a painkiller and ate the leaves as a vegetable.

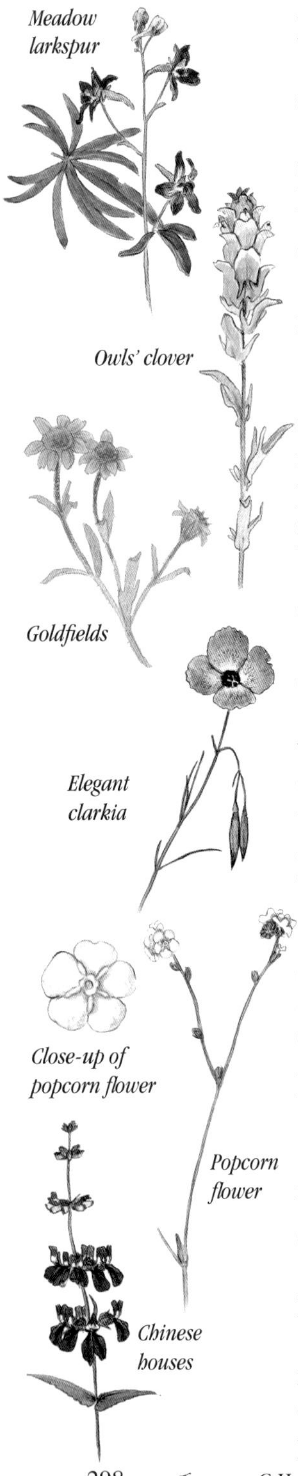

Hansen's Larkspur *(Delphinium hansenii)*

Habitat: well-drained soils; grassy slopes in chaparral and pine forests.

The Latin ***delphinus*** means "dolphin"–the flower buds resemble this marine mammal. There are many other Sierran larkspur species. This plant is very poisonous to cattle.

Owl's Clover or Escobita *(Orthocarpus sp.)*

Note: there are 4 or 5 different species of owl's clover in the river canyons of the Motherlode.

Habitat: fields and open woodlands.

Escobita, this plant's Spanish name, means "little broom" and refers to its flower cluster. Its common name, owl's clover, refers to the swollen head-like ends of the flower that seem to peer from the bract as an owl peers around from the leaves of a tree. Following a wet spring, meadows are carpeted with this beautiful flower.

Goldfields *(Lasthenia californica)*

Habitat: open fields or meadows and hillsides at low elevations.

Goldfields can be found in open areas with poor soils, where the grass is sparse. If the moisture is ample, it will form carpets of gold; hence its name, particularly appropriate for the Motherlode country.

Elegant Clarkia *(Clarkia unguiculata)*

Habitat: rocky or brushy slopes 100-1200' in lower foothills.

Many species of this genus are called "farewell to spring" as they signal the transition between spring and summer. Seen commonly along canyon roadsides. Name to honor William Clark of the Lewis and Clark expedition.

Popcorn Flower *(Plagiobothrys nothofulvus)*

Habitat: open places, commonly in grasslands and meadows.

Many species have a purple dye in the stems and roots. It is related to the forget-me-not.

Chinese Houses *(Collinsia heterophylla)*

Habitat: dry, open, and rocky slopes and shaded places at lower elevations.

This is one of the most common and most spectacular wildflowers of the Motherlode. The flowers grow in perfect rings of widely-spaced bands around the stem, forming a fairy tale pagoda of "Chinese Houses".

Baby Blue Eyes *(Nemophila menziesii)*

Habitat: grassy hillsides, meadows, and among brush.

Baby blue eyes is considered to be one of the most charming and delicate wildflowers in California. The tiny black dots serve as nectar guidelines for potential insect pollinators.

Baby blue eyes

California Buttercup *(Ranunculus californicus)*

Habitat: moist slopes and meadows.

The genus name, *Ranunculus*, means "little frog" and refers to the wet habitat where both the buttercup and frogs abound. There are several species in the river canyons of the Motherlode, but the most common is the California buttercup. The California Indians gathered their seeds in late June and afterwards winnowed, dried, and stored them. Before eating, they were parched and pulverized in a grinding hole, then often added to pinole, a seedy cereal.

California buttercup

Mule's Ears *(Wyethia angustifolia)*

Habitat: open hillsides, woods, and meadows in the foothills.

Only a little stretch of the imagination, is necessary to see the large basal leaves of this plant as alert mules ears. The California Indians parched and ground the large seeds of the mule's ears and made them into pinole, a seedy cereal. Young shoots were eaten raw, after peeling off the outer coating. A tea was made from the leaves to bathe fever victims.

Mule's ears

Indian-rhubarb *(Darmera peltata)*

Habitat: banks of mountain streams and foothill river canyons.

The fleshy leafstalks of this plant may be peeled and eaten as is, in a salad, or cooked and added to stews, although cooking destroys some of their flavor.

Indian-rhubarb

Mugwort *(Artemesia douglasiana)*

Habitat: moist, shaded areas of woods and along streamsides.

Well known since antiquity, mugwort is described on an Egyptian papyrus dated 1600 B.C. as a useful medicinal herb. Medieval legend says that sleeping on a pillow filled with mugwort allows a person to dream into their future. The Miwok Indians took small balls containing mugwort and other "medicine" plants and wore them strung on a necklace to prevent dreaming of the dead and to repel ghosts at night. Corpse handlers rubbed themselves with mugwort for the same reason. The leaves were also worn in the nostrils of mourners when crying, the pungent

Mugwort

odor clearing the head. Mugwort was used as a remedy for rheumatism, and even today has been taken to relieve obstructed menstruation and to quell the itching from a poison-oak rash. Chinese doctors rely upon mugwort for use in moxibustion, a process whereby the herb is made into incense, then burned and lightly applied to acupuncture points to stimulate them instead of using a needle. Also used by Maidu in their (acorn) granaries to keep out insects.

Soap plant

Soap Plant *(Chlorogalum pomeridianum)*

Habitat: dry open and stony ground.

Delicate flowers that open only in the afternoon grow from a stout branched stem 2 to 5 feet tall. The stem rises from a bulb with long narrow wavy edged leaves. The bulb had many uses for native peoples. The Maidu roasted the bulbs for food and used the fibers that cover the bulb for brushes. The crushed bulb was used to make glue or make a soapy lather for washing hair. This same soapy substance was introduced into slow moving streams to catch fish by suffocation. Juice from the leaves could also be used as a green tattoo dye when introduced into scratched skin.

California fuchsia

California Fuchia *(Epilobium canum)*

Habitat: hot rocky crevices and cobble bars along rivers.

The California fuchsia or hummingbird trumpet is a conspicuous plant of rocky canyon walls when its late summer blooms attract both the eye and hummingbirds. A member of the evening-primrose family, it is sometimes classified as a fireweed. Many selected forms of this drought-tolerant native are cultivated in today's gardens.

Dutchman's pipevine

Dutchman's Pipevine *(Aristolochia californica)*

Habitat: riparian, or about springs.

Dutchman's pipevine is a woody climber to 13 feet long and belongs to the birthwort family, because of its supposed efficacy for childbirth. The odd flowers trap fungus gnats briefly to ensure pollination. The leaves are host to horned caterpillar larvae of the beautiful pipevine swallowtail an abundant metallic blue-black butterfly.

LILY-LIKE MONOCOTYLEDONS

Brodiaea *(Brodiaea sp.)*

Habitat: open, grassy meadows and hillsides.

Brodiaea was named for James Brodie, an early Scotch botanist. The bulbs of this plant are thought to have been one of the most important underground food plants of the Nisenan. They were gathered in large quantities with digging sticks and eaten raw, fried, boiled, or roasted. When eaten raw, they are somewhat mucilaginous, and their flavor is improved if boiled slowly for a few minutes. But they are at their best when roasted slowly in hot ashes for a half hour to an hour, during which time they become rather sweet. Gophers are also fond of the bulbs. Brodiaeas are beautiful wildflowers and should be sampled only in emergencies or when growing in great abundance.

Brodiaea

Mariposa Lily *(Calochortus venustus)*

Habitat: sandy, rocky soil; dry, open slopes.

Mariposa, meaning "butterfly" in Spanish, lilies have a delicate beauty fine enough to have become the stuff of legend. Several thousand years ago it was believed they encouraged virtue and purity. Another myth warns that close sniffing of this lily will cause freckles to appear on one's nose. The bulbs of the mariposa were a very important food to the Nisenan, and in April, after budding, were dug with a stick by both men and women. They were roasted for about 20 minutes in hot ashes and when done, were like soft-boiled potatoes. These are one of the most spectacular wildflowers of the Motherlode, so it is wise to eat their bulbs only in emergency situations. They offer far more with their flowers than they ever could with their food.

Mariposa lily

Globe Lily or Fairy Lantern *(Calochortus albus)*

Habitat: shaded, rocky places; open woodlands.

This lily with its delicate globe shape, is often referred to as a fairy lantern.

Globe lily or fairy lantern

FERNS

Horsetails *(Equisetum arvense)*

Habitat: moist soil along streams and rivers; in marshes and other damp places.

Horsetails are considered to be a primitive family with a history better known than any other living order of plants. It existed as a large, tree-like plant, up to 60 feet tall, in the Carboniferous age, nearly 300 million years ago. Its present appearance has hardly changed, other than its height. The

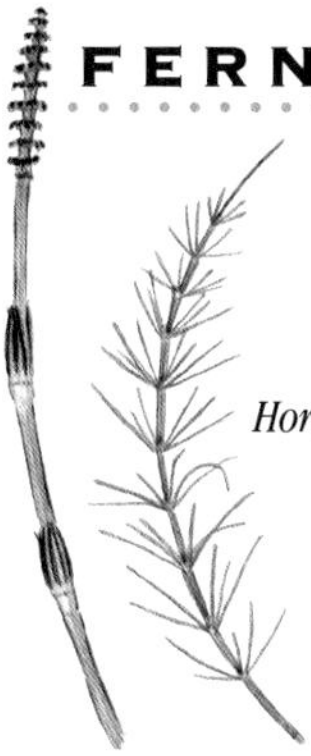

Horsetails

California Indians used the silica-covered stems to scour pots and pans (which is why sometimes they are referred to as "scouring rushes"). The young tips were used as a diuretic for bladder and kidney problems. Also, a strong tea boiled from the stems and applied externally is said to stop the bleeding of wounds and contains effective antiseptic and disinfectant properties. In Chinese medicine, a tea boiled from the stems is used as a pain reliever and to expel gas.

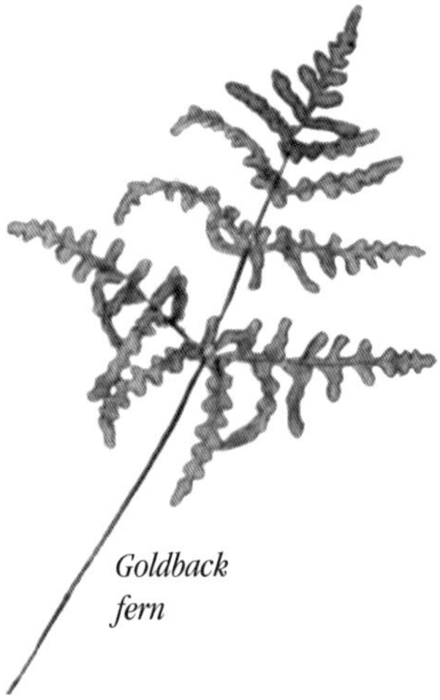
Goldback fern

Goldback Fern *(Pentagramma triangularis)*

Habitat: sun or shade in rocky soil and crevices.

The dark stems of the goldback fern were prized by Native Americans for use in basketry to add color. Indian children would make leafprints on their clothes by slapping the leaf on them with the bottom, spore-side down.

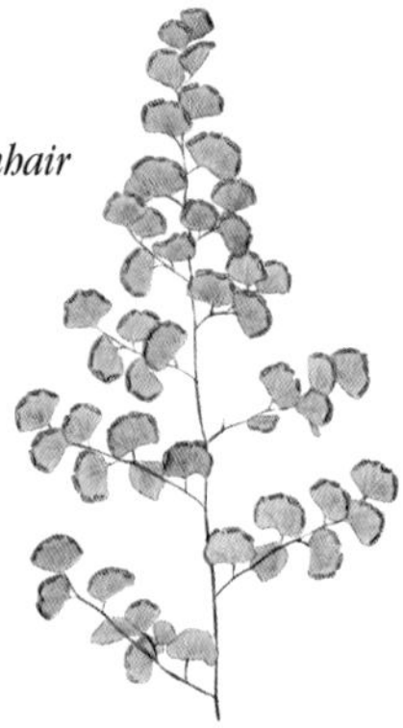
Maidenhair fern

Maidenhair Fern *(Adiantum jordani)*

Habitat: shade and damp soil; sometimes hanging vertically on wet limestone rocks, usually near a spray of water.

Their stems were treasured by the Miwoks for use in adding color to their baskets. The dried fronds may be made into tea and used for coughs, sore throats, and as a hair tonic.

Bracken fern

Bracken Fern *(Pteridium aquilinum)*

Habitat: open fields, woods, and burned areas.

Its vigor, fertility, and adaptability make the bracken fern the most common and widely known of all ferns. It is the first to poke up in the spring and produces fronds until the first frost. It grows abundantly where fire has burned groundcover. The California Indians cooked the rhizomes and young fronds for food and wove baskets and textiles from the long rhizomes. A greenish-yellow dye may be obtained from the stems. The old fronds are poisonous in large amounts, especially to grazing cattle. A strong tea made from the rhizomes and roots was used to expel worms and gas. Indian women also used this tea to relieve menstrual cramps. These lively ferns can be found carpeting fields from Alaska to the southernmost parts of the United States.

BIRDS

Great Blue Heron *(Ardea herodias)*

Great blue heron

Voice: a loud, harsh croak, repeated. **Nest:** mostly in colonies; a crude platform of sticks, usually high in an open tree near water.

In flight the blue-gray color, slow flapping of the large broad wings, and trailing long legs make identification of this heron easy. Either standing or flying the neck is crooked (whereas that of a crane is extended). The great blue may appcar along any open stretch of water, marsh or meadow, wading in the shallows or stalking slowly over grassland in search of food. The slender bill, 4-1/2" to 6" long, is an effective pincer, serving to grasp a fish in water, a frog on the bank, or even a mouse in dry grassland–all of which serve as food.

Water Ouzel or Dipper *(Cinclus mexicanus)*

Voice: call a short "bzeet", singly or in rapid series; male has elaborate varied song. **Nest:** on rocks near or over rushing water, of moss, entrance on side.

Water ouzel or dipper

This is our only "song" bird that lives solely on perennial cascading streams. The dense feathering that sheds water is its only aquatic adaptation, the feet being unwebbed. When perched on a midstream rock, the ouzel bobs down and up every few seconds. It flies along a winding stream course, keeping close over the water and uttering the short call repeatedly. To feed, the bird forages in the shallows or plunges right into the water, where it can walk on the bottom while searching for aquatic insects. The ouzel is a yearlong resident wherever streams remain unfrozen during winter, up into the lodgepole-fir belt. Its song may be heard at almost any season, being most impressive in winter when other bird voices are few. The nest is usually placed where moistened by spray, even behind a waterfall, so that its mossy exterior remains green so long as used.

Spotted Sandpiper *(Actitis macularia)*

Spotted sandpiper

Voice: a clear tweet-tweet-tweet, nest: on wet meadow or gravel, scant lining of grasses or none.

The pale brown and white body, inch-long bill, and incessant bobbing of the hind parts mark this little freshwater sandpiper. As it walks, the head moves fore-and-aft in unison with the feet. On taking to flight it makes an arc over the water to some more distant shore; after the first few strokes the wings are held spread, curving downward and moving only at the tips.

The bird forages in the shallows or on the shore close to water, picking up small aquatic animals or insects for food. It is seen singly or in pairs and does not flock. The male raises the four young.

Common merganser

Common Merganser *(Mergus merganser)*

Nest: in hollow tree or on ground, lined with grasses, roots and down.

This fish duck bears horny "teeth" and a hooked tip, useful for catching the various kinds of fishes taken for food. It dives and swims readily under the surface when searching for prey, but is clumsy on land. Over the years broods of mergansers have been reported at many places in the Sierra, but they are particularly common on the rivers here described. Trout fishermen may consider the bird a competitor, but its numbers are small and the total effect is slight.

Belted kingfisher

Belted Kingfisher *(Creyle alcyon)*

Voice: a loud rattle. **Nest:** near water on vertical sand or clay bank.

Sooner or later the kingfisher's rattling call may be heard on most waters. The bird perches on some bare branch or snag, then moves on over the water or circles among trees. Its prey is of large aquatic insects and small fishes usually caught by a direct plunge; sometimes the bird hovers on beating wings while searching.

Black phoebe

Black Phoebe *(Sayornis nigircans)*

Voice: a single plaintive "pser". **Song:** two pairs of similar notes, with alternate rising and falling inflection. **Nest:** on ledge or rock or flat surface in a building, a cup made of mud pellets mixed with grass.

The black phoebe is our only resident flycatcher, able to find insect food at all seasons. In spring it must be near water to obtain mud for nest making. Then it forages over a stream or pool and even takes insects from the water surface. In winter the bird occurs more widely, sometimes living around farmyards. This phoebe commonly hunts from exposed places, on streamside rocks, on bare branches or twigs, and on the roofs of small buildings, but in the heat of summer it seeks shady perches. Because of its special nesting needs it is of less uniform occurrence than many other birds, although man-made bridges and buildings have increased the places where it can live.

Cliff Swallow *(Petrochelidon pyrrhonata)*

Voice: while feeding, a low "shurr"; when disturbed at a nest, a plaintive "kleer" repeated. **Song:** squeaky notes. **Nest:** in colonies, on rough cliffs or under bridges or eaves; spherical with narrow-necked openings, of mud pellets.

This highly colonial swallow originally made nests on cliffs but now commonly uses rough-surfaced bridges, crowding a dozen to a hundred on some favorable site. Each nest is made of great numbers of mud pellets gathered singly at some water margin. The narrowed roundish entrance at the top leads into an expanded chamber provided with light fibrous lining. Nests are safe from most enemies, but the birds will fly about and utter complaining cries if a person approaches a colony. On the west slope Sierra adults arrive in March but nesting is delayed until early May. By then flying insects are more abundant, so that they can alternate feeding with nest building, incubation, and caring for the young.

Cliff swallow perched and in flight

Canyon Wren *(Catherpes mexicanus)*

Voice: call a short "bzert". **Song:** about 10 clear loud notes, descending in pitch and slowing at end. **Nest:** near stream in rock crevices, of twigs felted over with moss or other soft materials.

Anyone who visits a rock-walled foothill valley during the spring is likely to hear the loud clear song of this wren. Its color is striking - a pure white throat and reddish back. The bird hops in zigzag path on bent legs; every few seconds it slowly raises and then quickly depresses the body. When foraging it prowls into all manner of crevices in search of insects. The nest has a smoother exterior than that of other wrens.

Canyon wren

Wrentit *(Chamaea faciata)*

Voice: call is a wooden-sounding, rattled "churrrrrrr", or longer "krrrrrrrrrrr". **Song:** "pit-pit-pit-pit-pit-pit-trrrrrrrr", which has a bouncing ball-like quality as notes speed up into a trill; often repeated. Female song is similar but lacks the trill. **Nest:** comprised of a neat, compact cup of plant fibers in low bushes.

Known as the "Voice of the Chaparral", the song of the wrentit is one of most common sounds of the dry thickets and chaparral-covered hillsides. Heard more often that seen, the wrentit has a distinctive small round body and a long tail usually cocked at an angle. The chaparral couple mate for life and they rarely venture far from the nest area.

Wrentit

Anna's Hummingbird *(Calypte anna)*

Anna's hummingbird

Voice: call is a slightly emphatic to fairly hard "tik" or "tih" and a more smacking "tsick", in flight and perched. In flight chases, a rapid-paced, slightly buzzy twittering, "t-chissi-chissi-chissi", and variations. **Song:** a high-pitched, wiry to lisping squeaky warble from perch, often prolonged and repeated with pulsating succession. Year-round. **Nest:** a cup of plant down decorated with mosses and lichens, in tree or bushes.

A hardy denizen of the open-woodland, chaparral and residential gardens, annas are the only hummingbirds to withstand the winter and, amazingly, begin nesting as early as December and January. The flowers of manzanita and currant, insects, and fast food (hummingbird feeders) are a constant source of nutrition. During breeding, the casual observer may take great pleasure in watching the male anna's aerial skill as it performs a sky-diving territorial display to intimidate rival males or other trespassers.

Black-headed grosebeak

Black-headed Grosebeak *(Pheucticus melanocephalus)*

Voice: call is a sharp "eek". **Song:** a robin-like series warbled phrases, rising and falling. **Nest:** a loose structure of twigs in small trees or bushes.

It has been wonderfully said that the April return of the black-headed grosbeak at once fills the great spaces that have been silent with sweet and penetrating melody. As a spring and summer resident, these colorful, large-billed, finch-like birds can be found widely amongst deciduous and riparian habitats consisting of cottonwood, willow, oaks as well as old orchards and open oak-conifer forests. They mostly feed on insects during nesting and fruits in the late summer. They also frequent yard feeders containing black oil sunflower seeds. The low, sweet "whee, whee-you" note of the young can be heard from both the nest and when fed by the parents.

Spotted towhee

Spotted Towhee *(Pipilo maculates)*

Voice: the call is a descending and rapid mewing "queee, queee". **Song:** a few high-pitched introductory notes followed by harsh or buzzy trill. **Nest:** made of shreds of bark and plant fibers placed on the ground or low bushes.

With rich rufous sides and a red eye, this robin-sized bird is one of the most striking members of the sparrow family. Commonly found amongst brushy thickets and blackberry tangles, the towhee uses a technique known as "double-scratching" in which it repeatedly hops forwards and backwards, dragging its claws, in search of seeds and insects. Shy, but curious, the spotted towhees will often rise from below and perch high atop a shrub or small tree to exclaim its presence.

California Quail *(Callipepla californica)*

California quail

Voice: call notes include a rapid spitting "spwik wik wiw"; a sharp, metallic alarm "pit-pit"; soft clucking "ut, ut...". The **Song:** a nasal "chi-ca-go" or "put-way-doo" and often repeated. **Nest:** averaging 14 eggs, is a well concealed depression on the ground usually under bushes or within tall grass.

Often seen in familial groups, known as coveys, these smoky grey and brown pear-shaped birds with a distinctive head plume are commonly seen scurrying about the dense chaparral and riparian thickets. To avoid predators, they will often roost in trees or dense shrubs. The California quail is our state bird.

Acorn Woodpecker *(Melanerpes formicivorous)*

Acorn woodpecker

Voice: call is a loud "wack-a, wack-a or ja-cob, ja-cob" series. Also, a scratchy, drawn-out "krrrrit or krrrrit-kut", and a high, cawing "urrrk". **Drum:** a simple, slow roll of about 10-20 beats. **Nest:** in holes in trees and telephone poles.

With undulating flight and white wing patches, this clown-faced woodpecker is a conspicuous resident of the pine-oak woodlands and remarkable for its social habits, living over much of its range in communal groups, of up to 16 members, while maintaining and protecting large granaries in which thousands of acorns are drilled and stored for future use. A study of a single tree contained over 50,000 acorn-storage holes. They also feed on insects and it's not uncommon to see them sallying out over rivers and large streams for dragonflies and other large winged-insects.

Northern Flicker *(Colaptes auratus)*

Northern flicker

Voice: call is a piercing, descending "klee-yer" or "keeew"; also a soft, rolling "wirrror" or "whurdle" in flight and a soft, slow "wick-a wick-a wicka" given by interacting birds. **Drum:** a long simple roll of about 25 beats over a second, often interspersed with long "wick wick wick" series. **Nest:** tree holes and buildings.

No woodpecker spends more time feeding on ground than the flicker. Insects comprise 75 percent of its diet of which almost half are ants. They also eat grubs, caterpillars, beetles, grasshopper, and wasps. About 25 percent of their diet is from plants–mostly berries and fruits such as manzanita, ma-

Band-tailed pigeon

Northern pygmy owl front view and back view

Turkey vulture perched and in flight

drone, poison-oak, and acorns. Their seasonal abundance increases during the autumn and winter when small groups can be seen foraging on woodland floors and rural yards. The flicker's bright reddish-orange wing and tail feathers were used by California Indians for their head dresses.

Band-tailed Pigeon *(Columba fasciata)*

Voice: call is a low-pitched "whoo-whoo" delivered several times. **Nest:** a loose bulky platform of sticks, on a horizontal branch of a tree (usually an oak) from 8-40 feet up.

In the spring or fall, a common close encounter with the band-tailed pigeon usually comes when a flock suddenly takes flight on loud clapping wings and startles the passerby. Typically found in flocks 10 to 50 birds, they may be seen perched upright in the tops of oaks and pines or flying purposefully above the tree tops. Their abundance in any given year is largely dependant on the acorn crop. They'll also eat manzanita, madrone, coffeeberry and toyon berries.

Northern Pygmy Owl *(Glaucidium gnoma)*

Voice: a mellow, whistled, "took" or "took-took", repeated in a well-paced series. Also, gives a rapid series of "hoo" or "took" notes followed by a single "took", and heard most often early or late in the day. **Nest:** located in hole of tree usually an oak or pine.

Known as the "winged wolverine", this common little owl is extremely aggressive and brings real terror to the local birdlife. It is easily recognized by its long tail, dark streaked breast and prominent "false eyes" on the nape. Most active at dawn or dusk, its diet consists mainly of small birds but also include mammals, reptiles, insects, and it will not hesitate to attack prey larger in size. The call is easily imitated and readily attracts a mob of protesting songbirds. This technique is often used by birders to not only find an owl but to attract other birds into view.

Turkey Vulture *(Cathartes aura)*

Nest: in hole of cliff, no lining.

Turkey vultures, "buzzards", soar overhead with their large wings tilted upward. Whenever the air is warm they circle and spiral on upwelling currents with little change in the set of wings or tail. The individuals usually are spaced out, perhaps one per square mile, scanning the ground for any dead animals–ground squirrel, rabbit, horse, or cow. When one sees such food it glides down, rocking sideways while descending. Other vultures are attracted by this signal and soon converge toward the site. A large carcass may bring a dozen or more to tear off and devour the carrion. In morning and evening and on rainy days the birds perch on open trees in hunched posture with the head between the shoulders. During migration, late September and early October, they are often seen in large, loose flocks.

Red-tailed hawk perched and in flight

Red-tailed Hawk *(Buteo jamaicensis)*

Voice: a shrill long whistle. **Nest:** a bulky twig platform well up in trees or on cliffs.

Singly or in pairs, red-tails circle and glide high in open air as they watch for squirrels or rabbits on the ground. When prey is sighted, the hawk swoops and strikes with its large sharp claws. The larger animals are torn apart and eaten where killed, but smaller ones are carried off to a tree perch. Like other large flesh-eating birds, a red-tail may gorge a large meal that will suffice for several days. When not hunting, the hawk will perch high in a dead or live tree where it has a wide view. If disturbed, it leaps off and beats strongly with the big wings and soon begins to soar. Hunters mistakenly call this the "chicken hawk" and may shoot on sight, but the species is highly beneficial and protected by law.

Bald eagle

Bald Eagle *(Haliaettus leucocephalus)*

Voice: it has a remarkably weak call, rapidly repeated in a high, thin, hollow tone. **Nest:** sticks, often very large, in trees.

The bald eagle has been considered a winter visitor only but recent summer sightings suggest they have become breeders and year-round residents in the Central Sierra. Similar to the peregrine falcon, the bald eagle population crashed in the 1950s and 1960s as a result of pesticide use. With improved environmental stewardship and the will to survive, both of these magnificent birds have made a remarkable comeback, possibly exceeding historical populations. With fish being the primary source of food, bald eagles are typically found near lakes and large rivers. The bald eagle is the national symbol for the United States.

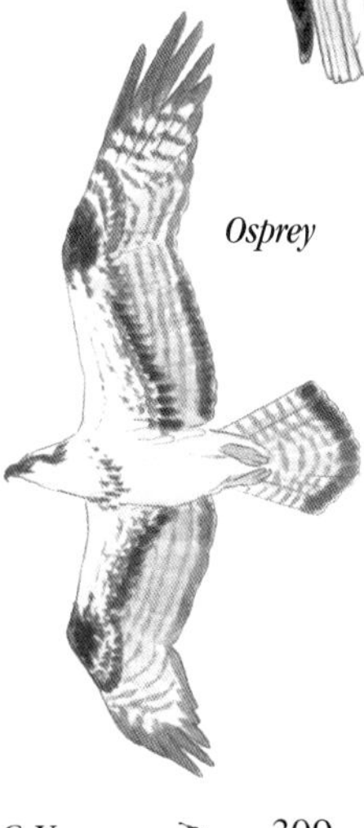

Osprey

Osprey *(Pandion haliaetus)*

Voice: distinctive whistles and categorized into 5 types: guard, alarm, excited, screaming, and solicitation. **Nest:** a huge platform of sticks on a dead tree.

With its distinctive brown and white plumage and exclusive habit of fish-eating, the osprey or "fish hawk" is one of the most easily identified raptors. It is commonly seen flying over fresh-water lakes, rivers, and reservoirs or seen diving into the water, feet first, to catch a fish. If successful, the osprey aerodynamically positions the fish head forward in its talons and flies to a favorite feeding perch. The osprey is a summer resident and migrates in fall and winter for the warm coasts of the Southern and Western U.S., Central America, and the Caribbean.

INSECTS

Lady beetle

Lady Beetle *(Coccinellidae)*

This family has dozens of color and dot variations. The lady beetle over-winters in the mountains in clumps, sometimes massive, on tree trunks, shrubs and grasses. It migrates into the valley, by catching wind currents, in the spring to eat aphids. Its body contains distasteful compounds to predators. Lady beetles are also poached by collectors for resale in the nursery trade.

Example of an engorged tick

Western black-legged tick

Western Black-legged Tick *(Ixodes pacificus)*

These ticks, that can transmit debilitating Lyme disease, are found on grasses, shrubs logs and leaf litter. To remove a tick that has attached itself to your skin grab it with tweezers as close as possible to your skin pulling firmly straight out. If a rash or flu like symptoms develop within 30 days see a doctor. Do a full body search after a hike in tick country.

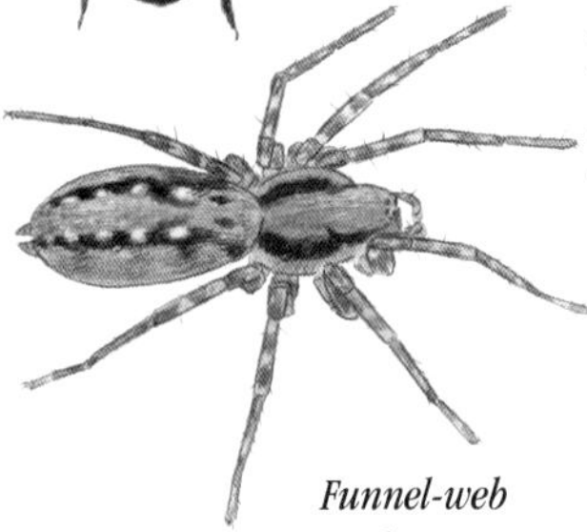

Funnel-web spider

Funnel-web Spider *(Novalena intermedia Agelenidea)*

These spiders spin broad sheets of silk with a funnel shaped retreat area that they hide in while waiting for prey to hit the sheet. The spider pounces on the victim dragging it into the funnel where it cannot escape.

Stonefly

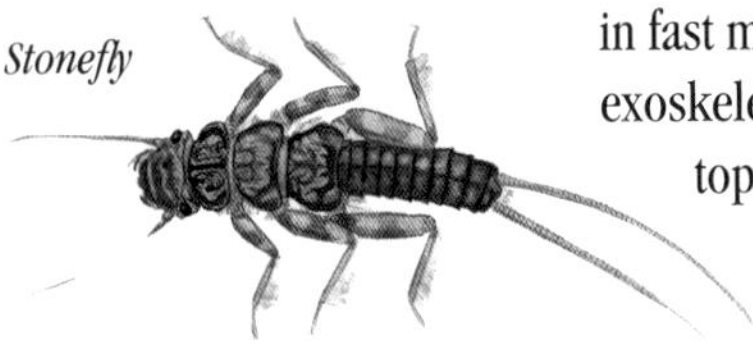

Stonefly *(Perlidae)*

The nymph form of this aquatic insect lives under rocks in fast moving water that contains more oxygen. The brittle exoskeleton shell of their bodies are found split open from top to bottom on river boulders after they have metamorphosed into a flying insects.

WATER LIFE

Crayfish *(Pacfastucus teniusulus)*

The crayfish's rigid upper-body with pincers is propelled by the flexible, segmented lower body used for swimming, carrying eggs, and young. They feed on fish, insects, snails and other animal matter.

Crayfish

Rainbow Trout *(Oncorhynchus mykiss irideus)*

Our only native trout in this region is found in all our small streams and rivers. When it migrates to the ocean it is called a steelhead.

Rainbow trout

Foothill Yellow-Legged Frog *(Rana boylei)*

This amphibian is found in clear foothill streams where the habitat is relatively natural and free of bullfrogs. Presently, the yellow-legged frog is quietly disappearing. It is on the federal endangered species list.

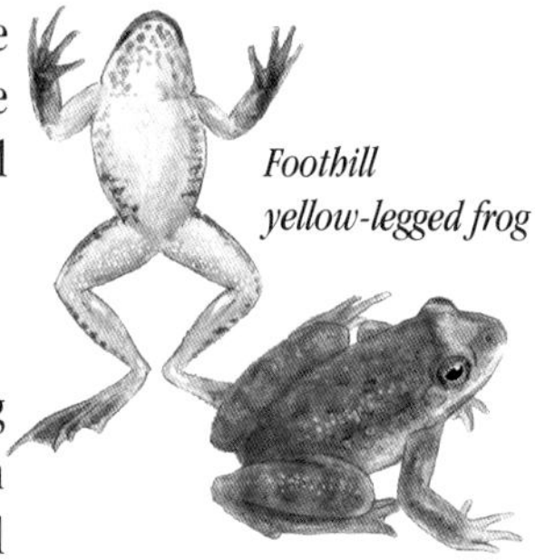

Foothill yellow-legged frog

Sierra Newt *(Taricha torosa sierrae)*

Seen on cloudy and rainy days in winter and early spring the "firebelly" travels from its moist summer hideaway in rotting logs or under rocks in the forest to streams. Its tail thins allowing it to swim with other adult newts to form mating balls. Beware of handling newts. Their skin contains the powerful neurotoxin tetrodotoxin deadly to all except garter snakes.

Sierra newt

REPTILES

Western Pond Turtle *(Clemmys mamarta)*

The only native freshwater turtle to California can often be seen sunning itself on rocks or logs along the river's edge. Eggs are laid in land nests. It survives drought in mud burrows and its diet includes aquatic plants, insects and carrion.

Western pond turtle

Northern Pacific Rattlesnake *(Crotalus oreganos oreganos)*

The buzz of this venomous heavy bodied fanged snake with slender neck and triangular shaped head is sure to get your attention. A new rattle segment is added with each shed skin at the end of the blunt tail. The rattler uses heat sensitive pits near the nostrils to detect prey and threats. In the event of a bite stay calm and see a doctor as quickly as possible.

Northern pacific rattlesnake

Pacific gopher snake head and tail

Pacific Gopher Snake *(Pituophis catenifer catinfer)*

This constrictor snake can easily be mistaken for a rattlesnake in appearance and its defensive behavior can mimic a passable imitation of the rattlesnake. When cornered, it hisses and roars like a bull. Look for the slender neck, head and sharp tail.

Gilberts skink

Gilberts Skink *(Eumecus gilberti gilberti)*

This secretive slim bodied lizard eats insects, larvae and spiders in the late afternoon.

MAMMALS

River otter

River Otter *(Lutra Canadensis)*

The playful family-oriented web-footed otter can be found swimming in pursuit of fish in the river, munching crayfish on river rocks or sliding down river banks on their dense fur coats. Their pups are born in burrows or a hollow tree.

Raccoon

Raccoon *(Procyon lotor)*

Solitary by nature except during the breeding season raccoons prefer to den in trees, leaving them at night to probe stream and bank with their sensitive fingers for clams, crayfish, insects and fish. They will also eat acorns and love fruits especially wild figs.

Black-tailed jackrabbit

Black-tailed Jackrabbit *(Lepus californicus)*

Our leaping jackrabbit is actually considered a hare because they are born with hair and escape from prey by running rather than hiding. Because their chisel-like incisors never stop growing they must be worn down by chewing.

California ground squirrel

California Ground Squirrel *(Spermophilus beechey)*

Often seen scampering along the ground or sitting in on upright posture on rocky outcrops near their burrows these sentinels of danger warn of threats with a distinctive bird-like chirping whistle.

Ringtail

Ringtail *(Bassariscus astutus)*

Almost completely nocturnal in behavior this rare omnivore feeds on berries, insects and mice. An agile climber, using its distinctive tail for balance, the ringtail may sometimes be seen sleeping in trees. Their nickname, miners cats, comes from the gold rush when the young were caught, tamed and used to rid the miners tents and cabins of mice.

Black bear

Black Bear *(Ursus americanus)*

The color of our largest nocturnal omnivore may vary considerably from blonde to black. Our local variety seems to favor the cinnamon color. The young, normally two, are born in the winter den every other year.

Columbian Black-tailed deer

Columbian Black-tailed Deer

(Odocoileus heminous columbianus)

Our local deer with their distinctive black tail are a subspecies of the mule deer. They generally browse in the early morning or evening. New antlers grow on the males in spring and are shed in the winter. Their sense of hearing and smell make up for poor sight.

Mountain lion

Mountain Lion *(Felis concolor)*

Our largest native cat also known as the cougar or puma will eat anything from mice to skunks to deer. They are curious observers. Their favorite method of attack is to slowly stalk their prey making a powerful leap to sink large canine teeth into the neck. **Caution:** humans in the crouching and running posture may look like prey.

Bobcat

Bobcat *(Lynx rufus)*

Widely found in the foothills the bobcat's main diet consists of rabbits, ground squirrels and rodents. Occasionally they can be observed capturing prey by pouncing from an ambush.

Coyote

Coyote *(Canis latrans)*

These wily tenacious predators have a well-earned reputation for mischief, having adapted to living on the fringes of populated areas. Young are raised in burrow dens. Both parents feed and teach the pups.

Gray fox

Gray Fox *(Urocyon cinereoargenteus)*

When threatened this shy fox found in the brushy wooded foothills can climb trees to avoid predators. They feed on small rodents, fruit, birds and eggs and usually den under large rocks, crevices or hollow logs.

Fishes and Fishing in the Forks of the American River:

Then and Now

By Eric Gerstung and updated by Bill Templin

The endemic fish fauna of the American River drainage, prior to the arrival of Europeans, was quite different than that of today. There were no fish in headwater lakes such as the Lochleven Lakes or higher elevation streams like Palisade Creek above impassable barriers (waterfalls over 8 feet high). There were no brown trout, brook trout, or kokanee salmon. There were no bass, sunfish, or catfish. All of the above were introduced from other parts of the world. There were, however, rainbow trout, its seagoing cousin, the steelhead, chinook salmon, white sturgeon, and Sacramento perch. The latter two occurred below Folsom. All but the Sacramento perch remain in the drainage today, though distribution has changed.

Non-game fish found in the American rivers indigenously were Sacramento squawfish, western sucker, hardhead, riffle sculpin, western roach, speckled dace, and Pacific lamprey. All but the lamprey are still present in the forks. Downstream from the forks several other species of non-game fish occupied the river when the Maidu were the only people here, notably Sacramento blackfish, Sacramento hitch, splittail, tule perch, Sacramento tui chub, and the thicktail chub. The thicktail chub is now extinct but all the others are still present in lower river. Europeans introduced carp, goldfish, mosquito fish, golden shiner, threadfin shad, and the fathead minnow to the drainage. These fish occur mostly in Folsom Lake or below it in the Lower American.

Other introduced gamefish including smallmouth bass, green sun-fish, bluegill sunfish, red-ear sunfish, white crappie, channel catfish, white catfish, brown bullhead, black bullhead, striped bass, and American shad. With the exception of the smallmouth bass, these fish are not usually found in the forks, but in Folsom Lake, the Lower American River, or several lakes and ponds tributary to the forks.

The most important fishery in the American River was that produced by the chinook salmon. Up until the early 1950s chinook salmon lived in the North and Middle Forks of the American River. There were two distinct runs–a fall run which came up after the first rains in November and a spring run which ascended the river during May.

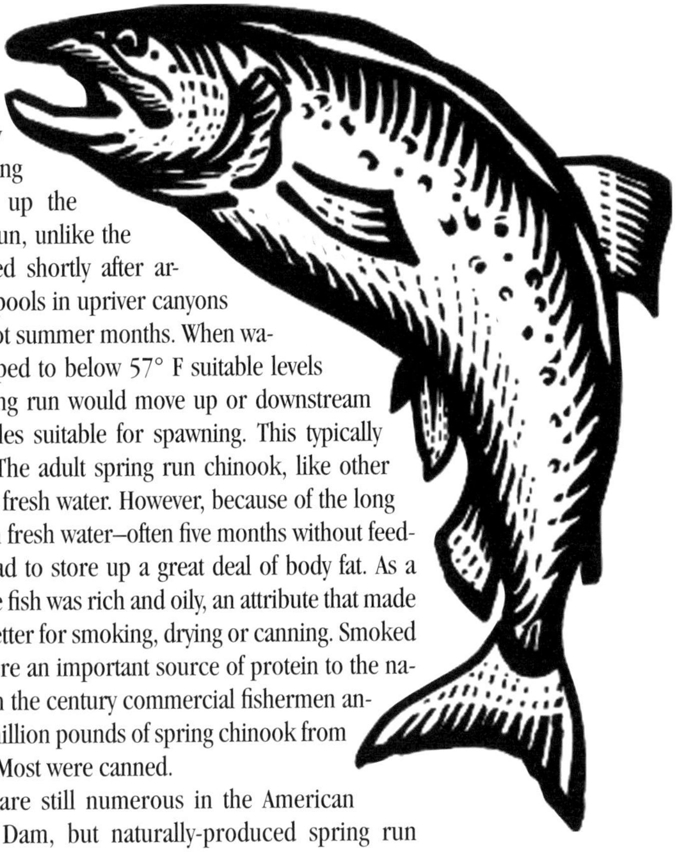

The fall run salmon spawned primarily in the lower river below the forks while the spring run spawned further up the drainage. The spring run, unlike the fall run which spawned shortly after arrival, sought out deep pools in upriver canyons where they spent the hot summer months. When water temperatures dropped to below 57° F suitable levels for spawning, the spring run would move up or downstream seeking out gravel riffles suitable for spawning. This typically occurred in October. The adult spring run chinook, like other salmon, do not feed in fresh water. However, because of the long residence time spent in fresh water–often five months without feeding - the spring run had to store up a great deal of body fat. As a result, the flesh of these fish was rich and oily, an attribute that made the spring run much better for smoking, drying or canning. Smoked or dried spring run were an important source of protein to the native Americans. Early in the century commercial fishermen annually caught several million pounds of spring chinook from the Sacramento River. Most were canned.

Fall run Chinook are still numerous in the American River below Nimbus Dam, but naturally-produced spring run fish no longer live in the American River or in most of the other northern California streams where they were formerly found. Only remnant populations remain in the upper Sacramento River and its Mill and Deer Creek tributaries and in several tributaries of the Klamath River. Surprisingly, Chinook salmon, that the California Department of Fish and Game supposedly sterilized in 2006 before stocking them in Folsom Reservoir, now appear to have spawned and their offspring are now (2010) being caught in the reservoir in the 12 to 14 inch size range.

Gold dredging can still interfere with fishing by making water muddy and by "flouring" the remnant mercury used in the early-day hydraulic mining. Spawning gravels in the American River and its forks were silted over by hydraulic mining that nearly exterminated the salmon and similar silting from gold dredging can adversely impact wild trout spawning today. After hydraulic mining was outlawed, a number of dams were constructed on the river: old Folsom Dam in 1895, the North Fork Ditch Company Dam in 1899, and the North Fork Debris Dam in 1939. The latter did not have a fish ladder, and fish ladders on the other two dams were nonfunctional most of the time. By the time Nimbus and Folsom dams were built in 1955, the

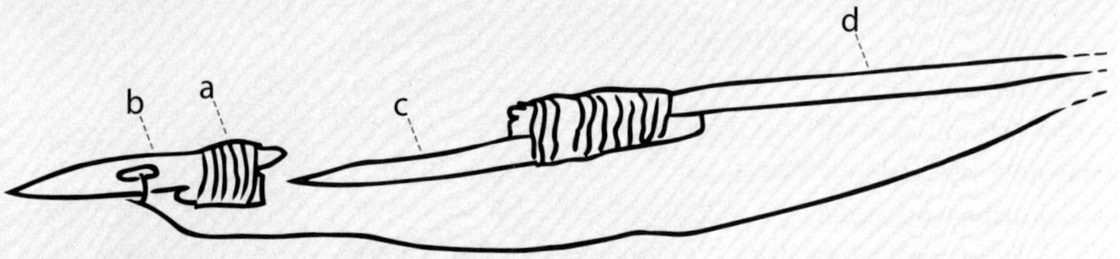

Salmon Harpoon
The bone-pointed harpoons were made with a large quill butt. a) tied to a point, b) with sinew, into which fits the point of the foreshaft, c) the foreshaft point was usually worked from the leg bone of a deer, lashed to the main shaft, d) string was attached to the main shaft and wrapped around it tightly when thrown.

spring-run had dwindled to a few fish. Water temperatures below Nimbus Dam are not suitable for spring run and consequently Nimbus Fish Hatchery was not designed to handle spring run. Spring run fish produced in other rivers occasionally stray into the American, but are not able to repopulate the river.

In contrast to the spring run, a small fall run of chinook salmon still exists below Nimbus Dam. The future of this run, however, is threatened by continuing diversions into the Folsom South Canal and releases of water for competing uses. Diversions and releases for competing water uses drastically reduces flows in the river and consequently also reduces the salmon runs.

The North Fork of the American River upstream from Colfax remains one of the few rivers in the northern Sierra Nevada not impaired by major dams or other development. The California Legislature in 1972 recognized this and included the North Fork upstream from Colfax-Iowa Hill Bridge in the State Wild and Scenic Rivers Act. Prior to this event a group of water development promoters had been attempting to persuade the Placer County Water Agency to build a 550 foot high dam on the North Fork at Giant Gap.

Had they been successful, Green Valley and thirteen miles of river would have been buried. Because the state act only applied to private land and did not prevent the Federal Energy Regulatory Commission (FERC) from permitting power development on federal lands, conservationists in Placer County, led by Matt Bailey of Dutch Flat, successfully lobbied Congress to add the North Fork to the National Wild and Scenic Rivers system.

Ironically, the congressional effort to protect the North Fork was spearheaded by the late Congressman Harold T. "Bizz" Johnson, an influential proponent of Auburn Dam. Further recognition was given to the North Fork in 1982, when the California Fish and Game Commission designated the North Fork as a Wild Trout Stream. Under this designation the river is managed for wild trout rather than for hatchery trout.

The wild trout fishery on the North Fork varies in quality from excellent in the upper half to fair in the lower reaches. The North Fork flows through a deep canyon throughout its length. Upstream from Colfax-Iowa Hill Bridge there is no road access to the river, though a half dozen or so riding and hiking trails provide access to a number of points along the river. Fishing upstream from Humbug Bar is generally excellent. Pan-sized rainbow trout are numerous, and a skilled angler generally has no trouble catching the limit. Brown trout and larger rainbows are also occasionally taken.

Bait and lures can be effective during the early portion of the season while flies–particularly nymphs–are best later in the summer. Downstream from Humbug Bar the river becomes progressively warmer and non-game species and small mouth bass make up an increasingly greater proportion of the fish populations. Water temperatures exceeding 80° F are not uncommon.

Bait and artificial lures can be used between the last Saturday in April and November 15 in all forks of the upper American River and downstream of Highway 49 year around. All reservoirs are open all year but they may not be accessible during winter road closures. The bag limit in reservoirs and during the regular trout and salmon season is five trout (or salmon in combination) and 10 in possession. For bass, the bag limit is 5 per day. Artificial lures with barbless hooks can be used in all waters year around. Anglers can fish with only artificial lures with barbless hooks in the streams above Highway 49 from November 16 to the last Friday preceding the last Saturday in April and the bag limit is 0.

There is some road access to the North Fork downstream from the Colfax-Iowa Hill Bridge. The Colfax-Foresthill road crosses the river below the mouth of Shirttail Canyon Creek and two jeep roads penetrate the canyon several miles downstream. Fishing for rainbow trout, generally pan-sized fish, is only fair and is typically limited to the early part of the season–before flows drop and the water warms up. Later in the summer a few trout can still be found in well-oxygenated whitewater reaches of streams. Smallmouth bass can be found in boulder-strewn runs and deep rocky pools. Although the average smallmouth is less than 10 inches long, occasionally fish up to 14 inches long are caught. Smallmouth can be easily caught with trout lures. The best fishing can be found by walking up or downstream a mile or so from bridge crossings.

Clementine, a narrow, five mile long reservoir situated on the North Fork two miles upstream from the Highway 49 bridge, is the place to catch a wider variety of warm-water game fish species. Smallmouth bass, typically 8 to 14 inches, bluegill ranging from 4 to 8 inches, and brown bullheads, usually 8 to 14 inches are fairly numerous. Green sunfish, largemouth bass, and white catfish are present but less numerous. Shore fishing is limited to the road terminus near the dam.

Due to heavy aquatic weed beds and a steep brushy shoreline without foot trails, a boat is needed to fish the remainder of the lake. Fishing is best early and late in the day when there are fewer speed-boats on the water. The lake and river downstream from the lake are open to fishing throughout the year.

The Middle Fork of the American River above French Meadows Reservoir has a nice population of wild rainbow trout. French Meadows Reservoir and Hell Hole Reservoir are stocked with rainbow and brown trout and kokanee salmon by the California Department of Fish and Game. All reservoirs in this watershed are open for fishing year-round to bait and artificial lures but access during the winter may be prevented by heavy snow on the roads. The Middle Fork of the American River downstream from its confluence of the Rubicon River–like the lower North Fork–had water temperatures more suitable for smallmouth bass than trout. However, the operation of the Placer County Water Agency hydroelectric project beginning in 1966, reversed the situation. Cold water drawn from the bottom of Hell Hole and French Meadows Reservoirs and released from Ralston Afterbay Powerhouse has made the Middle Fork too cold for smallmouth bass and much better for trout. Hard fighting wild rainbow and brown trout, typically from one to two pounds in size, can be caught by skilled anglers. Good fishing exists in the stream reach between Oxbow Powerhouse and Folsom Lake.

In the "peaking reach" between Oxbow Reservoir and Driver's Flat fishing is difficult during summer afternoons because of the frequency of passing commercial rafts that take over the river. A number of dirt roads provide access to the river in the vicinity of Foresthill. Daily flow fluctuations of several feet occur below Ralston Afterbay Powerhouse. Fishing is usually best when flows are gently rising, and poor during natural high storm flows and during peaking periods in response to high power generation and commercial rafting demands. Artificial flies, natural baits, and lures are generally effective. Fishing pressure is greatest in the more accessible reaches of the Middle Fork, but is not typically very heavy primarily because access is limited, can be difficult, and the existence of the high quality fishery in this area is not well known.

CHAPTER FOUR

American River History:
In Stories and Songs

The Native People

By Otis Wollan

Six thousand years ago, in the American River Canyons just outside of Auburn, the people were collecting seeds and digging wild onion and garlic to eat with their salmon. In the evening, as the day's salmon catch was smoking and hung for drying, the people told stories of how their ancestors had hunted and followed the four-leggeds for their food, but that now the gods had revealed the secrets of the plants that they could eat also. Now they could live in villages, and not travel so far. They ate salmon and fresh, steaming acorn bread that night.

The next day, the clouds gathered for a welcome Fall rain shower, and in the hurry of trying to get the drying salmon and the other stores under cover, one of the villagers dropped a stone tool in the mud.

Grinding rocks, like these in Bird Valley on the Middle Fork, are some of the few remaining testaments to the old ways.

Thousands of years later, a stone tool was found by one of the archeological teams from the Bureau of Reclamation as they catalogued all signs of human habitation in preparation for Auburn Dam's flooding of the canyons. Jim West, chief archeologist on the team, estimated the age of the stone tool from the clay deposit in which it was found is four to six thousand years old.

People have lived here for thousands of years, yet we know so little about them. The short time our European origin culture has been here is just a moment in time by comparison.

MAP OF THE Nisenan

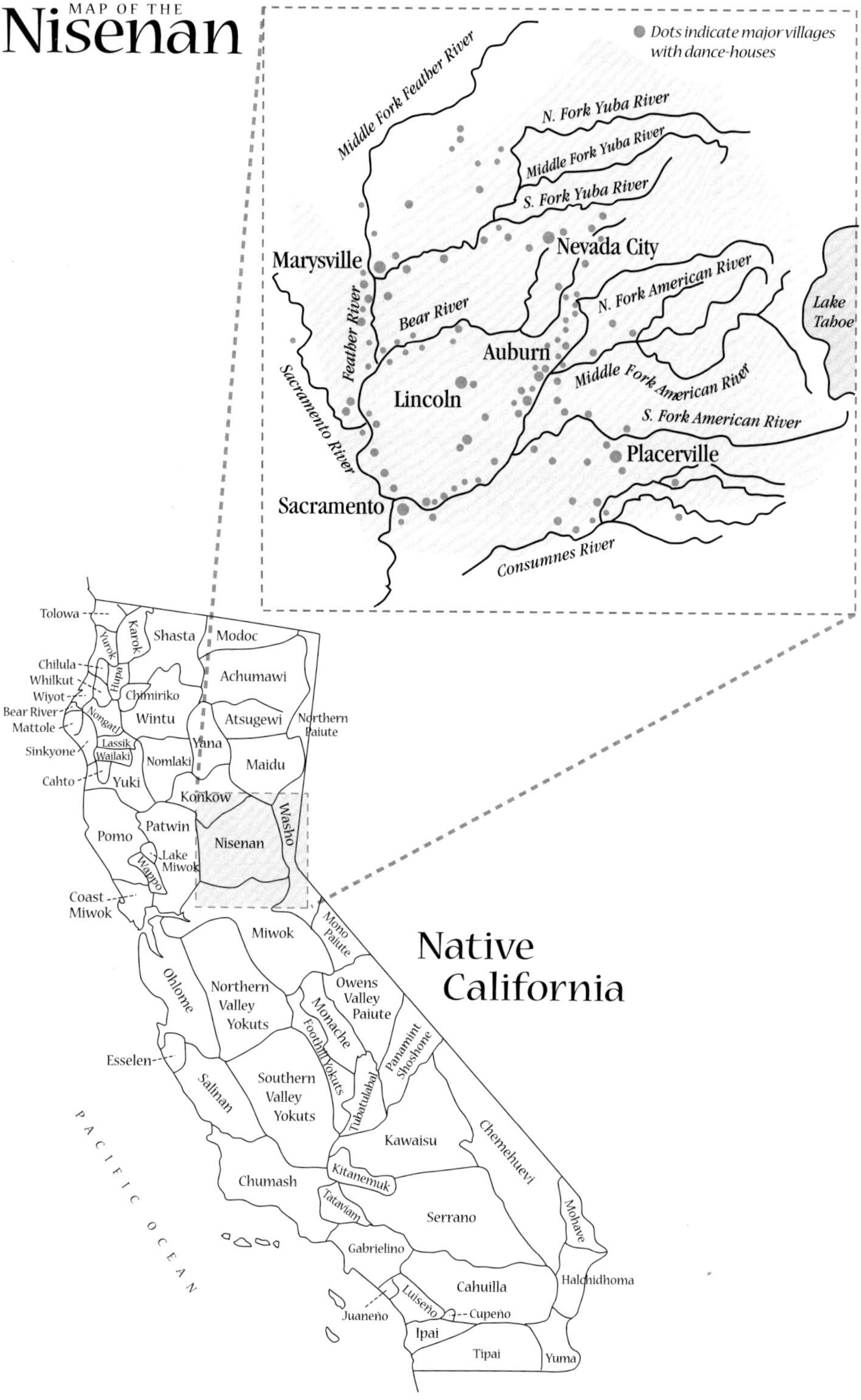

What were those people like? Who were they? How did they live, dress, eat, think? What did they dream? How did they treat the earth?

Walk out to the confluence of the North and Middle Forks of the American, just out of Auburn near Highway 49. Right there for thousands of years was a village.

Walk about until you find the grinding rocks. There are many grinding rocks right by the banks of the Middle Fork within a few feet of the confluence. Stop and take the time to imagine what that life must have been like.

Captain Tom's Auburn Wickiup, late 1800's
Brush and mud structures provided shelter from daytime heat.

Imagine the children, all playing by the river, and swimming in the pure water (that may not have changed much). All the surrounding hills are covered with acorn bearing oaks, canyon live oak, blue oak, and black oak. The big timber, Ponderosa Pine and Foothill Pine, with Douglas Fir in the North facing side canyons, stand tall. The under-story is free of scrub (unlike today). The brushy plants are regularly burned as a form of agriculture. Controlled burning provides better deer forage, easier access for humans, and a bountiful crop of the hard seeds from grasses and flowers on which the people depend for much of their food.

Imagine the Fall salmon run, with big salmon so plentiful that at Murderers' Bar Falls, they are simply gaffed out of the river as they sought their upstream gravel beds for spawning.

The cook fires are burning, and the salmon is being smoked. There is deer jerky drying in the sun. Acorn granaries are full, as usual (a two or three year surplus was common). Hazel nuts, pine nuts, tubers and roots seem to be in plenty.

A large k'um, or dance house, sits in the center of the village. Preparations for a dance are under way. Suddenly the deerskin over the door of the sweat lodge flies open, and out of the puff of smoke, a dozen men streak to the river for a cold plunge. They are fasting and sweating in preparation for a deer hunt.

9,000 *B.C.* | 8,000 | 7,000 | 6,000 | 5,000 | 4,000

EARLY HUNTING MAN
Nomadic people following animal migrations. Large, primitive tools and fluted point spears were used.

EARLY COLLECTING MAN
Milling Stones left by the "Mesilla" culture indicate hard seeds were collected for food.

Human beings have lived in these river canyonlands for almost ten thousand years. Large, primitive stone tools have been found; the oldest stone tool found in the proposed Auburn Reservoir Area is 6,000 years. A very sophisticated, biologically-rooted culture evolved, with a rich oral tradition, great stability, and a life that was in harmony with the earth.

Washo traders stop by the village on their trek over the Sierra crest. Dried fish from Pyramid Lake are traded for shell money the Nisenan had just gotten in trade from the Coast Miwok, and a few pieces of obsidian that the Yokut trader had brought by many months before.

That life went on for at least two thousand years, right here at the confluence village called *"Chulku"* and at the many other Nisenan villages nearby, at Auburn (*"Bisian"*), Clipper Gap (*"Didit"*), Colfax (*"Hakaka"*), Cool (*"Siyakayan"*), Coloma (*"Chapa"*), and all through this region.

Lizzie Enos

That life went on for generation after generation, until the Gold Rush, and it even continued after that in small, out-of-the-way pockets, until there was just one left that lived in the old way. The following is her story. It is as close as we can come to knowing what was here before we came.

OOTI: A MAIDU LEGACY

Photos and excerpt from the book by Richard Simpson

Lizzie Enos was a Maidu Indian. She was born in Placer County in 1880 and lived most of her life in the area of Meadow Vista and Clipper Gap. Her ancestors once populated an area from the Sacramento River eastward to the crest of the Sierra Nevada, almost touching Lake Tahoe. On the south were the converging American and Sacramento rivers, to the north Mount Lassen. Less than a hundred and fifty years ago this region was a natural wilderness where the Maidu culture flourished, a culture in which the spiritual and the mundane existed undivided. Springing from the Maidu myth of creation, the beliefs of the people lifted the earthly and tedious to a

3,000 2,000 1,000 0 *A.D.* 1,000 2,000

EARLY HORIZON
The "Windmiller" culture combined hunting, fishing, and seed collection, settling in the river valleys.

MIDDLE HORIZON
Stable villages developed trade routes; bow and arrow introduced.

LATE HORIZON
Large thriving villages with expanded trade routes.

place of reverence and celebration. According to those beliefs, the crushing of an acorn into meal, the crushing of ooti, became not an endless unbearable task, but a spiritual experience. The finding of the first acorn flower in spring signalled a time for festivals and dancing and celebration of life. The eating of ooti became a circle of remembrances, mysteries, and ever-changing associations.

Lizzie speaks for her people. She helps us understand that even the most simple everyday tasks are filled with miraculous importance and beauty. The following is her story of ooti.

Lizzie gathers acorns.

In the early time of legend, when Coyote was said to have swayed the people to his cunning ways and lost for them the good life, First Man, from World Maker's counsel, told the people of the acorn. He told them how the acorn should be gathered, how the shells were taken from them, how to pound the acorn into powder, how to sift them, how to take the bitter from them, how to bake them deep in coals, how to boil them in willow baskets, and how to make the water biscuit. All these things still survive in the mind of Lizzie, as if the past had never left her.

In the early days when villages had many houses, one could hear the endless music of the bone awl squeaking through the willow coils in the constant weaving of new baskets, and the constant repair of the old and worn. At the village, *Chukam Pakan*, only Lizzie makes this music now. She has spent many days weaving baskets, all made watertight of red and white willow, made strong and in all shapes and sizes suited to the job they must perform. A great pile of sound baskets now stands ready to be taken with the acorns to the pounding place.

Back from the green tufted bank of *Choopim Seyoo*, the little creek called Willow Water, sits a boulder full of acorn grinding holes. It is here, upon the boulder, that Lizzie will work throughout the day. From the village, *Maw Bawtatimaa,* to this boulder many women would come to sit and work. They sat and winnowed, gossiped, scolded children, pounded acorns until they had deep holes sculptured, now abandoned and filled with leaf mold, left their only mark in this hard black bedrock outcrop.

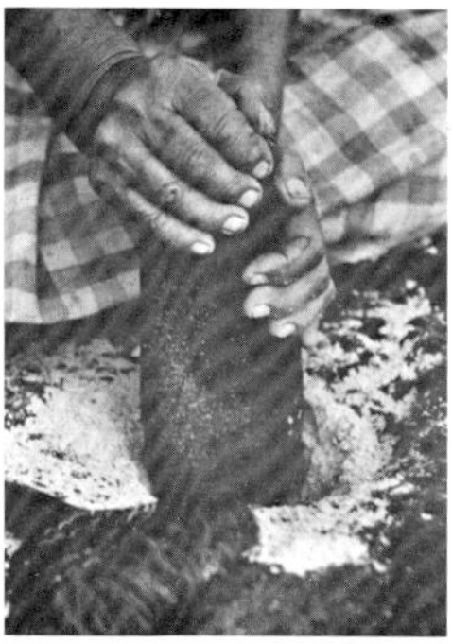

Lizzie uses a stone pestle to grind acorns into meal.

One of these holes is chosen. It is scrubbed hard with a soaproot brush until the lip and hollowed bowl shows blue against the older rain-worn rock around it.

Then Lizzie takes the first acorn in her fingers, points it down upon the boulder and strikes the white end twice with a small cracking rock. The acorn bulges and then splits open.

"My mother used to tell about this Indian lady that had gold cracking rock, big round one. She crack acorn with that for a long time I guess ... until this white man hear about it. White man come there and give that old lady fifty cents for it and take it away. But she don't care. That old lady had lotta those regular cracking rocks and fifty cents besides. Old time Indian never seem to care about gold like white people."

Lizzie pulls the split shell apart and the kernel falls into her palm. "When we crack and open this acorn, some of them black inside. Old timer never throw that away, just put it aside in one place. When they get maybe half sack they put that in running water about a week. Whole thing they put in there, and then take that out and boil it. After it boil they put salt on it and eat it that way. Is good. I used to eat with old people. Is good. Just taste like acorn bread."

The day moves on. Shells fall away and a basket fills with clean kernels, *Ootim Hai.*

When the final acorn has been hulled, Lizzie filled the grinding hole with kernels. Then she lifts the heavy stone pestle called *Bai* above her head, and, guiding the force of its weight back down into the hole, lets it fall to break the kernels, lifts it high and lets it fall to break and crush the kernels, lifts it high again and lets it fall, breaking, crushing, grinding the acorn kernels.

The ground kernels are scooped from the stone bowl and piled onto the flat winnowing basket. *Daw* is the Indian name for this special willow tool. The basket is whirled and tilted and bounced until the acorn meal arcs and spins in the air to find its own size there, then settles in a fine powder at the upper side of the basket as the larger particles fall over the lower edge and back into the hole to be reground.

Then the heavy pestle lifts and falls once more, thump, thump, thump, throughout the afternoon. And every little while the winnowing basket tilts and spins to interrupt the pounding, refining again and again the already sifted meal. So when the day is late and the shadows long, one basket has slowly filled with the finest yellow acorn flour, *Ootim Bat.*

Finished acorn meal is gathered together.

"Old people always have fine meal. `You eat better that way and it taste good that way,' my mother used to tell me. But I can't make it like they do. When they make acorn mush and it cold, it just like Jello. You can catch one side and it just come out in big chunk; then we eat it. Acorn dance song about that. Everybody dance and one man sing.

We dance, all of us. Men folks come into Round House with their costumes, come up in front, and the ladies circle around the outside of those men dancers. Oh look good! They just go slow and dance. Oh, they look good!

Old timer had a lot of songs. That Acorn Dance song just one of them they do all the time."

Lizzie leaves the acorn grinding rock for the day. Her basket is now filled with the new meal that tomorrow must be leeched of its bitterness.

Summer is here and deep sand lies stranded on the banks of the stream *Choopim Seyoo*, separated from clay and gravel like fine meal at the upper edge of the winnowing basket, fine sand to absorb the bitterness of the acorn. It is to such a place as this that Lizzie brings her baskets and newly ground meal.

She has built a fire on the gravel nearby, and over this fire her hand releases a spray of meal that sprinkles through the upward swirl of smoke and flame. She says the *Toomwey*, a prayer, speaks it as the meal is consumed by the heat of the fire and rises again as

Hot rocks are put into the basket to cook the acorn meal.

smoke to hang in the still morning air. Lizzie speaks this prayer to the spirits all around her.

Look at me from above
Look at me from these hills
Look at me from Heaven
And bless me

Lizzie then places cooking stones at the center of the fire to heat. These are the stones that will heat the water and cook the meal. "This be special rock. Common ones, when you make it hot and dip it in cold water, it break. But not that special rock. Just use same one over and over. *Koolem aw* we call that. *Aw* is the rock. *Koolem aw*, Powerful Rock."

Koolem aw got lotta little holes all over, only it not rough when you touch it. It is hard, that rock, but it have smooth feel like soapstone. That kind come from special place too. Used to be old camp, big Indian camp, up near Colfax with creek running through, and that creek got lotta those cooking rocks in there.

"In early days, maybe man and his wife they go up to that camp for Big Time, you know, dance or something. They had all kinds o' Big Time those old-time Indians. And when that over and they come back home, each bring down two or three of those rocks on their backs. That's the way they used to do. They have lot of it, that Powerful Rock."

Where the sand is deepest Lizzie smooths it flat and level. She smooths it around and around with her hand until a lip of sand circles the outer edge to form a shallow sand bowl as wide as an arm across.

As she works, Lizzie talks of the acorn and of the Big Prayer. "First acorn that fall, those green ones, they call that New Acorn. Old timers always have big doings for New Acorn.

Every woman from every camp bring New Acorn, and men folks kill lotta deers and rabbit. Women folks pound that acorn and they make New Acorn soup. That's the way they have big prayer. They don't say much, but they just talk a little bit and then you all go ahead and eat. Just same as white people.

Old timers used to do that, but late years we don't have that any more – we don't have New Acorn Prayer. That's why my mother used to say, 'Acorns sometime no more because you don't pray for it.' "

Dry pine needles are placed upon the sandy basin, strewn and patted down evenly to make a porous nest. Over this in turn a thin white cloth is spread. Then the meal, rich and yellow with bitterness, tumbles from Lizzie's basket onto the cloth. It is smoothed out with the hands until a layer of acorn meal covers the entire circle of the nest. At one edge of the unleeched meal, green Cedar boughs have been placed.

"This be where water pour. Water hit this bough and keep from making big hole that way. When you eat acorn mush or bread, little bit Cedar you can taste."

A basket of cool water is dipped from *Choopim Seyoo*. It is poured through the Cedar boughs and the first water fingers out upon the meal. Another basket of water pours, and another, until a little lake stands on this sandy bar.

Slowly the water sinks and goes into the meal. The water soaks the acorn particles, then sinks below the acorn meal, through the cloth, through the dry pine needles and disappears into the sand carrying with it the bitterness of the acorn.

After this, warm water is poured through the Cedar boughs, but never is it made hot enough to cook the bitterness into the meal. And so this little lake rises and sinks, rises and sinks, as the early morning sun comes bristling through the pine trees that stand back upon the hills.

When the last water disappears and the meal lies wet and not so yellow as before, Lizzie kneels at the edge and looks to find some trace of bitter. An extended finger sinks down to the bottom of the meal, then is pulled back out to touch her tongue. Quickly her hand travels here and there across the tiny flat, in and out, jabbing holes into the meal. The bitterness is gone. *Awntee*, the large cooking basket, is filled with the wet meal.

The cooked acorn meal is ready to be baked.

Water is poured into the basket and the meal stirred to a thin soup. It is then moved, along with a rinsing basket full of water, closer to the fire where the cooking stones have been heating at the center.

The hot stones are lifted from the coals, clamped in wooden tongs. Each stone is passed quickly through the rinsing water and then lowered into the soup, spreading a circle of heat to the bottom. One hot stone, then two, then three hot stones and four, and already wisps of steam rise from the surface of the cooking liquid.

Soon the stem becomes dense. With *Tawaal*, the paddle, the stones are turned and lifted as the soup grows even hotter. Back and forth, around and around the paddle goes, tumbling the stones over and over within the soup.

The surface lifts. Bubbles pop softly, making

The acorn mush is wrapped in grape leaves and cooked to make acorn bread, called Maat.

muddy sounds. Still the paddle goes until the cooking meal stirs stiff and thick, until large round bubbles stay open-mouthed and belch hot streams of steam into the air. It is done. It is *Oosaw*, acorn mush.

Lizzie pauses, listens to the hollow noises coming up from the heated stones and cooking meal, hears the hiss and grumble, sees the moisture lifting, moves the paddle now and then to keep the basket at the bottom free from burning. When the mush has become thick and still, the warm stones are lifted from the cooking basket. They are wiped off with a wet hand and dropped over the side onto a matting of Pine needles and Cedar boughs.

The mush is now ready to eat. It is soft and warm, and to be scooped up by the first two fingers pressed together; tasting good to the Indian. Every tasted mouthful is hinting of its process, hinting of the pounding rock, hinting of the Cedar boughs, hinting of the leeched-out bitter, hinting of the willow basket, hinting of the burning stones and ashes.

Sometimes those subtle tastes are later blended with the powder pounded from the glistening salt rocks. At other times the flavor is completely changed when the bright red Sourberry is crushed and added to it.

If this newly cooked mush becomes cool and rested, it jells to a substance firm, but never solid, eaten as quivering chunks or slices just the way the Acorn Dance song says: *Ootim Yaawn ye-koonai*–from the acorn blossom to the acorn mush, that's hard but wiggles.

But now the mush is still hot from the heated stones. From part of this hot mush Lizzie will make the Water Biscuit.

"Old timer used little basket just for making that Water Biscuit. Fill that little basket with hot mush and where the water be running clean and not too fast, dump it in there quick and let go. Get another basket full and dump it in. Keep doing that over and over till you get lotta little round biscuit.

Each little basket full of mush get kinda hard when it hit the cold water, you know. That's the way we make that kind. And they all look alike, that biscuit, same size, no different, all just look like clam.

Early days they call that *Saw*. Now we call it Water Biscuit. Indian eat it with deer meat, or rabbit, gray squirrel, things like that."

In the early times, a day like this would probably find more than one woman from the village working on the gravel bar. And with them too would be the children ranging in age from those cradled in the shade to the young girl just learning the skills needed to survive within her culture.

On this day, of course, there are no children. Only Lizzie works here. But if there were, the cooking stones would not lie cold on the pine needles as they do now. Lizzie would have fixed them for the children in a special way - just as her mother did long ago.

"That *Awmpes*, acorn mush cooked on those rocks. We like to eat when it just flake off dry, when we was little. Other times, old people, they put that in the water there, and that *Awmpes* come off of stones like it be thick skin or something. We used to pull it off and eat like nobody's business - little kids. Our mothers fix it that way for us, and then we just eating away and get belly full."

Part of the meal leeched of its bitterness that morning was held back from the hot stones of the cooking basket. This afternoon it will be baked to an unleavened bread, baked in the now smoldering coals of the morning fire.

Lizzie opens the hot ashes, makes a hollow there in the coals and lines this hole with green wild grape leaves brought from the marshy draw. The wet cake of leeched meal is firmly pressed into the bowl of leaves, then additional leaves are spread and pressed down upon the top. Over this, more hot ashes are heaped, and the still warm stones that circled the fire are moved in closer to contain the heat.

Upon all of this a new fire is built and Lizzie steps back to wait for it to turn to ashes. When the fire has burned down, Lizzie rakes away the coals and stones. With two sticks she lifts the steaming leafy acorn bread called *Maat*, lifts it from the smoke and ashes to a flat rock nearby. The limp cooked leaves are peeled off from around it.

The acorn bread is lifted from the coals.

"This cooked grape leaf good to eat. They used to use these Black Oak leaves too, big ones. And best kind were those Water Leaves, *Mawmbak*, white folks call it Indian Rhubarb.

In spring time we used to get Poison Oak leaves. Old people says, "Go get Poison Oak leaves." We used to strip it into baskets and bring it in. Never get any itch from that Poison Oak. Old people cover that acorn bread with it, put it in ashes, and then when it's

A composite photo by Richard Simpson with Lizzie's face as the hills.

done we used to eat that leaf. Never hurt us."

The acorn bread sits cooling on the flat rock. A dove calls across the valley to the setting sun. Lizzie rests on the bank of *Choopim Seyoo* and touches the Spirits in all things around her, hears the distant voice of the old storyteller.

Hears in memory his tale of a water bubble with changeable rainbow colors, a water bubble which became the God-like man *Aikat* who killed Thunder and married his daughters.

Remembers how the Deer Children killed Bear Lady who had killed their mother; how they floated up to heaven on tree cotton and found their mother there.

Recalls the warnings about the red-faced wild people called *Baawmkawle*, who stole good-looking children when the rain fell softly.

Remembers *Hunchup*, the witch doctor who killed half white girls with poison air, how he was killed and became a coyote.

Heard how the people killed the salt man, and where he died there still is salt.

Remembers the old man that raised tobacco on the hill; he who had gone to *Estawm Yan*, the Middle Hills, to hear the Spirits talk and to bring back new songs; he who told her the stories and legends of the Indian.

"This old man he be part Dreamer, and he knew lotta stories. When we was kids we pester all the time: 'Tell story, tell story!' And he tell them, good stories. But when that ol' man get tired telling he say, '*Aawpawkpawkawm aawm yoo-oolooshkit*.' That means, White Rock All Fall to Pieces. Then he wouldn't tell you no more, no matter how much you give him. You give him hundred dollars he wouldn't tell you no more. '*Hammu!*' he say. 'That's All!' "

The acorn bread is cool. The first star is in the sky. The dove has gone to sleep. Lizzie has gone home. It is dark and acorns are growing in the trees.

Lizzie died in 1968 at age eighty-seven.

Native Dance: A Way of Life

Time separates us from the native culture that preceded us on this land. A sense of time also separates us.

Nisenan lived unhurried in a land of abundance, bound to the seasons, driven by the rhythm of the salmon run, the acorn harvest, the deer migration, the pine and hazel nuts, the wild onion and garlic.

A K'um, or dance house, Auburn area, 1930's
Dance houses were at the center of every Nisenan village.

Everything had its time. Nisenan knew just what time it was, and what was to be done according to the time. Knowledge of the earth and her cycles was passed from generation to generation in song and story and dance and the day-to-day comings and goings that make up one's life. The Nisenan little ones soon learned how to tell what time it was.

Nisenan marked time with dances that flowed with the rhythm of the season. Maybe we can learn more about these people by visiting a few of their dances.

Every village had *a k'um*, or dance house. The following accounts of some of the Nisenan dances were written by Stephen Powers. After walking across the continent alone, Powers spent 1871 and 1872 studying the customs, habits, legends, and ideas of the California Indians. Some of that time was spent in the Mother Lode, with what remained of the Nisenan tribe. He describes their dances in articles originally written from 1872-1876 for a popular magazine of the time call the "Overland Journal":

"Of dances the Nisenan have a large number, each being celebrated in its yearly season. One of the most important of these is the acorn dance (*ka-mi-ni kon pe-wa la-koam*, literally "the

Miwok Dancers Autumn Big Time Festival, 1988, *held in North Columbia, California. Seasonal Big Time celebrations continue to be held regularly in California.*

all-eating dance"), which is observed in autumn, soon after the winter rains set in, to insure a bountiful crop of acorns the following year. Assembled together throughout their villages, from fifty to a hundred or more in a council-house, men, women, and children, they dance standing in two circles, the men in one and the women in the other. The former are decorated with all their wealth of feathers, the women with beads, etc. After a certain length of time the dance ceases, and two venerable, silver-haired priests come forward with gorgeous head-dresses and long mantles of black eagle's feathers, and take their stations on opposite sides of one of the posts supporting the roof. Resting their chins on this, with their faces turned up toward heaven, each, in turn, makes a solemn and earnest supplication to the spirits, chanting short sentences in their occult priestly language, to which the other occasionally makes response. At longer intervals the whole congregation responds "Ho!" equivalent to "amen", and there is a momentary pause of profound silence during which a pin could be heard to drop. Then the dance is resumed, and the whole multitude join in it, while one keeps time by stamping with his foot on a large hollow slab. These exercises continue for many hours and at intervals acorn-porridge is handed about, of which all partake liberally without leaving the dance-house. Of the religious character of these exercises there can be no doubt."[1]

"The most important is the first-grass dance (kam'min, the generic word for "dance", hence the dance of the year), which is

1. The Tribes of California, by Stephen Powers, University of California Press, 1976, pps. 285-6

held in autumn or winter, after the rains have fully set in and started the grass. None but a resident of California can appreciate the joyfulness of the feeling which gives rise to this festival, when, after the long, weary summer of drought, the first cool rain commences trickling down on the parched plains and the naked foothills, and they clothe themselves again with a soft, pale green. Assembled in the dance-house together, both men and women, the men dance with such extraordinary enthusiasm and persistence that they sometimes fall exhausted and lie in a trance for hours."[2]

Preparing to dance, Chaw'se, Grinding Rock State Park
The traditions are still active with the tribes of California, the young still learn from the old, and there is an active renaissance of the native cultures happening now.

"Then there is the clover dance which is celebrated in the blossom-time of clover, in concentric circles like the above, but outdoors, and not attended with anything that could be called religious ceremonies. The men often dance with a fanatic violence and persistence until they are reeking with perspiration, and then plunge into cold water or stretch themselves at full length on the ground in a manner that would insure a white man the rheumatism.

"Pretty early in the spring there comes a gala-day, which is the occasion of a great deal of enjoyment. It is called *we-da*, though that is only one and the most important of the exercises of the day. Its purpose is to prevent the snakes from biting them during the summer, and though held for so momentous a purpose, it is a very gay and sportive affair. First, the sports are initiated in the morning by the *han pa-wa-ho*, a grand spectacular ballet-dance, performed by the women and girls in the open air (as all the sports are). There is extremely little art in it, and nothing is represented except the wild, extravagant joy of this genial season. Collected in some sequestered mountain glade, where the grass is green and the trees throw a grateful shade around, with flowers in fillets encircling their heads and woven in their hair, and inhab-

2. p. 324, Powers

ited (aboriginally) only with narrow cinctures of woven bulrushes about the waists, a great company of girls join hands in a circle and begin a voluptuous, dithyrambic dance. Faster and faster, wilder and wilder grows the motion, keeping time with the accelerating chant, until finally they run riot over the whole place. They break asunder with screams and laughter, and every one of the spectators finds himself pelted with girls and flowers.

"The second act in the spectacle is the *kau-da*, a dance performed by men alone. After it is over, a number of women go around with baskets to solicit presents of acorn-bread, fish, shell-money, and other articles, wherewith to pay the singers, and on the liberality with which the spectators contribute depends their immunity from snake-bites during the coming summer. The third act, toward the close of the day, is the *weda*. A bevy of young maidens dance around two young men in succession, singing a very gay and lively chorus, and ever and anon they make a dash at him, catching him by the shoulders, laughing, stretching out their arms toward him, tantalizing him, etc. After this dance is ended, some old fellows go around among the women, soliciting presents for the singers, as above, and when the women are about to contribute, they are frequently seized themselves by the old fellows and dragged along sportively, to the vast amusement of the bystanders."[3]

At Chaw'se, the young dance with the old and new singers join in with the old to keep the traditional songs and dances alive.

"The dance for the dead is observed as far south as the American River, annually. As soon as life is extinct the body is burned, with all the person's possessions. Then the ashes are conveyed to some tribal burying-ground, and slightly covered up in the earth.

"When the dance for the dead is held by appointment at each place, generally in the spring, the ashes are uncovered and a fire is made directly over them. The first evening and morning the mourning women dance in a circle around the fire, holding in their hands their votive offerings; the second evening and morning they burn the offerings during the dance. The southern Nisenan custom is

3. pps. 324-5, Powers

to hold a "cry" at various villages and various times throughout the year, according to appointment, at which they sit in a circle on the ground, weeping and wailing. An effigy or effigies of the dead are rudely made of skins and cloths, and carried about over the hills and throughout the valleys, wherever the departed were most accustomed to resort during life, to recall the memory of the absent ones, and fill the breasts of the mourners with a more piercing sorrow. After this is done the effigies are burned, as the real bodies would have been."[4]

"Upon the ripening of manzanita berries comes the manzanita dance, which is like the clover dance described above.

Then there is the great spirit dance, which is held in propitiation of the demons. The reader must not for a moment confound this great spirit with the being so called by the Algonkin races, for he has nothing whatever to do with their cosmogony; he created nothing, is powerful only for evil, and is nothing more nor less than the chief of the imps or goblins supposed to haunt certain hills or other localities.

K'um at Grinding Rock State Park
Build by Miwok elders, aged 50 to 90, in as close to the old ways as possible. Roof beams are bound together by grape vine. Cedar bark slabs form the roofing.

Then there is a dance called *walin-hu pi-mi-ni*, (this will not bear translation), which is held in the open air at pleasure, chiefly in the clover season. The maidens dance this alone in the evening. They join hands in a circle and swing merrily around an old man seated upon the grass, chanting to a lively step; then presently they break the circle with screams and laughter, and flee in every direction. The young men waiting near pursue and capture each his mistress, and kindly, liberal night draws her sable curtain over the scene that ensues."[5]

The way in which a dance house was built gives us more insight into who these native Californians were. The following story is taken from Malcolm Margolin's wonderful anthology *The Way We Lived: California Indian Reminiscences, Stories and Songs.* Margolin's commentary appears in italics.[6]

4 pps. 328-9, Powers
5 pps. 286=7 Powers
6 Heyday Books, 1981

DANCE HOUSE CREATION

Life in many of the larger Central California villages centered around a communal building. Such buildings were huge--sometimes up to sixty feet in diameter. They were generally underground or partially underground, and a person passing down the sloping entrance way walked into a world of deep, earthen smells. The temperature was relatively constant throughout the year, the lighting always dim. During the day a narrow shaft of sunlight came through the smoke hole and swept slowly across the floor; a fire flickered at night, casting huge shadows upon the walls. In such dark, cavernous, mysterious places people gathered for ceremonies, public events, and sacred dances. These buildings were variously called "assembly houses," "earth lodges," "round houses," or "dance houses."

The Grinding Rock K'um
Built partially underground. In the old times, forest duff built up on the roof and the round house could barely be seen until you were upon it.

"When they want to build a dance house, all the important men get together in the *elkel* [chief's house] and talk about where they can get the trees. They have all the posts and ribs of the structure named, and the men mention the various logs they have seen that would meet the needs of the different parts. They do not speak of their decision to anyone, but go out and look at the tree that is to form the center pole. They will walk around the tree and examine every detail of it.

"Before any further steps are taken, the group goes to the captain of the village and asks his approval of their plan. He will not answer them for a long time, perhaps as much as an hour, and then he may ask them if they are in a position to build a dance house. They will tell him what food they have in store. He will ask "How do your women feel?" and they will reply that it is all right with them. This procedure is necessary because it is expensive to build a dance house, as they must feed all the neighboring people who assist in the construction and are invited to the dance that follows. The headman can stop the building of a house. Others might object to it, but their only protest is to move to another village.

"Having decided to build a house, the men begin to prepare the poles. These are cut down, trimmed, and barked, a fork being left at the top. The cutting of the poles may take a month. The one selected as the center pole is the last pole to be cut. Finally they select a place to dig the hole for the dwelling, and by this time the people have caught on to what is in the air without being told, and those who are next to the important men come to help.

Around the K'um, small structures were built for individual families. In the lower elevations and in the Valley, semi-subterranean mud structures and brush buildings were constructed; higher in the foothills, cedar and pine bark slab huts were built like those in the picture.

"The house is built in one day. The people have gathered and brought what food they could. They all get to work digging out the pit, each person working by digging with his club and carrying the earth out in the conical carrying baskets. Each works in that portion of the excavation toward which his own home lies. By working hard together, they finish the hole in three or four hours. Everyone helps, women, children, and men–all but the menstruating girls.

"Then important men have meanwhile gone to the location of the center pole and have dressed it as dancing man with a feather headdress. It is carried to the house pit by six or eight men on a stretcher made of grapevine, accompanied by two singers, who sing a march. They do not set the pole down till they get to the hole, where they set it upright in a special way and tamp it into place.

"Next they put the two "brothers" in place and then the other upright posts; then the ribs are put from ground to post and between posts, a man being ready at each joint to do the lashing. Then smaller sticks and finally wormwood are added, each person again working on that portion lying in the direction of his home. After the wormwood is laid over the ribs, the crannies are stuffed with moss, and earth is carried onto the roof and spread over it to a thickness of about three or four inches. It is packed down by constantly walking over it, so that in the end the house is nearly airtight except for the door and smoke hole. At the last the people from the several surrounding villages try to finish their side first, and this work is done in high spirits, the people teasing and making fun of one another. Those first finished raise a great shout and help the others to finish the work.

"The house is completed by night, and after this there is either feasting or a "sweat" or both. The hosts are expected to feed their guests for some time, and usually their entire supply of food is ex-

Photograph: Charlene Fontana Collection

Roundhouse which stood above the Colfax Indian Cemetery.

hausted by the occasion.

"The dance house is used communally by the dancing men and the people, but it belongs to the village chief. He does not live in it, but has it merely as a meeting house. His own house is the smaller sweat house.

"The building of the dance house was a joyous, boisterous affair. Men, women, and children crowded onto the site and worked shoulder-to-shoulder, excavating the hole, raising the posts, lashing the beams, and piling the earth onto the roof. Afterwards they feasted and celebrated. What seeming chaos! Yet the confusion was only apparent, as the preceding account suggests. The entire enterprise was well-ordered and carefully planned with the debates and deliberations, the hierarchy of "important" and "less important" men, the division of labor among families, the ritual context of every act.

"When completed, the dance house became the center of a village's social and religious activities. In both its construction and in its later use it united the various families into a symbolic whole. During the sacred dances that would be held for years to come, the dance house would continue to unite people with one another–and with the spirit world as well."

The Nisenan Culture

Who were these people? Maybe it would be helpful to go back to Stephen Powers, who was one of the earliest to try to understand the human side of our predecessors in California. On August 11, 1862, he writes:

"Unlike several tribes in the northwest part of the State, these are no misers, but quite the contrary, as are all the Southern California Indians. They never hoard up shell-money, beads, trinkets, or anything of a merely factitious value, unless it is for the purpose of burning them in honor of some great chieftain on his funeral pyre. In a bountiful acorn harvest they gather and store up in wicker granaries sufficient to last them two or three years; but frequently use the surplus above the winter's supply to gamble on, and often gamble away even the provisions which are immediately necessary. No Indian is despised so much as one who is close-fisted; nothing is more certain than that, if an Indian comes along hungry, they will divide with him to the uttermost crumb."[7]

"It is a humble and a lowly race which we approach, one of the lowest on earth; but I am greatly mistaken if the history of their lives does not teach wholesome and salutary lessons–lessons of barbaric providence, plenty, and contentment, of simple pleasures and enjoyments, and of the capacities of unprogressive savagery to fill out the measure of human happiness and to mass dense populations ..."[8]

Yet when we look to these early observers, we often learn more of the biases of the observer than the characteristics of the observed. What makes Stephen Powers such interesting reading is that his fascination and keen interest in the subject shine through his post-Victorian biases. No better example from his book exists than the following:

"Let the following facts bear witness to their low aboriginal estate: Robert Gordeon, a responsible citizen of Auburn, states that in 1849 he was surface-mining (near) Auburn and that a great proportion of the men and women who entered his camp were costumed strictly after the fashion-plates of Eden. This was in a region pretty well up in the mountains, where the aborigines had not yet come in contact with Europeans. Both sexes and all ages moved about his camp, absolutely in *puns natualibus*, with that perfect freedom and innocence which betoken unconsciousness of any impropriety. But these simple, unswathed mountaineers, according to the same good 'authority, were often of a magnificent physique, tall, sinewy fellows, who would have made the scale-beam kick at 180."[9]

These were a very domestic people, living amid a world that provided them with all they considered they needed and wanted. They lived in stable populations here for thousands of years, evolving their languages until distinct patterns were very localized. Again, from Powers:

"As to language, the Maidu shades away so gradually into the Nishinam that it is extremely difficult to draw the line anywhere. But it must be drawn somewhere, because a vocabulary taken down on the Feather River will lose three-fourths of its words before it reaches the Cosumnes. Even a vocabulary taken on Bear River will

7 pps. 324-5, Powers
8 p. 5, Powers
9 p. 317, Powers

lose half or more of its words in going to the Cosumnes, which denotes, as is the case, that the Nishinam language varies greatly within itself. It is probably less homogeneous and more thronged with dialects than any other tongue in California. Let an Indian go even from Georgetown to American Flat, or from Bear River to Auburn, and, with the exception of the numeral, he may not at first understand above one word in four or five or six." [10]

The following series of photos of Foothill Nisenan was collected by Brian Bibby and was displayed at the North Columbia Schoolhouse Cultural Center in North San Juan in 1988. "The Festival was conceived as a way of presenting the richness of the cultural continuum of foothill life, honoring the complex traditional arts of the native Americans of this area, and exploring the connections between art, culture, and natural history. Here you will see a gathering of artists, craftspeople, and performers whose work reflects a strong inter-action with the natural world of the Sierra Nevada foothills."

The Nisenan were masters of the picnic. A moveable feast was held for the smallest occasion. A simple meeting of someone from another tribe would call for a picnic at a favorite spot. All that was required was a cooking basket and some acorn flour. A fire and the surrounding forest provided all that was needed for the festivity.

They liked moving their camps often. Yet it seems that for all the movement, there was actually very little territory covered.

"It is seldom that a Nishinam, after all his infinite little migrations, dies a mile from the place of his birth. They are thoroughly home-loving and home-keeping, counting a certain valley or flat a home, like all California Indians."[11]

Their local nature led to their local languages, and local stories. The following stories are Maidu/Nisenan stories from Malcolm Margolin's book *The Way We Lived: California Indian Reminiscences, Stories and Songs*, Heyday Books, Berkeley, 1981. Malcolm Margolin's comments are printed in italic.

Nisenan: Football Big-Time

Games provided another excuse for people to get together. Larger villages often had areas leveled and cleared for ball games, and each locality throughout the state had its own version of shinny or "soccer". The Nisenan of the Sacramento Valley and Sierra Foothills favored a relay game in which each team tried to kick and carry its ball to a goal and back AGAIN to the starting point. The stakes were high (Native Californians loved to gamble) and the play was rough-and-tumble; nevertheless off the playing field restraint and ritual prevailed. Games were interspersed with ceremonial feasting, dancing, and socializing, and good form demanded that the losing team accept even the most crushing defeat with equanimity.

10 p. 314, Powers
11 p. 319, Powers

"In the early days the Indians had football 'big-time'. Very early in the morning the other team put up a great deal of money, (i.e. many beads). If they made goals at both ends of the field they won. Then they danced to make fun of us. When we finished we ate breakfast. After breakfast we played football again. At midday we rested, then we ate. When the sun came round to the west we were at it again. We did that for two or three days and only quit when we had lost our money, valuables, baskets, clothes, bows. Before we parted we ate, the men of this side treating the other side. Then the men of the other side treated this side. Only then did we go each on his way. That was football 'big time'."

NISENAN: FOOTBALL FREE-FOR-ALL

People throughout California certainly fall in love. Even in the puritanical northwestern part of the state, tender stories were told of poor young men who, by magic and hard work, accumulated enough of a bride price to marry the women they loved. Also, most groups in varying degrees were tolerant of premarital sex, homosexuality, certain cases of infidelity, polygamy, divorce, and remarriage. People of all ages relished sexual jokes and delighted in the raunchiest of Coyote stories. Among many groups there were certain seasons and certain ceremonies during which sexual looseness was not only permitted but even encouraged.

Sometimes a football game was called, the women playing the men, putting up valuables and even money to bet with each other. The men kicked the ball with the foot while the women caught it with the hand and ran with it. The men hugged the woman who carried the ball. When they tickled her belly, she threw the ball to another woman.

If that woman missed, a man kicked the ball with the foot. Another woman caught it with the hands and ran with it towards their

Photo by A. W. Chase or possibly Stephen Powers. Courtesy Smithsonian Institution.

Captain Tom, Auburn, before 1876
Woven rabbit skin blanket, abalone shell gorget, flicker quill headband aid hairpin with flicker quill pendant. Captain Tom was from Kotomyan, a village east of Auburn. The term "Captain" was used to identify headmen.

Courtesy State of California Dept. of Parks and Recreation.

Handgame, Bald Rock, Butte County, 1907
A group of Maidu (Concow) men engage in a traditional gambling game, with roundhouse in background. Left foreground Billy Day (Twobo), left rear Hood Smith, left leaning forward Lewis Parker, right foreground Peter Curz, right rear Johnny Johnson, far right sitting on bench Bill Foreman (also known as sili wah). This village was known as Billy Day's place. He was the father of artist Frank Day.

goal. Then a man hugged her again. When he threw her on the ground and rolled her around, she threw the ball. In that way another woman caught it and brought it towards their goal.

The men played with the foot, the women played with the hand: that was their playing together so that a man could hug the woman he loved. The women on their part took every opportunity to hug the men they loved; the game was like that so that this could be done.

Maidu: Sun and Moon

Everywhere in California the sun and moon were seen as people. The Maidu pictured them living in a house where they were subject to all the usual domestic inconveniences.

Sun and Moon were sister and brother. They did not rise at first. Many different animals were sent to try and see if they could make the two rise, but failed. None of them could get into the house in which the brother and sister lived. This house was of solid stone, and was far away to the east.

At last Gopher and Angle-Worm went. Angle-Worm made a tiny hole, boring down outside, and coming up inside the house. Gopher followed, carrying a bag of fleas. He opened it, and let half of the fleas out. They bit the brother and sister so that they moved from the floor where they were to the sleeping-platform. Then Gopher let out the rest of the fleas, and these made life so miserable for Sun and Moon, that they decided to leave the house. The sister was afraid to travel by night, so the brother said he would go then, and became the Moon. The sister travelled by day, and became the Sun.

The use of fleas to roust the sun and moon is typical of the Native Californians' religious sensibility. Theirs was a thoroughly domestic world. People seldom ventured more than twenty miles from their birthplace. Their major life experiences took place in a village and family context, and it was village and family that provided them with the metaphors by which they interpreted the workings of the world. Even the most awe-

Photographer unknown, Courtesy Rose Enos.

some mysteries - the regulation of the sun and moon, for example–were understood basically as domestic dramas.

Families near Clipper Gap, 1890
George Wilma (standing left), Kelly Jack and his wife Molly (standing right). Maidu elders have remarked on the fine appearance of the men and women of that time. One elder remembered how the women always had their hair fixed so nice. Their dresses are very much in style for the period. This is a professional portrait and it appears that having one's picture taken, professionally or not, was very popular among Maidu people from the late nineteenth century, as personal photo collections attest.

Maidu: The Creation

The Maidu creation epic begins with a vision of the world covered with water. A raft with two beings floats out from the north. A feathered rope drops from the sky, and Earth-Initiate climbs down into the raft. Who made the water, the raft, the trinity of Earth-Creators? Like many California creation epics, the Maidu account seems to begin in the middle of the story. Mysteriously, elements of the world seem to have always been present, their existence apparently beyond question or speculation.

In the beginning there was no sun, no moon, no stars. All was dark, and everywhere there was only water. A raft came floating on the water. It came from the north, and in it were two persons–Turtle and Pehe-ipe. The stream flowed very rapidly. Then from the sky a rope of feathers, called Pokelma, was let down, and down it came Earth-Initiate. When he reached the end of the rope, he tied it to the bow of the raft, and stepped in. His face was covered and was never seen, but his body shone like the sun. He sat down, and for a long time said nothing.

At last Turtle said, "Where do you come from?" and Earth-Initiate answered, "I come from above." Then Turtle said, "Brother, can you not make for me some good dry land, so that I may sometimes come up out of the water?" Then he asked an-

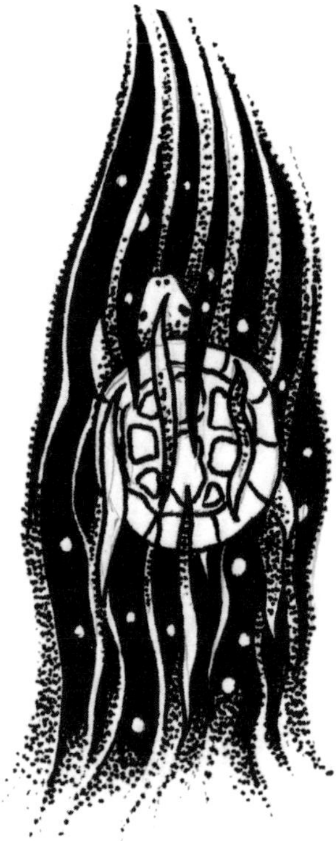

Artwork by Stan Padilla

other time, "Are there going to be any people in the world?" Earth-Initiate thought awhile, and then said, "Yes." Turtle asked, "How long before you are going to make people?" Earth-Initiate replied, "I don't know. You want to have some dry land: well, how am I going to get any earth to make it of?" Turle answered, "If you will tie a rock about my left arm, I'll dive for some." Earth-Initiate did as Turtle asked, and then, reaching around, took the end of a rope from somewhere, and tied it to Turtle. When Earth-Initiate came to the raft, there was no rope there: he just reached out and found one. Turtle said, "If the rope is not long enough, I'll jerk it once, and you must haul me up; if it is long enough, I'll give two jerks, and then you must pull me up quickly, as I shall have all the earth that I can carry." Just as Turtle went over the side of the boat, Pehe-ipe began to shout loudly.

Turtle was gone a long time. He was gone six years and when he came up, he was covered with green slime, he had been down so long. When he reached the top of the water, the only earth he had was a very little under his nails: the rest had all washed away. Earth-Initiate took with his right hand a stone knife from under his left armpit, and carefully scraped the earth out from under Turtle's nails. He put the earth in the palm of his hand, and rolled it about till it was round; it was as large as a small pebble. He laid it on the stern of the raft. By and by he went to look at it: it had now grown so that it could not be spanned by the arms. The fourth time he looked, it was as big as the world, the raft was aground, and all around were mountains as far as he could see. The raft came ashore at Tadoiko, and the place can be seen today.

'As in a dream," is perhaps the best way to describe the Maidu creation myth. Motives and actions are suffused with dreamlike indetermination and vagueness. Even Earth-Initiate seems oddly befuddled. "I don't know, " he answers when asked when people will be created, and his making the world out of mud seems a rather homey and spur-of-the-moment

affair. The Maidu earth-makers were far from omniscient and omnipotent. They appear, in fact, rather tentative and at times confused - as figures in a dream tend to be.

As for Pehe-ipe who shared the creation raft, throughout all of creation he remains uninvolved - a witness to this most awesome of events, never a participant. His name literally means "Father-of-the-Secret-Society." During Secret Society dances a Pehe-ipe impersonator appeared and played a major role: curiously, that of the clown!

Maidu: Tolowim-Woman and Butterfly Man

Native Californians had paradoxical and complex attitudes toward sex. On one hand people fell in love and had wide sexual experiences. On the other hand, sex was seen as threatening, dangerous, inimical to spiritual pursuits. People about to hunt, gamble, dance, seed power, collect medicine, or engage in any serious venture were warned to avoid love-making. Against the passion of the individual, the voice of society repeated its message: be prudent, moderate, obedient, restrained. Yet how difficult it was to heed that message! A woman gathering food in a meadow might stop now and then to indulge in a fantasy. How wonderful it would be, she might daydream, if an irresistible lover were suddenly to appear.

A Tolowim-woman went out to gather food. She had her child with her; and while she gathered the food, she stuck the point of the cradle-board in the ground, and left the child thus alone. As she was busy, a large butterfly flew past. The woman said to the child, "You stay here while I go and catch the butterfly. She ran after it, and chased it for a long time. She would almost catch it, and then just miss it. She wore a deer-skin robe. She thought, "Perhaps the reason why I cannot catch the butterfly is be-

Maidu Girl, Auburn, before 1876
Identified as Captain Tom's daughter, she wears a belt and headband of abalone shell pendants and necklace of large abalone pectorals over a pioneer style cotton dress typical of its day.

Photograph by A. W. Chase or possibly Stephen Powers. Courtesy Smithsonian Institution

Photographer unknown, Courtesy Rose Enos

Crease Ranch near Colfax, 1900
Back Row standing L-R: Jack Suehead, Antone Wiley, Oscar Williams, unknown, George Wilma, child standing unknown. Front row L-R: Roland Prout, Bob Yaime (reclining), Bert Prout, Perry Gilbert, Arthur "Dutch" Gilbert, Rube Gilbert. Antone Wiley was noted as an orator at ceremonial gatherings, particularly blessing the food.

cause I have this on." So she threw it away. Still, she could not catch the butterfly, and finally threw away her apron and hurried on. She had forgotten all about her child, and kept on chasing the butterfly till night came. Then she lay down under a tree and went to sleep.

When she awoke in the morning, she found a man lying beside her. He said, "You have followed me thus far, perhaps you would like to follow me always. If you would, you must pass through a lot of my people." All this time the child was where the woman had left it, and she had not thought of it at all. She got up, and followed the butterfly-man. By and by they came to a large valley, the southern side of which was full of butterflies. When the two travellers reached the edge of the valley, the man said, "No one has ever got through this valley. People die before they get through. Don't lose sight of me. Follow me closely."

They started and traveled for a long time. The butterfly-man said, "Keep tight hold of me, don't let go." When they had got halfway through, other butterflies came flying about in great numbers. They flew every, about their heads, and in their faces. They were fine fellows, and wanted to get the Tolowim-Woman for themselves. She saw them, watched them for a long time, and finally let go of her husband, and tried to seize one of these others. She missed him, and ran after him. There were thousands of others floating about; and she tried to seize, now one, now the other, but always failed, and so was lost in the valley.

She said, "When people speak of the olden times by and by, people will say that this woman lost her lover, and tried to get others but lost them, and went crazy and died." She went on then, and died before she got out of the valley. The butterfly-man she had lost went on, got through the valley, and came to his home.

To desert child and family and run with complete abandon after love and beauty-- this is indeed at the heart of many a daydream. But as the fate of the Tolowim-woman poignantly suggests, destruction awaits those who seek freedom and unrestrained joy. The moral is clear: freedom leads to ruination and one had best follow the middle way--the way of moderation and restraint, the way of the family.

Photographer unknown, Courtesy Rose Enos.

Dick Childs, Nevada City, 1910
Mr. Childs is seen examining a lengthy band of sewn flicker quills. These were generally worn as trailers down the back of ceremonial dancers who performed in the Hesi. His son Gus looks on.

Yuki: Initiation into the Ghost Society

A major event in a boy's life was his initiation into a secret society. Such societies flourished in north-central California, preserving sacred knowledge, ritual, songs, and dances, and passing them on to a younger generation. The Ghost Society, widespread among many different tribal groups, was apparently of an ancient origin. Ghost Society members impersonated the spirits of the dead–a dangerous and fearful undertaking–and cured illnesses caused by ghosts. Their dance costumes consisted of long black poles, elaborate feather work, and bodies painted with black, red, and white stripes. Such spectacular regalia combined life images with death images, thereby symbolizing the society's position as mediator between the world of the living and the world of the dead. By sponsoring initiation rites, the Ghost Society also mediated between the world of childhood and that of adulthood. A Yuki man, looking back upon his youth, recalls his initiation into the Ghost Society–although he is careful, of course, not to divulge any of the sacred knowledge that his grandfathers gave him at the time.

For the Ghost-Society Initiation everyone moved to the village of Ushichma'lha't, and the same day a dance house was put up.

Reclaiming of the Original Tribal Names

From mining days the Native Californians disliked the name "Digger." So in 1924 at a Big Time Festival at Ione, an effigy of "Digger" was burned and original tribal names were taken once again–Nisenan, Miwok, Wintu, Konkow, Pomo, Maidu, Yuki, Wappo, Yana, Nomlaki, and Patwin. The following caption accompanies this picture at Grinding Rock Park:

"From the arrival of the Spanish in 1769, California Native Americans have fought for survival. During the Gold Rush, some Sierra Indians actively defended themselves against miners' assaults. In the 1870's, others joined the Ghost Dance Cult in an attempt to bring back the dead, revitalizing their religion and culture at the same time."

During the 1920's, Miwok leader, William Fuller, led one group's struggle to get rid of a demeaning name. Fuller was joined in their effort by other Indian leaders including Charlie Maximo and Pedro O'Conner. In 1924, the despised "Digger Indian" was burned in effigy at an Ione Big Time celebration. Fuller later helped organize the Federated Indians of California. This organization was one of several groups seeking more compensation for lands lost in the 1850's and later, in addition to the token amounts won earlier in the federal treaties case. In 1963 and 1964, the Indian Claims Commission reached a compromise settlement of $29,000,000 for these lands–about 47 cents an acre."

Photographer unknown. Courtesy of State of California Dept. of Parks and Recreation

Maidu Dancers, Chico, 1919
Back L-R: George Nye, Isaiah Conway, Jody Conway, Herb Young
Front L-R: Billy Conway, Dewey Conway
Those standing are dressed for the Toto Dance. Billy Conway is dressed as the Yati (wind spirit) and Dewey is dressed similar to the Du (earth mother). This is one of at least two publicity photographs to advertise a performance by the group at the Majestic Theater in Chico.

The logs were cut and everybody helped in their erection. That night the old men discussed among themselves how they could best catch me the next day.

In the morning they went out to cut the large center post and took me along. They found a white oak in the canyon and cut its roots.

They had no steel axes and worked with a large stone. When they were about to fell the tree itself they ordered me up into it. I was to sit on the crotch with my arms folded. They wanted to test me and see if I was a man and make me into someone who would be a chief. But they made the tree fall as lightly as they could so as not to hurt me. Then they chopped of the top above the fork in which I still sat. Now, one of my uncles took off my boy's fawnskin and gave me a man's deerskin to wear. Then they took the log away. I lay flat on it. Thus they brought it into the dance house. They set it up it its hole and still I kept my place. They my maternal grandfather reached up and took me off, laid me on his lap and cried over me. Then I could not help but cry too.

When the sun went down, they built a large fire and sweated themselves, but did not trouble me. For four days I was in the dance house with many other boys, all of us eating nothing. My maternal grandfather, and also my paternal grandfather, Lamsch'ala, talked to me about the Ghost Society.

This was late in the fall, when the river first began to rise. After four days I was allowed to eat and drink again, but all winter they kept me hidden away in the dance house. Whenever I went outdoors my face was covered. All through the winter at intervals they had the Ghost Society performance for four days at a time. They made it for themselves, not to teach me. But my grandfathers told me to watch them and to see everything that they did. Between times they kept me well covered up. Every evening they sweated. This they did until late spring when the grass seeds were ripe.

Dunning Sticks
Wood whittled and painted with red and black pigment and tied with milkweed fiber string. These were tossed into a debtor's house by the creditor, as a reminder the debt should soon be paid.

The second time I went through the Initiation was at Suk'a. I was a big boy now. This time the ceremonies lasted only four days. After the meal at the end I belonged to the dance house [as a full initiate] and went with the others to bring wood for sweating. Between the first ceremony and this one my grandfathers had taught me fully all the songs that I must know.

The third time I took part I was a grown and married man. Now I took part in the building of the dance house and all the other work. I danced and helped to give orders. I was practicing to be an important man.

The first Ghost-Society-Initiation lasted from the time "when the river first began to rise" until the time "when the grass seeds were ripe"– from early December until May or June, a six month period during which the youth kept to the dance house and devoted himself exclusively to religious instruction. No one considered this excessive. Throughout life a proper person would put large amounts of time aside for dancing, singing, praying, fasting, and other ritual observances. For Indian people everywhere in California, such activities were a fully necessary for human life as the hunting of game or the gathering of acorns.

From Fire to Basket

By Roger Grogban

The baskets of the California Indians are known throughout the world for their beauty and quality. In the late 1800s and early 1900s the Euro-American began collecting Indian baskets as objects of art, generating a cottage industry that has left a legacy that can be seen in museums in California and around the world. But before the European first came to California, baskets traditionally made by the women, were an integral part of the native culture. Baskets were used for gathering, storing and cooking food. Large conical baskets carried on the back were used to gather grass seeds, acorns, pine nuts, berries, bulbs and other edible roots. Most of the food gathered was dried and then stored in baskets, including fish and meat that was either dried or smoked. At birth the infant was placed in a cradleboard, which was essentially a woven basket.

Acorns, one of the main staples of the Native Californian's diet, were stored outside in caches that were basically large basket granaries woven from wild grape vines. Much of the food was cooked in large watertight baskets, by heating rocks and placing them in the basket. The woman women would use a paddle to stir the rocks keeping them from burning a hole in the basket. Once the heat was transferred from the rock, a new hot rock was placed in the basket. This was repeated till the mixture was boiling and cooked.

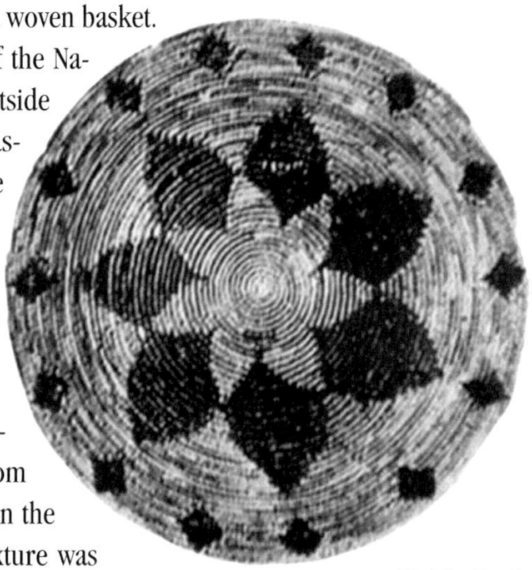

Maidu Basket

Fire was used as a tool to produce the required material for basket making. The flower stalks of deer grass and bear grass were two common plants used by many groups. The branches sprouting after a patch was burned were stronger and more flexible. Thousands of flower stalks were needed to supply basket material for a village. Seasonal low intensity burns were used to maintain large patches. The burning of deer grass produced a more viable plant, and it increased seed production, giving rise to even more stalks. Burning also inhibited other species of plants from invading the collection area.

Red Bud

Bushes such as redbud and ceanothus were used as basket material. Ceanothus was used to make burden baskets. A bush growing in the wild does not produce many straight branches. But when burned or cut the re-sprouting branches

Photographer John W. Hudson, Courtesy Field Museum of Natural History, 1926.

are straight and flexible without side branches. Growth coming off the side of a branch produces a greater density of wood, like a knot in a board, altering the uniformity of flexibility of the branch. Burned bushes were more productive than wild ones. One fire-tended bush would produce ten times the amount of material compared to a wild one.

Part of the beauty of the California Indian baskets is the dark red-wine color set against the tan or light brown background. These designs are geometric and often a representation of something seen in nature, such as an animal or insect. These dark designs are seen in most Native Californian baskets. One of the main sources of this dark color is from redbud. The new shoots of the redbud have a pigment in the epidermis giving it dark color, but as the branch matures the epidermis turns into gray bark.

Seed Gathering, Near Yankee Jim Town, 1902
A woman identified as Hunter Jim's daughter-in-law gathers grass seeds with a seed beater and conical burden basket. A wide variety of grass seeds were harvested throughout the summer months. Often parched and ground into flour to be eaten dry or mixed with water, heated and drunk as soup.

Some anthropologists contend the quality of basket making in California would not be possible without the use of fire. It was not enough to know what plants to use but when and how often to burn them. But fire was not only used to supply materials for baskets, it was an important factor in food production.

Acorn soup or mush was a staple of the Native Californian diet. To increase the harvest of acorns the Native Americans would burn the area beneath the oaks. At harvest time it was easy to see the acorns as they fell from the tree and on the ground. Burning also reduced the population of insects whose larva spend part of their life cycle inside the acorn.

Maidu basket weaving

Patches of edible bulbs were burned to promote division of the bulb. New growth from the seasonal burns provided excellent forage for animals and improved the chance of a successful hunt in the open space left after a burn.

Contemporary Native Californians are interested in the restoration of their culture. Many of the young people are learning their language, stories, and ceremonies from their elders and, along with this movement, there is a renewed interest in the art of basket making, not just learning to weave a basket, but the whole cultural complex of plants, when to burn, when to pick and how to prepare the grasses, branches, and roots. Along with the practical knowledge there is what we call a spiritual aspect to basket weaving. When collecting plants it is common to make some offering as a sign of gratitude and respect for the plants being used.

Though we cannot manage the land as the Native Californians did, and the landscape has been changed, we are beginning to rethink the place that fire plays in the Californian landscape. Prescribed burning helps reduce fire danger in our communities and helps establish Native Californian collection sites for basket materials, food and medicine. The Native Californians' practice of periodic burning with low intensity fires reduced the probability of catastrophic fire while increasing the productivity of the land to their advantage.

Nisenan baskets

The Botany of Native California

Originally titled 'Aboriginal Botany," *this section was written by Stephen Powers in 1877. It is reprinted with permission from Tribes of California by Stephen Powers, UC Press, Berkeley, 1976.*

As employed in this chapter, the word "botany" is somewhat loosely comprehensive, and is used for lack of a better. Under it are included all the forms of the vegetable world which the aborigines use for medicine, food, clothing, etc. Of course, savages have no systematic classification of botanical knowledge; there are no genera, no species. Every oak, pine, or grass has its separate name. The Indians never group individuals together, except occasionally by adding one of the words *cha, du, po' po, kom, wai, bak* (tree, bush, grass, seed, root, leaf), or something of that sort. But it is not to be supposed that the Indian is a superficial observer; he takes careful note of the forms and qualities of everything that grows on the face of the earth. True, he ascribes marvellous and impossible qualities to some plants, generally those which do not grow in his neighborhood, but this does not blind him to their real properties.

Acorns

And as his perception of individual differences is nice and minute, so his nomenclature is remarkably full. I assert without hesitation that an average intelligent Indian, even if not a shaman, (or medicine-man,) has at command a much greater catalogue of names than nine-tenths of Americans. Nothing escapes him; he has a name for everything, though he never cultivates any plants. And, indeed, his extensive knowledge is not especially to be wondered at, being taught him with severity. In times of great scarcity they are driven by the sore pangs of hunger to test everything that the soil produces, if perchance they may find something that will appease the gnawings of appetite. They therefore know the qualities of all herbs, shrubs, roots, leaves; whether they are poisonous or nutritive, whether purgative, astringent, sedative, or what not, or without any active principle. And they have often found out these things by bitter experience in their own persons. It is surprising what a number of roots, leaves, berries, and nuts, the squaw will discover. She will go out in the spring with nothing but

Photographer John W. Hudson, Courtesy Field Museum of Natural History, no. anthro 9514

a fire-hardened stick, and in an hour she will pick a breakfast of green stuff, into which there may enter fifteen or twenty ingredients. Her eye will be arrested by a minute plant that will yield her only a bulbous root as large as a large pea, but which the American would have passed unnoticed. The women are generally best acquainted with the edible matters, while the men are the authority as to the medicines.

There are seventy-three vegetable substances mentioned in this chapter. I am indebted to the kindness of Prof. H.N. Bolander, who identified for me many plants that I was unable to determine. There are a few specimens which are so scarce nowadays, owing to the ravages of stock, or so difficult to find in flower, that it was impossible to give their scientific names.

I will take this occasion to say that there are many substances popularly called "Indian medicines" which are humbugs, and which have been fathered upon the Indians by patent-medicine men. Whatever is set down in this chapter has been learned from the aborigines themselves.

In regard to medicinal herbs and plants, their usages are peculiar and sometimes amusing. As the practice of medicine among

Cooking Acorn, Foremans Ranch near Bidwell's Bar, March 21 or 22, 1903

A large feasting basket used for cooking acorn soup at special gatherings is seen in the foreground. Such large baskets were valuable items and would certainly be among the property of wealthy headmen who could afford to sponsor certain ceremonial gatherings. In this case a spring dinner was given with honored guests coming from Chico. Even though Euro-american pots and pans were available and used by Maidu people for cooking beans, potatoes and beef, baskets were best suited for the acorn process. It appears that American foods were prepared in American vessels and Maidu food prepared in Maidu containers. A bucket for carrying water, a pair of wooden tongs for lifting hot rocks from the fire and a smaller basket of water for dipping the hot stones to remove the ash are also visible.

Photographer John W. Hudson, Courtesy Field Museum of Natural History, no. anthro 9513

Give Back Feast (boye'to'ton), Foreman Ranch near Bidwell's Bar, March 21 or 22, 1903

"One of the customs was to give a feast in return for a former hospitality" (John Hudson). Four men carefully carry an obviously full basket of acorn soup from the cooking area. A rope encircling the basket aids in the handling and weight distribution. When all the food is assembled, it is blessed through a lengthy prayer.

them is a source of great profit and prestige, it is sought to be invested with mystery. The shamans are always crafty men, keen observers, reticent. An old doctor always clothes his art with a great deal of superstition, secrecy, and pompous solemnity. In answer to impertinent young questioners, he says his samples do not grow anywhere in that neighborhood; he is obliged to purchase them from tribes living at a great distance. I knew an old doctor and his wife, both as full of guile and subtlety as an egg is of meat, who always arose at the dead of night, crept stealthily out of camp and gathered their potent herbs, roots, etc., then returned before any one was stirring and concealed them.

The Indians referred to in this chapter are the Nishinam, of Bear River, and the flora is that of the extreme lower foothills of Placer County. Their general name for medicine is *wen'-neh*, which denotes "good", but they frequently use the word "medicine", even among themselves.

To begin with the oaks, the species which produces their favorite acorns is the *Quercus Gambelii*; Indian name, *Cha'-kua*. They generally select those trees which have a free, coarse bark and large acorns. About the middle of October the harvest begins, when the Indian, armed with a long, slender pole, ascends the tree and beats off the nuts. A tree which has been well whipped looks as if it had been scourged in a mighty hail-storm. The old men generally assist in carrying them home in their deep, conical baskets, and there the squaws' duties commence. Holding an acorn in a stone, she gives it a slight tap with a stone pestle, called *su'-neh*, to crack the shell, which she strips off rapidly. They are then dried and beaten to powder in small hollows on top of some great rock. The flour is soaked a few hours in a large hollow scooped in the sand, the water draining off and carrying away the bitterness; after which it is cooked into a kind of mush in baskets by means of hot stones, or baked as bread in an underground oven. The acorn which stands second in favor is that of the burr-oak (*Q. lobata; Indian, lauh*). In Placer County this oak seems to be more properly Q. Douglassii, as its branchlets are erect and rigid. There is an oak which they call *shu'-heh*, which seems to be something like a cross between the white and burr oak, having very white and coarsely rimose bark, and glabrous, shining, deeply sinuate leaves. Professor Bolander pronounces this also *Q. Gambelii*. The live-oak is *ha'-ha; Q. Wislizenia, ham'-mut*; the black oak, (*Q. Sonomensis*) ham '-chu. The acorns of these last three are eaten only when they can procure no others. There is one other very small species called chi' pis, growing in the mountains; but I cannot determine from their descriptions whether it is the chinquapin or the whortle-berry oak.

The nut-pine or silver-pine (*Pinus edulis*) is *toan, toan'-em cha*. It is a great favorite with them, the most useful tree they have, and they always regret to see an American cutting one down. The nuts are a choice article of food; and, burned and beaten to powder, or crushed up raw and spread on in a plaster, they form their specific for a burn or a scald. The pitch and the mistletoe (*Arceuthobium*) which grows on this pine are very valuable, in their estimation, for coughs, colds, and rheumatism. They set them afire, making a dense smudge, and then the patient, wrapped in a blanket, squats over it or stands on all fours over it, and works and shuffles his blanket so as to make the smoke circulate all through it, and come in contact with every portion of his body.

When an Indian has an arrow-wound, or wound or sore of any kind, he smears it with the pitch of this tree, and renews it when it wears off. In the spring, if food is scarce, they eat the buds on the ends of the limbs, the inner bark, and the core of the cone (*ta'-eh*), which is something like a cabbage-stalk when green. The cone-core and bunch-grass are boiled together for a hair-dye. They are as proud of their black hair as the Chinese; and when an old chief who is somewhat vain of his personal appearance, or one of the dandies of the tribe, finds his hair growing gray, he has his squaw boil up a decoction of this kind, and he sops his bleaching locks in it. The tar (*shin'-dak*), which is worn by widows in mourning, is made of *hit'*, pitch and burned acorns, powdered; it is removed by means of soap-root (*Chlorogalum pomeridianum*) and hot water.

Chip' pa is the willow, the long twigs of which are used both for arrows and basket-making. In making an arrow the hunter employs a rude kind of turning-lathe, a couple of sticks held in the hand, between which the twig intended for the arrow is tightly clamped and twisted around, which rubs off the bark and the alburnum, and makes it round. The long straight shoots of the buckeye (*po'-loh, po '-lem du*) are used for the same purpose. For the woof in basket-making they employ the wood of the redbud (*Cercis occidentalis ; pad'-dit*), which is split up with flints or the finger-nails into fine strings, used substantially as thread. The willow twig is passed round and round the basket, the butt of one lapping the tip of the other, while the redbud strings are sewn over the upper and under the lower.

Ko'-toh is the manzanita. Its berries are a favorite article of food, and are eaten raw, or pounded into flour in a basket, the seeds separated out, and the flour made into mush, or sacked and laid away for winter. They also make quite an agreeable article of cider from them, by soaking the flour in water several hours, and then draining it off.

Alder is *shu'-tum*; poison-oak is *chi'-tok*. They are less easily poisoned by the latter than Americans; their children handle it a great deal while little. They eat the leaves both as a preventive and as a cure for its effects, though it sometimes poisons them internally. The women use the leaves freely in cooking; they lay them over a pile of roots or a batch of acorn bread, then lay on hot stones and earth. The bright-red berries of the California holly (*Photinea arbutifolia; yo'-lus*) are eaten with relish; also the berries of the elder, nok, and wild grapes, *pi'-men*. They call a grape-vine a bush, *pi'-men-en du*.

Soap-root, *hauh*, is used for poisoning fish. They pound up the root fine, and mix it into pools where the fish and minnows have no way of escape, and at the same time stir up the bottom until the water becomes muddy. The minnows thrust their heads out of the water stupefied, and are easily scooped up. Buckeyes are used in the same manner. Soap-root is also used to heal and cleanse old sores, being heated and laid on hot. Both soap-root and buckeyes are eaten in times of great scarcity; they are roasted underground thirty-six hours or more to extract the poison.

For toothache the remedy is the root of the California buckthorn (*Frangula Californica; lu'-hum du*). It is heated as hot as can be borne, placed in the mouth against the offending member, and tightly gripped between the teeth.

Several sorts of mints, *hi'suh*, are used in a tea or decoction for colds or coughs. Ague is believed to be cured by a decoction for colds or coughs of the little mullen (*Eremocarpus setigerus; ba'-dah*), which grows on black adobe land in autumn. Colic is treated with a tea made from a greenish-gray lichen (*Parmelia saxicola;*

wa'-hat-tak), found growing on stones. For rheumatism they take the leaves and stems of a parasite vine (*Galium ; shesh-em*) which grows up in the middle of the chaparral bush, heat or burn them, and clap them hot on the place.

Yellow dock *hit'*, is a valuable specific in their pharmacopoeia. In case of acute pain of any description the root is heated hot and pressed upon the spot. In the spring the leaf is eaten boiled for greens, together with clover and many other things.

Bunch-grass, *bu' puh*, is the subject of superstition. They believe that the long, slender stalks of it, discharged as arrows from a little bow against a pregnant woman, will produce a miscarriage; also, that they will hasten the time of maturity in a maiden. There is another thing which they call *wo-ko'-mah*, probably wild parsnip, which they believe to be a deadly poison. It will produce nose-bleed, and the people who keep it in their houses will surely die. I will here state that I cannot discover that the Indians ever used poisons to any considerable extent to rid themselves of enemies; if they did, it was the old shamans, and they keep the matter a secret. The Indians profess to stand in great and perpetual dread of being poisoned by one another; and no one will taste anything handed to him by one who is not a member of his family, unless the other tastes it first; but they imagine a hundred cases of poisoning where one actually occurs.

Of grasses, they eat the seed of the wild oat, (*tu'-tu-tem kom*), but very sparingly. Wild clover, *chi'-wi; alfderilla, hat'-tis*; and a king of grass growing in wet places (*Melica; holl*) are all eaten raw when young and tender, or boiled for greens.

There are two kinds of mushrooms which they consider edible. The one of which they are fondest is called *pul'-kut,* and is a little round ball, from the size of a marble to that of a black walnut, found underground in chaparral and pine thickets. They eat it raw

Betsy, near Colfax, October 5, 1912

Her age estimated at 108, and blind, Betsy sits in front of her traditional conical hupu. A twined burden basket rests by her side. Despite the use of Euro-American style cabins by most Maidu at that time, Betsy preferred her traditional home. During her lifetime she had witnessed the first coming of non-Indians into the Maidu county and the subsequent loss of a majority of their homeland. She had experienced radical changes in a way of life and like others survived by adopting new strategies of how to cope. She was the grandmother of long time Nevada City resident Louis Kelly and the great, great grandmother of Rose (Kelly) Enos.

Photographer Banbrock (Auburn studio), Courtesy Rose Enos.

with great relish, or roast it in the ashes. Another kind is the *wa'-chub*, which grows in the ordinary form, brown on the upper side, chocolate-colored and deeply ribbed underneath, and easily peeled. It is eaten boiled.

Higher up in the mountains they find a root looking somewhat like a cork, a piece of which they sometimes wear suspended to their clothing as a charm. It is called *chuk'* or *cham' pu*. Indians of other tribes in the State invest different species of Angelica with talismanic attributes.

Under the popular name of grass-nut there is included a large number of plants with a small, round, bulbous root, all of which, with one exception, the Indians eat with much satisfaction. They are generally pried out of the ground with a sharp stick and eaten raw on the spot; but sometimes the women collect a quantity in a basket and make a roast in the ashes, or boil them. Most of them are by no means disagreeable to the civilized taste. There is the beaver-tail grass-nut (*Cyclobothra; wal'-lik*), the turkey-pea (*Sanicula tuberosa; tu'-en*), the purple-flowered grass-nut (*Brodiaea congesta; o'-kau*); the tule grass-nut (*ko'-ah*), a small bulb, with a single, wiry, cylindrical stalk, growing in wet places, which I could not identify; the climbing grass-nut (*Brodiaea volubilis; oam' pum wai*), sometimes planted by Americans for ornaments; the little soap-root (*Chlorogalum divaricatum; poy'-um*), the wild garlic (*Allium; ku'-ih*); the eight-leafed garlic (*shal*), the five-leafed garlic *(in'-shal*), and the three-leafed garlic (*wuk'-wi*); the yellow-blossom grass-nut (*Calliproa lutea; us'-tuh*); the long-leafed grass nut (*Brodiaea congesta*, although the Indians have a different name for it from that mentioned just above, namely, *yoang wai*); the white-flowered grass-nut (*Hesperoscordium lacteum; yuo'-wak wai*); and the wild onion (*Allium cepa; chan*). There is one other grass-nut, with a black bulb (*Anticlea; hak'-kul*), which the Indians consider poison, although it probably contains no more poison than other members of the liliaceous family.

The list of greens which they eat in the spring is also quite extensive. Besides the grasses and the yellow dock above mentioned, there is the mask-flower (*Mimulus luteus; pu'-shum*); two species of the Angelica (*hen and oam'-shu*), which are difficult to determine; the California poppy (*Eschscholtzia Californica; ta pu*), either boiled or roasted with hot stones, and then laid in water; the rock-lettuce (*Echeveris lanceolata; pit'-ti-tak*), eaten raw; the wild lettuce (*Claytonia perfoliata; yau*), and a species of Sanicula (*man'-ku*) the root of which, long and slightly tuberose, is also eaten. Of the wild lettuce a curious fact is to be noted. The Indians living in the mountains, about at the elevation of Auburn, gather it and lay it in quantities near the nests of certain large red ants, which have the habit of building conical heaps over their holes. After the ants have circulated all through it, they take it up, shake them off, and eat it with relish. They say the ants, in running over it, impart a sour taste to it, and make it as good as if it had vinegar on it. I never witnessed this done, but I have been told of it, at different times, by different Indians whom I have never known to deceive me.

Of seeds, they eat the following: A kind of coarse, wild grass (*Bromus virens; do'-doh*); a species of yellow-blooming, tarry-smelling weed (*Madaria; koam'-duk*), the seeds of which are as rich as butter; the yellow-blossom or crow-foot (*Ranunculus Californicus; tiss*), of which the seed is gathered by sweeping through it a long-handled basket or a gourd; a little weed which grows thick in ravines (*Bennosperma Californicum; poll*), gathered the same way; also a weed (*shi'-u*) with little white blossoms distributed all along the stalks, which are thickly covered with minute prickles - I know not what it is. All these seeds are generally parched a little, and then beaten to flour, and eaten without further cooking, or made into bread or mush. The dry, parched flour of the crow-foot seed has that peculiar, rich taste of parched corn.

There is an umbelliferous plant (*sho'-kum*), the root of which the Indians esteem very highly for food; more highly than any other, it being their nearest equivalent to potatoes. I know not if it is the true cammas; I think it is at least a species of it. It grows on rocky hillsides, blossoms in June and July, has an extremely delicate, fringe-like leaf, and a root about an inch long and a quarter as thick, sweetish-pungent and agreeable to the taste. In Penn Valley, Nevada County, they gather large quantities of it.

They are acquainted with the Yerba Santa, but attach no particular value to it.

There is a plant (*pum*) growing on a northern hillsides with a broad leaf, and a long white root as thick as one's little finger, which is highly esteemed as a medicine for internal pain of any kind, while the top affords edible greens. The Indians could not find a specimen of it.

Around old camps and corrals there is found a wild tobacco (*pan*), which Prof. Asa Gray pronounces *Nicotiana quadrivalvis* and Professor Bolander *N. plumbaginifolia*. It is smoked alone or mixed with dried manzanita leaves (*Arctostaphylos glauca*), and has a pungent, peppery taste in the pipe which is not disagreeable. Mr. A.W. Chase, in a letter to the author, states the Klamaths cultivate it–the only instance of aboriginal cultivation known in California. I think the Indians never cultivated it more than this, that they scattered the seeds about the camp and then took care not to injure the growing plants. I have even seen them growing finely on their earth-covered lodges. The pipe, *pan'-em-ku-lah*, is generally made of serpentine (or of wood nowadays), shaped like a cigar-holder, from four to six inches long, round, and with a bowl nearly an inch in diameter.

There are two plants used for textile purposes. One is a kind of tulegrass or small bulrush (*Juncus; dok'-kun*), which they hetcheled with flints or with their fingernails, bleached, and wove into breechcloths. For strings, cords, and nets they used the inner bark of the lowland milkweed (*Asclepias; pu*). When it is dry the Indian takes both ends of a stalk in his hand and crushes it in his teeth, or else passes it over a stone while he gently taps it with another; then strips off the bark and twists it into strands, then into cords. The rock milkweed (*oam' pu*) has a medicinal value; they use the root for the toothache the same way the root of the buckthorn is used.

It is necessary to state that most of the medicines above mentioned are of the class which the women are allowed to become somewhat acquainted with and to employ. There are several other substances which are more rare and valuable, or at least they deem them more valuable, and which the medicine-men alone know anything about. They are found far up in the mountains or in other localities, and may be called the medicines of commerce, having a tolerably well-settled value in shell-money. I regret that I was generally unable to secure sufficiently complete specimens to determine them. For instance, there is a root *(lu'-no)* which I should call seneca snakeroot, but of which I could secure only a little piece. A root as large as a pipestem and about four inches long is worth $1. A decoction of it is used for diarrhea, that scourge of aboriginal life, also for venereal diseases. There is a bush (*cha' pum*) found in the mountains, with a very pale, tea-green bark and minute golden specks on the small limbs, which is probably California sassafras, and which is very highly esteemed for coughs and colds, a tea of the bark being given. Another root (*pal'-lik*) – spikenard from its appearance – is made into a tea and drunk for diarrhea. This also is very valuable. There is still another root (*lit'-we*) found on the Truckee which is good for the dropsy.

Although it is not strictly germane to the topic, I may be permitted to state that the Indians have names for all the internal organs of the human body; and their ideas of their functions and of the operations of medicine are at least as respectable as those of the Chinese.

Native Animal Foods

The following articles are either eaten or used for medicine by the Nishinam of Placer County.

Nauh (*Helix Vancouwerensis*), snail; used for food.

Nauh (*H. Columbiana*), snail; used for food.

Shek (*Saturnia Caeanothi*), caterpillar; used for food.

Shek (*Arctia, two species*), caterpillar; used for food.

Shil'-lah (*Hyborynchus Perspicuus*), a small minnow. Sometimes the Indian shaman, after sucking a patient for a long time, pretends to vomit up one of these minnows (which, of course, he had previously concealed in his mouth), pretending that it had somehow been introduced into the system and had been the source of all the trouble.

Hol'-lih, crickets; used for food, roasted. Formerly they were often roasted in large numbers by firing the woods.

Pan'-nak, grubs found in decayed oak-trees; used for food.

Laih (*Engystoma*), a small frog; used for food.

Sho'-lah, slugs; eaten for food.

Ok'-o pe peh (*Phrynosoma*), a horned toad; given internally for medicine in certain stomachic affections.

Pit'-chak (*Sceloporus bi-seriatus*), another toad; used as the above.

Shol'-lo-koi-koi (*Gerhonotus multi-carinatus*), a lizard; used for medicine. Shol'-lo-koi-koi, another lizard; used as the above.

Kut (*Sphinx Ludoviciana*), a horned black worm; used for food. The Indian name denotes "a buck", so called on account of the horn.

Tai'-a-mun (*Coronella balteata*), a ring-snake; used by the Nishinam for medicine; eaten by the Washo of Nevada.

Earth-worms (*Lumbricus*), Indian name unknown to me; eaten in soup. The Nakum of Big Meadows dance and stamp violently, chanting all the while, to bring these worms to the surface.

Cham'-bau (*Ortyx Californicus*). After eating the flesh of this bird, roasted, the Nishinam dry the skins, and preserve them as a dainty for use in case of sickness.

The skunk (*Mephitis*) is eaten by the Nishinam, when properly caught and dressed.

The Gold Rush

Murderer's Bar: Repository of Mysterious Dead

By Harry C. Peterson

Hostile Indians, adventurous prospectors, the lure of gold, an ambush, an attack, a terrific struggle with odds twenty to one, a hastily-built fire, a collection of charred bones and the dank odor of burned flesh--all served as a prelude to the discovery of one of the richest mining placers on the whole Mother Lode.

Of all the weird names wished upon helpless localities in the early mining days, none was more uncanny than that of Murderer's Bar, which was the name given to this particular spot on the Middle Fork of the American River, not far from Auburn. That it should, after having been christened, turn out to be one of the treasure-places of the Middle Fork but intensifies the anomaly.

Like most of the richest gold camp discoveries, it was a place the prospectors were not specifically looking for. When Thomas M. Buckner left Kentucky in 1845 and migrated to Oregon, he had no intention whatsoever to prospect for gold except with a plow. California held no lure to him then. Oregon was the choice of most of the middle Westerners who wanted to do farming on a large scale.

The news reached Oregon quickly that Marshall had found gold. There were sixty-two young men wedded to the soil of Oregon who immediately divorced themselves from its obligations the minute they heard the news. They formed a party under the leadership of Captain Martin and, after a few hardships, reached Sutter's Fort, August 2, 1848.

They first went up to Sutter's Mill at Coloma to get their bearings. From there, a party of seven of the Oregonians, including Buckner, tramped over by the Spanish Dry Diggings and down into the canyon of the Middle Fork to what was later known as "Spanish Bar." Going across they gained the ridge on the other side and located the trail followed by the sailors

Courtesy International Museum of Photography at George Eastman House.

Maidu Headmen and Treaty Commissioners, 1851

By September 18, 1851 a series of federal treaties, authorized by Congress were made with Maidu groups at Bidwell's Rancho Chico and in the Yuba and Cosumnes River regions. On August 1, 1851 the headmen of several independent Maidu groups gathered at John Bidwell's ranch to sign. This ambrotype may have been taken that day. U.S. Indian agent O.M. Wozencraft may be one of the Euro-American men. Attending Maidu leaders and their tribal/village affiliations were listed as;
Luck-pan of Michopda, Wis-muk of Hololupi, Yo-lo-sa of Cheno, So-miela of Yutduc, Yon-ni-chi-no of Batsi, Mo-la-yo of Eskuin, We-no-ke of Toto, Wa-tel-li of Sunus, and Po-ma-ko of Simsawa.

The treaty promised 227 square miles of land and each person over age fifteen was to be given a variety of clothing, food, tools and livestock. None of the eighteen treaties made in California were ever ratified by Congress.

and went on to the present Bird's Valley. Here they camped.

Every morning they trudged down through the brush and dry grass to the river in the canyon below. They had nothing but the most primitive tools to work with--iron spoons, butcher knives and a tin pan. They confined their efforts to getting out the gold from the crevices of the bedrock that was exposed at that time of the year by the low water in the river.

The gold they found was rather coarse, and did not occur very evenly. Some crevices paid good, some not at all, but the average was promising; they considered themselves fortunate until their provisions suddenly began to get scarce. Like thousands of other miners later, they had not reckoned much on the fact that it would require much more cash to replenish their grub boxes than it did the first time.

Eighteen hundred and forty-eight was a hard winter. Even Captain Ezekiel Merritt, who had played a prominent part in the raising of the historic Bear Flag at Sonoma [revolt of

An 1852 daguerreotype of Spanish Flat, now the Auburn Placer Library area, taken by Joseph Blaney Starkweather.

1846], was forced to go up there to tide over the winter. He and Buckner took a liking to each other. Buckner told him of his trip up the river, and they decided to quietly go up together the minute winter broke. In April, the two, with Merritt's Indian servant, Peg, went overland.

This time Buckner and Merritt did not go all the way to Coloma, but cut off a few miles this side and descended into the canyon of the Middle Fork at that point. They followed along the river until they came to a place where a huge landslide had so changed the bed of the river that there was quite a little waterfall there.

The river was still running rather full, and though Buckner felt that the hole at the foot of the waterfall must of necessity contain an immense amount of gold that had been rolling into it for probably a century, they could find no way of getting it out. They tried putting buckets on long sticks, but, aside from losing their buckets, all they gained was a little valueless gravel.

They decided they would tackle it later in the year, but in the meantime remain around close by. They went down stream a short distance, until they reached the head of a large gravel bar on the south side of the river. Some distance down stream was a jutting point of rocks that hid the river beyond them.

For several days Captain Merritt, an experienced frontiersman, insisted that he saw evidences of Indians in the neighborhood and that they must be cautious. As a result he went in the lead and was just passing through the brush on the other side of the bar when he suddenly stopped. He was an exceedingly nervous man, and when excited he stammered. Buckner, just behind him, saw the captain's lips begin to pucker up and the

Courtesy Meriam Library, Special Collections, CSA-Chico

Indian Mission, Greenville, Plumas County, 1905
Maidu (and other) Indian children were enrolled in government boarding schools beginning in the 19th century. Even though Indian children could rightfully attend public schools, the government maintained boarding schools throughout the nation. The strict and sometimes harsh treatment of the children and the military atmosphere at the schools made them quite unpopular. Indians attempting to enter public schools often met with resistance.

tobacco juice to sputter and spray the atmosphere. He sensed that the captain had discovered something.

"B-b-b-by G-g-g-god! He-he-h-here's wh-wh-whi-white man-man-man's hair h-h-he-here! Ye-ye-ye-yes, an' Injun's ha-har, t- t-t-too!"

Buckner rushed up and looked at what Merritt was pointing to. Sure enough, there on the pebbly bar, away above high-water mark, was a white man's hair, and scattered around were many strands of an Indian's coarse black hair. Looking around they saw every evidence of a plundered camp, and evidence that the fight had been a terrific one; that not only had the white men of the party been killed, but that the Indian had suffered greatly, too.

Then Merritt and Buckner and the Indian boy, Peg, began a search for the bodies of the slain, but the only evidence they found was a mass of charred human bones. Every vestige of clothing and arms had disappeared. With their picks and shovels they dug a hole and buried the bones as they had found them, all mixed together.

This discovery made the little party more cautious than ever. Peg was sent ahead to see if by any chance there were Indians on the other side of the rocks just down the river. He came

Photograph courtesy of Mrs. Ruby Ray Eriksen

Early Pioneers of Placer County, Last Chance, 1906

Upper Left: Barney Cavanaugh, after whom Cavanaugh Ridge was named. William Anderson, after whom Anderson Ridge was named. Lower Left: John P. Ray who came to California from Virginia City in 1865. Andy Hauk who came to California soon after the discovery of gold helped to place the tombstone of Alan Grosch in the Last Chance Cemetery.

back and reported plenty of fresh signs but no live Indians. Merritt immediately picked out an open space where they could not be ambuscaded and made camp, and prepared for a surprise party that night, but the Indians failed to show up.

Encouraged, the three packed up and started down around the rocks. They had hardly made the turn when some seventy wild Indians appeared on the rocks above them and began a terrific yelling, and danced about in the most frightful manner imaginable. They had nothing but bows and arrows, and having seen Merritt's long rifle, and having apparently had experience with its death-dealing qualities, they made no definite attack with their arrows, but apparently tried to frighten the whites away. The Indians kept up the serenade for several hours, but Merritt and Buckner held their ground without apparently paying any attention to the savages, who finally got disgusted and silently disappeared.

Captain Merritt looked around him. The bar they were on had a fine grove of willows, some ash trees, and a great many smooth-barked, thrifty alders. It had all the necessities of a first class miners' camp, and Buckner was strong for staying there, but Merritt deemed it safer on the other side of the river; besides, he was a trifle superstitious, and the idea of all those bones with the ghastly memories they evoked, did not appeal to him. Across they must go.

Buckner decided the place's name must be marked so he took out his hunting knife, stripped off a section of bark from a large alder tree, and carved in large letters MURDERER'S BAR.

From that day to the present it has held that name. There was much mystery attached to the death of the unknown.

THE CALIFORNIA BLADES

By Eugene Markley

The war between the 49ers and Bear River Indians started in December of 1849. It was to become the largest conflict between the two cultures in the west slope region of the Northern Sierra, the end results of the conflict being the almost total extermination of a passive primitive culture by the warrior like Anglo-Saxon 49ers.

Before the onslaught of the gold rush, the native Maidu lived in scattered villages along the divides that separated the restless green rivers of the west slope. Along these divides or ridges were knolls and small vales. In the secret vales flowed small winding brooks. These creeks were fed by secluded springs of the most quaint nature. Surrounding these enclaves were miniature hills covered with immense stands of yellow pine, sugar pine and groves of black oak. These forest barriers guarded the hidden meadows and secret brooks. Into these sanctuaries came the large mammals of the low mountain to feed. Black tail deer and elk browsed the meadows, and black and grizzly bear ate the wild berries and dug for ground squirrels here. Trout and salmon lay among the dark rock faces as the creek meandered downward to the main westward flowing rivers. The Indians lived about these meadows building their conical shaped cedar bark huts slightly on the ridges. Here on the southwest slopes the sun would have a longer day with them.

Each native village consisted of from 30 to 60 individuals with an elder to give advice and guidance to the clan type group. Perhaps one can imagine a tranquil wilderness scene with deep forest, lush clearings and meandering streams where Auburn, Clipper Gap, Meadow Vista, Colfax and Gold Run now stand. The cedar bark huts were surrounded with great stores of food. Stacked sugar pine cones, containing their rich nuts often exceeded the size of the dwellings. Hanging in baskets on the sides of the huts were immense caches of manzanita berries. Large cribs made of branches and bark stood about the village housing great quantities of acorns gathered from the unsurpassed oak forest of the Sierra. Supporting the natural granaries, the Maidu caught the fish of the

Photographer unknown, Courtesy of Rose Enos.

Al Williams, 1920

Like many Maidu, Al served the United States in the armed forces. Al Williams and his family were from the Nevada City area.

hidden streams and slew the bear, elk, antelope and deer. Thus the natives were able to knit their society with mother earth in a sensitive way so as not to disrupt the timeless balance of nature.

By the winter of 1849-1850 the searching miners left the main rivers and combed the ridges and secondary streams along the divides looking for new sources of gold. The 49ers, not caring much about the natural order of life, soon commenced to destroy the great elk and deer herds of the hills and vales. Those surviving animals not reaching the stomach of the hungry miners sought isolated protection along the steep canyon walls. As the miners worked the high gravels the Indian fisheries were destroyed. As their main food supplies disappeared the Maidu, unaccustomed to such complete disregard of the earth and its creatures held great councils in the Bear River Canyon praying that the crazed white man would leave their lands.

As the winter of 1849-1850 set in, the starving Maidu began to look on the increasingly numerous 49ers as a dire threat to their very existence. The natives, thinking in a logical manner, reasoned that if the whites were taking their animals and fish from the forest, why could not they take the animals of the whites? Was it not true that the Great Spirit had given them the animals of the forest and the fish of the streams to nourish their bodies forever? Thus in response to hunger and equality the Maidu began to raid the stock of the 49ers. Mules, horses, oxen and cows became fair game to them.

By early December, 1849, the miners were being forced by storms down the slopes to warmer climes. They, in many instances, left behind food caches which the natives considered as theirs for had not the white man plenty to eat? So the cabins and brush huts of the 49ers were entered at will and the food consumed on the spot or carried away to their encampments. One group of miners decided to return to their cabin near present Colfax. On arriving at their cabin with a string of mules laden with food and mining supplies they encountered a band of Indians feasting in their cabin. As the angry miners rushed in, the food pillaging Indians rushed out in a grand melee. The 49ers sought to terminate the lives of the fleeing unwanted guests, but damp gun powder caused their weapons to misfire. The Indians, being surprised by the miners, fled in such haste that they did not have time to string their bows and slay the whites. Thus no blood was drawn with the first encounter.

When morning arrived the 49ers found not only their food caches consumed, but their laden pack mules were missing. The sorely disgusted 49ers set out in hasty pursuit. But after a distance of forest ridge travel the Indians' trail disappeared into the wilds of the Bear River Canyon. Upon returning home the frustrated miners spread the word among the foothills that the Indians were getting brave and needed punishment.

In mid winter of 1849-1850 a public meeting was held among the miners to determine what action they should take against the pillaging Maidu. Individually, the miners were at a loss to stop raids as the Indians became more brazen with success. For it was very easy for a small band of Indians to lose the clumsy miner in pursuit of his stock or grub stake. The 49ers decided a strong group of organized men was needed to invade the Indian sanctuary of the Bear River Canyon. Thus at Illinoistown the miners formed a military company with the gallant title of the California Blades. About 30 men signed on to punish the marauding Bear River Band.

Assembling a variety of weapons including muzzle loaders, yagers, cavalry pistols and swords, the California Blades, under an elected captain, went on the warpath. Northeast of Illinoistown they picked up a Maidu Indian trail. As they continued on three forested hills and small open meadows they gradually descended into the wilds of Bear River. Working around a small waterfall they stumbled on to a bench below the main ridge line. Here sat a village of the Maidu in complete solitude. A charge was made by the Blades and in seconds the Indians seemingly vanished from earth. Only a few old and decrepit individuals were rounded up by the whites.

Photograph courtesy of Placer County Museum

Mining Operation in the Placer or El Dorado County area.

There was much evidence scattered about the encampment of theft and plunder from the 49ers camps. Mule and oxen hides covered the dwellings and an ample supply of mule meat hung from racks throughout the camp. Besides the stolen goods there were great stores of acorns, manzanita berries and sugar pine cones. Now that the village was occupied by the somewhat lucky Blades, the question was what to do with the captured material. Some argued that the right course was to destroy the food supplies thus giving the Indians a direct punishment. Others argued that it would be inhuman to destroy the food supplies that would lead to wholesale starvation of the band. As the two sides were nearly equally divided on what to do, a vote was taken. The destructionists won by a single vote. An hour later the Indian encampment had been reduced to a smothering scattering of ashes.

Now with the California Blades on the offensive they raided camp after camp killing the males and taking the women and children captive. From mid winter to late summer of 1850 the Divide between the Bear River and the American was not safe for the natives. One encampment after the other was overrun and put to the torch. The aggressive California Blades literally burned the Maidu out of their homeland.

Surviving remnants of the Indians retaliated against the whites by swooping off fifty head of stock near Auburn. In early spring they seized three stores along the main ridge carrying off stores of food and a great number of mules and oxen. But the Indians were never able to mount an offensive against the militant miners. This was because of inferior weapons, their passive culture and lack of food sources.

By the summer of 1850 the Blades increased their operation and exterminated village after village as they sought to protect the white population from the original inhabitants. In late summer those Indians surviving the massacres retreated to the north side of the Bear River. Here for several years they were able to isolate themselves from the white hordes.

The victorious California Blades posted Indian scalps in all the wayside stations from Sacramento to Dutch Flat, "declaring the west slope free of Indian trouble." In the fall of 1850 the California Blades were disbanded, their warrior deeds soon lost in the pages of history of the Northern Sierra.

The Mystery of Yankee Jim

By Harry C. Peterson

When it comes to mysteries, to the mysterious appearance and disappearance of the genus man, probably no place on earth could touch the early gold diggings of California. A man could appear, remain a week, disappear completely, all without causing comment or inquiry as to his name, business, or destination.

Today the mysterious stranger in our midst is looked upon with much suspicion. We give him three major guesses and several minor ones; he is a bootlegger, a rum runner, or a Rutterite; he looks tricky, he is up to something, he is wicked, he is all wrong until we find out he is all right. Even then we are doubtful.

But in the early mines every man was a stranger, one to the other. Every man came with no intention of settling down in any one particular spot; he came with but one big idea, of getting the gold wherever he could get it regardless of place, time or trouble. He might have been a doctor "back-home," or a lawyer, or a judge, or even a minister. In those days there was but little variety in the miners' togs, at least while they were new. Some wore the blue denim overalls, blue denim much heavier than that of today, but also much softer in texture. But many, possibly the majority at first, wore great, roomy trousers of finely woven white cotton canvas, such as our old-time grain and sugar sacks were made of; a canvas cloth of great durability; tough, flexible, and capable of absorbing an immense amount of bacon grease, flour, dirt and pine pitch without cracking under the strain.

Now this idea of the miner wearing white pants I know is not according to the Hoyle of the modern western fiction writer, nor the scenarist, but then neither is the idea that a great many miners wore other than red flannel shirts seven days a week. Just the same it is a fact that the majority of shirts during the summer time were either blue or butternut in color--when new. During the winter the red shirts were more in demand as the color added warmth to the scene. There was some variety in the hats, some were cleaner than others; the more clean ones in camp the more tenderfeet were said to be in town.

Shaving in cold water without soap was an uncomfortable job, also useless, and all whiskers were not alike. Some grew out straight, some curled, some grew wavy, but they all grew,

Yankee Jim's, 1857

and grew and grew. Personality and whiskers distinguished man from man in the diggings. Where the stranger came from, what his name was, no one knew, no one cared a rap, no one inquired. Then again, during that hectic excitement it was hard to remember names, much more difficult than remembering characteristics, so they called a man by his most prominent cartoonistic feature, that feature that the cartoonist emphasizes in his drawings to carry across the printed page that man's personality or most distinguishing feature. It was the same in '49. A man was "Whiskey-nose Bill," "Lop-ear Louie," "Sneezer Bill," "Skinny Sam," or "Cock-eyed Dan," all names that distinguished one man from the other. "Faro Kate," "Nugget Nellie" and "Monte Belle" were among the names doing service for the feminine contingent that soon flocked to the mines.

Among the very first, if not the very first of these nicknamed unknowns was Yankee Jim, founder of one of Placer County's most famous early day mining camps. Gold had been discovered in the first part of 1848. The news reached the outer world slowly, because the news carried little weight with it until the gold itself reached the seaport at San Francisco and later New York. As a consequence the first preliminary "rush" to the mines was made by the men already in, or on their way to California at that time. Prior to this date ships with ever increasing frequency visited San Francisco for barter, for supports, or for fresh water, the latter usually taken aboard at Sausalito.

It was from these different sailing ships that California received many of its first visitors, visitors that had applied for shore leave from their captains and had not been able to find their ship again before it sailed. Among some of the most respected and prominent men of this state were some of these sailors, who, in a state of mental aberration, had wandered out into the country and became lost in the brush until they saw the masts of their ships disappear through the Golden Gate. Six months aboard a sailing ship with almost no stops was enough to cause almost any able-bodied man to "forget" where his ship lay waiting for him. By the last of 1848 most of these men, being usually in or near San Francisco or Monterey, had heard of Marshall's discovery. The more adventurous immediately left for the diggins; the others stayed within sound of the mandolin and guitar.

From all that can be learned, Yankee Jim was one of those who was adventurous; also he had other reasons for wanting to keep away from the "well-traveled roads." He went up into the

"Sunday in the Mines,"* *a painting by Charles Nahl

mountains alone and disappeared. Rumors soon began to filter down to Sutter's Fort that a mysterious miner, tall, lanky, of great strength and agility, uncommunicative, devoid of fear, neither seeking trouble nor avoiding it, was bringing into one of the mining camps of the North Fork many large specimens of gold. He would appear at a provision tent just after dark, buy such articles as he needed, pull out a leather pouch made from kangaroo skin, pour out enough gold to cover his purchases, pick up his packages, saunter around the camp for a short time, then suddenly drop from sight. He talked little, but he listened much. The little crowd of miners sized him up, dubbed him "Yankee Jim" and let it go at that. "Yankee Jim" did likewise; any name suited him just as long as it was not his right one.

His visits to the camp were not frequent; where his claim lay no one knew, but everybody was determined to find out. Whatever shortcomings Yankee Jim had, one was not the lack of woodcraft. When he disappeared into the darkness he seemed to simply melt out of sight. They tried to follow him, they lay in wait on all sides of the camp for him to come by, but they waited in vain. Yankee Jim passed without their knowledge. It was uncanny, this ability to be swallowed up in the dark with everybody watching. They searched all the neighboring creeks for him, but no trace was ever seen. Yankee Jim knew how to cover his tracks better than an Indian. This ability, along with the fact that he was getting gold of much coarser grain than any of them were, caused much speculation, many rumors and stories that did not lose their interest in the retelling. By the time the story had reached Sutter's Fort it had arrived at that stage where Yankee Jim suddenly appeared in the flame of the camp fire, stood with folded arms a moment, then stepped out into the midst of the astounded miners, walked to the "store," bought his grub, stepped into the flame again and "poof," he was gone. These weird descriptions of his coming and going must not all be laid to rumor. In those days of difficult transportation "much strength in little bottles" was the rule, and some of those bottles held the strength of Samson and the imagination of a Poe.

It was at Barne's Bar on the North Fork in the fall of '49 that "M.D." Fairchild and Ben Currier first heard of Yankee Jim. One thing they had heard was of much interest, and that was that Yankee Jim was getting his gold high up in the hills and not down on the river, and that the gold was different, more easily found and in greater profusion. While at Sutter's Fort they had been told by Jim Marshall, the discoverer of gold, that they must beware of the streams and rivers during the winter, that after a heavy rain they would suddenly rise, not a few feet, but sometimes fifteen or more in the narrow places, coming down without warning. This same warning had been given everyone passing through Sutter's Fort. Sam Brannan urged every miner to return to the settlements in the lowlands for the winter. Sam kept a store in almost every lowland settlement.

While most of the embryo miners heard Sam's warning, few determined to heed it; all hoped to find some place on top of a hill where they could mine in safety. Consequently, this idea that Yankee Jim had discovered such a place appealed to Currier and Fairchild. They joined forces with four other men and started out

Photograph courtesy of the California State Archives

Miners at Auburn Ravine, circa 1852

to locate the uncanny Yank. They told no one of their mission; it was not good policy to announce in advance that they had a hunch as to where gold was plentiful. That afternoon each man quietly laid out all his equipment so that it could easily be rolled up in the dark; then they all sat around smoking with the rest of the fellows, talking of the work they were going to do the next morning. But the next morning found them gone, bag and baggage. They had left during the night to parts unknown.

Keeping out of sight as much as possible, they reached the summit of the Foresthill Divide before dark. They were tired, so camped under some tall pines where the camp fire smoke would blend in with their branches and be unnoticed by their late comrades. At midnight a rainstorm suddenly swept their camp. Ben Currier and one of the other boys got up and piled some more wood on the fire. Just as Currier started to pull the blankets around him again he noticed a glimmer of light moving through the forest in the direction of the place they were headed for. Currier woke the rest of the party, they talked it over, and he, with a companion, was delegated to follow the light and find out what it meant.

It was a wet, dismal night in an unknown country, known to be full of Indians and otherwise. The country was rocky, full of decayed branches of trees, and terrible grizzly bear were known to abound in that district, but their fear was numbed by one thought: the light ahead might be that of Yankee Jim going to his golden lair. With scratched faces and bleeding hands the two stalkers followed through the darkness for several hours. Suddenly the light disappeared; they waited; a half hour passed, an hour, but the light failed to again show up. They were miles from their camp, wet and disgusted. They groped around in the dark and gathered up a lot of rocks and sticks. These they made into a pile at the foot of a tall pine tree so that they could again locate it by daylight. Cursing their luck, they began to work their way up the mountain side, knowing that they must first reach the ridge before they could locate their camp.

The break of day disclosed their party some miles away. Reaching them, they related their adventures. Immediately they reached the conclusion that they were close upon Yankee Jim; they rushed through their breakfast and without waiting for Currier and his companion to rest up, all set out to find the little pile of rocks that had been left as a marker the night before. Once they had located this they felt that one Yankee Jim would be their meat before nightfall; but he wasn't, for they never found their little pile of rock. They searched the vicinity well, only to discover that the man with the light had disappeared down a deep gorge. They were all afternoon getting to its bottom, and had no more than made camp when it began to storm again. For five days not a sound had been heard or a light seen that would indicate that Yankee Jim was near. A roaring fire soon had the blankets drying out, a good breakfast going and everybody was bubbling over with good nature when suddenly Currier looked up, gazed intently for a moment up the gorge, turned excitedly to his companions and exclaimed: "My God, boys! Indians!"

They hastily scattered the fire to stop the smoke from betraying their presence. With extreme caution they packed up their blankets and grub, wet or dry, it made no difference; Indians were Indians in those days. The most experienced men of the party were delegated to scout out the mysterious smoke. With great skill they managed to reach a point directly opposite the place from which the smoke had been ascending. It was across the stream, well hidden by bushes. For some time the scouting party waited in silence. Suddenly there was a cautious parting of the bushes. Somebody was peeking out, peering anxiously down towards the gorge where Currier's fire had been. A man of Currier's party raised his gun to fire, when Currier knocked up its barrel. "You fool! It's a white man!" It was a white man, wearing a most gorgeously colored skull cap, a cap that had so nearly cost him his life, for the gunner had taken it for an Indian head dress. The scouting party rose to their feet, hailed the man in the bushes who ducked from sight, reappearing, however, the moment he discovered the hail came from white men. He was very glad to see the Currier party, but Currier was disappointed, for this refined looking man with the silk skull cap in no way resembled the long searched-for Yankee Jim. They were invited across the stream. On the other side they found two men, Mr. Tuttle from Connecticut, who wore the cap, and Mr. Van Zandt of Oregon. These two men, having also heard of Yankee Jim, had come up there early in the season with the idea of trailing him also, but without success. In the meantime they had been quite successful in the gorge and invited the rest of the party to stay and try their luck. They decided to give up the hunt for Yankee Jim and settled down to work. They were soon making good, but Currier was still determined to do a little hunting on the side for the mysterious Yankee.

Currier took to spending his Sundays trailing among the gulches. One Sunday morning, in a little flat at the foot of a ravine, he was suddenly aware that he was staring at the feet and legs of a man projecting from a sort of temporary shelter made by standing long slaps of pine bark against a tree, an immense sugar pine, into the butt of which his fire had burned a deep cavity. It was the crudest of habitations, but satisfactory during good weather.

Apparently the man was asleep, so Currier approached and hailed him. Startled, the man arose and awkwardly greeted his visitor. His first greeting was, "How long, stranger, be ye expectin' to stay up this way?"

"Until I dig out my fortune from among these rocks. I am up here with a crowd of other fellows after gold and we have decided to stay here all winter and mine."

"Ain't ye afraid o' the Injuns up here?"

"We know how to take care of ourselves, we are well armed and when we came here we expected to take some chances."

Photograph courtesy of the California State Archives

Miner at Auburn Ravine, circa 1852

"Wal, ye sure take some in these hills. Maybe, stranger, you could let me have some bullets; I hain't but five left, and when them's gone I got nothin' but a knife to fight with, and an Injun arrow travels further than a knife thrust."

Currier made him happy by telling him he had several pounds of lead back at camp and would bring him up some the next day. A look of alarm came over the face of the lone camper.

"Stranger I like you because ye did not make me bargain for them bullets, but stranger, I have reasons for not wanting my whereabouts known, and I ask you to respect my wishes. If you will, I may be of much service to you in the immediate future." He dropped his dialect in his anxiety to escape from discovery by the other miners in the vicinity. Currier assured him that he would respect his wishes and left, to return the next morning with the promised lead for the bullets.

The sight of the much needed lead caused the tall, lanky stranger to loosen up his tongue. He confided to Currier, under promise of secrecy, his real name and birth place. His talk was rather rambling, drifting rapidly from one subject to another as though trying to keep away from anything pertaining to his own life, yet almost irresistibly coming back to that subject as though he wanted to unburden himself to somebody.

Between desire and caution, his talk conveyed but little to Currier other than that he had apparently been the black sheep of a New England family, that to escape punishment he had

Photograph courtesy of the California State Archives

Covered bridge formerly at Mineral Bar below Colfax, circa 1874

signed aboard a sailing ship bound for the South Seas, and that he had shifted from vessel to vessel until he found himself aboard one coming up the coast of California. At some seaport, most likely Monterey, he had deserted and slipped away into the interior and subsisted as best he could until he was sure his ship had left port. Then he emerged from hiding intent upon having a good time in the old town of Monterey.

He was a sailor, used to having a sweetheart in every port. He had none in Monterey, so started in to supply the deficiency. He had expected to be welcomed with open arms by the best families there, but the best families in those days were ultra conservative when it came to entertaining sailors. They chose with great care and this sailor boy was not one of the chosen. He picked out a Mexican girl. She had already annexed a sweetheart, but she failed to so inform the sailor. He discovered it when he felt a stiletto trying to edge its way in between his ribs. The fight did not last long; the sailor gave a twist of his body as he felt the knife approach, and it slipped to the ground under his feet. The boyfriend, without his knife, ran away.

The sailor decided he was not wanted in Monterey. For some time he wandered up and down the coast until there came the great news of the gold discoveries. Immediately he left for the mountains. Like many renegades, he seemed to have exceptional luck. He feared but one thing, and that was that someone should recognize him. Most of his talk was in the language of the sailor of his day, but at times he spoke with the finest of English. At others he dropped into the Cockney dialect, which later gave rise to the suspicion that he had been a "Sydney Duck" from the penal settlements of Australia, but Currier always felt that he was really a Yankee with a criminal record.

He admitted to Currier that he was the man known as Yankee Jim, that the name suited him and he intended to continue to so be known, but that he had no desire to have a gold rush to his locality, that if Currier would come up there alone he would show him some of the richest diggings in the mountains, practically taking Currier in as a partner on condition that no one else learned of it.

Just then it flashed into Currier's mind that only a short time before there had been found the skeleton of a man and a horse not very far from this spot, and that there was a bullet hole through that unknown skull, as well as through the skull of the skeleton of the horse. While it had never been charged that Yankee Jim had anything to do with the killing, yet somehow the idea of residing alone up in that canyon with a self-confessed bad man lost its lure, even if there was plenty of gold to be found there.

"What good is gold to a skeleton?" flashed through Currier's brain. He declined Yankee Jim's offer, though he kept his location secret until he was discovered by other parties.

Little by little Yankee Jim began to mix with the rest of the crowd. He threw off his reserve when he found hundreds of other men up there under assumed names. When he discovered that no one cared what anyone's past had been he seemed to take heart again. He established a little camp and it became known as Yankee Jim's and is still so known. It grew in importance, was a candidate for county seat at one time, and was the center of much political excitement. In 1853 Col. McClure introduced the hydraulic mining technique here; at the same time he planted out the 500 fruit trees he had just received from Philadelphia, many of which were still bearing a few years ago. In 1850, the "Mountain Courier" was established there, and a year later the rival paper "Placer Courier" was started. These two papers in one town, through their efforts, secured the 1857 Democratic convention.

In June, 1852, a fire swept over Yankee Jim's; he was cleaned out and he disappeared. He was a mystery while there, he remained a mystery after he left. Various fates were allotted to him, but that most generally accepted is that he was the man who attempted to steal the pilot boat Plutus in Wilmington Harbor, near Los Angeles, with the idea of using it as a pirate craft to prey upon small shipping up and down the coast. He was caught, given a jury trial, found guilty, and strung up.

He died as he had lived, just plain Yankee Jim.

THE GOLD RUSH IN SONG

These four songs are reprinted with permission from The Songs of the Gold Rush *by Dwyer and Lingenfelter, UC Press, Berkeley,*

Guitarist and songwriter John A. Stone came to the goldfields in 1850. After three years of hard luck, he unearthed a block of gold bearing quartz in 1853 weighing a whopping 700 pounds and worth $15,000. He laid down his pick and shovel immediately and took up a musical career, touring the Mother Lode with his popular group the "Sierra Nevada Rangers" and performing his humorous and satirical songs. Miners greatly enjoyed these parodies of their lives as a release to their often dismal living conditions and luckless prospecting.

Cal Hamlen, pictured fourth over in the front row, ran a butcher shop, taught music in Dutch Flat and also led Hamlen's Band.

Photograph courtesy of Placer County Museum

Community bands and amateur theatrical companies provided surprisingly good entertainment to their neighbors to supplement the performances of wandering troupes of entertainers.

WHEN I WENT OFF TO PROSPECT

J. A.. Stone | *Air: King of the Cannibal Islands* | *J. Broughham*

When I got there, the mining ground
Was staked and claimed for miles around,
And not a bed was to be found,
When I went off to prospect.
The town was crowded full of folks,
Which made me think 'twas not a hoax;
At my expense they cracked their jokes,
When I went off to prospect.

I left my jackass on the road,
Because he wouldn't carry the load;
I'd sooner pick a big horn toad,
When I went off to prospect.
My fancy shirt, with collar so nice,
I found was covered with body-lice;
I used unguentum once or twice,
But could not kill the grey-backs.

At Deadwood I got on a tight –
At Groundhog Glory I had a fight;
They drove me away from Hell's Delight,
When I went off to prospect.
From Bogus-Thunder I ran away –
At Devil's Basin I wouldn't stay;
My lousy shirt crawled off one day,
Which left me nearly naked.

Now all I got for running about,
Was two black eyes, and a bloody snout;
And that's the way it did turn out,
When I went off to prospect.
And now I'm loafing around dead broke,
My pistol and tools are all in soak,
And whisky bills at me they poke –
But I'll make it right in the morning.

PROSPECTING DREAM

J. A.. Stone *Air: Oh! Susanna* *S. C. Foster*

My matches, flour and chili beans lay scattered all around,
I felt so bad I wished to die as I lay on the ground;
My coffee rolled down by a rock, my pepper I could not find,
'Twas then I thought of Angeline, the girl I left behind.

I took my shovel, pick and pan to try a piece of ground,
I dream'd I struck the richest lead that ever had been found;
Then I wrote home that I had found a solid lead of gold,
And I'd be home in just a month, but what a lie I told!

I dug, I panned and tommed awhile, till I had but a dollar,
I struck it here, and right down there, I could not raise the color;
John Chinaman he bought me out, and pungled down the dust,
Then I had just an ounce in change to start out on a "bust".

I went to town and got drunk; in the morning, to my surprise,
I found that I had got a pair of roaring, big black eyes,
And I was strapp'd, had not a cent, not even pick or shovel,
My hair snarled up, my breeches torn, looked like the very devil.

I then took up a little farm and got a senorita,
Grey-eyed, hump-backed and black as tar – her name was Marguerita;
My pigs all died, hens flew away, Joaquin he stole my mules,
My ranch burnt "down", my blankets "up", likewise my farming tools.

I left my farm and hired out to be a hardware clerk,
I got kicked out "cos" couldn't write, so again I went to work;
But when they caught me stealing grub, a few went in to boot him,
And others round were singing out, "Hang him, hang him, shoot him!"

THE UNHAPPY MINER

J. A.. Stone — *Air: King of the Cannibal Islands* — *J. Broughham*

I mine from break of day,
But cannot make it pay,
Disheartened return to my cabin at night,
Where rattlesnakes crawl round,
My bed made on the ground,
And coiling up, lay ready to bite.

My poor old leaky lamp,
Is always cold and damp;
My blanket is covered with
something that crawls;
My bread will never rise,
My coffee-pot capsize.
I'd rather live inside of prison walls.

My boots are full of holes,
Like merchants have no soles;
My hands, once so soft, are harder'n stone;
My pants and woolen shirt,
Are only rags and dirt;
And must I live and die here alone?

I know how miners feel,
When pigs begin to squeal,
Or hens on their roosts to cackle and squall;
It makes my blood run cold,
To think it's all for gold,
And often wish that Gabriel would call!

It's "Starve or pay the dust,"
For merchants will not trust,
And then in the summer the diggings are dry;
Of course then I am broke,
Swelled up by poison oak;
It's even so, I really would not lie.

If I were home again,
To see green fields of grain,
And all kinds of fruit hanging
ripe on the trees;
I there would live and die,
The gold mines bid good-bye –
Forever free from bed-bugs and fleas.

THE DAYS OF '49

I had comrades then a saucy set,
They were rough I must confess,
But staunch and brave, as true as steel,
Like hunters from the west;
But they like many another fish,
Have now run out their line;
But like good old bricks they stood the kicks,
Of the days of '49.

There was Monte Pete, I'll ne'er forget
The luck that he always had,
He'd deal for you both night and day,
Or as long as you had a scad.
One night a pistol laid him out,
'Twas his last lay out in fine,
It caught Pete sure, right bang in the door,
In the days of '49.

There was another chap from New Orleans,
Big Reuben was his name,
On the plaza there with a sardine box,
He opened a faro game,
He dealt so fair that a millionaire,
He became in course of time,
Till death stept in and called the turn,
In the days of '49.

There was Kentuck Bill, one of the boys,
Who was always in for a game;
No matter whether he lost or won,
To him 'twas all the same,
He'd ante a slug; he'd pass the buck;
He'd go a hat full blind.
In the game of death Bill lost his breath,
In the days of '49.

There was New York Jake, the butcher boy,
So fond of getting tight;
Whenever Jake got full of gin
He was looking for a fight.
One night he ran against a knife
In the hands of old Bob Kline
And over Jake we had a wake
In the days of '49.

There was North Carolina Jess, a hard old case,
Who never would repent.
Jess was never known to miss a meal,
Or ever pay a cent.
But poor old Jess like all the rest,
To death did at last resign,
And in his bloom he went up the flume
In the days of '49.

There was Rackensack Jim who could out roar
  A buffalo bull you bet,
He roared all night; he roared all day;
  He may be roaring yet.
One night he fell in a prospect hole,
  'Twas a roaring bad design,
And in that hole Jim roared out his soul
  In the days of '49.

Since that time how things have changed
  In this land of liberty ,
Darkies didn't vote nor plead in court
  Nor rule this country,
But the Chinese question, the worst of all
  In those-days did not shine,
For the country was right and the boys all white
  In the days of '49.

The Charles Weed Photos of 1858

The American River Canyon was photographed in 1858 by Charles L. Weed. The photos were used by Thomas Armstrong to make the wood cuts in Hutchings California Magazine (1859-1860).

Photographs were taken in 1977 from the same vantage points as the Weed photos by the Bureau of Reclamation, and are shown side by side with the Weed photos. All photographs are from Bureau of Reclamation files.

Charles Weed photo

Maine Bar Claime Reclaimed

Top: In 1858, Maine Bar Claime boasted hotels, stores, baths, and up on the hill, the Maine Bar Fandango House.

Bottom: In 1977, restoration of the 49er miners' exploitation is well under way. This recent photo is taken from the same vantage point as the photo taken in 1858.

The Middle Fork of the American had a population of close to 10,000 men during the peak of Placer mining. The successful fluming of 13 river miles drew great attention. Once exposed the gold rich gravel bars were placer mined with pick, shovel, wheelbarrow, rocker and long tom. Undershot water wheels called "hurdy-gurdies" drove pumps which lifted water from the bottom of the pits to the flume.

The incredible story of the first flume is here lifted from the pages of Thompson and West's 1882 *History of Placer County, California.*

The Grand Fluming Operations

Excerpt from Thompson and West, 1882

These resulted in a final agreement between five companies, whose united membership was over 400, to join flumes, covering a length of more than a mile of the river. These were named, respectively, Vermont, Buckner's Bar, Sailor Claim, Murderer's Bar, and New York Bar Companies. As there were then no saw-mills in the country, this was certainly a vast undertaking under the circumstances; but from the cosmopolitan crowd arose the inventive genius necessary for the occasion. Stephen Tyler and a man named Lefingwell, members of the Murderer's Bar Company, proposed to their associates that, for the sum of $6.00 per linear foot, they would construct a flume twelve feet wide and three feet high, provided the company would grade and prepare the way for laying it. This proposal was accepted. Tyler and Lefingwell, immediately after the contract was made, went down to Sacramento, where they obtained an ordinary horse-power, such as were in those days used upon threshing machines, a circular saw, and about 150 bronco horses, which, in a few days were all brought to the locality of the scene of this magnificent project.

In 1858, the miners toiled with pick, shovel, and wheelbarrow along side the "hurdy-gurdy" undershot water wheel to extract the gold.

Charles Weed photo

A Model Saw-Mill

A 'saw-mill' was in time improvised, which for uniqueness, per-haps, was never surpassed. A log was placed upon the carriage way of the 'mill', an adjacent corral was levied upon for the 'motor', and as many bronco horses secured to the levers of the machine as could find room, while yelling vaqueros, with formidable whips, urged the frightened animals into their utmost efforts of strength and speed. The horses thus used could not endure a long term service, and, as the exhausted ones were turned out to pick their subsistence upon the hillsides under the watchful eye of a herdsman, fresh relays were drawn from the corral. Some few thousand feet of lumber were sawed by this method; but it was rough and came slowly. The motive power which drove the machinery of the newfangled mill daily became less effective, until, at length, the hills were covered with, starved, spirit-less, sorenecked, crippled and generally bunged-up frames of the equine race, instead of the trim, active little beasts fresh from a California caballada of a few weeks before. The contractors, finding that they could not accomplish the job in the manner begun, and the men who were building such high hopes of wealth to come from the river's bed, were getting anxious as the advancing season brought them nearer and nearer to the time when high water might be expected. An agreement was made that Tyler and Lefingwell would rive out puncheon from the sugar pine, and lay a flume with it, while the company would get canvas, sew it together and line it. The puncheon flooring alone would contain large cracks, through which the water would escape and which the canvas would entirely cover up.

Charles Weed photo

Grand Mountain Bar

Top: In 1858, Grand Mountain Bar shows the variety of mechanical transfer of the flume's energy from undershot wheel through pulley to the diggins.

Bottom: In 1977, the very same spot today, now known as Buckeye Bar, still shows signs of the mining activity, but nature has nearly healed the wounds.

Meanwhile the adjoining companies had been progressing in about the same ratio, some whip-sawing lumber, others spitting out puncheon, and some of them cutting poles to lay down as the flooring of the flume upon which to lay canvas. As the distance was more than a mile, the flume, twelve feet wide, with sides three feet

Charles Weed photo

Craniwells Claim

Top: In 1858, Craniwells Claim at Maine Bar shows the denuded hill-sides. Trees were cut for lumber and firewood, and little remained except the brush.

Bottom: In 1977, Maine Bar from the same spot shows a healthy regeneration of the forests, both conifers and oaks. A horse trail is seen in the foreground.

high, and canvas at that time not less than one dollar a yard, and all required sewing together, this involved a great expenditure as well as much labor. Sailors and all others who could or would use the "palm" were set at work at a half-ounce a day wages sewing the canvas flume lining.

The Grand Finale

At length, one bright Saturday in September, at 11 o'clock A.M. witnessed the completion of the structure, canvas-lined from head to foot, and the water flowing through it-- the realization of months of arduous toil and anxious hopes. The water would require a little time to drain off, and what more proper thing to do could there be than to wait until Monday morning before beginning general work? As high as $60 a pan had been obtained in digging a foundation to the bed-rock for some of the posts which held up the flume; two men owning interests had quietly slipped out of their blankets on Sunday morning, took a rocker and "prospected" returning before breakfast with nine pounds and a half of gold, and what could there be to prevent the real-ization of the golden dreams of a fortune won, in which all the participants of the scheme indulged? But a terrible disappointment was in store for them. Upon the mountain peaks to the eastward, where the river had its source, on Sunday evening gathered portentous clouds, and deluged the highlands with rain, all unknown to the hopeful men who were low down upon the stream.

The locality written of in the foregoing was not an exceptional place with regard to population and plans for garnering up the gold. Above, for many miles, were wing-dams, races through which the water of the river was directed by dams thrown clear across the stream, and obstructions of various sorts, one in succession above another. The copious rain-fall striking the bare granite slopes ran off with great rapidity and soon swelled the stream beyond the carrying capacity of some of the races high up on the river, and as the dams were not made to withstand great pressure, they soon gave way, not only letting down the resultant waters of the storm, but also that which had been held back. The carrying away of one precipitated upon the rest below a mass of water and debris, which, in turn, added its own accumulations to the flood, which at length, as it swept on in its downward course, became irresistible.

All of the old miners who were upon the middle fork of the American in 1850 remember the September flood. This swollen torrent reached the dam at Murderer's Bar early on the Monday morning when everybody were expecting to go to work in the bed of the river. The alarm was sounded and hundreds of men appeared upon the scene. Rapidly rose the seething waters, the flume running full, until it reached the top of the dam. Higher and higher it piled back of the rocky barrier that obstructed it, until a greater level was reached, when it began to pour over the dam and slowly fill up the bed of the stream that had been drained. The water reached the floor of the flume, which the fast disappearing dam was lightening of its burden of water, but little water now flowing through it. In a few moments more additional rocks are swept away from the crest of the dam, and the water speedily deepens under the flume, which is not solidly spiked to its foundation. Another moment the whole structure floats, breaks from its mooring, and moves down the river out of sight, like an enormous serpent, wriggling and twisting along the sinuous stream, held together by its lining of canvas.

Thus, in an hour's time, was the labor of hundreds of men for months destroyed, their fond hopes dissipated, and their bright dreams of wealth and home rudely dispelled.

Thousands of men witnessed the passage of the floating flume, which did not break up for several miles, and was the source for two or three years after which miners along the river supplied themselves with canvas.

Charles Weed photo

Craniwells Claim

Top: In 1858, dozens of miners leave the dinner house at Craniwells Claim. Many will make their way up to the fandango house at the top of the hill.

Bottom: In 1977, the same spot 120 years later shows hardly a sign of the booming mining town, and the fandango house is but a slight depression on the knoll.

Chinese in the Gold Fields

Russell Towle's "The Dutch Flat Chronicles" *and Jonathan H.X. Lee's* "Auburn's Joss House" *contributed immeasurably to this article*

By 1875 on the order of 100,000 Chinese, or Celestials, were scattered across the "Mountain of Gold", their name for California. China was then, and remains today, the most populous nation on the earth. Flood and famine had wrought disastrous misery upon her people for millennia, driving waves of emigrants away in search of a better life. The Chinese rushed into the goldfields along with the rest of the world at the prospect of making it rich quickly. Once here in the Golden State their impressive willingness to perform difficult, dirty, dangerous low-paid labor to build rail lines, levees and work the various types of gold mining operations were so successful that the "yellowman" was abused, denied citizenship, singled out for special taxes (1852 Foreign Miners Tax), and occasionally expelled (burned), from communities. The Chinese Exclusion Act, although vetoed by President Chester Arthur, was passed by Congress in 1882. This act was used to exclude Chinese from immigrating to the US for decades because they were considered a threat to white prosperity.

Industrious as the day is long, the Chinese were adept at panning gold from the tailings of the gold mining operations of other miners.

More than any other ethnic group at the time and despite their impressive contributions to our rail lines and levee systems, the Chinese were subject to extreme prejudice. Yet in spite of the anti-Chinese sentiments they managed to flourish on all levels and impart aspects of their rich Flowery Kingdom culture to California where West greets the East. Their religious beliefs Confucianism, Daoism and Buddhism, peculiar social customs, self-sufficient way of life and use of opium led the Chinese to create Chinatowns within the larger mining camps. Usually celebrated in carnival style whenever possible, Chinese Lu-

Photograph courtesy of the California State Archives

Miners at Auburn Ravine, circa 1852.

nar New Year festivities featured exploding firecrackers, musicians beating gongs, gambling, parades and numerous ritual ceremonies designed to placate their deities to bring about prosperity and harmony.

Auburn's Joss House Museum also known as the Chinese Ling Ying Association House, located on Sacramento Street in Old Town Auburn, offers a window into the Chinese-American history and culture.

Photograph courtesy of Placer County Museum

The Joss House as it stands in Auburn today.

Auburn Historic Museums

Placer County Courthouse Museum

101 Maple Street, Auburn 530-889-6507
Open Daily, 10:00 am – 4:00 pm. Closed on holidays

The Placer County Museum located on the first floor of the1898 County Courthouse presents a fascinating overview of Placer County history featuring, the Auburn-Foresthill "mudwagon" stagecoach, the Pate Collection of Native American artifacts, Hawver Cave fossils, rare gold nugget specimens, the restored Sheriff's Office and many other intriguing displays of local history.

Gold Country Mining Museum

1273 High St., Gold Country Fairgrounds, Auburn
Phone 530-887-0690
Open 11:00 am-4 pm Tuesday-Sunday. Closed on holidays

The Gold Country Museum focuses on Placer County's mining history with interactive displays that offer children and adults the opportunity to explore a mining tunnel, pan for gold and learn more about "placer" mining methods.

Bernhard Museum Complex

291 Auburn Folsom Road, Auburn 530-888-6891
Open 11:00 am-4 pm Tuesday-Sunday. Closed holidays

The Bernhard House is an 1890's era Victorian farmhouse originally constructed as the Travelers Rest Hotel in1851. The furnished residence, cavernous fieldstone, winery building, carriage barn, vineyard and garden provide an authentic glimpse of a working pioneer farm.

Auburn Joss House Chinese Museum

200 Sacramento Street, Old Town Auburn 530-823-0373
Open 1st Saturday of the month. 10:00 am-3:00 pm

Also know as the Chinese Ling Ying Association House, the museum features an altar with Confucius, Daoism and Buddhist deities, a Chinese kitchen and boarding house style accommodations for the temporary residence of Chinese immigrants.

Old Town Auburn Walking Tour

Meet at the Courthouse, 101 Maple Street, Every Saturday morning at 10:00 am sharp. Tour lasts about one hour.

Free admission to the museums and tour but donations are gratefully accepted to help maintain the high quality of the museum exhibits. For more information please call 530-889-6500 or visit www.placer.ca.gov/museum on the web.

"El Presidente"
or Mouth Peace for the River

Hunting Blind Justice with an entrained brain
That flows with the push and pull
Of those who use the law as an obstacle
Providing eddies for pools of diversity.
The way not all seeds sprout at once.

Leading Blind Justice with a band of river lovers,
Talented but penniless.
Leading Blind Justice through a landscape
Ruled by law, but where justice
Is for sale.

Armed with evenings of pizza, stuffed envelopes,
And newsletters folded and stamped.
Planning strategies to let the river speak–
With boats, bikes and paddles,
Or people in saddles or a flower sniffed.

Armed with letters to the Governor,
Letters to Senators, editors and any old Representative.

Keeping Blind Justice from being bought off.
Leading Blind Justice to the river
With a heart that practices
Listening to the wild

- For PARC President Tim Woodall by Roger Groghan

The American River:
"Worth More Than a Dam"

By Gary Estes and Tim Woodall

The North and Middle Forks are still threatened by the proposed Auburn Dam

Authorized in 1965 as part of the Central Valley Project, Auburn Dam was originally conceived as a thin-arch concrete dam, 698 feet high, located on the North Fork of the American River just below the City of Auburn. The U.S. Bureau of Reclamation (USBR) stopped construction of the dam's foundation due to seismic safety concerns after an earthquake struck Oroville in 1975. Geologists discovered the same fault

Auburn Dam site circa 1975

system responsible for the Oroville earthquake ran directly beneath the Auburn Dam site, and federal studies determined that 750,000 people in the Sacramento area were at risk from flooding if Auburn Dam failed. The dam was then re-designed

Auburn Dam site in 2008.

to be more earthquake-resistant, resulting in huge cost increases which Congress for more than three decades has refused to fund.

The multipurpose Auburn Dam was intended to provide Sacramento with increased protection from American River flooding. In recent years that flood risk has been greatly reduced, without construction of the proposed dam, by substantial strengthening of downstream American River levees and by construction of a new auxiliary spillway at Folsom Dam (scheduled for completion in 2017). These projects, which have proven far less expensive and destructive to the environment, will protect against a flood 50 percent larger than any experienced in the American River watershed since 1850.

The Auburn Dam's estimated water and power production also do not justify its exorbitant cost. Water yield would add less than one-half of 1% to California's water supply, at prices no local water agency would be willing to pay. The State's own Water Plan reports that investing in water conservation and reclamation would have the ability to produce 5 times more water than the Auburn Dam at a fraction of its estimated $6 to $10 billion cost. If completed, the Auburn Dam would be the most expensive dam ever built in the United States.

Although there is no longer an economic justification for the proposed dam, it still has political supporters and will continue to be a threat to the canyons until the project is de-authorized by Congress and the North and Middle Forks of the American River are afforded permanent protection.

The devastating impacts of the Dam include the flooding and losing forever:

- 48 miles of the North and Middle Forks of the American River and their canyons, which contain irreplaceable wildlife habitat and unique biodiversity.
- A landscape rich in Native American and Gold Rush history, with more than 1500 known historical and cultural sites.

- The river-based 35,000 acre Auburn State Recreation Area, enjoyed by almost one million annual visitors who come for hiking, mountain biking, trail running, rafting, kayaking, fishing, rock climbing, gold panning, swimming, picnicking, bird watching, photography, and more. The proposed reservoir would also create a steep and unsightly dead zone, or "bathtub ring," caused by widely fluctuating water levels.

Major Events in the History of the Auburn Dam

1967: Construction begins on a 265 foot high earthen cofferdam and a half-mile long diversion tunnel 33 feet in diameter to divert the river around the construction site. The North Fork is closed to public access downstream of the confluence of the North and Middle Forks due to the hazardous diversion tunnel.

1975: The coffer dam was completed and the river was diverted through the diversion tunnel.

1975: August 1 Oroville earthquake, measuring 5.7 magnitude, leads to new seismic safety studies.

1977: Construction stops due to earthquake safety concerns.

1980: U.S. Interior Department decides that Auburn Dam must be re-designed as a more expensive concrete gravity dam after geologists report that the original design could fail in a moderate quake similar to the one at Oroville.

1984: President Ronald Reagan establishes a new federal cost sharing policy requiring local sponsors of federal dam projects to pay 25% of project costs (later increased to 35% in 1996).

1986: A huge February storm hits the American River watershed, washing out the earthen cofferdam at the now-dormant Auburn Dam construction site and threatening Sacramento, leading to new flood risk concerns and additional studies on potential solutions. (However, a later review showed that the USBR had mismanaged Folsom Dam operations during the storm, and that if they had followed the correct flood control operation rules there would not have been a serious flood threat to Sacramento.)

1992: A proposal for a less expensive flood control-only dam at Auburn is rejected by a wide margin in Congress.

1996: The U.S. Geological Survey reports that potential ground movement at the dam site could be larger than earlier thought, raising the risk of dam failure in an earthquake.

1997: A report by the U.S. Department of Interior determines that the North and Middle Forks are eligible for National Wild & Scenic River designation.

1999-2000: Bill Lockyer, California State Attorney General, cites violations of federal and state law, including the public trust doctrine, in his request that Secretary of Interior Bruce Babbitt direct USBR to close the diversion tunnel, return the river to its historic channel, and restore public access to the river. USBR recognizes it has been in violation of the law and agrees to comply.

2003: Construction begins on the Placer County Water Agency (PCWA) American River Pump Station Project at the former dam site. The work includes excavation and reconstruction of a three quarter mile stretch of the natural river bed.

2006: Dam construction costs skyrocket to $6 to $10 billion according to a cost estimate report by USBR.

2007: The dam diversion tunnel is closed, and after 35 years, the river once again flows free in its historic channel as part of the PCWA American River Pump Station Project.

2008: The North Fork American River downstream of the Highway 49 Bridge is opened to the public for recreational use with State Parks opening China Bar river access at the former dam site.

2008: Construction begins on a new auxiliary spillway at Folsom Dam, which will greatly increase Sacramento's level of flood protection.

2008: The State Water Resources Control Board votes unanimously to revoke the Bureau of Reclamation's water rights for Auburn Dam.

2011: Congressman Tom McClintock vows to resurrect Auburn Dam.

Imagining the Future:

Three Options to Consider for the North and Middle Forks of the American River

What does the future hold for those stretches of the North and Middle Forks of the American River once doomed to be flooded by the proposed Auburn Dam? Authorized by Congress in 1965 but never constructed because of economic, environmental and seismic concerns, the dam remains a mothballed but still technically authorized federal project with a small remaining number of vocal supporters, despite the absence in today's world of any credible economic justification for its estimated $6 to $10 billion cost.

Long managed by the California Department of Parks and Recreation as the Auburn State Recreation Area (ASRA), the 30,000 acre former reservoir site has become an extremely popular recreation destination with approximately one million annual visitors enjoying a wide variety of recreational activities in ASRA's scenic foothill river canyons. This vital recreational resource is now an important contributor to the local economy and is deserving of a secure future, not one clouded by its continued status as the site of an "authorized" but obsolete dam project. What follows are three options for the permanent protection of these magnificent river canyons.

OPTION ONE:

Imagine: California Wild and Scenic River Protection of the North Fork for Future Generations

The California Wild and Scenic Rivers Act was established in 1972. Modeled after the National Wild and Scenic Rivers Act, the California law's purpose is to preserve designated rivers possessing extraordinary scenic, recreational, fishery or wildlife values in their free flowing state. Thirty-eight miles of

Rafters paddle Chamberlain Falls.

STATE WILD & SCENIC DESIGNATION IMPACTS	
WILL:	• Improve Local Economic Possibilities • Protect Scenic, Recreational, Fishery and Wildlife Resources from an Auburn Dam • Protect Existing Local Water Rights to uses within the Local Counties
WON'T:	• Change Local Land Use Authority or Take Private Property • Add Cost to Taxpayers • Change Hunting, Fishing or Gold Panning Regulations • Change Rafting, Hiking, Mountain Biking or Horseback Riding Recreational Use • Restrict Options to Fight Wildland Fires

the North Fork of the American River from its headwaters in the Pacific Crest near Lake Tahoe to the Colfax-Iowa Hill Bridge has been part of the state Wild and Scenic Rivers system since 1972.

The 16 miles of the North Fork from Colfax-Iowa Hill Bridge to Upper Lake Clementine, with its spectacular scenery and recreational opportunities, would be a logical addition to the California Wild and Scenic River system. This river canyon has unique and irreplaceable qualities that make it worthy of the highest level of protection achievable. California protection would also help ensure this river is never buried under a dam's reservoir by prohibiting state and local funding for the planning or construction of a dam.

The undammed free-flowing North Fork from its headwaters high in the Sierra Nevada Mountains to Upper Lake Clementine flows through a deep scenic canyon with easy river access next to the historic bridge crossings at Mineral Bar, Yankee Jim's and

Ponderosa. The legendary Class IV Chamberlain Falls whitewater run attracts kayakers and rafters from around the world to test their skills on the rocks and rapids of the North Fork Gorge. The 16 miles of proposed Wild & Scenic River feature whitewater experiences from beginner to advanced.

"Naturally functioning aquatic ecosystems are the lifeblood of our watersheds."

- Joe Medeiros, Professor Emeritus, Sierra College

The North Fork trails are a botanist's treasure chest of wildflower blooms in the spring. They offer easy river access to its crystal clear pools for fishing and summer swimming. The popular Codfish Creek Falls Trail has a useful American River ecology trail guide available on PARC's website. North Fork visitors are able to enjoy a full range of all popular river canyon recreational activities including fishing, camping, picnicking, swimming, mountain biking, horseback riding, recreational gold panning and much more.

California Wild & Scenic protection is a perfect opportunity to protect the natural ecosystems associated with the free flowing North Fork as it rises and falls with seasonal rainfall and snowmelt. This contributes to the resilience and flexibility of aquatic species that rely on the river for food and habitat and sets the stage for all the rich diverse ecosystems in the watershed that have adapted to abundant water conditions with seasonal drought. We must protect this adaptive biological diversity, especially with the uncertain future of climate change!

Join Protect American River Canyons in creating a living river legacy for future generations to inherit. For more information on the benefits of California Wild & Scenic protection and to add your name and email address to the growing list of Wild and Scenic supporters visit: www.parc-auburn.org

Photo left: Proud fishermen diplay their catch of the day.

Photo right: Roger Groghan dips nets in the river with Junior Rangers.

OPTION TWO:

National Wild and Scenic Rivers

The National Wild & Scenic Rivers Act was passed by Congress in 1968 to balance our nation's existing policy of developing rivers for power and water with a new policy of preserving the free flowing character and outstanding values of other rivers. Most of the California rivers and streams initially added to the federal system were threatened by massive dams and diversions, leading Congress to add these endangered rivers to the system in order to protect them. But wild and scenic status means much more than simply prohibiting dams. It is a management tool to protect and enhance the outstanding values for which the rivers were designated.

In January of 1993 the North and Middle Forks of the American River, within the boundaries of the Auburn State Recreation Area (ASRA), were determined to be eligible for National Wild & Scenic River designation in a study conducted by the Bureau of Reclamation.

An interagency team of land and river managing agencies found that both forks of the American River possessed outstandingly remarkable scenic, recreational, fish, wildlife, and ecological values.

Adding those segments of the North and Middle Forks that flow through ASRA (approximately 48 river miles) to the National Wild & Scenic River System makes sense. These rivers and their canyons are highly scenic and possess tremendous recreational value, making them a perfect fit for National Wild & Scenic designation.

OPTION THREE:

American River National Recreation Area

National Recreation Areas (NRA) are congressionally designated open space resources of national significance. There are currently 44 NRAs in the United States, including three in California: Golden Gate NRA, Santa Monica Mountains NRA, and Whiskeytown-Shasta-Trinity NRA.

In 1990, a study undertaken by the U.S. Bureau of Land Management (BLM) determined that the North, Middle, and South Forks of the American River upstream of Folsom Reservoir met all the eligibility criteria for becoming a National Recreation Area (NRA). The American River National Recreation Area Feasibility Study concluded:

"The combination of these three segments together meets all NRA criteria for designation and is feasible for management as an NRA with a combination of natural/cultural resources and recreation opportunities unequalled in any existing NRA."

The study also evaluated the addition of two lower segments – Folsom Lake State Recreation Area and the American River Parkway – to the upper three segments, and found that the addition of these two segments "would significantly enhance the American River's eligibility as an NRA."

Designation of all or some portion of the American River watershed as an NRA is deserving of serious consideration. Such a designation would result in a uniform management philosophy that emphasizes protection of natural and cultural resources while also promoting and enhancing access to the canyons' recreational treasures. NRA status would also help reduce, if not eliminate, any remaining uncertainty about the future of the North and Middle Fork canyons and leading to additional investment in the canyons' recreational amenities and increased visitation.

Protecting the American River Canyons Since the 1970s

protect american river canyons

Protect American River Canyons, or PARC, was originally founded by a dedicated group of Auburn area citizens in the 1970s to stop the construction of the Auburn Dam. With encouragement and leadership from Friends of the River, PARC focused on the theme *"The American River: Worth More Than a Dam"* by providing valuable information and research on the Auburn Dam.

PARC is a community-based 501(c) 3 non-profit organization dedicated to building community through collaboration and protection of the natural, recreational, cultural and historical resources of the North and Middle Forks of the American River and its canyons for all to enjoy and responsible care for.

PARC sponsors community watershed education programs, college scholarships, Confluence Festival events, restoration projects including the spring and fall river cleanups and visitor improvements; recreational activities including Paddle Safety Day, and seasonal hikes and outings that focus on American River ecology. PARC publishes this recreational guide book and a map to the Auburn State Recreation Area. PARC also publishes a seasonal newsletter, and offers beautiful visual presentations about the American River watershed.

PARC provides information on what you can do to help shape a positive future and protect the natural resources of the American River Canyons. PARC remains vigilant to the political threats to the river.

PARCland is American River land purchased in partnership with the Placer Land Trust as a symbolic gesture of our community's commitment to the Wild & Scenic values of the American River wilderness.

Become a PARC Member!

Membership in PARC keeps you informed on important canyon protection issues, canyon recreation opportunities and helps fund our community outreach programs. Join in the fun, in exploring and protecting the American River watershed! A regular annual membership is $25 payable to PARC P.O. Box 9312 Auburn, CA 95604. Visit our website at www.parc-auburn.org.

Local Organizations

California State Parks Foundation

The California State Parks Foundation (CSPF) is the only statewide independent nonprofit organization dedicated to protecting, enhancing and advocating for California's magnificent state parks. CSPF is committed to improving the quality of life for all Californians by expanding access to the natural beauty, rich culture and history, and recreational and educational opportunities offered by California's 280 state parks–the largest state parks system in the United States. CSPF cultivates stewardship of state parks by hosting annual Earth Day Restoration and cleanup programs and supporting volunteer enhancement programs.

Address: 1510 J Street, Suite 220, Sacramento, CA 95814
Website: www.calparks.org
Phone: 916-442-2119

Canyon Keepers

The Auburn State Recreation Canyon Keepers (ASRACK) are volunteers that assist State Parks rangers by providing information and assistance to Auburn SRA visitors. The Canyon Keepers conduct monthly hikes and meetings that are open to the public who want to learn more about canyon recreation, history and ecology. If you enjoy the American River Canyons, would like to learn more about the area, and are interested in helping others enjoy its natural beauty, please consider joining the Canyon Keepers. There are two membership levels: active and supporting. Please contact Canyon Keepers to learn more about activities, meetings and hikes.

Website: www.CanyonKeepers.org
Phone: 530-885-4527

Center for Sierra Nevada Conservation

Since 1986, the Center for Sierra Nevada Conservation, formerly Friends Aware of Wildlife Needs, has been a tireless voice for sound management of our public lands and wise government land use policies. From recreation to private forestry practices, to ecosystem management on our public lands, to the El Dorado County General Plan, CSNC members have worked countless hours to make sure that environmental values are not forgotten by land managers and politicians.

Website: www.sierranevadaconservation.org
Address: P.O. Box 603, Georgetown, CA 95634
Phone: 530-333-1113
Email: csnckaren@gmail.com

Friends of the River

Founded in 1973, Friends of the River (FOR) has been at the forefront of river conservation, successfully protecting or restoring 2,500 miles of California rivers. Working on behalf of rivers, FOR has been setting national precedents for effective environmental action to improve flows for rivers controlled by hydropower dams, restore fish populations, protect natural ecosystems and improve recreational opportunities. More than 95% of California's riverside wildlife habitat and wetlands have been lost to development. FOR has been a leader in training activists to save their rivers and a steadfast collaborator with PARC in the ongoing effort to protect the American River from the controversial Auburn Dam project.

Website: www.friendsoftheriver.org
Address: 1418 20th Street, Suite 100,
Sacramento, CA 95811
Phone: 916-442-3155
Email: info@friendsoftheriver.org

North Fork American River Alliance

In 1978 a citizen-based collection of river advocates successfully lobbied to have 38 miles of the upper North Fork designated National Wild & Scenic River. The river is national treasure of spectacular waterfalls, wild trout, rugged canyons, awesome vistas and California gold rush history. The North Fork American River Alliance (NFARA), is a volunteer non-profit corporation founded to preserve the wild, scenic and cultural heritage within the North Fork American River watershed. Working with private property owners, public agencies, land trusts and other interested parties NFARA's goal is to be a constructive voice in the management of the wild, scenic and cultural heritage of the North Fork. They actively participate in public workshops and public agency management plans, and form coalitions with groups and individuals focused on protecting the North Fork. They sponsor community education programs to inform the public about the values of the North Fork watershed and have adopted several trails, frequently organizing volunteer work parties.

Website: www.nfara.org
Address: P.O. Box 292, Gold Run, CA 95717
Phone: Jim Ricker, 530-389-8344
Email: info@nfara.org

Placer Land Trust

Natural Wonders Forever

Founded in 1991 to work with willing landowners and conservation partners to protect natural and agricultural lands in the Placer County region for future generations. In 2008, Placer Land Trust became the first nationally accredited land trust in the Sierra Nevada region. As a private charitable nonprofit organization, Placer Land Trust relies on community support and works with many individuals, businesses, organizations, and agencies to ensure that some of Placer County's natural wonders – such as the American River. Through voluntary conservation such as land acquisition and conservation easements, Placer Land Trust has permanently protected over 7,000 acres of land in Placer County. Placer Land Trust has protected approximately 1,275 acres in the American River Canyon, from its first project completed in partnership with Protect American River Canyons–the 30 acre Codfish Falls Trail Preserve near Ponderosa Bridge–the 160 acre Oest Ranch Cold Springs Preserve near Clipper Creek in 2012. The American River and its canyons and tributaries remain a focus of Placer Land Trust's conservation work today. Contact Placer Land Trust to learn more about how to help them protect our natural wonders forever.

Website: www.PlacerLandTrust.org
Address: 11661 Blocker Drive, Suite 110,
Auburn, CA 95603
Phone: 530-887-9222
Email: info@placerlandtrust.org

Placer Nature Center

For over 20 years, Placer Nature Center has facilitated environmental education programs, enjoyment, appreciation, and ultimate stewardship of natural resources by providing opportunities to school children, families, and community groups to learn about Placer County's nature's beauty, history, and immense value. For children, contact with nature is the strongest factor in determining their future stewardship in adulthood. So let your children hop the rocks of the American River, sit in the shade of an ancient oak tree, hear the breeze in the Foothill Pines, and become tomorrow's protectors of Placer County's rivers and streams, foothills and chaparral, mountains and canyons. Please contact us, and have your children's teacher contact us about our school and family programs and events.

Website: www.PlacerNatureCenter.org
Address: 3700 Christian Valley Road
Auburn, California 95602
Phone: 530-878-6053

Save the Auburn Ravine Salmon and Steelhead

SARSAS is trying to do with one stream, the Auburn Ravine, what must be done to all streams and rivers on the entire West Coast, make the entire length of the ravine navigable for Anadromous Fish. SARSAS holds monthly meetings in Auburn with guest speakers and cosponsors the autumn Calling Back the Salmon Celebration in Lincoln.

Website: www.sarsas.org
Address: P.O. Box 4269, Auburn 95604
Phone: 530-888-0281
Email: jlsanchez39@gmail.com

Sierra Club

Our mission is to explore, enjoy, and protect the wild places of the earth; to practice and promote the responsible use of the earth's ecosystems and resources; to educate and enlist humanity to protect and restore the quality of the natural and human environment; and to use all lawful means to carry out these objectives. The Placer Group of the Sierra Club covers Placer County west of the divide and works on air and water quality issues, wildlife habitat, open space, sustainable agriculture, and local government matters that impact the environment.

Contact: Marilyn Jasper, Chair, Placer Group
Website: www.sierraclub.org
Address: Sierra Club Placer Group,
P.O. Box 7167, Auburn, CA 95604.
Phone: 916-652-7005
Email: marilyn.jasper@mlc.sierraclub.org

Sierra Foothills Audubon Society

Sierra Foothills Audubon Society (SFAS) is dedicated to educating everyone about the variety and beauty of our natural environment and encourages all to protect our wildlife and natural places. SFAS has monthly meetings, sponsors outings and publishes *Phoebe Newsletter* six time a year.

Website: www.sierrafoothillsaudubon.com
Address: P. O. Box 1937
Grass Valley, CA 95945
Phone: 530-823-4670

Sierra Nevada Conservancy

The Sierra Nevada Conservancy (SNC) initiates, encourages, and supports efforts that improve the environmental, economic and social well-being of the Sierra Nevada Region, its communities and the citizens of California. The SNC is a California state agency created by bipartisan legislation (AB 2600) and signed into law in 2004. The SNC supports the Sierra Nevada Region by providing funding for local projects and offering technical assistance and other support for collaborative projects in partnership with local government, nonprofit organizations and Tribal entities.

Website: www.sierranevada.ca.gov
Address: 11521 Blocker Dr., Suite 205
Auburn, CA 95603
Phone: 530-823-4670

Public Land Management

Auburn State Recreation Area
501 El Dorado Street
Auburn, CA 95603
530-885-4527
www.parks.ca.gov

US Bureau of Reclamation
7794 Folsom Dam Road
Folsom, CA 95630
916-978-5100
www.usbr.gov/mp/ccao/offices.html

US Bureau of Land Management
Mother Lode Field Office
5152 Hillsdale Circle
El Dorado Hills, CA 95762
916-941-3101
www.blm.ca/gov

Tahoe National Forest American River Ranger District
22830 Foresthill Road
Foresthill, CA 95631
530-367-2224
www.fs.fed.us/r5/tahoe

US Forest Service
Georgetown Ranger District
7600 Wentworth Springs Road
Georgetown, CA 95634
530-333-4312
www.r5.psws.gov/eldorado

Placer County Water Agency
144 Ferguson Road
Auburn, CA 95603
530-823-4850
www.pcwa.net

Auburn Area Recreation District
103 Recreation Drive
Auburn, CA 95603
530-885-0611
www.auburnrec.com

El Dorado National Forest Georgetown Ranger Station
5061 Wentworth Springs Road
Georgetown, CA 95634
530-333-4312
www.enfia.org/eldorado-nationalforest-offices

RECOMMENDED READING

Ecology

Wildflowers of Nevada and Placer Counties, California

Published by the Redbud Chapter of the California Native Plant Society in 2007. www.redbud.cnps.org

A comprehensive botanists' delight of color photographs, accurate descriptions in simplified terms and comments about plant use to over 500 native and non-native species found in our area. Over 20 accessible trails including directions are recommended for viewing wildflowers.

Living Wild, Gardening Cooking and Healing with Native Plants of the Sierra Nevada

Written by Alicia Funk and Karen Kaufman and published in 2011 by Flicker Press. www.flickerpress.com

Preserves our knowledge of how to responsibly use wild plants for food, medicine and crafts and filled with color photographs, descriptions, recipes and samples of art projects using wild flora from our area.

Animal Tracks of Northern California

Written by Chris Stall. Published in 1989 by The Mountineers.

Features life-size drawings of some common animal, characteristic footprints.

Trail Guides for Hiking the American River Canyons

American River Canyon Hikes: Practical Guides to Trails in the Canyons of the North and Middle Forks of the American River

3rd edition by Jim Ferris, Michael Lynch, Sheila Toner, published in 2012 by the Auburn State Recreation Area Canyon Keepers.

Contains maps, trail descriptions, photos and historical information for popular Auburn State Recreation Area trails.

Georgetown Trails, the Auburn Outback and Placerville Paths, A Trilogy of Trail Guides

Written by Tom W. Petersen and self-published by Get Off Your Gass.com.

Includes countless popular and obscure American River watershed trails. This well-researched trilogy of is filled with insider trails descriptions, maps, hiking tips, historical and naturalist information.

North Fork Trails, Hiking trails of the North Fork American River Canyon

Written and self-published in 2012 by Ron Gould, 2nd edition.

Features the wild and scenic beauty and rich gold mining legacy of the historic trails of the North Fork popularized by the late North Fork American River champion Russell Towle. Abundant concise maps, directions, descriptions and historic information about the significance of the trails.

Take A Hike! A Guide to the Lesser Known, and Often More Challenging Trails in Placer and El Dorado County's Gold Country

Published in 2004 by Robert J. Griffis and Evan W. Jones.

Along with the excellent trail descriptions and photos, this book clearly rates the level of difficulty encountered when hiking these trails established by miners often looking for the quickest route to and from their mining claims.

The Sugar Pine Journals, Bogus Thunder Mountains, Sojourning in Rough Country and Hills of the Coyote

Republished in 2013.

A quartet of books containing unique anecdotal stories and essays of the Northern Sierra Mother Lode written by mountain man, Gene Markley. He led hundreds of hiking, nordic skiing and gorge scrambling outings to the gold camps, Native American sites and scenic wilderness of the American River canyons. His outings and books spawned a deep respect and conservation ethic for the protection of the Sierra Nevada mountains.

The Western States Trail Guide: A comprehensive guide to the 100 miles of trail between Squaw Valley and Auburn, California

Written by Hal V. Hall and published by the Western States Trail Foundation in 1992. www.WSTrail.org

Contains comprehensive trail maps, directions, descriptions and historical information about the Western States Trail.

Take a Hike!

Written by Robert J. Griffis and Evan W. Jones. Published in 2004 by Binding Plus.

A guide to the lesser know, and often more challenging, trails in the gold country in Placer and El Dorado counties.

History

The History of Placer County

Published 1882 by Tompson and West. Reproduced by Placer County Historical Society.

A detailed history of Placer County with illustrations and biographical sketches of its prominent people and pioneers.

Images of America: American River Canyon

Written by Rodi Lee and Michael G. Lynch. Published in 2012 by Arcadia Publishing.

Historic photos and descriptions of the American River Canyons, including gold mining, Mountain Quarries Mine and Railroad and Canyon Bridges.

Environment

Nature Noir: A Park Ranger's Patrol in the Sierra

Written by Jordan Fisher-Smith. Published by Houghton Mifflin Company in 2005.

A powerful and intimate account of a park ranger's experiences in the Auburn State Recreation Area. The book is filled with compelling and poetic descriptions of canyon ecology.

BIBLIOGRAPHY

Margolin, Malcolm. *The Way We Lived: California Indian Reminiscences, Stories and Songs.* Heyday Press.

Simpson, Richard. *Ooti: A Maidu Legacy.* Celestial Press.

Cassidy, John. *A Guide to Three Rivers.* Friends of the River.

Powers, Stephen. *The Tribes of California.* University of California Press.

Dwyer and Lingenfelter. *The Songs of the Gold Rush.* University of California Press.

Stall, Chris. *Animal Tracks of Northern California.* The Mountaineers.

Angel, Myron. *The History of Placer County*. Placer County Historical Society.

Muir Laws, John. *The Laws Field Guide to the Sierra Nevada*. Heyday Books in cooperation with the California Academy of Sciences.